A Companion to the Works of Thomas Mann

Studies in German Literature, Linguistics, and Culture

Edited by James Hardin
(*South Carolina*)

Camden House Companion Volumes

The Camden House Companions provide well-informed and up-to-date critical commentary on the most significant aspects of major works, periods, or literary figures. The Companions may be read profitably by the reader with a general interest in the subject. For the benefit of student and scholar, quotations are provided in the original language.

A Companion to the Works of
Thomas Mann

Edited by
Herbert Lehnert
and Eva Wessell

CAMDEN HOUSE

First published 2004
by Camden House

Camden House is an imprint of Boydell & Brewer Inc.
668 Mt. Hope Avenue, Rochester, NY 14620, USA
www.camden-house.com
and of Boydell & Brewer Limited
PO Box 9, Woodbridge, Suffolk IP12 3DF, UK
www.boydell.co.uk

ISBN: 1–57113–219–8

Library of Congress Cataloging-in-Publication Data

A companion to the works of Thomas Mann / edited by Herbert Lehnert
and Eva Wessell.
    p. cm. — (Studies in German literature, linguistics, and culture)
Includes bibliographical references and index.
ISBN 1–57113–219–8 (hardcover : alk. paper)
    1. Mann, Thomas, 1875–1955 — Criticism and interpretation.
I. Lehnert, Herbert, 1925– II. Wessell, Eva. III. Series: Studies in
German literature, linguistics, and culture (Unnumbered).

PT2625.A44Z397 2004
888'.912—dc22
                                                            2004005359

A catalogue record for this title is available from the British Library.

This publication is printed on acid-free paper.
Printed in the United States of America.

Contents

Foreword

THE *COMPANION TO THE WORKS OF THOMAS MANN* is meant for readers of Thomas Mann's works who want to become familiar with the present state of scholarly discussion of his texts. We mean to address scholars, teachers, students of German or comparative literature, but we also want to include the many readers of Mann's writings in the English-speaking world who do not read German. For this reason quotations of Mann's texts were paraphrased or translated whenever it was possible without loss of meaning. Often, the German original was provided as well when the flavor of the original text made a quotation in German imperative.

We have chosen the original German texts, not the various English translations, as the basis for our discussion. Thus references are always to the German edition (the thirteen-volume edition of 1960–1974, since the new Frankfurt edition is just beginning to appear). For this reason, the titles of Mann's works are given in their original form and only translated the first time they occur in each essay. Most English renderings of Mann's texts are by the individual contributors. Some contributors have used existing translations if they were close enough to Mann's meaning.

Although we attribute equal importance to Mann's shorter narratives, we wanted to distinguish those clearly from the long novels. Publication records are often confusing. "Der Tod in Venedig," for example, was designated a "Novelle" in its first printings. First published in the journal *Neue Rundschau* in 1911, it appeared in 1912 as a privately printed book (to add to the confusion: the text is a slightly older version than the one in the first printing) and in 1913 as a publicly available book with the revised text of the first printing. In 1922 it was included in a volume called "Novellen" with Mann's approval. Even though the title of this work is often quoted in italics, we decided to treat the work as a novella and place its title in quotation marks. We did the same with all the other shorter narratives, including "Herr und Hund" and "Die vertauschten Köpfe." The latter works appeared first in book form but were subsequently included in collected volumes of stories.

The essays by Manfred Dierks, Werner Frizen, Helmut Koopmann, and Peter Pütz were written in German and translated by the editors; the essay by Hans-Joachim Sandberg was also written in German and translated by Ronald Speirs, University of Birmingham. Several contributors have helped the editors with comments on other contributions, especially Werner Frizen, Jens Rieckmann, and Egon Schwarz. We wish to thank Douglas Milburn for stylistic help with some translations and the library of the University of California, Irvine, especially its Inter-Library Loan Department, for invaluable help.

H. L.
E. W.

Thomas Mann's Works

SOURCE: POTEMPA, GEORGE. *Thomas Mann Bibliographie. Das Werk.* Morsum, Sylt: Cicero Presse. Vol. 1, 1992; vol. 2, 1997.

All of Mann's novels were published by the Fischer Verlag, originally S. Fischer, Berlin. Because of its exile (1936–1950) the name of the publishing house varies: Bermann-Fischer Verlag: Vienna, 1936–1938; Bermann-Fischer Verlag: Stockholm, 1938–1947; Vienna, Amsterdam, 1947–1950; S. Fischer: Frankfurt am Main since 1950. Mann's American publisher: New York: Alfred A. Knopf.

Narratives

"Vision: Prosa-Skizze." Written for and published in Thomas Mann's student paper *Frühlingssturm*, 1893. First public printing 1958. English: "A Vision." *Six Early Stories*. Trans. Peter Constantine. Los Angeles: Sun & Moon Press, 1997.

"Gefallen: Novelle." Written and published 1894. English: "Fallen." *Six Early Stories*. Trans. Peter Constantine. Los Angeles: Sun & Moon Press, 1997.

"Der Wille zum Glück: Novelle." Written 1895, published 1896. English: "The Will to Happiness." Trans. Eric Roman. *Story* 34, 1961. Also trans. Peter Constantine. *Six Early Stories*. Los Angeles: Sun & Moon Press, 1997.

"Der kleine Herr Friedemann: Novelle." Written probably 1894–1896, published 1897. English: "Little Herr Friedemann." *Stories of Three Decades*. Trans. Helen T. Lowe-Porter. New York: Knopf, 1936. Also trans. David Luke. *Death in Venice and Other Stories by Thomas Mann*. New York: Bantam Books, 1988.

"Der Tod: Novelle." Written 1896, published 1897. English: "Death." *Six Early Stories*. Trans. Peter Constantine. Los Angeles: Sun & Moon Press, 1997.

"Enttäuschung: Novelle." Written 1895–1896, published 1898. English: "Disillusionment." Trans. Helen T. Lowe-Porter. *Stories of Three Decades*. New York: Knopf, 1936.

"Der Bajazzo: Novelle." Written 1895–1897, published 1897. English: "The Dilettante." *Stories of Three Decades*. Trans. Helen T. Lowe-Porter. New York: Knopf, 1936. Also trans. David Luke as "The Joker." *Death in Venice and Other Stories by Thomas Mann*. New York: Bantam Books, 1988.

"Luischen: Novelle." Written 1897, published 1900. English: "Little Lizzy." Trans. Helen T. Lowe-Porter. *Stories of Three Decades*. New York: Knopf, 1936.

"Tobias Mindernickel: Novelle." Written 1897, published 1898. English: Helen T. Lowe-Porter. *Stories of Three Decades*. New York: Knopf, 1936.

"Der Kleiderschrank: Novelle." Written 1898, published 1899. English: "The Wardrobe." Trans. Helen T. Lowe-Porter. *Stories of Three Decades*. New York: Knopf, 1936.

"Gerächt: Novellistische Studie." Written and published 1899. English: "A Revenge." Trans. Edgar Rosenberg. *Esquire,* December 1959. Also trans. Peter Constantine. *Six Early Stories*. Los Angeles: Sun & Moon Press, 1997.

"Der Weg zum Friedhof: Novelle." Written and published 1900. English: "The Way to the Churchyard." Trans. Helen T. Lowe-Porter. *Stories of Three Decades*. New York: Knopf, 1936. Also trans. David Luke as "The Road to the Churchyard." *Death in Venice and Other Stories by Thomas Mann*. New York: Bantam Books, 1988.

Buddenbrooks: Verfall einer Familie. Written 1897–1900, published 1901. English: *Buddenbrooks*. Trans. Helen T. Lowe-Porter. New York: Knopf, 1924. Also trans. John E. Woods as *Buddenbrooks: The Decline of a Family*. New York: Knopf, 1993.

"Tristan: Novelle." Written 1901, published 1903. Trans. Helen T. Lowe-Porter. *Stories of Three Decades*. New York: Knopf, 1936. Also trans. David Luke. *Death in Venice and Other Stories by Thomas Mann*. New York: Bantam Books, 1988.

"Gladius Dei: Novelle." Written 1901, published 1902. Trans. Helen T. Lowe-Porter. *Stories of Three Decades*. New York: Knopf, 1936. Also trans. David Luke. *Death in Venice and Other Stories by Thomas Mann*. New York: Bantam Books, 1988.

"Die Hungernden: Studie." Written 1902, published 1903. English: "The Hungry." Trans. Helen T. Lowe-Porter. *Stories of Three Decades*. New York: Knopf, 1936.

"Tonio Kröger." Written 1900–1902, published 1903. Trans. Helen T. Lowe-Porter. *Stories of Three Decades*. New York: Knopf, 1936. Also trans. David Luke. *Death in Venice and Other Stories by Thomas Mann*. New York: Bantam Books, 1988.

"Ein Glück: Studie." Written 1903, published 1904. English: "A Gleam." Trans. Helen T. Lowe-Porter. *Stories of Three Decades*. New York: Knopf, 1936.

"Das Wunderkind: Novelle." Written and published 1903. English: "The Infant Prodigy." Trans. Helen T. Lowe-Porter. *Stories of Three Decades*. New York: Knopf, 1936.

"Beim Propheten: Novelle." Written and published 1904. English: "At the Prophet's." Trans. Helen T. Lowe-Porter. *Stories of Three Decades*. New York: Knopf, 1936.

Fiorenza: Drei Akte. Written 1903–1905, published 1905. Trans. Helen T. Lowe-Porter. *Stories of Three Decades*. New York: Knopf, 1936.

"Schwere Stunde: Novelle." Written and published 1905. English: "A Weary Hour." Trans. Helen T. Lowe-Porter. *Stories of Three Decades*. New York: Knopf, 1936.

"Wälsungenblut: Novelle." Written 1905, private printing in 1921; first public printing in German in 1958. English: "The Blood of the Walsungs." Trans. Helen T. Lowe-Porter. *Stories of Three Decades*. New York: Knopf, 1936.

"Anekdote." Written and published 1908. English: "Anecdote." *Six Early Stories*. Trans. Peter Constantine. Los Angeles: Sun & Moon Press, 1997.

"Das Eisenbahnunglück: Novelle." Written 1908, published 1909. English: "Railway Accident." Trans. Helen T. Lowe-Porter. *Stories of Three Decades*. New York: Knopf, 1936.

Königliche Hoheit: Roman. Written 1906–1909, published 1909. English: *Royal Highness*. Trans. A. Cecil Curtis. London: Sidgwick & Jackson, 1916.

"Wie Jappe und Do Escobar sich prügelten: Novelle." Written 1910, published 1911. English: "The Fight between Jappe and Do Escobar." Trans. Helen T. Lowe-Porter. *Stories of Three Decades*. New York: Knopf, 1936.

"Der Tod in Venedig: Novelle." Written 1911–1912, published 1912. As book: *Der Tod in Venedig*, private printing 1912, public printing 1913. English: "Death in Venice." Trans. Helen T. Lowe-Porter. *Stories of Three Decades*. New York: Knopf, 1936. Also trans. David Luke. *Death in Venice and Other Stories by Thomas Mann*. New York: Bantam Books,

1988. And by Clayton Koelb. *Death in Venice: A New Translation: Backgrounds and Contexts, Criticism.* New York: W. W. Norton & Co., 1994.

Betrachtungen eines Unpolitischen. Written 1915–1918, published 1918. English: *Reflections of a Nonpolitical Man.* Trans. Walter D. Morris. New York: Frederick Ungar Publishing Co., 1983.

Herr und Hund: Ein Idyll. Written 1918, published as a book, private printing, 1919, public printing 1925. English: "Bashan and I." Trans. Herman George Scheffauer. London: W. Collins Sons and Co., 1923. Also trans. Helen T. Lowe-Porter as "A Man and His Dog." *Stories of Three Decades.* New York: Knopf, 1936.

"Gesang vom Kindchen: Ein Idyll." Written 1918–1919, published 1919 (Song of the Newborn, no English translation).

Der Zauberberg: Roman. Written 1913–1924, published 1924. English: *The Magic Mountain.* Trans. Helen Lowe Porter. New York: Knopf, 1927. Also trans. John E. Woods as *The Magic Mountain: A Novel.* New York: Knopf, 1995.

"Unordnung und frühes Leid: Novelle." Written and published 1925. English: "Disorder and Early Sorrow." Trans. Helen T. Lowe-Porter. *Stories of Three Decades.* New York: Knopf, 1936.

"Mario und der Zauberer: Ein tragisches Reiseerlebnis." Written 1929, published 1930 (also as book). English: "Mario and the Magician." Trans. Helen T. Lowe-Porter. *Stories of Three Decades.* New York: Knopf, 1936.

Joseph und seine Brüder: Roman. Written 1926–1943, published in 1933–1943 as individual novels: *Die Geschichten Jaakobs* (Berlin: S. Fischer, 1933); *Der junge Joseph* (Berlin: S. Fischer, 1934); *Joseph in Ägypten* (Vienna: Bermann-Fischer, 1936); *Joseph der Ernährer.* (Stockholm: Bermann-Fischer, 1943). English (all trans. Helen T. Lowe-Porter): *Joseph and His Brothers* (contains only *Die Geschichten Jaakobs*) (New York: Knopf, 1934); *Young Joseph: Joseph and His Brothers II* (New York: Knopf 1935); *Joseph in Egypt: Joseph and His Brothers III* (New York: Knopf, 1938); *Joseph the Provider: Joseph and His Brothers IV* (New York: Knopf, 1944).

Lotte in Weimar: Roman. Written 1936–1939, published Stockholm: Bermann-Fischer 1939. English: *The Beloved Returns: Lotte in Weimar.* Trans. Helen T. Lowe-Porter. New York: Knopf, 1940; as *Lotte in Weimar: The Beloved Returns.* Trans. Helen T. Lowe-Porter. Berkeley: U of California P, 1990.

Die vertauschten Köpfe: Eine indische Legende. Written and published as a book in 1940. English: *The Transposed Heads: A Legend of India.* Trans. Helen T. Lowe-Porter. New York: Knopf, 1941; *Stories of a Lifetime.* 2 vols. London: Secker & Warburg, 1961.

Das Gesetz: Erzählung. First printings as a book in German: Los Angeles: Pazifische Presse 1944; Stockholm: Bermann-Fischer, 1944. English: "Thou Shalt Have No Other Gods Before Me." Trans. Georg R. Marek. *The Ten Commandments.* New York: Simon and Schuster, 1943. Also trans. Helen T. Lowe-Porter. *Stories of a Lifetime.* 2 vols. London: Secker & Warburg, 1961.

Doktor Faustus: Das Leben des deutschen Tonsetzers Adrian Leverkühn, erzählt von einem Freunde. Written 1943–1947, published Stockholm: Bermann-Fischer, 1947 (first licensed edition published inside Germany: Berlin: Suhrkamp, 1948). English: *Doctor Faustus: The Life of the German Composer Adrian Leverkühn as Told by a Friend.* Trans. Helen T. Lowe-Porter. New York: Knopf 1948. Also trans. John E. Woods as *Doctor Faustus.* New York: Random House, 1997.

Die Entstehung des Doktor Faustus: Roman eines Romans. Written 1948, published 1949. English: *The Story of a Novel: The Genesis of Doctor Faustus.* Trans. Richard and Clara Winston. London: Secker & Warburg, 1961.

Der Erwählte: Roman. Written 1948–1950, published 1951. English: *The Holy Sinner.* Trans. Helen T. Lowe-Porter. New York: Knopf, 1951; reprint U of California P, 1992.

"Die Betrogene: Erzählung." Written 1952–1953, published 1953. English: "The Black Swan." Trans. Willard R. Trask. New York: Knopf, 1954. Also trans. Helen T. Lowe-Porter. *Stories of a Lifetime.* 2 vols. London: Secker & Warburg, 1961.

Bekenntnisse des Hochstaplers Felix Krull: Der Memoiren erster Teil. Written 1910–1954, published 1954. Frankfurt am Main: S. Fischer; earlier partial printings: Vienna: Rikola, 1922; Amsterdam: Querido 1937. English: *Confessions of Felix Krull, Confidence Man: The Early Years.* Trans. Denver Lindley. New York: Knopf, 1955.

Selected Essay Collections in German

(All published by Fischer Verlag or Bermann-Fischer.)

Rede und Antwort: Gesammelte Abhandlungen und kleine Aufsätze, 1922.

Bemühungen: Neue Folge der Gesammelten Abhandlungen und kleinen Aufsätze, 1925.

Die Forderung des Tages: Reden und Aufsätze aus den Jahren 1925–1929, 1930.

Leiden und Größe der Meister: Neue Aufsätze, 1935.

Achtung Europa! Aufsätze zur Zeit, 1938.

Deutsche Hörer! 55 Radiosendungen nach Deutschland, 1945.

Adel des Geistes: Sechzehn Versuche zum Problem der Humanität, 1945.

Neue Studien, 1948.

Altes und Neues, 1953.

Nachlese, 1956.

Selected Essay Collections in English
(American Editions)

Three Essays. Trans. Helen T. Lowe-Porter. New York: Knopf, 1929.

Past Masters and Other Papers. Trans. Helen T. Lowe-Porter. New York: Knopf, 1933.

Freud, Goethe, Wagner. Trans. Helen T. Lowe-Porter. New York: Knopf, 1937.

This Peace. Trans. Helen T. Lowe-Porter. New York: Knopf, 1938.

Order of the Day: Political Essays and Speeches of Two Decades. Trans. Helen T. Lowe-Porter, Agnes Meyer, and Eric Sutton. New York: Knopf, 1942.

Listen Germany! Twenty-Five Radio Messages to the German People over BBC. Trans. Konrad Katzenellenbogen [Konrad Kellen]. New York: Knopf, 1943.

Essays of Three Decades. Trans. Helen T. Lowe-Porter. New York: Knopf, 1947.

Last Essays. Trans. Helen T. Lowe-Porter, 1959.

Thomas Mann's Addresses: Delivered at the Library of Congress 1942–1949. Washington: Library of Congress, 1963.

Diaries

Tagebücher. All Frankfurt am Main: S. Fischer. Edited by Peter de Mendelssohn: *1918–1921* (1979), *1933–1934* (1977), *1935–1936* (1978), *1937–1939* (1980), *1940–1943.* Edited by Inge Jens: *1944–1946* (1986), *1946–1948* (1989), *1949–1950* (1991), *1951–1952* (1993), *1953–1955* (1995). Only a partial selection of the diaries is available in English: *Diaries 1918–1939.* Trans. Richard and Clara Winston. New York: H. N. Abrams, 1982.

Collected Works

The Fischer Verlag published several editions of collected works, which were available as single volumes beginning in 1922, and then again in Stockholm and Frankfurt in 1939–1986.

The edition used in this volume is:

Gesammelte Werke in dreizehn Bänden. Hrsg. Hans Bürgin and Peter de Mendelssohn. Frankfurt am Main: S. Fischer, 1974, 1990.

A new edition has been in the process of being published since 2001:

Große kommentierte Frankfurter Ausgabe. Werke — Briefe — Tagebücher. Frankfurt am Main: S. Fischer. It will contain all fictional and essayistic works, a selection of letters, and eventually a new edition of the diaries.

Abbreviations

Works by Thomas Mann:

Br. 1–3   Mann, Thomas. *Briefe 1889–1936.* Ed. Erika Mann. Frankfurt am Main: S. Fischer, 1961.

DüD 1–3   *Dichter über ihre Dichtungen: Thomas Mann.* 3 vols. Ed. Hans Wysling and Marianne Fischer. Munich: Heimeran; Frankfurt am Main: S. Fischer, 1975–81.

Essays 1–6   Mann, Thomas. *Essays,* 6 vols. Ed. Hermann Kurzke and Stephan Stachorski. Frankfurt am Main: S. Fischer, 1993–97.

GKFA   Mann, Thomas. *Große kommentierte Frankfurter Ausgabe. Werke — Briefe — Tagebücher.* Frankfurt am Main: S. Fischer, 2001– (in progress).

GW 1–13   Mann, Thomas. *Gesammelte Werke in dreizehn Bänden.* Frankfurt am Main: S. Fischer, 1974, 1990. [Original: *Gesammelte Werke in zwölf Bänden.* Frankfurt am Main: S. Fischer, 1960].

Nb 1; *Nb* 2   Mann, Thomas. *Notizbücher 1–6, 7–14.* Ed. Hans Wysling and Ivonne Schmidlin. Frankfurt am Main: S. Fischer, 1991–92.

Tb   Mann, Thomas. *Tagebücher 1918–21, 1933–55.* 10 vols. Ed. Peter de Mendelssohn and Inge Jens. Frankfurt am Main: S. Fischer, 1979–95.

TM/AM   *Thomas Mann-Agnes E. Meyer: Briefwechsel 1937–1955.* Ed. Hans Rudolf Vaget. Frankfurt am Main: S. Fischer, 1992.

TM/HM   *Thomas Mann-Heinrich Mann Briefwechsel 1900–1949.* Ed. Hans Wysling. Frankfurt am Main: Fischer Taschenbuchverlag, 1995.

TM/OG   Mann, Thomas. *Briefe an Otto Grautoff 1894–1901 und Ida Boy-Ed 1903–1928.* Ed. Peter de Mendelssohn. Frankfurt am Main: S. Fischer, 1975

TMJb 1–15 *Thomas Mann Jahrbuch*. Ed. Eckhard Heftrich, Hans Wysling, Thomas Sprecher, and Ruprecht Wimmer. Frankfurt am Main: Klostermann, 1988–2002.

TMS 1–26 *Thomas-Mann-Studien*. Vol. 1–26. Ed. Thomas Mann Archiv der ETH. Bern: Francke (vol. 1–8); Frankfurt am Main: Klostermann (vol. 9–26).

Works by Friedrich Nietzsche

KSA 1–15 Nietzsche, Friedrich. *Kritische Studienausgabe*. Ed. Giorgio Colli and Mazzini Montinari. 15 vols. Munich: Deutscher Taschenbuchverlag, 1988.

Introduction

Herbert Lehnert

T HOMAS MANN'S FIRST NOVEL, *Buddenbrooks,* was published in 1901,[1] and his fame began with its second edition in 1903. Not yet thirty, he found himself a success. Before this recognition he had published vivid stories about odd characters who did not fit into ordinary society. These stories were experiments with the lives of outsiders distanced from society, from a society in which God was dead, and the proper meaning of love and death had to be re-discovered. In the novels outsiders relate to normal people. In *Buddenbrooks* we are shown how the distance from bourgeois society might develop. The connection between the viewpoints of outsiders and those of writers is explicit in the novellas "Tristan," "Tonio Kröger" (both 1903), and "Der Tod in Venedig" (Death in Venice, 1912). Characters living in tension with their society are found in "Wälsungenblut" (Blood of the Walsungs, written in 1905), *Joseph und seine Brüder* (Joseph and His Brothers, 1933–43), *Lotte in Weimar* (1939), and *Doktor Faustus* (1947).

For Mann, society is held together by love and power, and the extraordinary individual has to reckon with both. The unstable relationship between the extraordinary individual and love, power, and society stands at the center of all of Mann's works. Another major theme, in the absence of a binding religion, is the fascination with death. In the Buddenbrook family the acquisition of wealth — that is, power — is favored over sexual love. In *Königliche Hoheit* (Royal Highness, 1909) an outsider's distance is healed by love. In *Der Zauberberg* (The Magic Mountain, 1924) a young middle-class man is thrown out of his normalcy by illicit love and curiosity about death. In "Die vertauschten Köpfe" (The Transposed Heads, 1940) a gifted Brahman and an ordinary person are friends, until sexual desire for a pretty but ordinary girl separates them, with inordinate consequences. Gregorius, the protagonist of *Der Erwählte* (The Holy Sinner, 1951) is what the German title says, "The chosen one." Like all other outsiders in Mann's work, Gregorius clashes with the normal world through sexuality. The medieval model serves Mann to play with the social disapproval, the "sinfulness," of extraordinariness. But this play with sin and human superiority is undertaken with a parodistic veneration for humane religion. The first person narrator in *Bekenntnisse des Hochstaplers Felix Krull* (Confessions of Felix Krull, Confidence Man, 1954) considers himself a chosen person, and this is playfully balanced with his fraudulent existence. Rosalie von Tümmler in "Die Betrogene" (literally, The Betrayed One, translated as *The Black Swan,* 1953) ends her ordinary life with illicit desire, and her stepping out of bounds lets her be reconciled with death. Mann's readers experience individuals who wrestle with a world filled with rules that bind, a world with an appearance of stability that is constantly questioned. Even though Mann's texts are situated in the past, this past is not depicted nostalgically — it is a society as unstable as ours.

Two of Mann's earliest stories, "Der Wille zum Glück" (The Will to Happiness, 1896) and "Enttäuschung" (Disillusionment, 1898) carry implied references to Friedrich Nietzsche; both also are concerned with sexual tension. Clear traces of Nietzsche's philosophy are noticeable in an essay the eighteen-year-old Mann wrote for a student paper. In all these early literary activities he competed with his older brother, Heinrich, who had rebelled against their father by refusing to take over the family firm. Heinrich had left home and, as a book dealer's apprentice, had engaged in intensive self-study for a literary career. Thomas, four years younger than Heinrich, showed no inclination to fill in for his brother. He resisted by performing poorly at school and soon followed his brother in reading Schopenhauer and Nietzsche. He also wrote poetry in the style of Heinrich Heine and prose in the manner of the Austrian Hermann Bahr (1863–1934), the prophet of literary modernism.

Thomas and Heinrich Mann belonged to a generation of young writers who questioned the values of a staid and inflexible bourgeois order in the face of rapid social change. One such change was Darwinism, which shattered the belief in God the creator of a stable world. Nietzsche had attacked the veracity of traditional worldviews. God was not only dead, he proclaimed; we all had killed him.[2] Since the old slave-morality was based on the idea of sinning against a God who had now vanished, Nietzsche demanded the creation of a new morality.

The young writers who formed a new phase of German literature, Hauptmann, Schnitzler, George, Hofmannsthal, Heinrich and Thomas Mann, entered the German literary scene in the last decade of the nineteenth century. The reading of Nietzsche had sanctioned their rebellion against the bourgeois family tradition and its patriarchal morality. Thomas Mann's *Buddenbrooks* questions, even condemns, the ambience created by such a tradition. However, the narrator tells the story in a way that lovingly evokes sympathy for the family in his reader. The family's bourgeois ambition self-destructs, but the novel does not attack the bourgeois social system itself. *Buddenbrooks* is not an anti-bourgeois propaganda piece. And yet, the reader is made uneasy about the values and standards the novel portrays. The scholarship dedicated to Thomas Mann's fiction has learned to penetrate the seemingly conservative surface of Mann's works. Mann's language is filtered through a narrator who, while sharing the world of his readers, also remains distant from it. He thereby unobtrusively questions the foundation of the language he employs, and therefore also the foundation of his readers' world. Mann called this distanced position of the narrator irony; it is an ambivalent form of irony, not the usual brand with its mere opposite signifiers but rather one that allows for multiple meanings.

Mann appreciated Nietzsche's "psychological" criticism of the contemporary world, which exposed a bankrupt moral order, and he accepted Nietzsche's high valuation of creativity, intellectual insight, and affirmation of self. But he desired even more to become a successful writer, and that meant addressing his readers on their own terms. Mann's language is thus rarely provocative but seemingly realistic; as such it was appropriate for addressing the conservative public of the time. The provocative avant-garde Expressionist writers who came to dominate the literary scene in Germany since 1910 often found this objectionable, and critics from both the Right and the Left tended to misjudge Mann's work, finding it dated. They declared it inadequate because it did not provide utopian visions of social change such as the dominant ideologies of the twentieth century, fascism and Leninist socialism.

Thomas Mann was affected by the humanist dimension of these ideologies: cultural elitism on the Right, humane all-sympathy on the Left. He was even more affected by the void that had been left behind when the Christian religion ceased to serve as a general framework of values in Western society. *Der Zauberberg* plays with this empty space by placing Nietzsche's idea of God's death into the soul of a simple young man, Hans Castorp, in whom it turns into a fascination with death. Mann has his character explore and play with various ideologies, all of which cancel each other out in the end. *Der Zauberberg* reflects Mann's desire to keep his imagination free of all intellectual commitments in order to protect his work (more than his person) from the ideologies that so strongly influenced the thoughts and imagination of his contemporaries.

The outsider theme in Mann's fiction was generated by both the literary fashion of his time and by a very personal trait. The literary fashion was decadence, a perception of weakness of the will or the nerves, medically called neurasthenia. Neurasthenia was believed to be an actual physical condition but also a reaction to the increasing complexity of modern life. The other, more personal characteristic, which nurtured Mann's exploration of the outsider theme and with it the contradictory structure of all his work, was his own sexuality: he was bisexual with a dominant homoerotic trait. I use the word "homoerotic" rather than "homosexual" because Thomas Mann, in all likelihood, never consummated any of his homoerotic relationships.[3]

Decadence was seen as a positive, even desirable, expression of modernity by artists such as Oscar Wilde. As such, it functioned as a welcome opposition to the restrictive morality of the middle class, and was a condition reserved for creative artists or dilettantes who wanted to be different. Nietzsche saw decadence only in negative terms. In *Der Fall Wagner* (The Case of Wagner, 1888) he offered a definition of the decadent style in regard to the modernist music of Richard Wagner: decadence meant "life" had gone out of all cultural forms and creations, "so that life no longer lived in the whole" (dass das Leben nicht mehr im Ganzen wohnt).[4] Nietzsche took this formula from the fashionable French writer Paul Bourget (1852–1935) who by "the whole" meant the closed worldview of his Catholic faith. Bourget recommended a return to the church, but Nietzsche and Thomas Mann had no such designs. The "whole" for Nietzsche may have been "life," nature, or the universe, but here he was merely concerned with denying the value of Wagner's music, a value that, he claimed, lay only in details that never condensed into a meaningful aggregate.[5] Wagner's music represented modernity, which itself must be defined as decadent. Because God no longer anchored the modern world, nor lent it a sense of wholeness, and since modern science offered no substitute, there was no longer any "wholeness" to be found.

Nietzsche's tragic vision was indebted to Arthur Schopenhauer, one of his mentors. Mann had also read Schopenhauer and taken in his pessimistic worldview. A godless world, Schopenhauer taught, was dominated by the "Will," a force present in all beings that were compelled to fight for their existence. Thus the world was a chaotic struggle of everything against everything, and human society was held together only tenuously by the power of the state. Only pity with the subjects of this ill-designed world, and art, the artificial world transcending the chaotic Will, could give some sense to life. This godless, skeptical worldview, even its metaphysical aspect, which allowed for a vision of the world as a "whole" with hints of unknown forces outside of human rationality, made a lasting impression on Mann. This can be seen in some of the major characters in his fiction: Thomas Buddenbrook reads a chapter by Schopenhauer, and in presenting Hans Castorp's resistance toward Settembrini's optimistic rationality in *Der Zauberberg,* Mann was guided by the views of the pessimist. The many affinities of Mann's fiction with the writings of Carl Gustav Jung (1875–1961), which have occupied some Thomas Mann scholars, turned out to have been caused by Schopenhauer's laying a common ground for both.[6]

Rejecting Schopenhauer's denigration of life, Nietzsche transposed Schopenhauer's irrational Will into the "Will to Power," a will to take charge of one's own world. Nietzsche dreamt of an elite group of superior human beings, *Übermenschen,* who would exert power over the dependent masses and give directions through a new morality. Nietzsche's "psychology" meant to tear the existing falsehoods of a loveless world apart in favor of a future dominated by free, creative men, capable of a tragic view of the world and of human existence.

Mann did not care for Nietzsche's dream of strong men.[7] But, he was nevertheless attracted by Nietzsche's sharp criticism of society and his dream of a creative renewal beyond the decadence of the present. He realized that Nietzsche's judgment stemmed from a personal condition similar to his own: Nietzsche never experienced fulfilled sexual love, and Mann did not expect to satisfy his own homoerotic desire. Both compensated their want by writing. Mann admired Nietzsche's greatness, not in the least because he knew its origin so intimately. Even when Mann felt forced to reconsider Nietzsche's influence in his essay "Nietzsche's Philosophie im Lichte unserer Erfahrung" (Nietzsche's Philosophy in the Light of Our Experience, 1947), he pointed out Nietzsche's "errors" but left no doubt about his greatness.

One of Mann's early plans — he jotted down the first existing notes for it in one of his notebooks during the writing of *Buddenbrooks*[8] — was to write about the Italian reformer and martyr Girolamo Savonarola (1452–98). This came to fruition in 1905 with the drama *Fiorenza,* the two protagonists of which confront two examples of Nietzsche's dream world: Lorenzo de Medici, a strong Renaissance man whose affinity to Nietzsche is indicated in the text by once being called "Dionysos,"[9] and the Prior, Savonarola, who prevails through a different form of the Will to Power. Lorenzo is a powerful and ruthless Renaissance ruler who is dying and expresses fear of his imminent death, while the Prior is modeled after the powerful ascetic priest in section fifteen of Nietzsche's essay "Was bedeuten asketische Ideale?" (What do Ascetic Ideals Mean?).[10] The Prior's last words in the play are "I love fire," an allusion both to Savonarola's burning of artworks during his future rule of Florence and to his eventual execution. Both forms of the "Will to Power" end in death.

After *Buddenbrooks* was completed Mann planned a society novel to be titled "Maja," for which extensive notes exist. Some of these notes bear the alternate title "Die Geliebten" (The Beloved). The character Albrecht in these notes resembles Mann's brother Heinrich, with whom he was competing for domination of the German literary scene. Albrecht belies the Nietzschean cult of Life, beauty, instinct, and strength, exhibiting the neurasthenia that Heinrich attributed to himself.[11] Another of Thomas's fictionalized portraits of Heinrich, again with the name of Albrecht, is the reigning grand duke in *Königliche Hoheit,* whose "vornehm" (distinguished) aloofness is caused by his neurasthenia rather than based on strength. The condition almost causes him to abdicate in favor of his younger brother; even the word abdication itself appears in the text (*GW 2,* 156). A poet appearing in the same novel, suggesting Heinrich, is a false Nietzschean: he exhibits strength only on paper. The fictional portrayal of the competition between the younger brother and the elder shows the potential for viciousness that would eventually spill over into real life. Book reviews by Thomas contained deprecatory allusions to Heinrich's writings, without naming them or him.

The sibling rivalry between Heinrich and Thomas Mann was aggravated by Heinrich's heterosexuality. While Thomas in his writings camouflaged his desires as well as the need to suppress them (for example in making little Herr Friedemann a cripple), Heinrich could fantasize openly about his. Writing, in Thomas's opinion, should not be easy. He expected his brother to transform his desires differently but with no less effort. When Thomas read Heinrich's trilogy *Die Göttinnen* (The Goddesses) and his social novel *Die Jagd nach Liebe* (The Hunt for Love), both published in 1903, he found them hastily written, deficient in content and style. Heinrich, his brother felt, had ceased to be the model of a distinctive writer that he once had been; he had begun to write down to his readers, stimulating their lasciviousness. This went against Nietzsche's writings, which had deeply affected both brothers. Nietzsche had written for a new creative aristocracy that was to break the old social conventions and push aside the old morality, not in favor of licentiousness but to create a new humanity of a higher order. Writing down to one's audience meant serving primitive instincts. Thomas's opinion is contained in his letter to Heinrich of 5 December 1903. In order to guard against the possibility that Heinrich would dismiss his criticism as plain old-fashioned moralism, Thomas specifically refers to Nietzsche's ideas of a new morality. It is clear that he wanted to be understood in Nietzsche's terms.

Heinrich's *Die Jagd nach Liebe* was a society novel dealing with frustrated love, and set in Munich, as Thomas's "Maja" was planned to have been. The main theme of "Maja" was the frustrated love of a woman protagonist for a flirtatious young man. For his novelistic plans Mann used notations of his relationship with a male friend, the painter Paul Ehrenberg. Thomas's text, if he had developed it beyond mere notes, would have been quite different. Still, the publication of Heinrich's novel was most likely one reason for the shelving of "Maja." Another reason was Thomas's marriage, which for a while meant the end of his frustrated homoerotic desires.

Much happened in Thomas Mann's life during the years between the publication of *Buddenbrooks* late in 1900 (with the date of 1901) and his marriage in February of 1905: a frustrating homoerotic friendship with Paul Ehrenberg, a temporary love relationship with a young English woman in Florence, and, since the fall of 1903, the courting of Katia Pringsheim. Besides making plans for the society novel "Maja" and for the Savonarola drama *Fiorenza,* Mann produced two novellas during that time which present the outsider theme in contrast: "Tristan," in which art means death, and "Tonio Kröger," in which a writer, though bitterly complaining about his alienated existence, finds his life's task in putting his love for the common people, the non-artists, the insiders, into his writing. "Tonio Kröger" assigns literature the mission of introducing love into the miserable Schopenhauerian world.

The writer from his distant outsider point of view looks into the center of the world ("das Innere der Welt"), Schopenhauer's "Will," and sees comedy and misery ("Komik und Elend," *GW* 8, 290). But in the end he promises to apply love when bringing into form what he has seen (*GW* 8, 338). "Tristan" and "Tonio Kröger" were probably written side by side. They were both published in 1903. *Fiorenza* was written from mid 1903 to January 1905.

Mann's marriage in February of 1905 ended his outsider existence, but his idea of proper modern writing still required the distance from society that an outsider position afforded. Only from a distant vantage point could modern society, with its constant changes, be adequately observed. Mann even felt that he had to justify his marriage, asserting in a letter to his brother of 23 December 1904 that it would not impede his writing. He assured Heinrich, who could still serve him as his artistic conscience, that he was not simply craving happiness ("Glück") but meeting life ("Leben"). "Leben" was a key word in Nietzsche's philosophy contrasting flexible, chaotic life with fixed morality and set conventions, condemning the latter. But Mann assigns his own meaning to the word "Leben." Nietzsche would not have considered the social reality of family life inspiration for creativity. Thomas's apology to Heinrich means that he, like Heinrich, recognized Nietzsche's distance from bourgeois society obligatory for the modern artist. In his innermost self Thomas Mann knew that his art was a translation of his outsider position, induced by his sexual otherness. He played with the danger of losing his creativity together with his outsider position in plans for subsidiary plots for "Maja" or new novellas. Several of his notes for such future works written in the fall of 1904 are concerned with a writer who degenerates because of the fame he has attained. In one, written about the time when Mann was courting Katia, an artist, sick with syphilis, courts a pure sweet girl and shoots himself shortly before the wedding.[12] Syphilis stands for the impurity of the outsider; it was also Nietzsche's illness. Another note, written probably in the spring of 1905, after the marriage, tells us that the idea began to fascinate Mann; the syphilitic writer, after having approached the pure sweet girl, has made a pact with the devil; the syphilitic poison in his blood acts as stimulus and inspiration. He creates great works, but in the end the devil takes him by means of syphilitic paralysis.[13]

In 1905, during the first year of his marriage, Mann wrote the novella "Wälsungenblut" (Blood of the Walsungs, privately printed 1921, first publication 1958), another variation on the outsider problem. On protestation of his father-in-law Mann withdrew the work after it had been printed.

The novel *Königliche Hoheit* was in progress since 1906 and was published in 1909; Mann's earliest notebook entries concerning it are from 1903. This story of a prince, protected from crude reality, occupied with merely ceremonial duties, was originally planned as another outsider story, symbolizing the "formal" existence of the writer. Mann had the prince shake off his outsider status by falling in love and earning the respect of his future wife, a commoner and a rich heiress. He looks forward to an "austere happiness" (strenges Glück) with his bride (*GW 2*, 363). "Austere happiness" also describes the fulfillment the novel's author could find in a relationship that excluded his dominant sexual desire.

Thomas Mann found security in his family, living with a wife of high intelligence who nevertheless devoted herself entirely to the service of her husband's career and to the psychic well-being of their six children. But the austere happiness remained brittle. This intimate conflict in Mann was the driving force behind his greatest novella, "Der Tod in Venedig." On a trip to Venice in 1911 Mann was accompanied by his wife Katia and his brother Heinrich. Katia represented Mann's new socially adjusted role and Heinrich the stimulus for his ambition as writer. On the beach of the Lido of Venice Mann fell voyeuristically in love with a boy but left soon with his company. In the novella this experience is transferred to the writer Gustav von Aschenbach and imaginatively amplified. Aschenbach goes to Venice to escape a bout of writer's block. A dignified traveler, he arrives in Venice alone. He has achieved fame by an extraordinary discipline and commands national authority. He has even been honored with the rank of nobility, and his books have become required readings in public schools. Even though Aschenbach never touches or speaks to the boy with whom he falls in love, he loses his bearings and his sense of dignity by allowing his desire to take control of him. His death, seeing the beloved boy as Hermes, leader of the dead, beckoning him before the empty horizon of the sea, destroys as well as fulfills his life. Succumbing to the cholera ironically preserves his dignity before the world. In a way "Der Tod in Venedig" answers Mann's fears of losing his creative powers by adjusting to social normalcy contained in the plans for novellas jotted down in 1904. This answer became a tightly woven text that contained his fears by transforming them. Aschenbach's public authority cannot satisfy his innermost emotional needs. These needs are anarchic and defy discipline but can be transformed into the imaginative artistic construct. While the text narrated a breakdown of discipline, it confirmed Mann's self-control. Creativity requires a well-maintained inner distance from the world; it cannot be absorbed in serving society. "Der Tod in Venedig" both praises and condemns Mann's decision to suppress his dominant sexual desire in order to establish a conventional bourgeois facade for achieving fame and authority. It contradicts Nietzsche's vision of man employing his creativity to attain a higher state of being. The work also was an early answer to Heinrich Mann's call to use the writer's authority for a political agenda: propagandizing for the democratization of Germany.

From about 1904 on, Heinrich Mann had engaged himself in efforts to bring about liberal democracy in Germany. Heinrich's manifesto "Geist und Tat" (Intellect and Action, 1911) exhorted German writers of high literature to further democratic developments in Germany and polemicize against the traditional complacency of the German bourgeoisie. Reactionary forces should no longer be allowed to remain in power. Heinrich characterized German authors writing on unpolitical subjects as apostatizing literati. He meant this label to fit his brother. Thomas did not react; at least there is no record of him having done so. (He burned his diaries from that period in 1945.)

For the time being, the personal relations of the brothers remained intact, sometimes even cordial. Heinrich answered Thomas's aggressive letter of December 1903 defensively but with dignity.[14] He defended his brother against a poor review of *Fiorenza* in 1906. But his review of "Der Tod in Venedig" reads like a prose poem about the need for the abdication of the authority of the genius in a decadent environment. It begins, ominously, with a discussion of Zola's novelistic history of the empire of Napoleon the Third. The review can be read as Heinrich's praise for the artistic achievement of his brother's novella, but also as a demand that Thomas reject the German "Kaiserreich."[15]

Heinrich had understood that "Der Tod in Venedig" contained an answer to his essay "Geist und Tat." In Thomas's text the government has given a social role to the eminent artist Gustav von Aschenbach, whom Heinrich, in his review, refers to as the "genius." Aschenbach's writings are standard readings in the public schools, but their value as described in Thomas's text is moralistic, not political, and Aschenbach even loses his moral superiority.

In his essay "Zola" (1915), which was to cause the most severe break between the brothers, Heinrich used the word *Nationaldichter* for writers who supported the German war effort in 1914. He aimed at the ambition of his brother, his desire to become *the* writer of national prominence. Considering the goals that Thomas Mann pursued from 1909 to 1914 — a novel on Frederick the Second of Prussia and an essay judging the contemporary literary scene from a superior point of view — one would have to agree that the mantle of *Nationaldichter* indeed was his aim (as it was Heinrich's). The novel on Frederick of Prussia was to have shown Frederick's superiority, which was based on his intelligence and his human weaknesses as well. But the project did not materialize; instead, Mann turned to the depiction of a false superiority. *Bekenntnisse des Hochstaplers Felix Krull* is a narrative about a confidence man of questionable bourgeois origin whose success is the result of his ability to act as a nobleman. The beginnings of the text contain parodic allusions to Goethe's autobiography *Dichtung und Wahrheit* (Poetry and Truth, 1811–14). *Krull* plays with the authority of Goethe's genius and, at the same time, with the deceptiveness of art. Nietzsche had given art both a positive and a negative value: art was good because it deceived, as life itself did; but art was problematic because it never was what it pretended to be.

The memoirs of the confidence man, narrated in the first person, soon assumed novel size. The bourgeois standard of value that Krull displays is belied by the sexual instruction he receives from the prostitute Rozsa. Her teaching is to prepare him for later sexual exploits. Mann abandoned the novel at this point, in 1913, in order to write *Der Zauberberg*. In the continuation of the novel about the confidence man, written late in Mann's life, Krull's heterosexual adventures paradoxically convey homosexual desires. As in the "Maja" notes, Mann has a woman, Madame Houpflé, express her author's desire for adolescent boys (*GW 7*, 445). In another passage, he has Krull evoke the desire of a Scottish Lord who resembles the author, only thinly disguised. Krull's superiority and noblesse are false. The playfulness of Mann's representation of Krull's falsehood can be read both as a making fun of Nietzsche's attempt to achieve a new form of nobility and as a criticism of the social and moral orientation of the bourgeois world before the First World War.

Besides the Frederick novel, another unfinished work that betrays Mann's aim to become *Nationaldichter* is the plan of an essay on literature under the title "Geist und Kunst" (Intellect and Art). This title is also found among the fictional works of Gustav von Aschenbach in "Der Tod in Venedig." "Geist und Kunst" was intended to discuss the question of how deceptive art can be serious business. Nietzsche's *Der Fall Wagner* and his psychology of demasking remain the models for Mann's argumentation. Establishing the value of playing with contrasts and contradictions rather than overwhelming the reader with unambiguous rhetorical persuasion seems to have been the essay's goal. One of the notes lists a series of contrasts, among them those of intellect and nature, intellect and art, and naive and sentimental. The last and most challenging one is "Plastik und Kritik" (plasticity and criticism). "Plastik" meant full-bodied, fictional writing, persuading the reader by creating concrete images in his mind, while "Kritik" meant writing from an intellectual distance, analyzing the common world and its general assumptions, while using Nietzsche's psychology of demasking as a model.[16] To demonstrate the tension between these two contrasting literary modes in his writing had always been Mann's hidden goal. Such literature could rise above mere entertainment while not losing readers by boring them with abstractions. Wagner's music, which aimed for effect, always served Mann as the model for his own way of writing, but one of which he remained somewhat suspicious; much as Wagner's, his work might be read as catering to the sympathies of his readers. But Nietzsche's demasking psychology allowed him to address his audience's intellect as well, making the intellectual aspect of his writing as challenging as Nietzsche's and its artfulness as effective as Wagner's. The plan for the essay on "Geist und Kunst" was never executed, most probably because Mann wanted to draw in and judge too many contemporary phenomena. Among them were the fashion of art for art's sake and the "Lebensphilosophie" that Nietzsche's followers pursued after his death. With the "Geist und Kunst" essay Mann had the intention of instructing, but the modernism that was taking hold at the time resisted such directives.

Work on the novel *Der Zauberberg* began in 1913. Mann claimed that the plan was originally a parody of "Der Tod in Venedig." His protagonist was to be a simple young German rather than an artist. But the figure of Hans Castorp, cast out of his ordinary life, soon began to fascinate his author. Castorp's magic mountain, a sanatorium, became a symbol of European decadence, and Hans Castorp's very German resistance to the rhetoric of an Italian liberal became a kind of answer to the unanswerable question, "What is German?" Here there was potential for the great national novel, to be read by the readers of "higher" German literature, the educated class or *Bildungsbürger,* the core of which were the higher civil servants. The brothers Mann fought one another for their attention. Heinrich wanted those *Bildungsbürger* to become political and to take power away from established authority; literature was to be the instrument of political change. Thomas, by contrast, was satisfied with the existing order, since it offered sufficient freedom for a writer. He was convinced that political involvement would reduce the writer's "ironic" distance and his freedom to assume any or all positions.

Who were the *Bildungsbürger,* the readers of "high" German literature? Middle-level civil servants with modest incomes formed the core of the class, and they were less affected than the richer classes by a capitalist ideology that considered wealth the standard of value. These people also had little interest in progressive social ideologies aimed at changing the governmental system of which they were part. But they also had come in contact, during their university educations, with criticism of the then-current values of society, and this served to balance their political conservatism. As civil servants they believed in government under the law. Such readers appreciated texts that played with contrasting worldviews rather than presenting defined and specific utopias. They enjoyed novels that invited them to understand not only the ordinary member of the middle class but also the outsider, and to value both on their own terms.

The *Bildungsbürger* measured their value by their ability to participate in culture, and culture included high literature, a literature not produced to meet average tastes. They considered themselves a separate class by virtue of their university degrees and titles. Although it was not easy for a person of the lower classes to gain access to a university, the path was not closed in principle. Thomas Mann himself advocated free access to higher education even in his essay *Betrachtungen eines Unpolitischen* (Reflections of a Nonpolitical Mann, 1918), his defense of a specific German culture free of politics. He located the idea of freedom exclusively in the mind of the individual, maintaining that political movements tended to stimulate envy and greediness (*GW* 12, 259).

If Mann's works were written for the *Bildungsbürger,* a class that no longer exists in its original fashion, why should we read him? Did German *Bildungsbürger* not fail dismally in protecting their culture from National Socialist barbarism? And is the historically conditioned inclination of the *Bildungsbürger* to lean on authority not responsible for their tolerating a totalitarian regime? And did Mann not write specifically for those more conservative, authoritarian *Bildungsbürger?* It is true that Mann's fictional worlds give the appearance of stability: while the Buddenbrook family declines, the Hagenströms rise; while Hans Castorp is surrounded by the sick and dying, an orderly world exists below his mountain. But even in these cases foregrounds and backgrounds are constructed as dichotomies; stability is cancelled by an irritant. This, in variations, is true everywhere in Mann's work. In *Der Zauberberg* Hans Castorp's illicit love for a libertine woman is grounded in homosexual desire and linked with his religious and Romantic fascination with death. There is always an anarchic ingredient in the seemingly stable social backgrounds of Mann's fiction. For Mann, like Nietzsche, culture is in constant need of creative renewal.

Thomas Mann's dream of a better future meant the rule of culture in human affairs, of a culture generated by free human beings who determine their own future, guided by a humane morality of love and tolerance. Such a dream stood already at the core of his critique of the lifestyle of the grand-bourgeoisie in *Buddenbrooks,* and such a dream is the driving force in Mann's great novel *Joseph und seine Brüder.* The knowledge that Mann, as a person, was less humane than appears from his writings does not change the picture; fictional texts owe their existence to being separated from their author.

European culture, including the contemplation of new moralitics, was severely shaken by the First World War. The war was initially seen by both brothers Mann as the cultural catastrophe that it was. When it broke out in August of 1914 Thomas used the word "madness" (*Wahnsinn*) to describe it.[17] While Heinrich, convinced that Germany would inevitably lose the war, immediately voiced his aversion to war against his beloved France, Thomas shifted, and, moved by popular patriotic enthusiasm, spoke in a letter of 22 August 1914 of a cleansing experience, an elevation and liberation from the rotten pre-war civilization saturated by comfort.[18] Writing to Heinrich on 18 September he called the conflict a "people's war" (*Volkskrieg*), using Romantic terminology.[19] After this letter, the relationship between the brothers ruptured; apparently there had also been a face-to-face altercation.

Heinrich put his enmity into his essay "Zola," which appeared in November 1915. In it he alludes to Thomas's first war essay "Gedanken im Kriege" (Reflections in War, 1914), which probably repeated much of what he had said to Heinrich in the hostile discussion that had ended their relationship. Thomas lauded the German war of liberation from Western civilization, liberalism, capitalism, and decadence in favor of culture, as he had conceived it in *Der Zauberberg*. This contrast of creative and tragic culture with rational and comfortable civilization reflected Nietzsche's thinking. *Die Betrachtungen eines Unpolitischen*, Mann's long war essay, displays a strong national German bias, but also declares a certain cosmopolitan openness to be an inherent part of German culture. Mann called the ideological form of liberalism "democracy" and his own anti-ideological stance "conservative." He suggested a Romantic form of democracy he called a "people's state" (*Volksstaat*) (*GW* 12, 272–82).

The bitter enmity of the brothers affected Thomas more deeply than Heinrich. It lasted until 1922 when they reconciled. In the Weimar Republic the two cooperated, helping when the Prussian Academy of Arts established a section for poetry and writing, giving the profession of letters official status. Heinrich became president of the section.

After the First World War Thomas Mann took a while to reorient himself. He had difficulties accepting the victory of the Western allies; he understood it as a victory of capitalism over German culture. *Betrachtungen eines Unpolitischen* had been published in the fall of 1918, only weeks before the German capitulation. The book was successful among the *Bildungsbürger*, but was naturally not much liked by the more liberal and radical intellectuals. But during the Bavarian revolution and civil war, including the short period of a Bavarian *Räterepublik* (soviet republic) run by anarchists and then by communists, Mann's house and family in Munich were protected by leftist intellectuals. In 1919 the University of Bonn awarded him a honorary doctorate. The faculty meant to honor Mann's *Betrachtungen* but would not say so openly because Bonn was under British occupation. However, when Mann realized that the German rightist parties' brand of conservatism was a regressive political ideology that had no interest in preserving an open and tolerant, non-ideological culture, he moved away from the nationalist orientation of his *Betrachtungen*.

National Socialism originated in Munich, where Mann made his home. He resisted this movement from its very beginnings. He could not tolerate its regressiveness, because his Nietzschean view of culture required constant cultural renewal. Some right-wing writers and National Socialists also claimed Nietzsche's anti-democratic notions for their movement. This would become an irritation for Mann, especially after 1933 when Hitler seized power in Germany.

In 1921 in his hometown of Lübeck, Mann held his first public speech; he spoke about Goethe and Tolstoy.[20] He repeated the speech in many places in Germany. By including the great Russian author, Mann continued the cosmopolitan line of thought set forth in *Betrachtungen*, though Goethe won higher praise than his Russian counterpart. Goethe and Tolstoy shared a love of education inspired by Rousseau: the Rousseau of *Émile* rather than the Rousseau of the *Contrat social* that Mann had ridiculed in *Betrachtun-*

gen.[21] Both Goethe and Tolstoy offered examples of how life could be turned into writing and writing into education. A writer whose imagination is free of social or monetary interests can set the national mood and become a spiritual leader. Mann's conception of the possible role of a writer in national life is less comprehensive than Nietzsche's idea of a creative ruling elite and involves less activism than advocated by Heinrich; it was a more realistic conception, but also a step in Heinrich's direction.

Mann first publicly voiced support for the Weimar Republic in 1922, in a speech honoring Gerhart Hauptmann titled "Von deutscher Republik" (On German Republic). He advocated a republican form of government as the appropriate political model for a nation that had found itself in patriotic fervor at the outbreak of the war and that, in addition, could no longer see itself ruled by a monarchy that had degenerated into theatricality. Mann presented the Romantic monarchist Novalis and the American Walt Whitman (whose poems had just appeared in a new translation) as examples of the kind of cultural nationalism he had in mind. In this speech Mann still tried to avoid the word "democracy," using the term "Humanität" (humaneness) instead (*Essays* 2, 133), but he soon learned that the preservation of culture and *Humanität* against rightist intolerance required not only political involvement, but explicit support for democracy.

Mann's speech was addressed to the majority of *Bildungsbürger* who leaned toward the right. "Republicanism" and "democracy" were catchwords in their eyes: they opposed and ridiculed these forms of government because they saw them forced on Germany by the victors. Mann's support of the republic was widely seen as a move away from the patriotic conservatism that had governed his *Betrachtungen*. Yet he refused to admit to any such shift. He claimed that he had addressed the relationship between politics and culture in *Betrachtungen*, and he did so now by exposing the politics of the right. Any change was merely one of words, not of substance.

In 1925, Mann turned the speech about Goethe and Tolstoy into an essay under the title "Goethe and Tolstoi: Fragmente zum Problem der Humanität." He added a section in which he struck out against "German Fascism," calling it "romantic barbarism" (*GW* 9, 169). In 1930, when the National Socialists gained seats in the Reichstag and the agony of the Weimar Republic began, Mann traveled to Berlin and delivered his "Deutsche Ansprache. Ein Apell an die Vernunft" (German Address. An Appeal to Reason). The political place of the German "Bürger," he concluded, was now at the side of the Social Democratic Party (*Essays* 3, 278). In 1932, with the republic in its death throes, Mann, undaunted, commemorated the hundredth anniversary of Goethe's death by giving two speeches. He reminded the audiences of the aged Goethe's interest in progress, and implored his fellow Germans to think in terms of a democratic future.[22] During 1932 and up until January 1933, Mann condemned National Socialism and supported a humanitarian socialism in newspaper articles, answers to public queries, and speeches (*Essays* 3, 343–58). With this support of socialism, Mann moved beyond Nietzsche, who regarded Socialism as an impediment to the higher development of man.

Mann had taken up *Der Zauberberg* again in 1919 and finished the novel in 1924. The original counterpart figure to the humanist Settembrini in the first conception, a Lutheran minister, now became Naphta, a Jewish Jesuit who in a seeming contradiction is both a scholar of medieval thought and a supporter of a communist revolution. The change was a reflection of Mann's experience of revolutionary postwar turmoil. Although socialist intellectuals find this absurd, as Marxism means progress to them, Mann understood communism in terms of a pre-capitalist medieval communal economy. The idea suggested to Mann by Gustav Landauer's *Aufruf zum Sozialismus* (Call for Socialism, 1911) is not far-fetched: communism developed practices analogous to those of the church: excommunication and the inquisition; and the medieval economy exerted means of control. Naphta's criticism of Settembrini's liberal humanism often hits the mark. His Jewishness represents alienation, as Jewishness generally does in Mann's fictional world. Naphta reveals capitalist modernity as an ideology, and it is humorous that Mann has him do that from the points of view of both the right and of the totalitarian left.

Nietzsche's cult of Life is represented in *Der Zauberberg* by a Dionysian figure, Mynheer Peeperkorn, whose role in the text becomes satirical when he commits suicide because he feels impotent. Such a depiction implies skepticism toward Nietzsche's cult of Life as a foundation for new values. But Nietzsche's overcoming of Wagner's lure is offered by the narrator as a link to Germany's future: Wagner's Romantic music stands for the nostalgic desire for a return of the pre-war world; Nietzsche's rejection of his beloved friend stands for rejection of political nostalgia and a courageous acceptance of change. Neither Wagner nor Nietzsche are named, but they are clearly meant. At the end we see Hans Castorp participate in the destruction of the First World War, paradoxically singing a Romantic theme song of dreams, home, and death. The novel does not only have an open ending, it is a novel of openness.

The novel tetralogy *Joseph und seine Brüder*, conceived by Mann in the early twenties, was begun in 1926 and completed in 1943. The novel's four volumes were published in 1933, 1934, 1936, and 1943 while he lived in Swiss and American exile. *Joseph* reflects the difficulties a creative narcissist like Mann had in dealing with the world. His character Joseph overcomes his love of self: strengthened by his conviction of having to fulfill a divine task, he becomes a leader, engages himself in the service of his fellow human beings, and in the end saves his family — but not without pitfalls along the way. In a way the novel answers Heinrich Mann's call for writers to become politically engaged in his essay "Geist und Tat" of 1911. The biblical model allowed Mann to depict Joseph's position in Egypt — borrowing his power from the king — as the political ideal of the *Bildungsbürger,* a genial authority for the common good. The last volume, *Joseph der Ernährer* (Joseph the Provider), telling of Joseph's social programs, alludes to Franklin Delano Roosevelt, whom Mann had met personally: Mann wanted to see Roosevelt as a social democratic leader. *Joseph und seine Brüder* can be read as the fictional wish fulfillment of the creative imagination empowered to set the world right. The transformation of the artistic Joseph into a leader and an economist, however, is not presented as a general model: Joseph does not win the primary religious blessing from his father Jacob. That Joseph becomes an economist assigns him to this world and excludes him from the religious future of his people.

Mann's exile had begun late in February of 1933, after Hitler had been appointed to form a government and had used the burning of the Reichstag as a pretext for assuming dictatorial power and for abolishing the civil rights of the Weimar constitution. The political police in Munich had prepared an order to incarcerate Mann in the concentration camp at Dachau, but Mann, on a winter vacation in Switzerland, heeded dire warnings not to return.

Mann was deeply shaken by his banishment from his home country; more so than by the loss of his house and savings. Even more galling was a public protest of the Munich Wagnerians against a speech he had given there before his departure and again in Amsterdam and Paris. This protest action, while being signed by a few Nazis, was not the result of a National Socialist campaign but an action by Munich *Bildungsbürger,* instigated by the opera director and conductor Hans Knappertsbusch. In his essay on Wagner, Mann had confessed his lifelong attachment to Wagner's music, but he had also described Wagner in terms that fell short of the kind of exaltation the signers considered appropriate. The Munich protest hit Mann in the center of his being. Mann had judged his value for the German nation to lie in his sophisticated writing: enough Wagner to be popular among *Bildungsbürger,* enough Nietzsche to challenge them with ironic detachment. Just this combination the Munich protesters had rejected.

Mann resolved at first to withdraw completely into private life. He settled in Switzerland, near Zurich. After weeks of being unable to write, he continued *Joseph und seine Brüder.* In 1934, he seriously considered an essay or letter to the London *Times* exposing the Nazi regime as a threat to all culture. He decided to refrain from such direct attack because his books were still published and read in Germany: there was still a chance to exert an influence on his fellow Germans. Instead of the political statement, he combined a diary of his first cruise to America with essayistic comments on Cervantes's *Don Quixote* (1604–14) for a feature published in the *Neue Zürcher Zeitung.* In it he retells the episode of the Morisco Ricote who mourns the loss of his homeland after having been driven out of Spain for religious and racist reasons. Spain, Mann writes, pretending to report on Cervantes's opinion, will not become purer but poorer by the "eradication" (*Ausmerzung*) of its Jewish citizens (*Essays* 4, 129). This early protest against National Socialist policies had to be veiled because it was to appear in a conservative newspaper in neutral Switzerland.

The German Ministry of Propaganda, fearful of negative publicity, prevented the revocation of Mann's German citizenship demanded by the Munich Gestapo. Other writers, among them Thomas's brother Heinrich and Thomas's older children Erika and Klaus, were similarly threatened. Mann became a Czech citizen in December 1936. When a dean of Bonn University informed him that Nazi law required the repeal of his honorary doctorate, Mann responded in a letter charging Bonn and all other German universities with sharing in the country's responsibility for supporting a regime that was devastating Germany morally, culturally, and economically (*Essays* 4, 184). In this letter, he proudly announced that Harvard University had bestowed an honorary degree on him; it had happened in 1935, when he was honored together with Albert Einstein. Warning of the threat of war entailed by Germany's rearmament, Mann ended his letter with an invocation that God may help his misused country to make peace. This letter was first published in the *Neue Zürcher Zeitung* in January 1937, gaining worldwide publicity.

During another journey to the United States in 1938, Mann delivered the lecture "Vom kommenden Sieg der Demokratie" (Of the Coming Victory of Democracy) in several cities. When Hitler occupied Austria that same year, Thomas and Katia Mann no longer felt safe in Switzerland. They relocated to New Jersey, where Mann was appointed Lecturer in the Humanities at Princeton University, and they lived there from 1938 to 1941.

In 1939 Mann finished the novel *Lotte in Weimar,* which had been in progress since 1936, when it had interrupted the writing of *Joseph und seine Brüder.* In the final scene of the Weimar novel, a dreamlike, unreal Goethe comforts the disappointed Lotte for having been distant throughout her visit, speaking in the language of his poetry. Thus, the novel grows into a confession: Mann, playfully identifying himself with Goethe, wants to be appreciated for his works, not for his person; only his creative language has worth. Implied is a criticism of Nietzsche's assertion that the aim and purpose of all culture is to produce great men. Rather, the individual should serve culture and with it all of mankind. This idea permeates *Joseph und seine Brüder;* it is radically opposed to the *Führer* principle in National Socialism and its hero worship.

In 1941 the Manns moved to California and settled in Pacific Palisades in western Los Angeles, and in 1944 Mann and his wife became United States citizens. He appreciated the reception he had received in America, but he never fully embraced capitalist democracy. After Roosevelt's death and the war's end, he came to increasingly oppose the course the country took: the return to a free enterprise economy, the imperial foreign policy designed to protect American trade, and, especially, the Cold War with its ideologically driven anti-communism. He also opposed the Korean War, but in this case kept his opposition to himself. Mann favored a democratic socialism and a rapprochement with the Soviet Union: he knew that Stalin's Russia was a totalitarian state, and abhorred this, but he wanted to believe that a humane aspect was part of socialism.

Mann's daughter Erika, who had become his valuable assistant, could not obtain American citizenship. The FBI, relying on informers, was convinced — incorrectly — that she was a communist, and she feared being refused re-entry if she traveled abroad with her father. After Mann himself was attacked for participating in several peace movements, some of which had been communist inspired without his knowledge, he emigrated to Switzerland in 1952.

At this time, his relationship with Germany was still uneasy. His books were being read there again, and he had visited Germany in 1949, but his radio broadcasts during the war, carried by the BBC from Great Britain, had not endeared him to his home country. The estrangement had actually increased now, making him a new kind of outsider. Mann had produced his speeches for the BBC beginning in November 1940; since March 1941 they had been recorded in his own voice. In those speeches, he vituperated the German people for following Hitler, the "false victor" (*Falschsieger*) (*GW* 12, 993), predicting Germany's eventual defeat even in 1940 when German war fortunes were at their peak. In January 1942 he cited a report of the gassing of Jews. Once, on 27 June 1943, he praised the protest movement at the University of Munich and mentioned the executions of students and faculty with deep empathy. For a moment he distinguished between the Germans and the National Socialists (*GW* 12, 1076–77), but only for a moment. Deep down he saw the National Socialists as a bad caricature of Nietzsche's vision of the creative ruler. A 1939 essay titled "Bruder Hitler" (published in English as "A Brother") depicted Hitler as an evil artist, and in the speech "Deutschland und die Deutschen" (Germany and the Germans) of 1945 Mann refused to distinguish between a good old Germany and the bad new one. Many Germans opposed to Hitler's regime appreciated his radio addresses, but many others, whether opponents of the National Socialist regime or not, felt that he no longer was one of them.

Between 1943 and 1947 Mann wrote the novel that had been on his mind since 1904, the story of a creative artist inspired by the Devil, *Doktor Faustus*. It is the biography of a German composer with allusions to the biographies of Nietzsche and Thomas Mann himself. Mann had admired Nietzsche's call for cultural renewal, but he also criticized Nietzsche's ideas throughout his work. Mann had also appreciated — to a degree — Nietzsche's immoralism as a stance free of all set principles. Now he needed to restore such morals as were needed to condemn Hitler and his followers. The novel reflects all these mixed notions. Mann's ambivalent feelings for Nietzsche, the lifelong companion of his thoughts, corresponded to the ambivalence that had complicated his relationship to his homeland. How could he remain a cultural German while harboring embittered feelings toward the German *Bildungsbürger*? Since he had encouraged the American entrance into the war, he had even broken with those Germans who were not Nazis. Yet that separation was not complete: deep down Thomas Mann had remained a German.

The novel's narrative voice, the narrator himself, was not the exiled Mann but Zeitblom, a passive *Bildungsbürger* opposed to National Socialism. The object of his fictional biography, Adrian Leverkühn, the absolute artist, more distanced from society than his author, is nevertheless a scion of Germany, carrying allusions to Luther and Dürer. The narrator Zeitblom is a classical philologist like Nietzsche; like him he enters military service with a Naumburg artillery regiment. Leverkühn grows up in a countryside similar to the one of Nietzsche's youth; he gives up theology; he contracts syphilis. But unlike Nietzsche, who was a composer of minor talent, Leverkühn becomes a composer of genius. As a composer he connects with Nietzsche on a symbolic level; his compositions are not written for the public but rather for a small elite that appreciates their creative power. Like Nietzsche, Leverkühn completes his works under the stress of painful migraines, and he spends the last ten years of his life insane, being taken care of by his mother.

As a model for the absolute artist, Leverkühn forsakes all love that provides warmth, all love that is mutual. By living exclusively for his art, he becomes alienated from his society, with only few exceptions. One such case is his singular homosexual love affair with a character shaped after a friend and love-interest of Mann's, Paul Ehrenberg.

Leverkühn's yearning for divine love takes up the theme of missing love that Mann had first explored in *Buddenbrooks*. While love is missing in the earlier novel because of a bourgeois ideology that values economics over human relations, it is missing here because of an ideology of creative superiority. In this sense *Doktor Faustus*, the Nietzsche-novel, also carries a critique of Nietzsche's vision. The novel leaves it open whether the god who may grant his grace is dead or living. This ambiguity, this openness, is signaled when Leverkühn, in his last sane moments, breaks down on the piano with outstretched arms as if crucified, while seemingly being pushed by the devil (*GW* 6, 667). This open, undecided position characterizes Mann's work as a whole and elevates it above ideological fashions that raged in politics and literature during his lifetime.

The self-accusation in the novel is both unjust and just. Mann had fought the Nazis as well as he could. But despite all his implied and open criticism, he had been an admirer of Nietzsche all his life. In spite of his efforts to ward off Nazi power, he had been a part of a German artistic and intellectual elite that had failed to lead the country toward civilized relations with the rest of the world. Guided by Wagner and Nietzsche, the concern of this elite had been breaking through conventions and artistic traditions for the sake of individual greatness. This is the guilt that Adrian Leverkühn confesses in his final sermon to his friends and admirers (*GW* 6, 662). What the novel condemns is part of Mann's self: the veneration of the ideal of the absolute artist by way of music composed in total formality.[23]

In several letters written when the novel was still only available in Switzerland, Mann articulated his expectation that his German readers would recognize that he had not deserted his native country.[24] But they did not: on the contrary, the novel was initially viewed in Germany more as an accusation than as self-criticism. Mann's relationship with Germany remained tense for years. In 1947, Mann avoided German soil despite visiting in Switzerland. In 1949 he did visit, delivering a speech on the occasion of the bicentennial of Goethe's birth, both in Frankfurt am Main and in Weimar (then in communist East Germany). This led to unfortunate accusations related to the Cold War. The situation changed only somewhat in Mann's final years, for instance when an address on the occasion of the hundred and fiftieth anniversary of Schiller's death was well received. Some protest was still raised branding Mann an emigrant and a traitor, but it remained muted. The fragment *Bekenntnisse des Hochstaplers Felix Krull,* published in 1954, found enthusiastic readers.

Mann's last novel *Der Erwählte,* written while he was still in California and published in English under the title *The Holy Sinner,* takes up the theme of the guilt and redemption of the extraordinary person in the form of a parody of the German medieval epic of Hartmann von Aue, *Gregorius,* which in turn follows a French source. This mixture of sources allows Mann to create the ambience of a half-legendary European cosmopolitanism. It is a tale of sin and grace, the sin being an unwitting sexual transgression.

Mann's last completed work, the novella *Die Betrogene,* was begun in Pacific Palisades and completed in Switzerland. The central character refuses to consider herself betrayed after bleedings she had mistakenly perceived to be the result of rejuvenated love turn out to be a sign of death. This text can be read as Mann's testament, appreciating life while facing death.

Mann died in 1955 in Zurich. The Schiller-speech he had given after his eightieth birthday celebration and the award of honorary citizenship of his hometown of Lübeck had finally brought the reconciliation with his homeland he had desired.

Thomas Mann research has become so vast that an overview is no longer useful. Since Mann's diaries became known (published 1977–95) and his carefully maintained front has become transparent, Mann's biography plays a greater role in the understanding of his works than ever before. The Thomas Mann Archiv der Eidgenössischen Technischen Hochschule, Zürich (Schönberggasse 15, 8001 Zürich, Switzerland), holds Mann's literary estate. An enormous amount of material from the archive has been published.

There is a correlation between biography and the history of a writer's time and his work. Contemporary literary theory tends to pull scholars away from interpretations of an author's intentions in its historical setting in favor of establishing unusual relations between a fictional text and its surrounding culture. Such approach can be valuable, but eliminating intentions embedded in the text also opens the trap of missing the communicative nature of language — including that of fictional language.

Thomas Mann's work forms a discourse with his audience, the *Bildungsbürger*. Our world is decidedly different, but Mann's worldview, that of a cultural citizen, does provide an alternative to contemporary ideological doctrines. From Nietzsche, Thomas Mann had inherited the idea that human greatness should determine the course of human development. Mann remained fascinated by the idea, but in all of his works he also pointed out the negative consequences of such a stand. He appreciated the value of community in socialism but had to recognize the tyranny of its practice. He distrusted the restoration of the capitalist economy in the United States after Roosevelt's death, as he distrusted all ideologies. Surely a worldview such as Mann's, which refuses to be static and committed, but affirms the value of human beings above all, is one that should not be alien to us.

Discourse analysis can cast light on the difference between Mann's cultural outlook and ours, provided it does not shy away from carefully exploring the historical circumstances. Since much of the Mann-research was performed by scholars who share in the values and prejudices of the German *Bildungsbürger*, a clear understanding of Germany's upper-class discourse, and of the way Mann yielded to it or resisted it, can open new vistas not only on Mann's work but also on the people of the social strata for whom his work was written. In spite of the vast secondary material on Mann's work, there is no consensus on its meaning.

The contributions in this volume are meant to inform the reader of the present state of research on Thomas Mann's work and to present new views.

In my essay, "Thomas Mann's Beginnings and *Buddenbrooks*," I trace the development of Mann's early work, beginning with rebellion against his grand bourgeois family, in which he followed his older brother Heinrich. With *Buddenbrooks* Thomas decried the bourgeois family's material ambition and neglect of love, yet sympathized with family life at the same time. Mann's early novellas are concerned with the alienation of the outsider as artist or as dilettante, a theme traced to Mann's feeling of being isolated from society because of his sexuality.

Ehrhard Bahr presents in his contribution "Art and Society in Thomas Mann's Early Novellas" close readings of novellas written from 1900 to 1904, with special emphasis on "Tonio Kröger," and of the dramatic dialogue "Fiorenza." Bahr juxtaposes the religion of art (*Kunstreligion*), which was fashionable at the time in the wake of the success of Wagner's musical dramas, to Mann's perspectivism.

The theme of love in Mann's work before "Der Tod in Venedig," including the notes for the unwritten novel "Maja," is the concern of Wolfgang Lederer's essay "Love in Society: Thomas Mann's Early Stories." Lederer provides insight into Mann's psyche, his conflict between homoerotic love and aversion against its physical aspect, his desire to marry, and his regret over losing his independence as expressed in "Wälsungenblut."

Clayton Koelb discusses how "Der Tod in Venedig" arose from a crisis of Mann's discontent with his work in 1911. Koelb's close reading shows how themes from classical antiquity not only enter the plot but also shape the structure. Mann's "free indirect style," which is reminiscent of that of Gustave Flaubert, allows the reader to identify with Aschenbach (the vituperative outside narrator is not the only narrator) and gain insight into a love that only exists in Aschenbach's imagination.

Hans-Joachim Sandberg discovers in his essay "'Mein "Friedrich" — das ist was Anderes': Thomas Mann's Unwritten Novel about Frederick the Great, King of Prussia" a relationship between Mann's studies of Schiller in 1905 and his unwritten novel on Frederick II. The "greatness" of Frederick was rarely questioned in the Wilhelminian empire, but Mann, while identifying with Frederick's work ethic, understood greatness in his own terms.

In her essay "Magic and Reflections: Thomas Mann's *The Magic Mountain* and His War Essays," Eva Wessell discusses the origin of *Der Zauberberg*, which grew from a parody of "Der Tod in Venedig" into an essayistic investigation of Germany's role in the world. After the outbreak of the First World War this discussion became more direct and explicit in the war essays, culminating in *Betrachtungen eines Unpolitischen*, a defense in cultural terms of Germany's self isolation. After the war, Mann recovered the narrative structure of *Der Zauberberg*, with its original tolerance. Indeed, the war scene at the end of the novel even has anti-war character.

In his "Thomas Mann's Autobiographical Stories," Helmut Koopmann reads a number of texts that are autobiographical or close to it. Koopmann shows how Mann represents his time and his world while representing himself. In "Das Eisenbahnunglück" (The Railway Accident, 1909), Mann even humorously compares himself with Wilhelm II, criticizing the emperor's pompousness, while in "Herr und Hund" (1919), the story of the dog

Baushan, he conservatively blends out the contemporary background, that of the First World War.

Peter Pütz's essay "*Joseph and His Brothers*" lets us see how biblical themes can be used to reflect a very modern worldview. The mythical world is not as solidly determined as the world of modernity has become under the influence of science. In narrative myth, above and below, ascent and descent, appear interchangeable, and this view corresponds to the changes with which our world must cope. Views of the world from changing perspectives will see the same thing in different, even contrastive aspects. The text plays with the question whether God is found inside or outside of human consciousness. Mann narrates the "thinking out" (hervordenken) of God, which he has the patriarchs of Genesis do, not as arbitrary invention but as the recognition of a potentiality, a symbolic creation.

Werner Frizen is the editor of the novel *Lotte in Weimar*, which has long been known in English under the title *The Beloved Returns*. His essay on that text is informed by his knowledge of Mann's sources and of the historical background. Thus he can show the extent to which Mann changed the historical record, and what that change means.

Much of Manfred Dierks's work is concerned with Mann's psychology, applying Heinz Kohut's analysis of narcissism. Mann's success as a performer, when reading from his works in public, produced a peculiar relationship with his audience that had consequences for his political attitudes, which is the topic of Dierks's essay in this volume, "Thomas Mann's Late Politics." When Mann supported democracy in Germany or, in the United States, democracy's victory over fascism Mann held fast to a cultural authoritarianism that derived from his position above the audience when lecturing. Dierks exemplifies this analysis with an interpretation of "Mario und der Zauberer" (1930), a text that is informed by Schopenhauer. The magician Cipolla both represents and satirizes Mann's own cultural authority.

In his essay "'German' Music and German Catastrophe: A Re-Reading of *Doctor Faustus*," Hans Rudolf Vaget explains the origin of *Doktor Faustus* from Mann's worried ambivalence between identification with German culture and critical distance from it during the time of the novel's composition, at the end of the Second World War. Vaget reads the novel as one of a Germany identified with music, bringing out the "sinister consequences" of that identification, the rejection of the "world." As Leverkühn regresses from composing cosmopolitan music to composing German music characterized by total formalism, his music forms a symbolic parallel to the German catastrophe.

Thomas Mann limited himself in the expression of his homoerotic desire to voyeuristic adventures. His diary of the summer of 1950 describes some such adventures in detail, together with the contrasting emotions connected with them.[25] Diary entries about gazing experiences are found at other times in Mann's diary. Jens Rieckmann's essay "The Gaze of Love, Longing, and

Desire in Thomas Mann's 'The Transposed Heads' and 'The Black Swan'" discusses reflections of such voyeurism in "Die vertauschten Köpfe" and "Die Betrogene."

Egon Schwarz, in his contribution to this volume, enlivens Mann's most lively novel *Bekenntnisse des Hochstaplers Felix Krull* still more by close readings of selected scenes and by pointing to the significance of others. The episode of the young Krull being introduced to the actor-singer Müller-Rosé belongs to the portion of the novel written before 1913, and expresses the Nietzschean suspicion of artistry, while the description of the almost androgynous Andromache, in the circus scene from the portion written after 1951, reflects the serious artistic discipline of the artist-outsider. Krull is unreliable as a lover, but his seductive speech on love asks for redemption from narcissism, perhaps even speaking for the author. The vivacious Krull novel plays with contrasts, as all of Mann's serious texts do. The narcissistic protagonist, looking out for himself, displays some features of the picaresque novel but is quite different from the Spanish model. Schwarz sees this text more as a satire of the ambience of Europe before the outbreak of the First World War, before its self-destruction in that conflagration and the one that followed, ending in Hitler's barbarism.

Does our contention that reading Mann is relevant for our world of the twenty-first century hold when his construction of women characters is assessed? Or does he turn out to be a male writer merely reflecting a male worldview? This question is answered by Hannelore Mundt in her essay "Female Identities and Autobiographical Impulses in Thomas Mann's Works": yes and no. Mann's writings reflect the prejudices of his age, the expectation of a passive woman who subordinates herself to a male-dominated world. But the reflections of this prejudice in his writings are countervailed by two tendencies: first, the recognition that his society suppressed the sexuality and intellectual freedom of women, and second, a tendency to use a female character for a camouflaged expression of his own suppressed desires. These tendencies can come into conflict, as in the character of Mut-em-enet in *Joseph in Ägypten,* whose characterization turns into misogyny in spite of Mann's identification with her sexual deprivation.

My essay "Betrayed or Not Betrayed: A Testament?" answers the question in its title in the affirmative. Mann's last completed text presents a monistic religious message, delivered by Rosalie, the protagonist, by submission of herself to the whole of being in death, in contrast to her daughter Anna, who resists nature through her intellectual art. Both Rosalie's eventual turn to monism and Anna's dualistic preference of mind over body have equal value. The text also issues an implicit message calling for more sexual freedom, a call that can be heard in all of Mann's work.

Finally, my essay "Thomas Mann's Comedies" contrasts the novel *Königliche Hoheit,* with its praise of marriage, to *Der Erwählte,* with its humorous treatment of sin and atonement. I read *Der Erwählte* not as a supplement to *Doktor Faustus* but as a refutation of the autobiographical streak in *Faustus*. Through his protagonist, Gregorius, Mann asks forgiveness for the sin of extraordinariness. The Pope's humane intentions after his elevation are appreciated by all, including the reader.

Since we are aware of Mann's frustrated homoerotic desires, interpretations of his works — including the interpretations in this volume — have relied much on their autobiographical motivations. However, Mann's fiction never depicts his life or his experiences directly, but always transforms them, and it is the transformation that counts for its artistic value. In the essay "Bilse und ich" (Bilse and I, 1906), Mann, while defending himself against the charge of using living models for his writings, assures his reader that in his writings he speaks only of himself, "von mir, von mir" (*Essays* 1, 51). This sounds egotistic, and perhaps it is. It takes a strong self to place an imagined world against the real one. However, in Mann, the very act of questioning reality did not stop at his own self.

In his lecture "Meine Zeit" (The Years of My Life, 1950) Mann reacted to an accusation by German theologians (we do not know who accused him) that his work was unchristian. Defining "Christian" as the "presumption of considering one's life as guilt, indebtedness, obligation [. . .], as an object of religious uneasiness" (Schuld, Verschuldung, Schuldigkeit [. . .], als den Gegenstand religiösen Unbehagens), he objected to the theologians because his works had "evolved from their beginnings as a yearning for atonement, cleansing and justification." Their "playful, skeptical, artistic and humorous" appearance was only external, quite different from the "impulse to whom they owe their existence" (*Essays* 6, 160). This is especially valid for *Doktor Faustus*. Leverkühn's music is perfected art, a breakthrough into total form. Leverkühn's greatness, which Zeitblom admires, fulfills Nietzsche's vision of a culture geared toward production of great human beings. *Doktor Faustus* can be read as Mann's confession of guilt for sharing Nietzsche's vision, his "Vornehmheit," the departure from the common ground of the Christian heritage of communality. But this did not mean that Mann embraced the Christian doctrines.

Art cannot help being deceit, because there is no absolute truth. But deceptive art plays with potentials that may yet harbor truths. These are no truths that answer the question "what am I to do," which permeates Mann's 1954 essay on Chekhov (*Essays* 6, 266, 273, 274, 279). They are often contradictory truths whose validity does not go farther than hinting at a connection of truth and artistic form (*Essays* 6, 270, 275). The uncertainty with which Mann hints at a possible worldly purpose of artistic form in his essay on Chekhov is actually the same playful "irony" that had made him resist the ideologies of the twentieth century and has established the enduring modernity of his work. But as much as he fought for artistic freedom, against his brother's admonition that writings achieve value only when they propagate a moral-political message, and as much as he denied the effect of the writer's social engagement in his masterpiece, "Der Tod in Venedig," Thomas Mann, as a person, as a citizen, as an essayist, and — in spite of all his playful uncertainty — as a writer of fiction, did advocate a world of free human beings, free from the exploitation of man by man.

Notes

[1] The year of publication following the title refers to the first German edition, not to the translation. Translations of titles in this volume may or may not correspond to those of published translations. See the list of Mann's works.

[2] Nietzsche, *KSA* 3, 480–82. *Die fröhliche Wissenschaft* (The Gay Science, 1881; Book 5, 1886), 125.

[3] See Karl Werner Böhm, *Zwischen Selbstzucht und Verlangen: Thomas Mann und das Stigma Homosexualität* (Würzburg: Königshausen & Neumann, 1991). Böhm insists on the word "homosexual" because he believes that the desire, and not the consummation, should be the determining factor. His book contributes much to the understanding of Mann's works by describing the literary effects of Mann's renunciation of homosexual desire ("Triebverzicht"). After thoroughly considering the evidence, Böhm considers this renunciation a fact. I prefer the word "homoerotic" because it implies renunciation.

[4] Nietzsche, *KSA* 6, 27.

[5] Nietzsche, *KSA* 6, 28–29.

[6] Manfred Dierks, *Studien zu Mythos und Psychologie bei Thomas Mann*, TMS 2 (1972), 172, 257–60.

[7] *Tb* 1 July 1936: "Ich hatte nie ein Verhältnis zum Zarathustra." See also 5 July 1936.

[8] *Nb* 1 (1–6), 114, 116, 127, 135, 181, 187.

[9] *GW* 8, 1027. Mann's collected works, *Gesammelte Werke in dreizehn Bänden* (Frankfurt am Main: S. Fischer, 1974, 1990), will henceforth be cited in the text with the abbreviation *GW* and volume and page number.

[10] In *Zur Genealogie der Moral* (On the Genealogy of Morals, 1887), *KSA* 5, 283–85.

[11] *Nb* 2 (7–14), 43–44.

[12] *Nb* 2 (7–14), 107, 121–22. These two notes are the first indication of the plan for *Doktor Faustus,* which Mann actualized in 1943–47.

[13] Cf. Hans Rudolf Vaget's essay in this volume.

[14] Peter Paul Schneider, "'Wo ich Deine Zuständigkeit leugnen muß. . . .' Die bislang unbekannte Antwort Heinrich Manns auf Thomas Manns Abrechnungsbrief vom 5. Dezember 1903." In *"In Spuren gehen . . .": Festschrift für Helmut Koopmann,* ed. Andrea Bartl et al. (Tübingen: Niemeyer, 1998), 231–53.

[15] *TM/HM,* 363–65.

[16] Hans Wysling, "'Geist und Kunst,'" *TMS* 1 (1967), 123–233. Note 124, "Gegensätze," 218.

[17] *TM/HM,* 169.

[18] *DüD* 1, 454.

[19] *TM/HM,* 172.

[20] *Essays* 2, 45–84. This edition will henceforth be documented in the text as *Essays* with volume and page number.

[21] Cf. *Essays* 2, 49, with *GW* 12, 219.

[22] "Goethe als Repräsentant des bürgerlichen Zeitalters" (Goethe as a Representative of the Bourgeois Age, 1932), *GW* 9, 332.

[23] Cf. the somewhat different interpretation by Hans Rudolf Vaget in this volume.

[24] *DüD* 3, 103.

[25] Especially *Tb* 6 August 1950.

Thomas Mann's Beginnings and *Buddenbrooks*

Herbert Lehnert

T O UNDERSTAND THE anarchic undercurrent in the writings of the young Thomas Mann, let us consider two differing testaments by his father. In an 1879 will, the wholesale merchant Thomas Johann Heinrich Mann, senator of the Free Hanseatic City of Lübeck, made his wife and children his heirs. His principle property was the firm "Johann Siegmund Mann," which he wished to have continued. One of his children was to join the firm upon reaching maturity;[1] he certainly had his sons Heinrich and Thomas in mind. Twelve years later, in 1891, ill with bladder cancer and facing an operation, he decided otherwise: he ordered his business to be liquidated. He appointed guardians to invest the result of the sale, to administer the fortune and regularly pay the interest out to his widow, who was to pass a share on to each of their five children. The senator determined the dowries of his daughters and designated a certain sum for the "establishment" of his sons. He charged the guardians to promote a *practical* (his emphasis) education of his sons in order to keep them from the bohemian lifestyle that tempted his older son Heinrich. Specifically, the guardians were to oppose Heinrich's "so called literary activity," which, the senator felt, did not meet the prerequisites for a professional writer, as he understood them: "sufficient studies and knowledge." In addenda to his will, the senator reproached Heinrich for perceived indolence and recklessness against others (meaning himself). Thomas, his second son, fared a little better. He, the father mused, could be influenced by quiet reasoning and would find his way to a practical occupation.[2] But he did not entrust Thomas with the family firm either. The guardians, solid Lübeck burghers, never considered a writer's career "establishment" in the sense of the senator's will, thus never paid their legacies to either Heinrich or Thomas, but kept the control of the senator's fortune until it dissipated in the German inflation of 1923. The modest monthly interest the brothers did receive allowed them to subsist and write until they had earned sufficient income from their publications.

Their father had directed his rage against the life goals of both brothers in his testament. But they respected his superior intelligence, and did not hate, but instead even continued to hold him in admiration. The senator's rage had been caused by his disappointment in his older son's unwillingness to continue the firm, to continue his life's work, and with it the lifestyle of the family. The brothers' reaction was ambivalent. They did not break away from the bourgeois establishment entirely. But they also felt rejected by it and thus driven to profoundly question its value system.

The immediate cause of the senator's rage had been that Heinrich had left school, feeling that it did not prepare him to become a writer. The senator sent him away from home as a bookseller's apprentice, a position that was not to Heinrich's liking, but gave him access to the latest literary journals, which he used to pursue his literary education. Thomas was sixteen years old when his father died. He too wanted to become a writer, and rebelled against school, with its oppressive drill methods of learning and middle-class teachers. He shared Heinrich's literary interests, emulating his brother's self-education at home. Thomas's early literary tastes closely resemble Heinrich's. They shared enthusiasm for the witty and ironic outsider-poet Heinrich Heine. In 1890, Heinrich read the pessimistic philosophy of Schopenhauer, and soon afterwards he discovered the contemporary philosopher of a new way of thinking, Friedrich Nietzsche.[3] From the multivolume work of the Danish critic and scholar Georg Brandes Heinrich gleaned his knowledge of nineteenth-century literature, and Brandes certainly informed Thomas also. There can be little doubt that Thomas also read Schopenhauer and Nietzsche during his years at school in Lübeck, although documentary evidence for his reception of Nietzsche exists only beginning in 1894, and the exact time of his first reading of Schopenhauer is unknown. Thomas's readings of contemporary French novels were most probably undertaken at Heinrich's recommendation.[4] Independently he became interested in Norwegian literature, which left traces in his 1901 novel *Buddenbrooks*.

How the young Thomas Mann spent his time in school, instead of learning the prescribed lessons, can be gauged by his contributions to a student paper, "Frühlingssturm" (Gale of Spring), that he produced with friends. The essay "Heinrich Heine, der 'Gute'" (Heinrich Heine, the "Good Man," 1893), printed there, is an astonishingly mature piece for an eighteen year old. The young author's target was a defense of Heine published in a Berlin newspaper by a Dr. Conrad Scipio. While conceding Heine's immorality, Scipio, in an attempt to neutralize anti-Semitic attacks on the poet, claimed that Heine was a patriot and a believer. The young Thomas Mann wanted to go further: the poet did not have to be made "good" in the eyes of decent burghers; he was simply great: neither bound by common morality nor by allegiance to a religious faith. For instance, he could admire Luther, even though he was not a Protestant.[5] Mann's argumentation shows an affinity with, one could even say a strong influence of, Nietzsche's thinking. This influence becomes obvious when the young writer declares his "usual" philosophical position, which rejects the absolute use of concepts like good and evil, ugly and beautiful.

Literature was a device both brothers used to rebel against the values of the bourgeois world into which they were born. Heinrich railed against its repressive sexuality;[6] Thomas did also in his own way. The first public reflection of Heinrich's sexually charged opposition to established morality was a poem that appeared in the periodical *Die Gesellschaft,* a journal that had the reputation of being open to the most modern literary tendencies. Heinrich addresses the desperation of a girl who has been forsaken by her lover. The repressiveness of traditional morality is expressed in the poem "Geh schlafen," in which the girl receives a whispered admonition to "go to sleep" by drowning herself in a lake.[7] This publication by his older brother stimulated Thomas to write a poem of his own, also involving death by drowning. However, in Thomas's poem the suicide is male. Through a common friend, Ludwig Ewers, Thomas sent his poem to his older brother, asking for his opinion. Heinrich's verdict, in his answer to Ewers — not directly to Thomas — was contemptuously negative: "Blödsinn" (imbecility). He noticed homoeroticism in his brother's poem and considered that condition merely pubertal and immature.[8] The harsh condemnation must have left a wound in Thomas that never fully healed, even though he long continued to admire his mentor.

During the same year, the nineteen-year-old Heinrich Mann transformed his desire for a mutual sexual relationship, as well as his frustration with prostitutes, into a problematic and fictionalized self-portrait. Under the influence of the writer and critic Hermann Bahr, who proclaimed a new psychology in the vein of the fashionable novelist and critic Paul Bourget,[9] the young bookseller's apprentice wrote the story "Haltlos" (Drifting) in 1890, which was not published during his lifetime, although he must have shared it with his brother. The title "Haltlos," literally "without support," "without guidance," expresses the condition of the alienated young son of a wealthy family at odds with the entire world, a condition of free-floating weakness, a kind of negative freedom apart from family and social order. This condition can also be called decadence, a word fashionable at the time as an indicator not only of alienation from the world of the bourgeois fathers, but also of intellectual status. In biological or medical terms it was "neurasthenia," a weakness of the nerves, which explained a person's lack of ability to cope with the modern, rapidly changing world, the world of the progressively minded fathers.[10]

"Haltlos" imagines a love story between an alienated young man and a similarly alienated young woman. The "new psychology" proclaimed by Hermann Bahr was Heinrich's model for representing the erratic consciousness of the protagonist who lacks a stable bourgeois identity. The love relationship in the story is meant to show how the prevalent social order impedes the development of a new morality. The young man who, like his author, has visited prostitutes and has thereby developed a bad conscience, enters into a relationship with a poor but intelligent and loving shopgirl. But what starts out as a new kind of a liberated relationship is cut short. When he supplies the girl with money in an emergency, he falls back on the bourgeois attitude of his upbringing, behaving as if he had bought her, an attitude that colors their first sexual union. She shames him by returning his money, even though she will have to support herself and her sick mother as a fallen woman, a prostitute, in the future. She accepts this destiny because she wants to have spent the one night with her lover as a free woman. While Heinrich Mann here accuses bourgeois society of being obsessed with money, to the exclusion of true mutual love, he also accuses the young man of inability to separate himself from the values of his class.[11]

Thomas continued to emulate his brother. Most writings of this period are lost; an exception is Thomas's prose poem "Vision" (1893), which he published in his student newspaper, "Frühlingssturm." It was stimulated by Heinrich's unrhymed poem "Die Hand," which had been published in 1892.[12] Both texts are erotic fantasies about a girl's hand. Thomas had reacted to his brother's vituperation and was now moving into more socially acceptable territory. If one compares the texts, Thomas turns out to present poetic images much more vividly than his brother. He was competing.

The relationship between the brothers was friendly when the two met in Munich in 1894 after Thomas had finally finished the tenth grade at the age of nineteen. The death of the father had freed Heinrich from having to learn the bookseller's trade and allowed him to pursue his career as a writer. That same year, Heinrich even began to develop an envious respect for his younger brother because Thomas published the story "Gefallen" (Fallen, 1894) in the avant-garde journal *Die Gesellschaft,* where Heinrich so far had only placed a poem. Heinrich's prose until then had appeared only in insignificant periodicals and daily newspapers.

"Gefallen" turns out to have been an answer of sorts to Heinrich's "Haltlos." Repressed sexuality must have been an even more painful experience for Thomas Mann than it was for the heterosexual Heinrich, who merely suffered from his inability to have love experiences with compatible women. Thomas had reacted to the jolt of disapproval by his role model. He masked his sexual frustration by converting it into a heterosexual plot line. While Heinrich in his story had criticized the inability of the young man to live a new sexual morality, Thomas's "Gefallen" is characterized by more distance. It pitches an idealistic young man with ideas of reforming morality against another male who is affected by the fall of a woman. After freely entering into a love affair with the young student Selten, a young actress decides to sell herself for the considerable sum she can command as an actress. Doing so, she becomes a "femme fatale" for Selten, who narrates the story from the perspective of years later, having grown up and become a physician, but also a cynic, unable to love. The actress had accepted the role of courtesan her society proscribed for her and left her young lover emotionally stranded.

In the frame narrative, a bohemian gathering of younger men, a student accuses society of injustice toward women. His name "Laube" probably refers to Heinrich Rudolf Laube (1806–1884), a writer of the anti-Romantic and anti-Classicist, emancipatory literary movement "Young Germany." The cynic Dr. Selten has developed the opinion that if a woman falls for love today, tomorrow she will fall for money. The story of his disappointment in love is to counter the naive idealism of Laube (*GW* 8, 42).

Mann's story seems to carry a conservative message at first glance: society is as it is; there is no use trying to change it. But Selten is no reactionary; he does not criticize the greater sexual freedom of the actress but rather the young woman's use of it for monetary gain without regard for him. Selten intends to throw doubt on the belief that merely the liberation of women will produce the desired freedom of love. His girlfriend was more concerned with her position in society than with him. It is the moralistic bourgeois society as a whole that restricts individual fulfillment. Here is the hidden force that drives the story. The double standard is merely one restriction of sexuality.

No straightforward moral conservatism is to be expected of Thomas Mann, for whom Nietzsche's *Zur Genealogie der Moral* (On the Genealogy of Morals, 1887) was a source of orientation. While he made use of his sexual frustration, transforming it into the character of Selten, there is no reason to believe that he considers Selten's cynicism a solution. Neither does he agree with the ideological eagerness of the young male feminist Laube. He represents this character with ironic detachment, but that detachment does not exclude the reader's sympathy for Laube's sense of moral renewal. In this early story we have the "ironic" Thomas Mann who keeps equal distance from the conventions of society and from modernists who promise a better world in one stroke. In "Gefallen" there is even the first example in Mann's work of the Wagnerian leitmotif, here combined with an anti-Romantic modernist attitude. The thematic interplay in Wagner's musical dramas became a challenge for Thomas Mann's writing. Fiction was a task of composing, of weaving themes together, into each other, varying them with each context. In "Gefallen" the lilac motif is introduced as a sign of spring; the fragrance of its flowers accompanies the love affair in a Romantic manner (*GW* 8, 18, 23, 29). The student establishes a union with the lilac bush, talking with it and receiving promises of happiness (*GW* 8, 35). But the Romantic motif of unity with nature dissolves into modern indifference. When the same bush exudes a "sweet whiff of love" after the lover's disappointment, it makes him raise his fist toward smiling heaven. He crushes the blossoms with their "lying fragrance" (*GW* 8, 40). To make sure that post-

Romanticism prevails, the text has Selten again grasping and crushing lilac blossoms at the end of his story (*GW* 8, 42).

Thomas Mann was familiar with the technique of psychological description, as his brother Heinrich had learned it from Paul Bourget through Hermann Bahr. When the key word of this technique, "états d'âme" (states of the soul), appears in Thomas Mann's text (*GW* 8, 24), it is used almost mockingly. Thomas, the willing follower of his brother on the road to modernity, does not want to follow too closely.

It is the task of the modern writer, the follower of Nietzsche, to destroy both Romantic illusions and ideological simplifications. Literature must keep its distance from life in society. "Gefallen" allows us insight into much of the character of Thomas Mann's ensuing work. The autobiographical momentum for seeking love in a world full of hostility is translated into a detached complexity informed by Nietzsche's immoralism and Schopenhauer's atheistic pessimism. Both encourage distance from all contemporary values. At its core, Thomas Mann's fiction is not conservative but anarchic.

To keep his distance was the lesson Thomas had learned from Heinrich's reaction to his youthful poems with their intimate feelings. Heinrich's rejection of these poems had made Thomas vulnerable. He needed the role of the withdrawn, ironic author, hiding additional meaning under the realistic surface, especially because his society had made taboo the kind of love to which he was most attracted.[13] His innermost desires could be expressed by camouflaging them as fictional representations of deprived characters who deviated from social standards.[14] But Mann wanted his fiction understood as addressing all readers, not only those who shared his particular suffering.

The brothers lived together in Italy for a while, and some of their stories have an Italian setting. Thomas's story "Enttäuschung" (Disillusionment) was first published in 1898 in the small volume of his early stories *Der kleine Herr Friedemann* (Little Herr Friedemann), which was his first book. The story was probably written earlier, in 1895.[15] The setting of "Enttäuschung" is Venice. There, the first person narrator meets a middle-aged man who contrasts the fame of Venice with the many unfulfilled expectations of his lifetime. During his childhood in a minister's house, his world had been determined by an unbridgeable gap between divine good and satanic evil. He expected reality to be structured by such contrasts as well, and literature nourished his exaggerated expectations (*GW* 8, 64).

The disappointment of the stranger is caused by the language of traditional metaphysics (*GW* 8, 67). Judgments such as good and evil, beautiful and ugly, presuppose a world whose substance is guaranteed by a living God. Mann's stranger represents the experience of the world as it appears to the reader of Nietzsche, whose God is dead but who still carries a nostalgic memory of a divinely ordered world. Comfort comes from a creative mind: only at night by looking at the stars does the stranger feel some satisfaction.

When he disregards the earth and its life, he can dream of another reality that can be produced against the background of a modern cosmic worldview indifferent to human desire or feelings. The story presents a challenge to a self-created worldview and represents a new creative humanism.

This is less Schopenhauer's philosophy than Nietzsche's.[16] There are indeed clear pointers toward Nietzsche. The dialogue takes place on the Piazza di San Marco, which Nietzsche called his favorite study.[17] Nietzsche was the son of a minister, grew up in a small town like the stranger (*GW* 8, 64), and he was known to be insane at the time the story was written. The somewhat peculiar behavior of the stranger may hint at insanity. Nevertheless, the text does not attempt a portrait of Nietzsche; it rather embodies the effect of reading him.

Thomas Mann's story "Der Wille zum Glück" (The Will to Happiness, 1896) carries a reference to Nietzsche's "Will to Power" in its very title. The narrative form of Mann's text answers to a story by Heinrich Mann, "Das Wunderbare" (The Miraculous, 1896). In both "Das Wunderbare" and "Der Wille zum Glück" the principle story is narrated by a schoolmate of the protagonist; the schoolmate's narration frames the embedded story.[18] Heinrich's story is a fantasy about what his fate would have been had he given in to his father's desire, obtained a law degree, and stayed within bourgeois expectations. The narrative expresses the hope that his artistic spirit would have protected him from falling into philistine complacency. "Der Wille zum Glück," by contrast, is a pessimistic answer to Heinrich's optimistic view of the transforming power of art. Both stories are concerned with an escape from the artistic condition. In Heinrich's story the escape is successful, in Thomas's it is tragic.

Thomas has his story begin with the friends finding themselves to be outsiders in school, experiencing Nietzsche's "pathos of distance," and cultivating a secret love for Heine.[19] One of the friends is named Paolo Hofmann, the name Paolo indicating a foreign parent; the other is the first-person narrator. Paolo the schoolboy translates his strong sexual desire into the drawing of a voluptuous female figure (*GW* 8, 45); later, as an acknowledged painter, he produces a nude for which he is praised because of the effect of the tone the female body displays (*GW* 8, 49). He is in love with an attractive girl of Jewish parentage whose father prevents marriage because of Paolo's health: he has a heart condition.

Paolo's heart condition indicates his outsider role as an artist, which he does not accept. The story expresses disapproval of the artist's desire for normality, symbolized by sexual fulfillment, even if the object of love is an outsider herself, a young Jewish woman. If one considers Mann's later biography, this is highly ironic: he would marry a woman of Jewish descent. But he does not allow Paolo to possess the standard of value of a true artist. He betrays himself by praising the sculptor Bernini: "Is there a greater decorator?" (*GW* 8, 60). The passage alludes to Nietzsche calling Bernini the "ruin of sculpture," comparing him to Wagner, the "ruin of music" in *Der Fall Wagner* (The Case of Wagner, 1888).[20] Paolo admires the artist as decorator who appeals to the masses, as he has excluded himself from the artistic elite that transforms desire rather than popularizing it.

Another representation of the use of art as inappropriate compensation for desire is the story "Der kleine Herr Friedemann" (Little Herr Friedemann, 1897), which was most probably conceived very early and rewritten several times. A story called "Der kleine Professor" (Little Professor) is mentioned in Mann's letters beginning in 1894. The final version was accepted by the *Neue Deutsche Rundschau*, a leading modernist journal published by the S. Fischer publishing house, thus establishing Mann's connection to his lifelong publisher.

A model for the protagonist, Johannes Friedemann, was most probably the apothecary Gieshübler in Theodor Fontane's *Effi Briest* (1894/95) who is almost a hunchback and a *Schöngeist*, an aesthete, an *homme de lettre*.[21] Friedemann's hunchback marks him as an outsider. But he is born normal, and thus has normal sexual desire. The scene in the very beginning, when the nurse in her alcoholic stupor lets the baby fall from a table, is used as a satire both of the literary movement of naturalism and of the bourgeoisie. The real fault lies with the mother, who leaves the baby with inadequate help. Another half-hidden satirical theme lies in the use of Friedemann's *three* sisters who cannot marry. They live off a meager inheritance and thus do not offer an attractive dowry; they are also rather ugly. The sisters will appear again in *Buddenbrooks* with the same names. In the long novel their increasing bitterness is played out, and its cause becomes obvious. Love in the bourgeois social order, this satirical textual element says, is tied to beauty and money, mainly money.

While growing up, Friedemann learns the meaning of being an outsider. Sixteen years old, he realizes that because of his deformity he has no erotic chances in the world. He makes a rational decision to renounce sex and to substitute beauty for it, beauty as found in nature and in culture. He loves visiting the theater. The narrator calls him an Epicurean at this point, a designation that has two sources. In a notebook in which Mann kept ideas and material to use in his writings, he quoted a passage from the introduction to Paul Bourget's novel *Le Disciple* (1889), in which the modern dilettante is described as "un epicurien intellectuel et raffiné."[22] Bourget was a critic of decadence, of the scions of rich families who fled into an unproductive cult of art, leaving religion and national tradition behind, whom he called dilettantes. The loss of religion did not concern the Mann brothers, who had absorbed Nietzsche; although they did not share Bourget's reactionary tendencies, they found his description of the decadent sons of the bourgeoisie very applicable to themselves. If they disregarded their own literary productivity, they matched Bourget's image of godless modernists, withdrawn into themselves, who had substituted art for life. The character Friedemann, who is not creative, had become an Epicurean dilettante in this sense, except that he had not chosen his outsider position; it was forced upon him. This was the autobiographical element in Thomas Mann's conception.

The other source for the label "Epicurean" is most likely a passage from Nietzsche's essay "Was bedeuten asketische Ideale?" (What Do Ascetic Ideals Mean?) from *Zur Genealogie der Moral*. This passage provides almost a program for Mann's text. Nietzsche criticizes Schopenhauer's uncritical reception of Kant's definition of beauty: that what pleases without interest. Beauty, Nietzsche implies, always has a sexual connotation. Schopenhauer's description of the aesthetic experience as disinterested deliverance from suffering induced by the Will, Nietzsche suggests, in reality betrays a Schopenhauer tortured by sex, much more than he was willing to admit. Art does not cancel out sexual desire.

"Der kleine Herr Friedemann"[23] unmasks the use of dilettantism, a concern with art that is not creative and acts as substitute religion. Friedemann's plan for a life of serenity without sex is shattered when he falls in love with Gerda, a beautiful young married woman of society who is an outsider like he. He is smitten when he finds his seat next to hers in the theater during a performance of Wagner's *Lohengrin* (1850).[24] By weaving a Wagner opera into the representation of Friedemann's infatuation, Mann follows the example of his brother, who had used *Tannhäuser* (1845) in his first novel *In einer Familie* (1894). In both texts Wagner's music contributes to the sexual arousal of the male protagonists. In "Der kleine Herr Friedemann" the emancipated woman has sympathy for Friedemann, the fellow outsider. She invites him to play music with her. But she rejects him when, talking alone with her in a garden, next to a river, he declares his passion. A union with the stigmatized man would humiliate her socially, blow her camouflage, her marriage of convenience. She pushes him back and he lets himself fall into the water to end a life that fills him with disgust. But his death, his returning to Schopenhauer's Will is not a redemption. The text makes that clear by having the crickets that had fallen silent when Friedemann had hit the water soon continue their chirping (*GW* 8, 105). Nature is indifferent.

Thomas Mann worked hard on these early texts. The story "Der Bajazzo" (1897; the title is translated as The Dilettante, The Joker, and The Buffoon) is the revised version of an older text of 1895. It contains autobiographical memories of his childhood and youth. The unnamed first-person narrator grows up to be an uncreative dilettante, not capable of creating art but only of imitating it. He enjoys his distance from people who have a profession,[25] but whom he considers not gifted enough for leisure and enjoyment (*GW* 8, 122). But the boy's expectation that a life apart from society and its duties will produce happiness fails as dismally as Friedemann's.

Isolation means boredom, and a frustrated sexuality makes his isolation unbearable.

One of the story's passages is remarkable because it shows that Mann's admiration for Wagner's art, which he translated into his writing style, carries with it the potential of satirizing it. At one point in his travels the narrator mocks a Wagner musical drama on the piano as an audience of enthusiastic fellow hotel guests looks on. The pompous pantomimes and rolling harmonies in the description of this incident (*GW* 8, 118) show that Mann recognized the ostentatious side of Wagner's work. Implied or open criticism of Wagner was always possible, but it did not impede Mann's lifelong fascination with Wagner's music.

The story "Der Tod" (Death, 1897) is a fictional diary that reduces the aesthetic expectation of death as something "great and beautiful, and of a ferocious majesty" (*GW* 8, 74) to a meek, almost comical reality: death appears in the dreams of the protagonist as a dentist (*GW* 8, 74–75). Religiously tinted idealism is mocked. Nevertheless, the story plays with idealism in the sense that consciousness has power over physical reality. The protagonist apparently wills his death. Since his diary stops, the reader must assume that he has succeeded.

In the summer of 1897 in Rome, while Thomas was living with his brother Heinrich, and *Buddenbrooks* was in the conceptual phase, he wrote two stories, "Luischen" (Little Lizzy) and "Tobias Mindernickel." Both are more satirical than previous stories, perhaps because of Heinrich's influence. In a letter to Heinrich of 6 February 1908, Thomas remembers writing "Luischen" at the fountain in the park of the Villa Borghese in Rome.[26] His story, Thomas remembered, had impressed Heinrich. However, it was rejected by several journals and was not published until 1900.[27] Its satirical intention breaks grotesquely through a realistic surface. One can read the text as pre-expressionist;[28] it presents a caricature of a bourgeois husband, a lawyer grotesquely overweight and impotent, who idolizes his beautiful but frivolous wife with a love beyond his strength. This endearment is expressed as quite genuine and stands in contrast to the banal language used elsewhere in this text (*GW* 8, 172). Naturally she deceives him. Her lover is a dilettante, a semi-artist, a composer of popular melodies.

The narrator of "Luischen" speaks with two different voices. One voice condemns artists who want to be happy and lovable human beings, well adapted to society (*GW* 8, 172–73). The narrator's other voice mocks common morality with lines like "he, on his part, had not had enough morality in himself to resist her lure" (*GW* 8, 172–73). The denouement is presented with comical effect in the line "The fat man collapsed, making the planks clatter" (*GW* 8, 186). But the reader, who has been led to sympathize with the sexually frustrated husband, recognizes his moment of death as an insight into the true nature of the world. The betrayed husband realizes the truth about the sexual relationship between his wife and her lover with the help of music. For a moment, the semi-artist composer rises to an artistic level. Instead of dissolving dissonance in the usual tonal way, he surprises his audience with a modern tonal effect. In the first printing of the story this effect was a chord from Wagner's *Tristan und Isolde* (1865).[29] Mann replaced this direct reference in later editions by a similar effect. Chromatic, almost atonal, music, music outside of conventional rules, expresses the truth of sexual desire regardless of the asexual love of the husband. While banality wins out, his intense but misapplied love attains tragic value.

Another play with banality is contained in the story "Tobias Mindernik-kel" (1898). Mindernickel (lesser nickel), an impoverished burgher living in a poor neighborhood where he is mocked by children, is not "up to existence" (dem Dasein nicht gewachsen) (*GW* 8, 143). Pity and charity are his ways to gain some bearing: he bandages a boy who hurts himself while pursuing and taunting him. In this way he can touch a boy without fear of being accused of homosexuality[30] and gain a measure of power over him in the way Nietzsche had described charity in *Zur Genealogie der Moral*, as the Will to Power of the weak.[31] In order to exercise his suppressed Will to Power, Mindernickel buys a dog whom he names Esau, and for whom he cares with diligence, expecting the dog's absolute submission. Mindernickel's attempts to compensate for his own weakness by exercising authority over a weak creature hint at the authoritarianism of Wilhelminian Germany. After having beaten his dog, Mindernickel assumes the attitude of Napoleon (*GW* 8, 147), another ironic-humorous reference to Nietzsche: Napoleon was Nietzsche's hero and represented to him the promise of a higher development in man. Mindernickel fails to assert his superiority, and the dog retains his vivacious nature. Mindernickel, unable to tolerate an unfettered life, beats and eventually kills the dog. "Tobias Mindernickel" can be read as a parody of Nietzsche's morality, the "slave morality" of the weak, who may use charity as a means for the "Will to Power."

There may be significance in Mindernickel's naming of the dog after the betrayed brother in Genesis. The heterosexual Heinrich, like Mindernickel's dog, can follow his nature, and is envied by the outsider who is driven to the point of rage. Or, Thomas Mann can see himself in the role of the dog who is beaten for his nature (Heinrich's condemnation of his homoerotic poems). Or, yet again, Thomas is cast in the role of Jacob, who will prevail over the older brother. The naming of the dog evokes various versions of the brother problem.

After finishing *Buddenbrooks* Mann returned to the series of grotesque, pre-expressionist stories. In "Der Weg zum Friedhof" (The Road to the Cemetery, 1900) the superior stance of the narrating voice covering an unfortunate and oppressed human being prevails over, and is at the same time contrasted to, the sympathetic representation of the downtrodden character

Lobgott Piepsam, who, like Tobias Mindernickel, is unable to cope with existence. The lonesome and unfortunate alcoholic Piepsam confronts a young bicyclist with blond hair, blue eyes, and ordinary self-assurance, whom the narrator calls simply "das Leben" (Life) (*GW* 8, 191), for the right of way on the (realistic and symbolic) road to the cemetery. The confrontation with "Life" turns out to be too much for Piepsam. He collapses still shouting threats, evoking the Last Judgment (*GW* 8, 195). The reference to Revelations reminds the reader of section fifteen of the first treatise of Nietzsche's *Zur Genealogie der Moral,* where Nietzsche explains how the slave morality lets the weak enjoy the eternal punishment of the strong.[32]

Critics have identified the blond bicyclist representing "Life" with Mann's friend Paul Ehrenberg. This would assign Mann the role of the decadent Piepsam. But Mann himself made bicycle tours at that time, alone or with Ehrenberg. While Mann was not blond, that attribute merely signifies the well-adjusted German insider. We understand Mann's intentions much better if we do not associate him with the decadent outsider in his prose. Rather, author and reader are to identify with both the cyclist, who is engaged in Life, and Piepsam, who is heading for the cemetery. The humorous narrator comes closer to Mann's own voice than either character.

"Der Kleiderschrank: Eine Geschichte voller Rätsel" (The Wardrobe: An Enigmatic Story, 1899) is a fairy tale with realistic elements. This combination is more hidden in Mann's other works, but they all tend to have it to some degree. The protagonist, Albrecht von der Qualen, travels on an express train from Berlin to Rome, with a ticket to Florence. But on a sudden impulse he leaves his train in the station of a city unknown to him. The narrator describes him as living a life beyond time and space: von der Qualen does not possess a watch and does not want to know where he is. "Everything must be suspended in air" is the thought by which he lives. The narrator calls this motto an obscure phrase, but assures the reader that the protagonist connects much with it. (*GW* 8, 153). At the very end of the text, the narrator repeats the phrase and questions whether the protagonist did not just dream the whole story while he continued on his journey. "Reality," particles of a world the reader can reconstruct, is suspended in favor of the freedom of imagination.

This freedom is linked to suffering and death. The protagonist's name, "van der Qualen," evokes the German word for pain. Since several physicians have given him only months to live, there must be a reason for his pain, but we are not told what it is. When van der Qualen walks into the unknown city, he crosses a bridge and watches a boatman pass underneath. Immediately he knows that this is not an ordinary river. The narrator does not say so, but the reader guesses that this is the river Styx, and on it Charon is rowing his boat, waiting for van der Qualen.[33] The bridge he crosses has classical statues on its parapet. The bridge and the two towers flanking an old city gate are identifiable: both are found in the city of Lübeck. But the rooms in which van der Qualen has his encounter with the girl telling him stories is located in Munich, as Mann told us in his "Lebensabriß" (A Sketch of My Life, 1930).[34] Van der Qualen's first name is Albrecht, the name Mann would give to a character resembling Heinrich in his notes for "Maja" and in his later novel *Königliche Hoheit* (Royal Highness, 1909). Albrecht van der Qualen represents the outsider status of both brothers, their lack of a home and their uneasiness in their social environment. In contrast to their real situation, the fictional character is wealthy and thus as free as the brothers would have wished to be.

There is a half-hidden allusion to Hans Christian Andersen. During the narrator's description of van der Qualen's route through town, he mentions the rain-slick sidewalks, and remarks that van der Qualen is not wearing galoshes but durable and yet elegant boots (*GW* 8, 155). He does not wear Andersen's "Galoshes of Fortune."[35] The galoshes in Andersen's tale fail to deliver on their promise of good fortune; in this tale there is no such promise.

A naked and attractive young woman makes her fairy-tale appearance in the wardrobe of van der Qualen's rented room, but her stories are not fairy tales but sad narratives of failed loves. When the sexual stimulus coming from her stories and her nakedness overwhelms her listener and he reaches for her, she does not resist but suspends her storytelling for a while (*GW* 8, 161). The proper relationship to the fairy or muse is to merely listen and become completely immersed in her, and doing so makes the heart of the sick van der Qualen beat stronger, slower, and softer (*GW* 8, 159). Stories heal. Literature, the formed, disciplined freedom of the imagination, can absorb the suffering of the world. Its suspension of time and place, its ability to convey distance from cruel life, the struggle of all against all, can take the place of religion and keep the fear of death at bay. But it requires the transformation of sexual desire, because sexuality means service to Schopenhauer's Will to Life, the source of all suffering. It also means social commitment, service to society and reality, and with it comes banality. The girl does not resist; she lets herself be misused. This implies an early warning to Heinrich, the same warning Thomas made explicit in his letter of 5 December 1903.

Thomas Mann's early texts are stories of outsiders. Their aim is to experiment with the possibilities for a writer who had stepped out of the bourgeois world of his family and thus had assumed the ironic distance of an outsider. While Mann's sexuality emphasized his outsider condition, it did not create it. Mann's joy, expressed in a letter to Grautoff of 6 April 1897, that with "Der kleine Herr Friedemann" he had gained artistic freedom by having found the masks with which he could present himself to an audience,[36] does not merely mean that he had found a camouflage for his homoerotic feelings. Mann's outsider stories experiment with the way a writer

ought to see the world from a distance. Only then will he be able to transform it. The world under God's direction, his wrath, was no longer common
to author and reader; it had lost its tie to solid traditional values. The new
question that arose was: how can we live in Schopenhauer's world, filled
with the struggle of all against all? Will we be able to re-establish values
through the power of human creativity, as Nietzsche had demanded?
Nietzsche had not shown how this could be done; and neither can fictional
writing. But it can experiment with such questions.

"Der kleine Herr Friedemann" had caught the attention of the publishing house Samuel Fischer in Berlin. Fischer published the works of the
successful young dramatist Gerhart Hauptmann and had built a reputation
of attracting good young writers. In May of 1897, Samuel Fischer himself
wrote to Thomas Mann that he liked this text. He promised to publish it
with other stories by Mann as a small book, and encouraged him to write a
novel.[37] Soon, in the summer of 1897, Thomas Mann began to plan for his
first novel, *Buddenbrooks: Verfall einer Familie* (Buddenbrooks: Decline of
a Family), which was eventually published late in 1900 with a date of 1901.

We know much about the writing of Mann's first novel. Mann used to
jot down sudden ideas that came to him when he was away from his desk.
He used small pocket-notebooks for that purpose. A notebook of 1897 with
early notes for *Buddenbrooks* has been preserved. We also have a sheaf of
papers with other notes for the novel.[38] Some of them must have been written in the summer and fall of 1897. Thus we are able to reconstruct fairly
well what went on in Thomas Mann's mind when the opportunity to publish
a novel with the renowned house of Fischer arose. Such reconstruction
contradicts later commentaries by Mann that insist, it was the sensitive
latecomer Hanno Buddenbrook who originally had the central role in the
novel's conception.[39] This claim has been widely accepted, but is of limited
value. The first notebook entries are not about the boy Hanno at all, but
they list strange characteristics of Christian, the bohemian brother of
Hanno's father, the senator. Following the notes about Christian, there are
only a few concerned with Hanno. Immediately following these are detailed
descriptions of the characters of the first two Buddenbrook generations; on
page seven of Mann's second notebook one entry is devoted to Thomas, the
senator and protagonist of the third generation.[40] These notes record spontaneous ideas as they came into Mann's mind; they do not follow any
chronological order. Several notes show family trees depicting the three
generations, with dates.[41] A very early note in the Buddenbrook papers
clearly shows the plan for a family novel.[42]

Perhaps Mann's recollection of his interest in the story of the weakly
Hanno Buddenbrook does give us a clue to the novel's conception. A novel,
he realized, must depict more of society than his novelistic stories had done
so far. Since the young author was indebted to his family for most of his

societal insights, the idea of a family novel offered itself. As mentioned, the first jottings in his second notebook intended for *Buddenbrooks* describe the eccentricities of Christian Buddenbrook, who had a model in the Mann family, Friedrich Buddenbrook, a brother of Thomas's and Heinrich's father. In the novel Christian serves as a the most obvious indication of the decline of the family, and the theme of decline had been connected with the idea of a family novel from the beginning of its conception. Mann's later remembrance of planning the story of Hanno, the boy dilettante disgusted with bourgeois values, refers to his reluctance to take over the family firm. Hanno is Thomas Mann in the very limited sense of the family son unable to play the expected role. This inability is expressed by Hanno's weakness and sentimentality, certainly an exaggeration of traits of the young Thomas Mann at that age. The first note concerning Hanno in the second notebook provides evidence of this: Hanno "is expected to recite Lübeck street names,"[43] and in the text, the father conducts just such an examination of his son (*GW* 1, 510–11). The father wants to direct Hanno toward practical matters, and the boy resists because he senses his father's purpose: to prepare him for a role as a Lübeck merchant. Mann's resistance to the same kind of role, and his accompanying guilt feelings, are translated into the theme of the family's decline into decadence.

It has been established that *Buddenbrooks* contains a parody of Richard Wagner's *Der Ring des Nibelungen* (1869–76); Mann himself let it be known.[44] Neither a satirical treatment of decadent neurasthenia with Christian in the center, nor the transformed representation of his resistance to the family would produce a great work. So he looked to an admired example of greatness, Wagner's *Ring*. A great novel would be a composition with musically woven themes. On a smaller scale, in "Der kleine Herr Friedemann," Mann had already woven the sexual theme into the text in ways resembling a musical composition. Mann admired Wagner, but the young author was aware of the danger of attempting something on grand scale the composer was known for: it could lead him to pomposity of expression, to a false greatness. After all, he had read Nietzsche's *Der Fall Wagner*.

Nietzsche's treatise contains a passage in which the author jokes about the imagined effect of translating Wagner's mythical plots into bourgeois modernity.[45] Mann's parody of Wagner's *Ring* as a story of the hope and disappointments of a bourgeois family could begin by paralleling the building of Walhalla with the process of moving into a new house. This consideration led to Mann's inclusion of the housewarming party and required him to show the family rising as well as falling. *Buddenbrooks* as a parody of Richard Wagner's *Ring des Nibelungen* — not in the negative sense the word parody often carries — makes the work a symbolist rather than a realistic novel, in the sense that its structure is more self-referential than referential. The decline of the Buddenbrook family has limited historical significance.

The German bourgeoisie in general and the burghers of Lübeck in particular were on the rise after 1871, while the Buddenbrooks firm is in decline.

Nevertheless, the theme of breaking away from the family tradition has more than a private significance. Mann's novel was to be a modern, post-Nietzschean text imbued with the ambition to show the inadequacy of common orientations and the necessity of achieving the essential distance for experimenting with new ones. The business acumen of the male members of the Buddenbrook family declines as they become more distanced from the conventions and goals of bourgeois society. To buy and sell for one's profit requires one to be comfortably integrated with the world as traditionally understood and interpreted. Distance from this world means the alienation experienced by an outsider.

The text has Christian, the dilettante, say publicly that every business-man is a "crook" (Gauner) (*GW* 1, 318). Christian's statement causes his brother Thomas, the head of the firm, to fall into a rage at him. Thomas's need to remove his brother from the firm and from the town are indications of what he much later admits to himself: that he is not the naive merchant either (*GW* 1, 469–73). Christian's lifestyle represents a danger that Thomas recognizes in himself (*GW* 1, 580). Perhaps the clearest demonstration of the opposition between a naive agreement with the world and distance from it occurs in the narration of Hanno's school day. The students cheat. When they are successful and receive a satisfactory grade, they consider themselves good students (*GW* 1, 728–31). However, a student who is caught cheating is "condemned" (gerichtet), and "all regarded him with a mixture of disgust, pity and horror" (*GW* 1, 733). Even Hanno, despite seeing through this falsehood, cannot extricate himself from the general reaction. The narrator comments:

> Whoever among these twenty-five young men was of an upstanding constitution, who was strong and competent for life as it is, took things completely as they were; he was not offended by them and considered everything a matter of course. But there were eyes that were fixed upon a point with gloomy contemplation. (*GW* 1, 733)

Hanno Buddenbrook begins to suffer from his distance from the world.

The novel's first words, "What is this?" (Was ist das) (*GW* 1, 9), question the grand bourgeois society in which they are spoken. They belong to the Christian tradition, which is questioned in *Buddenbrooks*. The question is taken from Martin Luther's catechism, where it explains the article of faith in God the creator.[46] The scene is of the assembled family Buddenbrook awaiting the dinner guests for the housewarming party. The older Budden-brook, himself not a believer, has staged the examination of his eight-year-old granddaughter Antonie, called Tony, in order to poke fun at his son's pietist beliefs. On the symbolic level of the novel, the old man, born in the enlightened eighteenth century, carries allusions to Goethe and (by his predilection for Napoleon) to the free spirit of Nietzsche. Luther's catechism, as Tony recites it, requires thanks to God for all possessions, including houses, fields, and livestock. The free spirit of the old man finds the rural ambiance of Luther's language inadequate and even laughable. In contrast to him, his son, Johann Buddenbrook the Younger, can no longer live by the enlightened rationality of his father; he needs an ideology to justify his drive toward profit; he needs a higher being to sanctify his wealth, his successes.[47] The validity of the article of faith and its explanation is further questioned by the young Tony's way of reciting it. After having been helped over one hurdle, the words come to her smoothly. While she rattles them off, the narrator compares Tony's feeling with gliding down a hill on a sled (*GW* 1, 9). The Christian faith has become a meaningless routine in the bourgeois world, where profit and wealth are the only real principles. The younger Buddenbrook confirms this at the end of the day, when he sides with his father in the further exclusion of his half-brother from the family and its new wealth. If his faith conflicts with a business decision, he thinks of profit rather than Christian love.

The novel suggests an alternative religion in the episode of Thomas Buddenbrook's reading of Schopenhauer's chapter "Über den Tod und sein Verhältnis zur Unzerstörbarkeit unseres Wesens an sich" (On Death and its Relationship to the Indestructibility of Our Being, 1844). Thomas, the senator, understands Schopenhauer's treatise of the immortality of the will in the spirit of Nietzsche's cult of life. Death would relieve him of his failed existence and free him to an eternal presence from which he could enter into a new and happier life. But his bourgeois instincts resist such insights (*GW* 1, 659). He returns to the belief of his forebears, which leaves him dissatisfied (*GW* 1, 661). In the last scene of the novel a group of frustrated women is all that is left of the splendor of the Buddenbrook family. Tony doubts the religious idea of meeting again in heaven. The old teacher Sesemi Weichbrodt rises up against Tony's doubt, maintaining her victory against the lifelong temptations of reason: "It is so!" The narrator's irony when describing the old maid Sesemi renders the question with which the text began unanswerable. The novel does not offer a faith; neither does it sustain a valid ideology.

This is even true of what appears to be the main theme in the novel. The decline referred to in the novel's subtitle is a synonym for "decadence," and the decadence of a family is degeneration. But both brothers Mann were proud of living decadently at a distance from normalcy, from the "herd" as Nietzsche liked to say. On the other hand, Nietzsche's expression "Pathos der Distanz"[48] does not only mean the passionate desire to be different from the trite majority, but it also implies the anguish of being isolated. While Christian gives in to his neurasthenia, Thomas covers his up by acting the superior, successful businessman. Hanno withdraws; his friend Kai, who also comes from a decadent family, actively enjoys his distance and translates it into writing. Decadence, decline, degeneration are conditions that are fateful, but also, by providing distance, make individual creativity possible.

The theme of fateful decline is discussed early in the text during the housewarming party, when the second Buddenbrook describes the misfortune of the previous owners of the house as fated (*GW* 1, 24–25). The older Buddenbrook immediately objects, calling fateful decline just one of his son's "idées"(*GW* 1, 25). He himself needs neither "idées" nor religion. Belief in fate does not agree with the Christian faith. The second Buddenbrook's apparent belief in fate merely indicates his need to hold on to some kind of ideology. Fate comes up again when hail destroys the harvest in Pöppenrade and frustrates the senator's business coup. Here, fate is not an inevitable force, but misfortune has become a part of Thomas Buddenbrook's soul. He accepts this accident as something that belongs to him. That is why the text has him say, "It is good that way" (Es ist gut so), even repeating it, with the narrator adding: "exhaling, satisfied, relieved" (ausatmend, befriedigt, befreit) (*GW* 1, 494). Fate is only a strand in the musical theme of decline, which is not fully destined. The multiperspectivity by which fate may be regarded is apparent when Thomas speaks to his sister about the "irony of fate" (*GW* 1, 598). He means the selling of the family house to the competitor Hagenström. But Thomas has motivated the sale not long before by perfectly rational business calculations (*GW* 1, 583). Both irony and fate are Romantic views of the family's decline. They are embellishments, not a validation.

The text offers a spectacular example of Romantic downfall for comparison: Edgar Allan Poe's "The Fall of the House of Usher" (1840), which Mann's character, Hanno's friend the young Kai Graf Mölln, reads and intends to use as a model for his future novel of the fall of the Buddenbrooks. But nothing like the collapse of the Usher castle happens in *Buddenbrooks*. Senator Thomas has a stroke walking in the street, and falls in the dirt; Hanno dies of common typhoid fever; the Buddenbrook houses are simply sold; and at very end there is the assembly of frustrated women.

Some critics want to see the decline of the male Buddenbrooks compensated by their intellectual enrichment. Thomas Mann himself in 1940 wanted to see his novel in that light (*GW* 13, 141). While Thomas Buddenbrook has more intelligence than his ancestors, Christian's narcissistic insights can hardly be seen as signs of healthy differentiation toward higher intelligence. Hanno is extremely sensitive but not creative (*GW* 1, 743). There is no progression. What Christian and Thomas have in common is not their intelligence but distance from their commercial family background, a distance that drives Christian from home. Thomas uses his creative gifts for the family business: he pulls the firm and the family to its highest point, but his creativity means distance from his fellow burghers, a distance that produces alienation and stagnation. A genius withers in daily routine. Thomas Buddenbrook hides his stagnation by acting, by using a mask, through which he confirms his decadence, like the image Nietzsche painted of Wagner as the master of small details who lost the sense of the whole.[49] Hanno can see through his father's false front (*GW* 1, 626–27). His sensitivity has alienated him from his social environment. He represents the danger of distancing oneself from the world, while his friend Kai is able to use this condition creatively.

Why is this novel of decline fascinating to read? Because of its representation. The same family the plot puts to doom is depicted sympathetically and warmly, though with a dose of melancholy. There are passages in which even Christian elicits empathy, and others in which the disciplined Senator Thomas appears all too human. The reader is led to a sympathy for the family that artfully balances the severe criticism that the plot of the novel implies: the Buddenbrooks renounce love for the sake of acquiring wealth, and with it power. This criticism amounts to a condemnation of the bourgeois lifestyle.

All of the family members feel obliged to render the sacrifice of their happiness, to deny their humanity. Marriages for love are in the background of the plot. Gotthold, a son of a former love marriage by the old Buddenbrook, himself married for love. Because he thus compromised the status of the family, he is punished by exclusion. His inheritance is cut, and his three daughters remain unmarried for lack of attractive dowries. Thomas Buddenbrook loves Anna, a pretty, lower-class flower girl, but there is no question of marrying her. The novel contrasts her fertility with the frigidity of Thomas's wife Gerda.[50] Thomas proves his hidden attachment when he builds his new house opposite the flower store where he met his first love. While the senator lies in state, Anna, pregnant again, comes to see him. Her former beauty is still apparent; in a musical repetition the text evokes the description that was first given in the love-and-departure scene (cf. *GW* 1, 168 with 689). But now the dead senator's face is "flayed" (zerschunden). Anna's feelings are delicately alluded to in the text: "Finally she said: 'Yes . . .,' sobbed once, a single time, very briefly and indistinctly, turned and left" (*GW* 1, 690). She is still attached to her former lover, and sons from her would have provided heirs to the firm.

The representation of the destruction of Tony Buddenbrook's love is the novel's most prominent accusation of the bourgeois lifestyle in the novel. Her sacrifice for the family's grandeur becomes entirely futile. The novel uses a musical technique to keep this futility in the memory of the reader: she retains the words of Morten, her true love, in her memory, and utters them repeatedly through the years.[51]

The renunciation of love links *Buddenbrooks* to Wagner's *Der Ring des Nibelungen* thematically. The greatness of the house of Buddenbrooks was tied to money as that of Valhalla was tied to stolen gold. With Gerda Buddenbrook and her son Hanno, the family pride dissolves into music, Wagnerian music. The ring in Wagner's musical dramas represents power. A ring also appears in *Buddenbrooks,* and it also means power, but a power of a very different sort. In a fairy-tale Kai narrates, the protagonist catches a bubble rising from a swamp. In his hand it becomes a ring that effects "magic transformations, disenchantments, and deliverances" (*GW* 1, 623–24). Art, the young Thomas Mann must have believed, delivers one from woeful reality by transforming life into lasting shapes.

Notes

[1] The "Protokoll" of the will by Senator Mann is kept in the "Archiv der Hansestadt Lübeck" (Akten des Notars Dr. Robert Peacock). A copy was made available to me by Dr. Manfred Eickhölter, Heinrich und Thomas Mann Centrum, Lübeck.

[2] "Testamentsentwürfe des Senators Thomas Johann Heinrich Mann." Thomas Mann, *Buddenbrooks: Verfall einer Familie. Kommentar. GFKA* 1.2, 629–35.

[3] Heinrich Mann, *Briefe an Ludwig Ewers 1889–1913,* ed. Ulrich Dietzel and Rosemarie Eggert (Berlin: Aufbau-Verlag, 1980), 202. Gerhard Schäffner, *Heinrich Mann-Dichterjugend: Eine werkbiographische Untersuchung* (Heidelberg: Winter, 1995), 80–81, 87, a biographical account of the development of the young Heinrich Mann as a writer, clings to the traditional view of the conservative early Heinrich Mann, based on his having been the editor of the nationalistic and anti-Semitic journal *Das 20. Jahrhundert* (1894–96). Schäffner de-emphasizes the impact of this early reading of Schopenhauer and Nietzsche.

[4] Michael Wieler, "Der französische Einfluß: Zu den frühesten Werken Thomas Manns am Beispiel des Dilettantismus," *TMJb* 9 (1996): 173–87.

[5] *GW* 8, 712. Hereafter cited in the text. See also Harald Höbusch, *Thomas Mann: Kunst, Kritik, Politik, 1893–1913* (Tübingen: Francke, 2000), 17–33.

[6] Schäffner, *Heinrich Mann-Dichterjugend,* 56–86.

[7] Heinrich Mann, "Geh schlafen," *Die Gesellschaft* 6 (1890): 1663.

[8] Heinrich Mann, *Briefe an Ludwig Ewers,* 195.

[9] Hermann Bahr, "Die neue Psychologie." *Moderne Dichtung,* August and September 1890. Reprinted in: *Das junge Wien: Österreichische Literatur- und Kunstkritik 1887–1902.* Ed. Gotthard Wunberg (Tübingen: Niemeyer, 1976), 92–101.

[10] Joachim Radkau, "Neugier der Nerven. Thomas Mann als Interpret des 'nervösen Zeitalters,'" *TMJb* 9 (1996): 29–53.

[11] For another, more detailed, interpretation see Schäffner, *Dichterjugend,* 61–70. Schäffner draws too many biographical conclusions from this (and other) fictional texts.

[12] This poem was discovered by Michael Wieler, along with the fact that it was the model for Thomas's prose poem. Wieler, "Der französische Einfluß," 184–85.

[13] Cf. Howard Nemerov, "Themes and Methods in the Early Stories of Thomas Mann," *Poetry and Fiction: Essays* (New Brunswick: Rutgers UP, 1963), 297: "The suppressed erotic nature in these persons reaches out and forces the world to destroy them."

[14] Heinrich Detering, *Das offene Geheimnis: Zur literarischen Produktivität eines Tabus von Winckelmann bis zu Thomas Mann* (Göttingen: Wallstein, 1994).

[15] The date of origin of "Enttäuschung" is not certain. The title "'Begegnung,'" written in "Porto d'Anzio September [18]95" which is mentioned in a letter to Otto Grautoff of January 1896 (*TM/OG*, 61) could refer to an earlier draft.

[16] However, Edo Reents, "Von der Welt als Vorstellung zur Welt als Wille: Schopenhauer und Thomas Manns *Enttäuschung*," *TMJb* 8 (1995): 209–40, finds resemblances between Schopenhauer's biography and the stranger in the story.

[17] Nietzsche, *KSA* 5, 353.

[18] Hans Rudolf Vaget, "Intertextualität im Frühwerk Thomas Manns" und Heinrich Manns 'Das Wunderbare,'" *Zeitschrift für deutsche Philologie* 101 (1982): 193–216.

[19] Nietzsche, *KSA* 5, 205. Reed, *Thomas Mann: The Uses of Tradition* (Oxford: Clarendon Press, 1996), 23, discovered a quotation from Heine's poem "Unterwelt" (from *Neue Gedichte*) in *GW* 8, 50. This poem makes fun of the marriage of Proserpina and Pluto. The last section addresses the reader's longing: "Zuweilen dünkt es mich als trübe / Geheime Sehnsucht deinen Blick." Heinrich Heine, *Sämtliche Schriften*, vol. 4 (Munich: Hanser, 1968–1976), 398. The poem ends with the claim that "verfehltes Leben, verfehlte Liebe" (failed life, failed love) is unalterable.

[20] Nietzsche, *KSA* 6, 46. Cf. *Menschliches, Allzumenschliches* I (Human, All too Human, 1878), Aphorism 161, *KSA* 2, 151, where Bernini serves as an example of an overrated artist.

[21] Hans Rudolf Vaget, "Thomas Mann und Theodor Fontane: Eine Rezeptionsästhetische Studie zu 'Der kleine Herr Friedemann,'" *Modern Language Notes* 90 (1975): 448–71; Theodor Fontane, *Sämtliche Werke*, vol. 4 (Munich: Hanser, 1962–64), 52, 62.

[22] *Nb* 1 (1–6), 17.

[23] Guided by reception-theory, Vaget, "Mann-Fontane," 460–62, reads the story as *Kontrafaktur*, a reversal of the figures of Gieshübler and, to some degree, Wüllstetten in Fontane's *Effi Briest*. "Wie, wenn dieser stille Epikureer statt der liebenswürdigen Effi einer anderen Frau begegnete, einer Dekadenten?" (457) (How would it be if this quiet epicurean met another woman, a decadent?). I agree that Fontane's novel had a role in the conception of the story. I suggest, however, that this inspiration might be seen in a more playful, less stringent manner. Heinrich Mann's novel *In einer Familie* (1894) was as much an inspiration for it as Fontane's novel. Eckhard Heftrich, in *Vom Verfall zur Apokalypse: Über Thomas Mann* (Frankfurt am Main: Klostermann, 1982), 36, associates the name "Friedemann" with Wagner's Bayreuth home "Wahnfried" and with "Friedmund," a name that Siegmund in Wagner's *Die Walküre* considers as suitable for himself.

[24] The dates given for Wagner's musical dramas are the dates of the first performance.

[25] Cf. Harvey Goldman, *Max Weber und Thomas Mann: Calling and the Shaping of the Self* (Berkeley: U of California P, 1988), 60.

[26] Probably the same one that inspired Rilke's famous poem "Römische Fontäne" in *Neue Gedichte*.

[27] TM/HM, 131; Hans Rudolf Vaget, *Thomas Mann. Kommentar zu sämtlichen Erzählungen*, 96.

[28] Joachim Wich, "Groteske Verkehrung des 'Vergnügens am tragischen Gegenstand.' Thomas Manns Novelle *Luischen* als Beispiel," *Deutsche Vierteljahrsschrift für Literaturwissenschaft und Geistesgeschichte* 50 (1976): 234–36; Nemerov, "Themes and Methods in the Early Stories of Thomas Mann," 292.

[29] Jan Cölln, "Gerichtstag der Literatur," *Jahrbuch der deutschen Schillergesellschaft* 45 (2001): 335.

[30] Wolfgang Lederer has commented on the passage that Mindernickel displays occasional tenderness, such as when he is "permitted" to touch the injured boy. His deprivation has been that he cannot touch anybody, boy or dog, without the excuse that he is just coming to their aid. This relates to the fear of homoeroticism (which largely explains why some men, such as Walt Whitman, Henry James, and many others became nurses of injured soldiers). Mindernickel names his dog Esau, the brother of Jacob in Genesis. This relates to Thomas Mann's forbidden infatuation with Heinrich, whom he also could not touch (*GW* 8, 143).

[31] "The happiness of the smallest superiority" (das Glück der kleinsten Überlegenheit) (Nietzsche, *KSA* 5, 383). Cf. Vaget, *Thomas Mann: Kommentar zu sämtlichen Erzählungen*, 71, who points to Nietzsche's *Menschliches, Allzumenschliches* I, Aphorism 103, *KSA* 2, 100.

[32] *KSA* 5, 283–85.

[33] Henry Hatfield, "Charon und der Kleiderschrank." *Modern Language Notes* 65 (1950): 100–102.

[34] *Essays* 3, 184, cf. Peter de Mendelssohn, *Der Zauberer: Das Leben des deutschen Schriftstellers Thomas Mann*, vol. 1, ed. Cristina Klostermann (Frankfurt am Main: S. Fischer, 1996), 510–14, and *GW* 8, 155.

[35] Manfred Dierks, *Studien zu Mythos und Psychologie bei Thomas Mann*, TMS 2 (1972), 45.

[36] *TM/OG*, 90.

[37] Samuel Fischer and Hedwig Fischer, *Briefwechsel mit Autoren* (Frankfurt am Main: S. Fischer, 1989), 394.

[38] Notebook 2 is contained in *Nb* 1–6; the Buddenbrook papers are now in *GKFA* 1.2.

[39] *Essays* 3, 20–21; *GW* 11, 554.

[40] *Nb* 1 (1–6), 59–62.

[41] *GKFA* 1.2, 425–26.

[42] *GKFA* 1.2, 425. Also quoted in Mendelssohn, *Der Zauberer* 1, 467.

[43] *Nb* 1 (1–6), 60.

[44] Hans Rudolf Vaget, "Im Schatten Wagners," *Im Schatten Wagners: Thomas Mann über Richard Wagner: Texte und Zeugnisse 1895–1955*, ed. Hans Rudolf Vaget (Frankfurt am Main: Fischer Taschenbuch Verlag, 1999), 316–18; *DüD* 1, 38–39, 46.

[45] Nietzsche, *KSA* 6, 34.

[46] Eberhard Lämmert, "Thomas Mann: Buddenbrooks," *Der deutsche Roman: Vom Barock bis zur Gegenwart,* ed. Benno von Wiese (Düsseldorf: Bagel, 1963), 190–96.

[47] Richard Sheppard, "Realism plus Mythology: A Reconsideration of the Problem of 'Verfall' in Thomas Mann's *Buddenbrooks*," *Modern Language Review* 87 (1994): 936–38.

[48] Nietzsche, *KSA* 5, 205, and elsewhere.

[49] Nietzsche, *KSA* 6, 27–30.

[50] Cf. Heftrich, *Verfall,* 57–63.

[51] Cf. Peter Pütz, "'Der Geist der Erzählung': Zur Poetik Fontanes und Thomas Manns," *Theodor Fontane und Thomas Mann: Die Vorträge des internationalen Kolloquiums in Lübeck 1997, TMS* 18 (1998), 99–111.

Art and Society in Thomas Mann's Early Novellas

Ehrhard Bahr

IN ONE OF THOMAS MANN'S early short stories from around the turn of the century, "Das Wunderkind" (1903), an older gentleman compares his own futile attempts at producing a melody on the piano with the perfection of the child prodigy who has just performed:

> One must remember that genius ["Genie"] comes from above. God grants his gift. There is nothing one can do about it, and it is not a disgrace being an ordinary human being. It is something like with the Christ child. One may kneel before a child without feeling ashamed. How strangely comforting that is![1]

What the old gentleman claims as an excuse for his failures at the keyboard is the cult of genius, the belief that genius originates in a divine realm. The implicit argument is that not everyone can be expected to be a genius. His language, colored by a naïvely Christian Sunday-school mentality, borrows from the adoration of the infant Jesus[2] and reveals a semi-religious appreciation of genius that protects and excuses his own failings. The performance of the child prodigy is received in sentimentally religious terms: the performer becomes literally a "Wunderkind" (child of miracles or miracle child) before the old man's eyes.

In another short story, "Gladius Dei" (1902), the protagonist, a religious fanatic in a black coat with a monk's hood, stomps through the streets of Munich. Visiting a church and leaving it again after a short but intense prayer, he stumbles upon an art shop displaying the reproduction of a painting of a voluptuous Madonna with the Christ child. He overhears the cynical conversation of two students describing in explicit sexual terms the effect of the sensuous painting of the Madonna. The students speculate about the artist's model as a woman of easy virtue. Three days later, the fanatic monk-like figure returns to the art shop and demands that the photographic reproduction of the painting be removed from the window and burned, together with all the other works of art displayed, because it offends his religious feelings. Before he is forcefully removed from the premises by a burly janitor who serves as bouncer, the religious fanatic mounts an extensive diatribe against art as desecration of religion. Hieronymus, as he is called, shares his features and his first name in the German version of the story with Girolamo Savonarola (1452–1498), the scourge of Florence. In a prophetic vision, Savonarola's German imitator sees a sword of fire over the city of Munich and predicts its ultimate destruction using a Latin quotation, the words of his role model: "Gladius Dei super terram [. . .] cito et velociter" (May God's sword come over the earth [. . .] quickly and soon) (*GW* 8, 215).[3]

Hieronymus sees art as the very anathema of religion, negating the truth of religious faith. His target is the overrefined aestheticism and the art business of the *fin de siècle*. He envisions a type of art that serves religion as "the holy torch which turns its light upon all the [. . .] abysses of life," as "the godly fire laid to the world" (*GW* 8, 211–12). He considers modern art blasphemous and shallow, leading the faithful astray and making them doubt the dogmas of the church, in this particular case, the dogma of the Immaculate Conception. Hieronymus's protest may be a direct reference to the Catholic laity and its religious revival movement at the turn of the century,[4] as is the dogma of the Immaculate Conception, which was pronounced in 1854.[5]

These passages display the extreme poles of the perspectives on art and society represented in the short stories and novellas Thomas Mann wrote between 1902 and 1904: on the one hand, art as substitute for religion, employing the cult of the artist as creator endowed by God, and, on the other hand, modern art as the negation of true religion, and the artist as shameless charlatan, interested only in promoting his own career, while indulging in the sins of the flesh and thereby desecrating the ideas and symbols dear to the devoted followers of religion. These two competing ideologies, in extreme opposition to each other, reflect general tendencies around the turn of the century and evoke specific reactions and commentary in Mann's fiction, as he sought to position himself not only as an artist and writer among the various literary schools of this time, but also in his relationship to bourgeois society. There is a strong autobiographical element in Mann's early novellas. Not only did he try to define his craft as an author by writing them, but they also served to rehearse his stance toward society. Although he considered himself an outsider, he did not claim the pose of an ivory-tower saint or aesthete. He displayed a concern for humanity as represented in the society of his day, and exploited the tensions between artist and society for the purposes of his craft.

Bourgeois life in Central Europe at the turn of the century had been adversely affected by the process of modernization: rapidly increasing industrialization, the application of technology to new areas of production, cycles of financial crises, and the claim of the rising working class for a share of political power. This process was part of the secularization of the European mind in the nineteenth century. This secularization affected especially the role of religion in society. As the German historian Thomas Nipperdey argued, "The unity of religion and society became fragmented, the individual citizen began identifying with different groups, the realms of societal life became separate [. . .] and religion lost its function; it became a special form of identification."[6] To compensate for this loss, intellectuals around the turn of the century began to embrace art as a means to provide meaning to life and a new opportunity for pseudo-religious devotion. They developed the concept of a "Kunst-Religion" (religion of art), inherited from Romanticism, or a non-Christian "Kultur-Religion," worshipping literature, music, and the visual arts. Especially the educated Protestant middle class began to question the Bible as revelation and turned to literature, music, and philosophy as sources of inspiration, seeking edification, from the Weimar classics to Nietzsche.[7] The Nietzsche cult produced special "varieties of Nietzschean religion" that benefited from this displacement of traditional religion by secular culture.[8]

Transcending everyday life through art became one of the tenets of literature, with *l'art pour l'art* as one of its extremes, expressionism the other. Architecture resorted to historicism, camouflaging modern buildings such as railroad stations and banks as Gothic cathedrals and Italian Renaissance palaces, while in opera, Richard Wagner provided the middle class with a medium to transfer its familial and political conflicts into a myth of a supposedly common Germanic past. On the other hand, the churches became associated with political movements, as evidenced by the *Kulturkampf* against the Catholic Church, or by the anti-Semitism of the Christian Social Movement founded by the reactionary Protestant minister Adolf Stoecker.

Nineteenth-century German philosophers had reflected on the function of art in modern society. Both Schopenhauer and Nietzsche had singled out "genius" as the force to resist "the normative pressure of industrial society" and focused on the artist to provide new visions for mankind.[9] Yet Nietzsche went one step beyond this positive appraisal of the artist when he demanded the highest standards for artistic creativity and began to expose Richard Wagner, whom he had first admired as the prototype of the modern artist, as instead a "great actor," the "artist of décadence," and the "Cagliostro of modernity" in *Der Fall Wagner* (The Case of Wagner, 1888).[10] For Nietzsche, Wagner was not creative enough, and therefore he called him an "imitative actor" and a "master of miniature."[11] He spoke of the "duplicity of art,"[12] referring not only to the principles of the Apollonian and Dionysian, but also to the newly perceived ambivalence of art in general, the art, "in which falsehood is sanctified," as Nietzsche would later say.[13] Mann exploited these tensions between Nietzsche and Wagner for use in his own works that could be considered a rewriting of Wagner in the spirit of Nietzsche.[14]

As T. J. Reed pointed out, Mann's work "rested [. . .] on foundations in the art and thought of the nineteenth century."[15] Schopenhauer, Nietzsche, and Wagner were the often-cited "triple constellation" (*Dreigestirn*) of his life and work, his fiction and his critical essays. He was their "reverent disciple," as he confirmed in *Betrachtungen eines Unpolitischen* (Reflections of a Nonpolitical Man, 1918; *GW* 12, 79), although there were other role models, such as Heine, Goethe, Fontane, and Tolstoy. While the Nietzschean influence is dated fairly precisely with his short story "Der Wille zum Glück" (The Will to Happiness) in 1896,[16] his first contacts with Schopenhauer may have been through Nietzsche and Wagner, that is, earlier than his recorded "Schopenhauer experience" during the writing of his first novel, *Buddenbrooks*, in 1899. He saw productions of Wagner at the local theater in Lübeck as early as 1892, and they constituted major events of his youth, introducing the young music lover to *Lohengrin, Tannhäuser,* and *Meistersinger.* When he moved to Munich in 1894, the local opera provided even more opportunities, with the added attraction of first-rate productions. Mann's first visit to Bayreuth, occasioned by the chance acquirement of a ticket for a performance of *Parsifal,* was in 1909.[17]

The Nietzschean polarity of art is present throughout Thomas Mann's short stories and novellas between 1902 and 1904. It is the polarity between the Apollonian and Dionysian that takes the form of the polarity between creative and imitative art, or between life and morality in Mann. Yet this polarity is not static, but is constantly deconstructed, even within the same story. In "Das Wunderkind," quoted above, the naïve concept of art as expressed by an old gentleman is only one among others. The narrator records a spectrum of opinions that includes even a condemnation of the artist as a type. The music critic delivers a critique worthy of Nietzsche that stresses the bipolarity of "dignity" and "toadyism," "charlatanry" and "holy inspiration," "contempt" and "secret rapture" in the child prodigy's presentation and character (*GW* 8, 346). "What is the artist? A buffoon [*Hanswurst*]," he exclaims (*GW* 8, 347). Repeating this negative verdict on a more pedantic level, the piano teacher identifies the prodigy's compositions as derivative of Chopin, and finds fault with his technique. The businessman calculating the receipts of the evening admits that, besides financial profits, art brings some luster to life. A young girl, overwhelmed by the erotic appeal of the music, feels sexually frustrated because she cannot project her desire onto the prepubescent "Wunderkind," while a military officer, reflecting on the essence of authority, claps his heels together and pays his respect to the prodigy as an equal in his own right. The only people untouched by the performance are three members of the aristocracy: a young, blond, blue-eyed woman and her two brothers, young lieutenants. One of them kicks up his heels in a primitive dance on the sidewalk, but an unkempt girl, a self-declared artist, dismisses this coltish display as childish in comparison to the child prodigy's performance. Claiming the latter's artistry for herself, she declares: "We are all 'Wunderkinder,' we creative artists" (*GW* 8, 348). Yet, she is unsure of her contempt for the three aristocrats who have nothing to show for their exceptionality but their blond hair and blue eyes — leitmotifs of unreflective life and characteristic of Nietzsche's "noble race" in *Zur Genealogie der Moral* (On the Genealogy of Morals, 1887).[18] The artist follows the three young people with envy in her eyes until they disappear around a corner. Her words echo the sentiment of the old gentleman, but reveal an intense identification with the creativity of the "Wunderkind," while the old gentleman admires the player's skill at the keyboard only superficially.

Although the various opinions recorded show the ambivalence of art in society, the narrator's voice is even more critical, contributing to an even more polarized perspective. He exposes the "Wunderkind" as a skillful manipulator of his audience. His whole performance is a calculated play on the naïve impressionability of the audience, exploiting its sentimentality and ignorance and seducing the senses of the viewers in a shameless display of his precocious bisexuality expressed through his effeminate body language and dress. With "a mighty publicity machine" (*gewaltiger Reklameapparat*), the "Wunderkind" is shown by the narrator to present the artist as actor and fraudulent magician, as Nietzsche had accused Wagner of being. For this reason, the music composed and played by the child prodigy is also said to exploit cheap effects. In the case of his "Fantaisie," the narrator reveals to his readers the erotically charged modulation of the C-sharp passage, reminiscent of Wagner's music in that it subliminally captures the gullible audience, while it is mesmerized by the "Wunderkind's" flirtatious glance of the eye (*GW* 8, 344).

In "Gladius Dei," there is a similar bias conveyed by the narrator, who appears to argue against his protagonist. With the very first sentence, the narrator introduces himself as a spokesman for Munich as the city of the arts: "Munich was radiant" ("München leuchtete") (*GW* 8, 197). He does not tire of describing this radiance in repeated words of praise for the flourishing of the arts in this Florence of the North. These words are an homage to the function of art as transcendence of everyday life. Without any reservation, the narrator declares that art rules over this city. Almost four pages are invested in this praise which ends as it began on the first page: "München leuchtete" (*GW* 8, 200). There are, however, narrative shifts; first, hardly noticeable, when Hieronymus is introduced in terms of an "apparent realism." But a move toward symbolic typicality is evident in the referentiality of the description of the protagonist, whose features are compared to an old painting in Florence. An entirely new perspective emerges when the narrator relates the protagonist's mission, taking a biblical stance and speaking of "a command and summons from on high." He assumes the perspective of Hieronymus, referring to "God's will," which sends him off to perform his sacrificial duty: "And since God would have it so, he set forth [. . .] and went" (*GW* 8, 204–5). For the confrontation in the art shop, the narrator chooses a completely different voice, a satirical perspective — with anti-Semitic undertones — when Blüthenzweig, the owner of the shop, is characterized in his features and mannerisms.[19] Hieronymus's speech is a powerful and convincing counterargument to the narrator's homage at the beginning of the story. But the satiric stance prevails — and is especially noticeable when the protagonist is forcefully removed from the art shop — until shortly before the end, when the narrator yields to the Savonarola perspective of the protagonist. Hieronymus's vision reveals a burning of the accumulated works or art and literature, and he welcomes the destruction by fire as punishment of the sinful city.

Mann classified the novellas he composed between 1902 and 1904 as belonging to "the Tonio Kröger group," which he characterized as "the work of a young man in the second half of [his] twenties." The stories, he wrote,

> all wear the impress of much melancholy and ironic reflection on the subject of art and the artist: his isolation and equivocal position in the world of reality, considered socially and metaphysically and as a result of his double bond with nature and spirit.[20]

Mann presented "Tonio Kröger" (1903) as the symbolic center and masterpiece of this group.

Another story belonging to this group is "Beim Propheten" (At the Prophet's), written in 1904. The titular protagonist Daniel, who never appears, is modeled on Ludwig Derleth (1870–1948), who at that time moved in the Bohemian circles of Munich and published in Stefan George's *Blätter für die Kunst,* the most prominent periodical of *l'art pour l'art* in Germany. This novella is perhaps the most autobiographical and realistic story of the Tonio Kröger group, because the novelist in the audience, the central figure of the novella, is an obviously ironic self-portrait of Mann, while the rich lady and her daughter Sonja have Hedwig Pringsheim and her daughter Katia, his future mother-in-law and his future wife, as models: Mann and Katia Pringsheim became engaged on October 4, 1904.[21] There is additional biographical referentiality in terms of the locale and other characters and circumstances: Derleth lived, under similar circumstances to the fictional Daniel, in a fifth-floor apartment in one of Munich's bohemian suburbs; he had a sister who, like Daniel's sister Maria Josepha, was totally devoted to him; and he was given to mailing out invitations for readings that he gave of literary manifestos similar to the one in the story entitled "Daniel's Proclamations."[22]

Most important for the "religion of art" celebrated on the occasion of this reading is the "religious aura" of the locale: the date is the evening of Good Friday, the place a combination of art gallery and chapel.[23] As an altar there is "a white-covered table holding a crucifix" and "a seven-branched candlestick." The display of "a goblet of red wine, and a piece of raisin cake on a plate" (*GW* 8, 365) turns the occasion into a parody of the Christian Eucharist.[24] A gilded plaster column serves as pulpit: "The capital of the column was covered with an altar-cloth of blood-red silk, and on that lay," like a Bible, "Daniel's Proclamations" (*GW* 8, 366). But beyond this obviously satiric description of the locale, there is again "the artist problem, the dialectic contrast of *Geist* [mind] and art on the one side and life on the other" (*GW* 13, 145), which plays the central role also in this short sketch.

The novelist, Mann's fictional doppelganger, is an established writer who belongs "to quite a different sphere and [is] present only by chance, being on good terms with life and having written a book which was read in middle-class circles" (*GW* 8, 363). He is the first well-adjusted artist we encounter in the Tonio Kröger group, while Daniel stands for the opposite. Even in his absence, he represents the merging of decadence, symbolism, and aestheticism, being one of the "young geniuses, criminals of the dream," who live in "cheap studios with symbolic decorations, where solitary and rebellious artists, inwardly consumed, hungry and proud, wrestle with devastatingly ultimate ideals in a fog of cigarette smoke" (*GW* 8, 362).

The narrator does not hesitate to pronounce his verdict in the first paragraph, denouncing the events to come:

> This is the end: ice, purity, and nothingness. No compact is binding here, no concession given, no forbearance granted and no values considered. Here is the air so rarified and pure that the miasmas of life cannot endure. Here rules defiance, absolute logic prevails, the enthroned, desperate I, liberty, madness and death.[25]

This initial indictment by the narrator sets the tone of the story, but the narrative perspectives presented include those of the guests as well as that of the novelist. Although the perspectives change several times, the novelist's point of view is dominating and prevails. He does not perceive any resonance from "Daniel's Proclamations" in the audience. Regardless of the proclamations' murderous message, they are received as a literary conceit, a harmless fiction. The narrator ventures some guesses at the audience's reaction, but they remain vague, with the exception of a reference to the novelist that describes him as an unsympathetic outsider who has a "vision of a ham sandwich" (*GW* 8, 369). When Daniel's loyal disciple finally dismisses the audience with the exhortation to plunder the world as soldiers of a Christ as *imperator maximus,* the narrator does not criticize the crowd's disregard of this invitation to barbarous vandalism. The audience acts as if released from a slightly embarrassing but entertaining performance that has taxed its physical endurance. The narrator records the audience's passivity without further comment, except for that of the novelist, who is singled out for more critical scrutiny.

The novelist makes up for the lost evening by attending to his private affairs. He successfully exploits the opportunity to further matters of the heart, endearing himself to the rich lady and her daughter. His comments are most revealing when he reflects on genius and must admit that all the conditions of genius are present in Daniel:

> The isolation, the freedom, the spiritual passion, the magnificent vision, the belief in himself, yes, even the approximation to crime and madness. What is there lacking? Perhaps the human element? A little feeling, a little yearning, a little love?[26]

This passage reads like a parody of the novelist's lifestyle. He has the qualities that are missing in Daniel, but the qualities that have made him a successful novelist are trivial: "a little feeling, a little yearning, a little love." Demonstrating this well-adjusted but smug attitude toward his art and profession, he does not neglect his physical well-being for the sake of matters of the heart, as he rushes off to dinner with the words: "Now I am as hungry as a wolf for my supper" (*GW* 8, 370). With deceptively good-natured humor, the narrator concludes: "He certainly was on good terms with life" (*GW* 8, 370). It is a kind of ironic self-criticism that the author could well afford as a successful novelist and fiancé, engaged to a young woman from a prominent upper-class family. Although the success of the *Buddenbrooks* novel had earned Mann the acceptance of his middle-class readership, there is no narratorial endorsement of his new status, as the last sentence indicates. It is too easy to read this sketch as a condemnation of *l'art pour l'art* and an attack on Stefan George and his disciples. "Beim Propheten" contains also a good measure of serious self-criticism. But as the author pushes his own agenda, he also displays a healthy self-confidence in his craft. The interplay of narrative perspectives reveals an artistic program that endorses the author's occasional identification with the audience as well as his obvious disassociation from Daniel, the invisible prophet of the novella, and his kind of "religion of art."

"Tristan" (1903), also part of the Tonio Kröger group, shows a new concern regarding the worship of art. Art is associated here with the Wagnerian theme of *Liebestod,* from the perspective of "a burlesque"[27] on the one hand and, combined with a serious criticism of decadent aestheticism, a tolerant, if not accepting stance toward unreflective life and middle-class values, on the other. With the two names — Tristan in the title and "Einfried," reminiscent of Wagner's villa "Wahnfried" in Bayreuth — in the very first sentence, the Wagnerian plot is set into action. The fact that "Einfried" is a sanatorium adds the Nietzschean element of decadence. As Nietzsche had said, "Wagner's art is sick."[28] The novella is conceived to prove this point. Whether it is Wagner or the Wagnerians who are its target remains open.[29]

Detlev Spinell, the Tristan figure in Mann's novella, is not introduced by name until the stage is set for the drama, that is, until Gabriele, the Isolde figure, and her husband, Herr Klöterjahn, the King Mark of this drama, have arrived and been described in detail, together with the personnel of the sanatorium. Herr Klöterjahn, a businessman from a town at the Baltic Sea, has brought his young wife Gabriele to Einfried for the cure of a lung ailment. Her trachea is mentioned, but not the word tuberculosis (although it is on everybody's mind).

The Spinell character is not part of this exposition, although there are vague references to his name and profession: "Even an author is here, an excentric sort of man, with a name like some kind of mineral or precious stone, who is stealing time from God Almighty" (*GW* 8, 217). His name is finally mentioned after eight pages. A description of his appearance and biography is added perfunctorily, almost as an afterthought, by the narrator, addressing the reader directly: "Imagine a dark-complexioned man at the beginning of his thirties, impressively tall, with hair already distinctly gray at the temples [. . .] His doe-like brown eyes had a gentle expression; the nose was thick and rather too fleshy" (*GW* 8, 223). Because of his "round, white, bloated face," he is stuck with the nickname, "the decomposed baby" ("der verweste Säugling"), as one of the other male patients maliciously calls him. Spinell is described as an aesthete, carried away by beautiful sights, which he welcomes with theatrical exclamations, and as the author of a slim, "very artful" novel, displayed for everyone who enters his room to see (*GW* 8, 224). His birthplace in Galicia, mentioned by the director of the sanatorium with some contempt — "he comes only from Lemberg" — is a signal for his Jewish background, challenging and confirming the anti-Semitic resentment of the reader (*GW* 8, 225).[30]

The climactic scene of *Liebestod* is an intertextual reenactment of the second act of Richard Wagner's *Tristan und Isolde* (1865). Spinell encourages Gabriele to play the piano, in spite of her doctor's orders. She plays Chopin and then the never-mentioned Wagner. Mutely, Spinell shows her the title page of the score. Gabriele plays the beginning, then the second scene of Act II: "sie fuhren fort in den trunkenen Gesängen des Mysterienspiels" (*GW* 8, 246). Critics have reconstructed in detail the intertextuality of this scene.[31] One striking example may suffice to illustrate this technique, consisting of direct quotations, single word borrowings, and paraphrases:

WAGNER:	MANN:
Nun banne das Bangen	Banne Du das Bannen,
Holder Tod	holder Tod! Löse nun
Sehnender Verlangter	die Sehnenden ganz von
Liebestod!	der Not des Erwachens!
In Deinen Armen	(*GW* 8, 246)

Dir geweiht
Unheilig Erbarmen
Von Erwachens Not befreit.
(*Tristan und Isolde*, II, 2)

Only Gabriele-Isolde will meet the Wagnerian love-death as a result of this encounter. Spinell-Tristan will survive. The "Liebestod" remains an aesthetic experience for him. There is a serious angle to this Wagner parody. While Gabriele is dying, the text foregrounds the burlesque encounter between her husband and Spinell, who has scolded Klöterjahn for having suppressed and destroyed the delicate beauty of his wife. Not only does Spinell see Gabriele as a work of art, but he worships her in a strange fusion of art and religion as a "sacred relic" ("unantastbares und unverletzliches Heiligtum") (*GW* 8, 252).

When Klöterjahn made Gabriele a housewife and mother, he debased her, in Spinell's words, to the service of everyday life and sacrificed her to "that stupid, clumsy and contemptible idol called nature" (*GW* 8, 254). But he, Spinell, had lifted her "out of the depths of degradation," and it had been his doing that she is now passing away "under the deathly kiss of beauty" (*GW* 8, 254). Spinell understands his hatred of Klöterjahn and his son as a hatred of "cheap, ridiculous, yet triumphant life, the everlasting antipode and deadly enemy of beauty" (*GW* 8, 254). He predicts Klöterjahn's offspring will become "a well-fed, trading, tax-paying citizen; a capable, philistine pillar of society; in any case a tone-deaf, normally functioning individual, unscrupulous and confident, sturdy and stupid." Bourgeois life is "the everlasting antagonist and deadly enemy of beauty" (*GW* 8, 254).

Klöterjahn repudiates Spinell's point of view as "idiotic nonsense." He "would hack him into pieces if it were not against the law" (*GW* 8, 258). In the end, Anton Klöterjahn, junior, Gabriele's healthy baby, is victorious as a representation of the power of unreflective life over art. Looking at the approaching Spinell, the baby, sitting in his stroller, bursts out with joy and laughter. His health contrasts with the writer's nickname "decomposed baby." Fleeing, Spinell's hesitating steps disguise that "inwardly he is running away" (*GW* 8, 262).

That the religion of art in its decadent Wagnerian form is rejected in favor of a society of businessmen and taxpayers is certainly not the moral of this novella. Mann never committed himself to either the side of Spinell as the irresponsible aesthete or that of Klöterjahn as the self-complacent bourgeois. He presents them in the perspective of constant equivocation of Nietzschean irony. There is Spinell's irresponsibility on the one hand, when he asks Gabriele to play the piano for the sake of beauty, while she rightly worries that it might affect her health: "Suppose it were to be bad for me" (*GW* 8, 242). On the other hand, there is Klöterjahn's ridiculous name, his lack of culture and abundance of health. Yet the narrator speaks of his "good, warm, honest human feeling" (*GW* 8, 260).

In his essay "Bilse und ich" (1906), in which Mann defended his use of real people as models for fictional characters, he labeled Spinell a satirical figure whose aestheticism, "that defunct artificiality," he claimed to consider "the danger of all dangers."[32] But in a late letter he called Spinell "the higher principle" when compared to Klöterjahn.[33] The common denominator in these contrastive self-interpretations is found in the same passage of "Bilse und ich": "I punished myself in this character." He criticized both the narrowness of the bourgeois lifestyle and the asocial escapism of modernist art.

Mann classified his only drama *Fiorenza* (1905) as belonging among the works of the next period, which he dated from the end of 1904 to 1907 and called "the period of *Royal Highness* (Mann, "Preface," vi). Yet he had already published from the material in 1902: the short story "Gladius Dei" was an offshoot of *Fiorenza* but set in contemporary Munich. He included *Fiorenza* in the second volume of *Novellen,* the 1922 edition of his short fiction, as well as in *Stories of Three Decades,* the English translation of 1936, because it partook "of the character of both drama and tale" (Mann, "Preface," vi). *Fiorenza* took seven years to complete, and Mann invested more time in it than any other project during this period; it was finished shortly before his wedding in 1905. Although the first performance of the drama in Frankfurt in 1907 was a moderate success, later performances more or less failed and none ever satisfied the author. But as a dialogue text it expresses the topic of art and society as well as any text of the Tonio Kröger group.

Thirty years later Mann explained the purpose of the historical setting of the drama "as pretext for an exposition of opposed elements in [his] nature: creation and criticism, art and knowledge, form and analysis, the craving to be at once both sinner and judge" (Mann, "Preface," vi–vii). Yet *Fiorenza* also reflects the German cult of the Italian Renaissance that was part of the decadence of the *fin de siècle* as we can observe it in texts by Stefan George, Hugo von Hofmannsthal, and Rainer Maria Rilke. In Mann's hands, the story of Savonarola and his opponents receives a new twist. The scene is set in Florence on a day in April of 1492, the day on which Lorenzo de Medici is going to die. The drama culminates in the encounter between Lorenzo, the ruler of Florence, and Savonarola, the prior of San Marco in Act III. In his dying hour the Magnifico has called for the fanatic monk who had condemned him from the pulpit for his worship of the arts, literature, Greek philosophy, and the sciences, as well as for his sinful life in the pursuit of beautiful women. A strange reversal of roles takes place during this encounter: the Prior, as Savonarola is called in the play, claims to be "an artist who is at the same time a saint." He tries to distance himself from "the art of the eyes" by maintaining that his "art is holy," consisting of "knowledge and a flaming denial" (*GW* 8, 1060). While the Prior perceives a conflict between the spirit ("Geist") and beauty, Lorenzo argues that spirit and beauty must not be opposed: even if they are enemies, they are "warring brothers" (*GW* 8, 1063). Even though the Prior rejects that characterization, he cannot deny that they are united in the worship of their egos, their pursuit of ascetic ideals to overcome deficiencies, and in their contempt of the masses. When the Prior hears Lorenzo's confession, the Magnifico agrees to the conditions of grace with the exception of the last: to make Florence free from the lordship of his house. When Lorenzo hears that the Prior wants to be lord in Florence, he protests in the name of life, accusing the Prior of bringing death to the city in the name of the spirit: "It is death whom you proclaim as spirit, and all the life of life is art."[34] In his dying paroxysm Lorenzo calls for the arrest and death of the Prior, but in vain. Savonarola is liberated by the masses, but his victory is questioned by Fiore, Lorenzo's mistress, his old nemesis who had rejected and thus driven him into his life of asceticism. She warns him: "The fire that you fan will consume you, consume your own body, to purify you, save the world from you. If that prospect horrifies you — desist! Instead of willing nothingness, rather cease willing at all. Desist from the use of power! Renounce! Be a monk!" (*GW* 8, 1067). But Mann's Prior answers: "I love fire," meaning the burning of the vanities during his rule of Florence, but also prophesying his own end.

In a letter of December 17, 1900, Mann revealed the formula for his play: "Christ and Fra Giramolo (Savonarola) are one and the same: weakness turned genius gains power over life."[35] Later, in *Betrachtungen eines Unpolitischen*, Mann describes Savonarola as "Nietzsche's ascetic priest" — who is compared to the "radical litterateur of the most recent type" — that is to say, the "Zivilisationsliterat," Mann's most feared and disliked personification of the modern writer around 1918 (*GW* 12, 94). The critic Erich Heller has identified the Nietzsche-Freud influence on the psychological construction of the drama, explaining that Lorenzo is suffering from the same problem as Savonarola. Heller quoted from Nietzsche's *Jenseits von Gut und Böse* (Beyond Good and Evil, 1886) to explain the two characters' trauma and compensations as well as their sexual drives and sublimation.[36] What appears as the administration of confession in Act III becomes, in Heller's words, a panegyric to the Will to Power, and reveals the meaning of the allegory: Lorenzo and Savonarola, each in his way, are the impure spirit struggling from a position of seemingly preordained defeat for mastery over life, over Fiore, over Florence.[37] Heller considered *Fiorenza* a "momentous failure," blaming it for placing the characters and their "great gestures of the human spirit" into "a spiritual vacuum," while T. J. Reed considered it "difficult to take seriously" as a Renaissance drama.[38] Yet the play is an important variation on the theme of art and its religious valorization within society. It plays against the "Renaissanceism" of the period without endorsing Savonarola. Although Mann's fictional character has the last word as in "Gladius Dei," the drama is less ambiguous, as it anticipates Savonarola's self-willed destruction rather than his victory. The blame for the drama's failure should be placed on the rather abstract discussion of the protagonists and the lack of truly dramatic action.

"Tonio Kröger" was to become the "symbol" and "mouthpiece" of Mann's novellas of this period, one that he characterized as "a phase of the spirit and the expression in some sense, in art, of the attitude of a generation of artists." In his own words, "Tonio Kröger" was his signature piece of this period, expressing "adolescence in its melancholy penetration and its yearning for the simple and normal life" (Mann, "Preface," vi). But more important, in this novella the conflict between art and society, the problem of the other novellas of this period, is resolved. The protagonist "learns to move across the realms of the artistic and the bourgeois in a way that avoids not only [. . .] tragedy but also [. . .] impasse."[39]

From the beginning, art and bourgeois society, represented by the titular protagonist Tonio Kröger on the one hand and Hans Hansen, his schoolmate and adored friend on the other, are opposed as in any of the early short novellas or stories. There is also the quasi-religious dedication to art, the language of sacrifice required in this kind of worship, or, as Erich Heller called it, "the idiom of religion."[40] This dedication demands from the artist a special "credo," the willingness to be "something extra-human and inhuman" ("irgendetwas Außermenschliches und Unmenschliches") (GW 8, 295–96). The artist must stand in a "strangely distant and aloof relationship to mankind" in order to practice his art. Like a monk, he takes a vow of chastity.

In part four, which is a conversation between Tonio and a Russian painter named Lisaweta, Tonio elaborates on his concept of the artist, comparing the artist to the papal castrati, who sing like angels. According to him, literature is not a profession "but a curse." One does not become a genuine artist, but is "predestined and damned" to be one (GW 8, 297). He argues against the naïve belief in art as a gift that the old gentleman in "Das Wunderkind" professes, and characterizes this gift "as very dubious and [based] upon extremely sinister conditions" (GW 8, 298), like the mutilation of the papal castrati.

Tonio Kröger eventually finds a way to live in both worlds — the bourgeois and the artistic — without being at home in either, approaching both art and society with "Bürgerliebe," a kind of "bourgeois love of the human, the living and banal" (GW 8, 338). In his eyes, "the bourgeois are stupid," yet he cannot help loving them and longing "after the bliss of the banal" (GW 8, 337). Stereotyped as North Germanic, or as safely domesticated versions of Nietzsche's "blond beasts," they are the "blond and blue-eyed, the fair and living, the happy, the lovely, and the ordinary ones" whom he can never join but will love forever as an outsider (GW 8, 338).

Tonio has come a long and arduous way to reach this stage. The novella presents the different stations along the way, from the sufferings of youth to the insights expressed by the mature artist at the end of the novella. At the outset, Tonio is in love with Hans Hansen, his counter-image, and it is said that he has already suffered much because of him: "He who loves most is the inferior and must suffer — this simple and hard fact of life had already been imparted to his fourteen-year-old soul."[41] The reason for his love is in the first place that "Hans was handsome," but in second place that he was "in every respect his own counterpart and foil" (*GW* 8, 275). The narrator relates his qualities and accomplishments in detail:

> Hans Hansen was a first-rate student, and a regular fellow to boot, who was excellent at horse-back riding, gymnastics, and swimming, and was very popular. His teachers were almost tender with him, calling him by his first name, and favored him in every way; the other students curried favor with him; even grown-up gentlemen and ladies stopped him in the streets.[42]

This list of contrasts is repeated again and again whenever Tonio Kröger meets a representative of bourgeois society, be it his father, or Ingeborg Holm, or the Danish guests at the bath-hotel — perhaps not in such glowing terms as Hans is described, but nevertheless unequivocally positive, when his father is concerned, or conventionally romantic, when blonde, little Ingeborg enters his life and dreams.

Two prototypal markers characterize the relationship between Tonio and Hans Hansen: Schiller's drama *Don Carlos* (1786) and illustrated books about horses. Tonio identifies with King Philip the Second of Spain, who cries because of Marquis Posa's betrayal, while Hans prefers the photos of horses in motion. It is remarkable that Tonio makes no attempt to be like Hans Hansen. But he wants Hans to love him just as he is, and wants him to read *Don Carlos,* so that they will have something to talk about.

Tonio has internalized the ethical values of his father's world; although they are the opposite of his own. Whenever his father scolds him, he identifies with the criticism: "After all, we are not gypsies living in a green wagon [Zigeuner im grünen Wagen], we are respectable people, belonging to Consul Kröger's family, the family of the Krögers" (*GW* 8, 275). The often cited "Zigeuner im grünen Wagen" represent the proverbial "Bohemian" aspect of an artist's life, his isolation from the bourgeois. It characterizes his mother's world, which Tonio considers "somewhat wanton" (*GW* 8, 275). Half-German, half-Spanish, he is a combination of the blonde and dark nationalities of his parents, and this is presented as a factor contributing to his artistic nature. Even his first name and family name are markers for this almost stereotypical combination.

In most respects, Tonio resembles his dark-haired mother, who represents the artistic side, playing the piano and mandolin, but he does not identify with her values. Although he appreciates her acceptance of his mediocre performance in school, he prefers his father's criticism and punishment. Since he is not willing to change, he fully realizes that his socialization in the bourgeois world is fraught with never-ending problems, because he is unwilling to adapt to majority taste (*GW* 8, 275).

With Ingeborg, his heterosexual love interest, he encounters the same pattern of a relationship as with Hans Hansen. Hopelessly in love with her, he realizes that she will never even notice him, except as a ridiculous figure at their weekly dancing class. She belongs to the world of the blondes and is accordingly stereotyped as a "simple, pert, commonplace little personality" (*GW* 8, 287). Tonio, however, intends to love her as long as he lives, although he is separated from her by an unbridgeable gulf.

The exceptions to the rule of the blondes are his mother, Magdalena Vermehren, the girl that is always falling down while dancing, and finally the pale Danish girl at Aalsgaard who shares this unfortunate trait with Magdalena, repeating her pratfalls and triggering Tonio's memories. These girls are, like Tonio, outsiders in the extrovert world of the well-adjusted blondes. He loves his artistic "dark and fiery mother" because she approves of his outsider status. In this respect, Magdalena and the Danish girl are like his mother, understanding him and accepting him as he is because they share his values and appreciate his artistic accomplishments.

Only Lisaweta Iwanowna, the Russian painter in Munich, is in a class by herself. She functions as Tonio's sounding board, being the artist that Tonio desires to be and representing the religious strength of Russian literature, so much admired by Tonio. His self-image at this stage is that of the decadent Western writer who is plagued by doubt and the "disgust of knowledge" ("Erkenntnisekel") (*GW* 8, 300). This disgust is caused by the knowledge of his limitations as artist, the disproportion between his passionate feelings and the cold observations of his art.[43] Combining Schopenhauer's and Nietzsche's psychology, Kröger faces the end of his illusions and is overcome by despair about a world that defies unambiguous interpretation.

His conversation with Lisaweta in section four proposes a program for literature that is beset by the problems of artistic decadence. It reads almost like a programmatic essay, while the rest of the concluding narrative shows Tonio's response to decadence. At this stage, he sees human misery but perceives it in a comical perspective that is summarized in two words: "Komik und Elend" ("the comedy and the misery of life") (*GW* 8, 290).[44] Tonio Kröger identifies his own life as a man of letters with that of Hamlet the Dane, saying that the case of the Danish prince was that of a typical literary man: "He knew what it meant to be called to knowledge without being born to it" (*GW* 8, 300).[45] Lisaweta provides a diagnosis of Tonio's mental state and suggests the solution to his problems: "You are a bourgeois on the wrong path, a bourgeois gone astray" ("ein verirrter Bürger") (*GW* 8, 305).

After his long conversation with the Russian painter, Tonio decides to return to his origins, the city on the Baltic Sea and Denmark, the land of Hamlet and his blond countrymen. Here he experiences a return of his youthful longings during a dance at the bath-hotel. In a vision he believes to see Hans Hansen and Ingeborg Holm, now dancing as a married couple;

even Magdalena reappears in form of a Danish girl, taking a hard fall as before. This vision provides Tonio Kröger with the truth of the simple and heartfelt feelings of his youth. He writes to Lisaweta of his newfound identity that combines his "love of 'life'" with his existence as a bourgeois. The result is "a bourgeois who strayed off into art, a bohemian who feels nostalgic yearnings for a respectable upbringing, an artist with a bad conscience" (*GW* 8, 337). This reconciliation makes a true poet (*Dichter*) out of the decadent writer (*Literat*), and Tonio Kröger does not hesitate to celebrate this balance of artist and bourgeois in biblical language. He compares his newfound *Bürgerliebe* to "that love of which it stands written that one may speak with the tongues of men and of angels and yet having it not is as sounding brass and tinkling cymbals."[46] In spite of the implied criticism of the display of religious pretense or religious fanaticism in artistic production and self-representation in the other novellas, Tonio Kröger nevertheless expresses in his new art the kind of *Bürgerliebe* that he denied by implication to other decadent artists. Even the art of the "true poet" (*Dichter*) at the beginning of the twentieth century cannot do without this legitimation by religion, claiming the existence of truth, albeit precarious, in literature. It requires the authority of the language of First Corinthians 13 in Luther's translation, which uses the German word "Liebe" (love) instead of the English word "charity," as in the King James version, to legitimize and sustain Tonio Kröger's literature with *Bürgerliebe*.[47]

Later Mann declared in a letter of 1931 (and again in 1943) that the conflict between the bourgeois and the artistic way of life had "ceased to be of great import to [him]."[48] He never abandoned this combination of the creative but irresponsible way of the artist with the conforming and loyal, but narrow way of the bourgeois as the basis for the artist's claim to truth and transcendence. He no longer resorted to religion for the legitimation of his fiction, but still created artists who were members of the bourgeois gone astray in both "Der Tod in Venedig" (1912) and *Doktor Faustus* (1947). In the latter, the character Adrian Leverkühn's self-indictment concerns his outsider status as condition of his creativity. Mann entrusted the problem of truth and transcendence to the narrator, or even to a fictional character, for instance Zeitblom in *Doktor Faustus*. That Zeitblom prays at the end of the novel clearly indicates the transcendence that was dear to the author. No criticism hurt Thomas Mann more than that of the German reviewer who in 1949 called his fictional cosmos a "world without transcendence."[49] The relationship of art to society remained ambivalent in his view, to say the least. In "Der Tod in Venedig," art — that is, "that page and a half of choicest prose" — is the result of a production that Aschenbach considers "a debauch" (*GW* 8, 493), yet the news of Aschenbach's death is received by a "shocked and respectful" society (*GW* 8, 525). In *Doktor Faustus*, the artistic "breakthrough" is achieved by way of the pact with the devil. Art is placed in the realm of the immoral and demonic, but it no longer serves as substitute for religion. Leverkühn's final composition proves this point. In league with the devil, the composer must not love, but he seeks "an art *per du* with humanity" (*GW* 6, 429).

The specific theme of "Kunstreligion" — that is, art as substitute for religion — dates back to an earlier period. As a historical indicator it places Mann's early novellas and the drama *Fiorenza* into a specific time period at the turn of the century, which they reflect with a great sense of critical awareness and a unique combination of individual identification and distance. This combination, however, distinguishes them as more than mere period pieces; they are integral parts of a narrative oeuvre that is characterized by continuity and change.

Notes

[1] *GW* 8, 344–45. Mann's collected works (*GW* 1–13) will hereafter be cited in the text.

[2] Friedhelm Marx, "Künstler, Propheten, Heilige: Thomas Mann und die Kunstreligion der Jahrhundertwende," *TMJb* 11 (1998): 58.

[3] The quotation is from Savonarola's *Compendium Revelationum* (1495).

[4] Ulrich Linse, "Säkularisierung oder neue Religiosität? Zur religiösen Situation in Deutschland um 1900," *Recherches Germaniques* 27 (1997): 135.

[5] Hans Rudolf Vaget, *Thomas Mann-Kommentar zu sämtlichen Erzählungen* (Munich: Winkler, 1984), 99.

[6] Thomas Nipperdey, *Deutsche Geschichte 1866–1918*, vol. 1, 2nd ed. (Munich: Beck, 1991), 506.

[7] Linse, *Säkularisierung*, 122–23.

[8] Steven Aschheim, *The Nietzsche Legacy in Germany 1890–1990*. (Berkeley/Los Angeles: U of California P, 1992), 201.

[9] Fritz Weber, "Heroes, Meadows and Machinery: Fin-de-Siècle Music," *Fin de Siècle and Its Legacy,* ed. Mikulas Teich and Roy Porter (Cambridge: Cambridge UP, 1990), 217.

[10] Nietzsche, *KSA* 6, 29; 21; 23.

[11] Nietzsche, *KSA* 6, 37 and *KSA* 6, 28.

[12] Nietzsche, *KSA* 1, 25.

[13] Nietzsche, *KSA* 5, 402.

[14] See Hans Rudolf Vaget, "Im Schatten Wagners," *Im Schatten Wagners: Thomas Mann Über Richard Wagner: Texte und Zeugnisse 1895–1955,* ed. Hans Rudolf Vaget (Frankfurt am Main: S. Fischer, 1999), 313, and Gerhard Kaiser, "Thomas Manns 'Wälsungenblut' und Richard Wagners *Ring*: Erzählen als kritische Interpretation," *TMJb* 12 (1999): 239, 249–51, 253–54, 257–58. Vaget considers Mann to have been influenced by Nietzsche in his literary production as a kind of rewriting of Wagner, while Kaiser makes a case for the early novellas as critical re-interpretations

of Wagner. There is no doubt that Nietzsche inspired Mann to write in the vein of Wagner. As Vaget says, "Nietzsche machte Lust, Wagner gleichsam fortzuschreiben. Und indem [Mann] dieser Lust frönte, wurde ihm Wagner eine unversiegbare Quelle der Inspiration und Kreativität" (313).

[15] T. J. Reed, *The Uses of Tradition* (Oxford: Clarendon Press, 1974), 1.

[16] See R. A. Nichols, *Nietzsche in the Early Work of Thomas Mann* (Berkeley/Los Angeles: U of California P, 1955), 7–10. Others have dated Nietzsche's influence as early as 1891 by tracing it to Mann's brother Heinrich. The same applies to Schopenhauer's influence.

[17] *Im Schatten Wagners,* ed. Hans Rudolf Vaget, provides an excellent review of all passages in Mann's works, letters, and diaries that deal with the composer. For the period from Mann's early years in Lübeck to his years in Munich until 1905, see 15–39. See also Vaget's essay "Im Schatten Wagners" in the same volume, 301–35, esp. 308–12.

[18] *KSA* 5, 262–64.

[19] See Wolfgang Frühwald, "Der christliche Jüngling im Kunstladen: Milieu- und Stilparodie in Thomas Manns Erzählung 'Gladius Dei,'" *Bild und Gedanke: Festschrift für Gerhart Baumann zum 60. Geburtstag,* ed. Günter Schnitzler et al. (Munich: Fink, 1980), 332. Peter-Klaus Schuster, "'München leuchtete': Die Erneuerung christlicher Kunst in München um 1900," *München leuchtete: Karl Caspar und die Erneuerung christlicher Kunst in München um 1900,* ed. Peter-Klaus Schuster (Munich: Prestel, 1984), offers a convincing counterproposal with his reference to the commercial art house of Hanfstaengl in Munich, which specialized in reproductions of art. According to Schuster, "Blüthenzweig" is an ironic transcription of the name "Hanfstaengl" (30–32). For the anti-Semitic stereotypes involved in the name "Blüthenzweig" and the character's physical attributes and mannerisms see Yahya Elsaghe, *Die imaginäre Nation: Thomas Mann und das "Deutsche"* (Munich: Fink, 2000), 124–35.

[20] Thomas Mann, "Preface" [1936]. *Stories of Three Decades,* trans. H. T. Lowe-Porter (New York: Knopf, 1938), vi. Hereafter cited in the text.

[21] Marx, "Künstler, Propheten, Heilige," 52–54.

[22] Hermann Wiegmann, *Die Erzählungen Thomas Manns: Interpretationen und Realien* (Bielefeld: Aisthesis, 1992), 148–49; Esther H. Lesér, *Thomas Mann's Fiction: An Intellectual Biography* (London/Toronto: Associated U Presses, 1989), 239–40.

[23] Marx, "Künstler, Propheten, Heilige," 51–52.

[24] Marx, "Künstler, Propheten, Heilige," 55.

[25] "Hier ist das Ende, das Eis, die Reinheit und das Nichts. Hier gilt kein Vertrag, kein Zugeständnis, keine Nachsicht, kein Maß und kein Wert. Hier ist die Luft so dünn und keusch, daß die Miasmen des Lebens nicht mehr gedeihen. Hier herrscht der Trotz, die äußerste Konsequenz, das verzweifelt thronende Ich, die Freiheit, der Wahnsinn und der Tod" (*GW* 8, 362).

[26] "Die Einsamkeit, die Freiheit, die geistige Leidenschaft, die großartige Optik, der Glaube an sich selbst, sogar die Nähe von Verbrechen und Wahnsinn. Was fehlt? Vielleicht das Menschliche? Ein wenig Gefühl, Sehnsucht, Liebe?" (*GW* 8, 370).

[27] *DüD* 1, 171.

[28] "Wagners Kunst ist krank" (*KSA* 6, 22).

[29] See Vaget, *Kommentar*, 87, 90.

[30] For the anti-Semitic stereotypes involved in the representation of Spinell, see Elsaghe, 94–106.

[31] Among the various critics, see especially Ulrich Dittmann, *Thomas Mann: "Tristan," Erläuterungen und Dokumente* (Stuttgart: Reclam, 1979), 58–62; Thomas Klugkist, *Glühende Konstruktion: Thomas Manns Tristan und das "Dreigestirn": Schopenhauer, Nietzsche und Wagner,* Epistemata 157 (Würzburg: Königshausen & Neumann, 1995), 65–68; James Northcote-Bade, *Die Wagner-Mythen im Frühwerk Thomas Manns* (Bonn: Bouvier, 1975), 47–52; Bruno Roßbach, *Spiegelungen eines Bewusstseins: Der Erzähler in Thomas Manns "Tristan,"* Marburger Studien zur Germanistik 10 (Marburg: Hitzeroth, 1989), 159–64; Frank W. Young, *Montage and Motif in Thomas Mann's "Tristan"* (Bonn: Bouvier, 1975), 115–23.

[32] *Essays* 1, 43.

[33] *DüD* 1, 174.

[34] "Der Tod ist es, den du als Geist verkündigst, und alles Lebens Leben ist die Kunst" (*GW* 8, 1066).

[35] *DüD* 1, 177.

[36] Erich Heller, *Thomas Mann: The Ironic German* (Cleveland/New York: Meridian, 1961), 89.

[37] Heller, *The Ironic German*, 90.

[38] Heller, *The Ironic German*, 92; Reed, *The Uses of Tradition*, 94.

[39] Martin Travers, *Thomas Mann.* Modern Novelists (New York: St. Martin's Press, 1992), 43.

[40] Heller, *The Ironic German*, 84.

[41] "Wer am meisten liebt, ist der Unterlegene und muss leiden, — diese schlichte und harte Lehre hatte seine vierzehnjährige Seele bereits vom Leben entgegengenommen" (*GW* 8, 273).

[42] "Hans Hansen war ein vortrefflicher Schüler und ausserdem ein frischer Gesell, der ritt, turnte, schwamm wie ein Held und der sich der allgemeinen Beliebtheit erfreute. Die Lehrer waren ihm beinahe mit Zärtlichkeit zugetan, nannten ihn mit Vornamen und förderten ihn auf alle Weise, die Kameraden waren auf seine Gunst bedacht, und auf der Straße hielten ihn Herren und Damen an" (*GW* 8, 275–76).

[43] See Hellmut Haug, *Erkenntnisekel: Zum frühen Werk Thomas Manns* (Tübingen: Niemeyer, 1969), 59–64. Haug notices the strange combination of sentimental self-pity and rigorous self-criticism in Tonio Kröger as well as the proximity of genius and criminality.

[44] According to Reed's *The Uses of Tradition*, this mixture of "Komik und Elend" is Tonio Kröger's speciality: "Even at the close of the story, when he has successfully

come to terms with his deep-rooted feelings for the representatives of 'normal' life, he still speaks of his future literary creations as 'tragische und lächerliche Gestalten und solche, die beides zugleich sind — und diesen bin ich sehr zugetan'" (*GW* 8, 338; Reed, 21).

[45] R. A. Nichols in *Nietzsche in the Early Work of Thomas Mann* addresses the issue of Mann's association of Nietzsche with Hamlet and explains the common relationship to Hamlet as "the nature of the connection between Kröger and Nietzsche" (23).

[46] "Jene Liebe selbst, von der geschrieben steht, daß einer mit Menschen- und Engelszungen reden koennte und ohne sie doch nur ein tönendes Erz und eine klingende Schelle sei" (*GW* 8, 338).

[47] The source is probably a quote from Goethe in Johann Peter Eckermann's *Unterhaltungen mit Goethe* (Conversations with Goethe). This is a passage dated December 25, 1825, concerning August von Platen, and containing the same citation from First Corinthians 13 (see Vaget, *Kommentar*, 108).

[48] *DüD* 1, 161, 166.

[49] *Br* 3, 398.

Love in Society: Thomas Mann's Early Stories

Wolfgang Lederer

THE KIND READER, looking back over the early stories of Thomas Mann — those light, delicious, bittersweet concoctions — may well be struck by the recognition that they are also a veritable freak show of crippled bodies and lives. And the thought may arise that their author must have been an unhappy young man indeed. Nor need we guess as to this, for he has told us himself: those years were a time of "numbness, emptiness, ice,"[1] and also, he adds, of intellect and art, but that did not compensate for the lack of human warmth. The future looked bleak — recall Tonio Kröger's "for some there just is no right way." But be assured: his luck is about to change.

Not, of course, all at once or right away.

Thus the little study "Gerächt" (Avenged, 1899),[2] written when Mann was twenty-four, still emanates that same bitterness. Its twenty-year-old narrator, claiming to be tired of sexual excesses, is cultivating a "pure," meaning a purely intellectual, friendship with an older Russian woman of "unambiguous and resolute ugliness." This in itself should exclude all sensuality, but even so an "evil excitement" at times troubles the atmosphere. To clarify matters once and for all, the narrator bluntly explains to her that he appreciates the compatibility of their spirits but feels an abhorrence for her body. She accepts his declaration with apparent calm but returns his frankness by revealing that she had once had a sexual affair. He suddenly finds himself aroused by the thought that "this woman let someone make love to her. Her body has been embraced by a man," and he suggests that they, too, should have intercourse. She rejects his advances and departs, "a mocking smile on her ugly lips." The narrator, stupefied, taps his forehead and goes to bed.

Thomas Mann repeatedly protested that all his writings were based on his own life. "About *me* I am writing, about *me*" (*GW* 10, 22; Mann's emphasis), but we may question how much of this story is truly "lived." Was there in fact a time of "debauchery" in the life of young Thomas when he was about twenty years old? His autobiographies do speak of a "late and violent outbreak of sexuality" at that age (*GW* 11, 111), but he is never specific as to its nature. The abrupt and clumsy proposal issued by the narrator certainly does not suggest sexual experience, and his tepid reaction to being rejected sounds more like relief than disappointment. As to the Russian woman, she — like her "sister" Lisaweta Iwanowna in "Tonio Kröger" — probably never existed (*GW* 13, 144). No — what was autobiographical in this story was only the mood of bitter alienation and disenchantment.

But now a profound change was about to occur, a development that in the course of a few years would lead Mann to a new and different view of himself and the world. He later described the beginnings of this veritable revolution with the calm of distant retrospect: "At that time [he is speaking of his mid-twenties] I befriended two young people who were acquaintances of my sisters [. . .]. My affection for the younger one, Paul [. . .] was something like a resurrection of my sentiments for that blond school friend [. . .] but thanks to greater intellectual affinity it turned out much happier [. . .]. Their [Carl and Paul's] refined gentleness overcame my melancholy, shyness, and irritability. . . . It was a good time" (*GW* 11, 107).

A calm and rational account, which omits all the passion, suffering, and bliss that were actually involved.

The "blond school friend" — that was Armin Martens, for whom Thomas had felt a deep and silent, totally unrequited love, such as Tonio Kröger's love for the blond and athletic Hans Hansen, a love that fills him with "longing and melancholy envy and a little contempt and a great, chaste happiness" (*GW* 8, 281). It is that same love that, felt by Hans Castorp for Pribislav Hippe, will lay the emotional basis for *Der Zauberberg* (The Magic Mountain, 1924).

Paul Ehrenberg bore a striking resemblance to Armin Martens. He was "the same type,"[3] and he was so forthcoming that Thomas and he were shortly *per Du* — the familiar form of address Thomas would grant but a handful of friends in his entire life. He attributed to Paul — a good painter and a fair violinist — amiability, sincerity, decency, an artistic indifference to money, and "a certain purity which radiated from the beautiful, steel-blue eyes in his . . . youthfully attractive face" (*GW* 6, 265–66). By December of 1900 he happily calls Paul his "staunchly loyal comrade,"[4] but a few weeks later things sounds more uncertain. In a letter to his brother Heinrich he writes: I shall have a winter behind me of incredible inner turmoil. Depressions of a truly bad kind, with utterly serious plans for doing away with myself, have alternated with an indescribable, pure, and unexpected exultation. This was due to experiences which I cannot relate, of which the very hint sounds like bragging. But they have proven to me [. . .] that there is after all something honest, warm, and decent in me and not just "irony."[5] A week later he considers dedicating a soon-to-be-published volume of novellas to Paul, "in order to offer him something [. . .] perhaps also to let him see my power, to shame him a little [. . .]. It is crazy and ridiculous. At this point I keep writing nothing but 'he' and 'him' and 'his,' and all that's missing is that I capitalize it and frame it in gold, and with that the era 'Timpe' would have reemerged in shining glory."[6]

The era Timpe?

Timpe was another school friend with whom Thomas had been secretly enamored, and his present infatuation with Paul was bringing back "all the suffering and longing" of those school days. "It is all a matter of metaphysics, music, and pubertal eroticism. I never seem to emerge from puberty [. . .]. What is involved is not a love affair, at least not in the ordinary sense, but a friendship which, to my amazement, is understood, reciprocated, rewarded, but which [. . .] during certain hours of depression and loneliness assumes an all too painful aspect. Grautoff claims that I am simply in love like a teenager."[7]

And by April 1901: "It is only from old habit that, at my desk, I still compose negativistic irony, but otherwise I praise, I love, and live [. . .]. The whole thing is simply a feast [. . .]. My need for [. . .] devotion, trust, a squeeze of the hand . . . it is now feasting."[8] That summer, during a stay in Florence, Thomas, to his own surprise, found himself flirting with a "blond, enchanting" English girl, Mary Smith. A tender relationship developed, "including some talk of consolidating it through marriage. What eventually stopped me was the feeling that it might be premature" (GW 11, 117–18). Mary vanished, having planted the seed of a development that would mature some years later.

Meanwhile Thomas returned to Munich, and to Paul, and to the project of a novel to be called "Die Geliebten" (The Loved Ones); or, expanded into a "Gesellschaftsroman" (a novel of society), it was to be titled "Maja" (Maya). The original stimulus for it was a newspaper report about a married woman who, jealous of her lover, had shot him on a streetcar. The theme of jealousy was a painfully acute one for Thomas because Paul, an incurable flirt, gave him much occasion for it. Thomas scribbled scores of entries into his little notebook, some of them observations to be used in the novel, some simply recordings of the day's events. But increasingly these became amalgamated and confused.

Paul, under the name of Rudolf, was to become the faithless lover of the novel. The jilted husband, Albrecht, a sickly admirer of Renaissance sensuality, brutality, and splendor, would be modeled after Heinrich. And the jealous wife, Adelaide? Progressively, in the notes, she fuses with Thomas, and he becomes Adelaide.

Thus we read the plaintive "she suffers continuous pain at the impossibility of faithfulness on earth [. . .]. Her envy for the fullness of his manly existence, while she just feels and loves." (Nb 2 [7–14], 47). Similar complaints alternate with dithyrambs, such as:

> These are the days of living feeling!
> You have enriched my life — it blooms.
> I thank you, my salvation, luck, and star!

> Here is my heart, and here my hand
> I love you! Oh my God [. . .] I love you!
> Is it so fair, so sweet, so dear, to be human?
> (*Nb* 2 [7–14], 44, 46)

It is nevertheless a modest bliss: "To be calm and filled with a happiness that considers it quite natural to read along with him in the same book" (*Nb* 2 [7–14], 47). Other entries clearly refer to novelistic technique: "He must be made to appear most lovable, so that his death (the murder on the streetcar) makes the reader despondent, sad" (*Nb* 2 [7–14], 53). But always again the agony of doubt: "Her painful suspiciousness devalues all his sympathy. His invitations, his visits when she is ill, his attentions — are they not all just 'to be nice?' [. . .] And not from a drive, from a need, from love?" (*Nb* 2 [7–14], 53).

And the giveaway: "P's appointment calendar with notations of his social obligations — she reads them, sees also her own name" (*Nb* 2 [7–14], 55). P's appointment calendar? But the hero of the novel is to be called Rudolf! "He" (Paul/Rudolf) becomes ever more disappointing to "her" (Thomas/Adelaide), and the pain eventually finds expression in a letter to Paul: "*Where* is the human being who will say *Yes* to me as to a fellow who is not terribly lovable, who is moody, self-derogatory, unbelieving, distrustful, but sensitive and ravenously hungry for sympathy? Who will say yes — *unflinchingly?* Without letting himself be intimidated and estranged by apparent coldness? [. . .]. Deep silence."[9] In his notebook he wrote: "That letter to him, very daring. As a consequence his prompt visit . . . his care not to shame *her* in any way" (*Nb* 2 [7–14], 57). And yet: "It may be that, in spite of his noble behavior, she has spoiled more with that letter than she has mended. He is after all a bit embarrassed . . . his openness a bit diminished" (*Nb* 2 [7–14], 58).

Genuine love and contempt, misery and brief bliss — they continue to be recorded in meticulous and astutely insightful observations, such as may come in handy for future literary efforts. And while "Die Geliebten" was never written but "merely" lived, many of these notes were eventually incorporated into Mann's literary works; not just in concurrent fiction such as "Tonio Kröger" (1903) or the play *Fiorenza* (1905), but years later the sufferings of young Thomas would be inserted verbatim into the lovesick moanings of Potiphar's wife (1937), and the faithless flirt Paul would get his comeuppance as Rudi Schwerdtfeger in *Doktor Faustus* (1947).

This last use — or abuse — of reality could raise a question: Rudi Schwerdtfeger does seduce Adrian Leverkühn into a brief sexual affair. Did Paul ever seduce Thomas Mann sexually?

There is no evidence for such an occurrence at all. The most physically intimate scene recorded in the notes occurs in the context of a minor discord, following which "as I was leaning out of the open window, he said loudly: 'Kindly move over a bit, to make room for me too!' He leaned on the windowsill next to me and began [. . .] a comradely conversation. Finally he had again managed things such that he could comfortably rest his arm on my shoulder. I let it happen" (*Nb* 2 [7–14], 66). This carefully minimized physical contact is in line with Kai's stroking a hair from Hanno's forehead with a ruler (rather than with his finger) (*GW* 1, 710); with the fact that Tonio and Hans Hansen never touch; that Hans Castorp relates to Pribislav Hippe only by means of a pencil and even avoids calling his cousin by his first name; that Joseph identifies with the flower "touch-me-not"; that even the seductive sensualist Felix Krull turns down any homosexual approaches. No, though Thomas Mann was all his life moved and inspired by homoerotic feelings, cherished male beauty above all other, and at one point even publicly proposed homoeroticism as the political basis for the Weimar Republic (1922; *GW* 11, 847–50), he had a finicky aversion to sweaty male physicality.[10] He could not imagine what it would be like to be in bed with a man[11] and wrote, for instance, regarding his enthusiastic contemplation of a young workman's naked torso, that he "afterwards had thoughts about the unreal, illusionary, and aesthetic quality of such an inclination. Its goal seems to lie in contemplation and an admiration which, though erotic, will have nothing to do with common sense or even just sensuality. This is probably due to the impact of reality-awareness on fantasy: it permits the delight, but confines it to the image."[12]

In his essay "Über die Ehe" (On Marriage, 1925) he wrote: "There is no blessing on [homosexuality] other than that of beauty, and that is a death-blessing. It lacks the blessing of nature and of life [. . .] and this non-blessing hovers unmistakably over the free, all-too-free love [. . .]. Nothing comes of it; it does not lay the foundations for anything." And he contrasts the fickleness of homosexuality to the fidelity that constitutes "the enormous moral superiority of a love that, commanded by nature, is capable of marriage and procreation" (*GW* 10, 197–98).

Was he brainwashed by the society in which he lived into denying or repressing his homosexual instincts?

The chances are that such matters were never mentioned in his parental home. The exuberant, romantic-homoerotic friendships of the early 1800s were a thing of the past — such as, for instance, the abundant kisses and turgid expressions of love between Hans Christian Andersen and the Grand Duke of Weimar, of which nobody thought ill,[13] and the sexual revolution of the turn of the nineteenth century was just beginning. But by the time Mann was living in Munich, in the late 1890s, the wild and brilliant Otto Gross preached sexual liberation and claimed that "primary homosexuality" was an experience necessary for emotional and sexual health. Gross's erotic feasts were happening in Schwabing, right under Mann's nose.[14] Later Hans

Blüher wrote *Die Rolle der Erotik in der männlichen Gesellschaft* (The Role of Eroticism in Male Society, 1917)[15] and another book on the heavily homosexual youth movement, the Wandervögel; Thomas Mann read his books, listened to his lectures, and borrowed some of his ideas.[16] In France, André Gide published his *Corydon* (1924), and Thomas Mann conveyed to him the pleasure with which he had studied "this spiritual apology for an emotional sphere which, as I too believe, cannot be despised or condemned except by barbarians and ignorants."[17] That Gide, in spite of his frank confessions, enjoyed a position of respect in his country "belongs to the most admirable and remarkable phenomena of today's intellectual life" (*GW* 10, 711, 1929), wrote Mann; and during a stay in Paris he noted with interest that the Rue Royale was "erotic territory, hunting ground of prostitutes and especially of the male homosexual ones, whose number would about equal that to be found in Berlin" (*GW* 11, 52, 1926). He read portions of Proust's *À la recherche du temps perdu* (1913–27),[18] and in his long walks and talks with Gide discussed with disapproval Proust's practice of transforming boys he loved into girls, and of confounding homosexuality and effeminacy.[19]

When Thomas was twenty-one, Havelock Ellis's *Sexual Inversion* (1896) was published in Berlin, and that same year Magnus Hirschfeld produced his study on homosexuality, *Sappho und Sokrates* (1896). We do not know to what extent Mann was aware of these, but shortly thereafter a number of major scandals attracted widespread attention in Germany: Friedrich Alfred Krupp, head of the armaments firm of that name and a friend of Kaiser Wilhelm the Second, was denounced for entertaining "a private pleasure palace on Capri" to which he brought boys from the laboring classes;[20] and an acquaintance of Thomas Mann's, Maximilian Harden, published articles insinuating that a cabal of homosexuals of highest rank surrounded the Emperor himself. At the same time a kind of "gay liberation movement" was active, attempting to abolish the draconian laws against homosexuality that, in Germany and Britain, furnished the newspapers with salacious accounts of trials in which famous artists, industrialists, military men, and diplomats were "outed" and severely punished. The sheer number of such cases suggested that an underground world of "vice" was alive and well.[21] It would therefore seem that Mann could have found ways to "act out" homosexually had he so desired. (He felt he had already revealed himself quite plainly homoerotically.[22]) But he did not desire to do so, and he was not the only one to draw this line. His contemporary Stefan George, a masterly and sonorous poet, not only idealized heroic male beauty, but literally deified — and thereby rendered tabu — a fourteen-year-old youth he named Maximin. What was involved, he insisted, was not sexuality but Plato's "pedagogic eros," a distant worship.[23] Thomas Mann had a somewhat rivalrous feeling toward George, but he respected his integrity; and he was utterly enthusiastic about another "chaste" poet, Walt Whitman (*GW* 13, 296–97, Sept.

1923). It was in line with Mann's own principles and character that he, too, would observe the limit between Eros and Sexus, not only with Paul Ehrenberg but also with two later loves, Klaus Heuser[24] and Franzl Westermeier. During the tumultuous years of "Die Geliebten" (roughly between 1900 and 1904), and despite their emotional trials, Mann was continuously at work. He completed *Buddenbrooks* (1901), wrote "Tonio Kröger," started the play *Fiorenza,* and wrote a number of short stories. Some of these, such as "Ein Glück" (A Happiness, 1904), he considered rather misbegotten.[25] It is the story of a shy little officer's wife (an outsider, like Thomas), who, hurt and shamed when her flirtatious husband (flirtatious like Paul?) carries on outrageously at a ball, is deeply moved when the soubrette with whom he had been publicly and suggestively intimate comes to her to ask her pardon and to kiss her hand — implying a deeper understanding between the two women than between husband and wife.

Another story, a charming little vignette called "Das Wunderkind" (The Infant Prodigy, 1903), he liked better. Light as a feather and sparkling like a diamond, it hides behind its humorous appeal a risky excursion into forbidden territory, foreshadowing "Der Tod in Venedig" (Death in Venice, 1912). The eight-year-old Greek "prodigy" thanks the audience for the welcoming applause "with a tiny, shy and sweet girl's curtsy, even though he is a boy," and the applause that rewards his somewhat orgiastic playing (like Hanno's?) is in part an appreciation of his "dainty hips." An old man finds it "agreeable" to admire the child, but "he dares not think how sweet that is! 'Sweet' would be shameful for a vigorous old gentleman." A young girl, listening, is amazed at the passionate quality of the boy's playing, which arouses in her the fantasy of being kissed by her brother. "Sweet," in contrast to "agreeable," must not be "dared" because it would suggest erotic feelings toward the androgynous child; and a passionate kiss from the girl's brother would be incestuous — two themes that were of enduring fascination for Thomas Mann.

But of more immediate significance for his life was a short-story he had written a bit earlier, a "study" called "Die Hungernden" (The Hungry Ones, 1903; *GW* 8, 263–70). In its first line we are told that the "hero" of the tale, Detlev, is filled with an awareness of his "superfluity." He is superfluous because the "blue-eyed little painter" and Lilli, the couple with whom he is attending a ball, are so involved with each other that they are glad to be left alone. He departs, filled with a "a painful yearning for union" ("leidende Einheitssehnsucht") and aware that he emanates "a cold breath of insurmountable alienation." The "blue-eyed little painter" is, of course, the very image of Paul Ehrenberg, and Detlev's painful mixture of yearning and cold alienation, though supposedly directed toward (the equally blue-eyed) Lilly, marks him as an alias of Thomas. He tries to convince himself that he despises the blue-eyed ones, "who do not need the intellect," yet like an evil spirit he ogles them from afar and yearns to be like them. As an artist he is under the curse that commands: "You may not be, you must observe; you may not live, you must create; you may not love, you must comprehend!" There is to be nothing in his life but "numbness, emptiness, ice, and spirit, and art" — the formulation he used to characterize the pre-Ehrenberg years but which now seems to apply again. Clearly, the relationship with Paul has not lived up to his hopes, has not met his neediness; and symbolizing his "walking out" on Paul, Detlev walks out of the opera house where the ball is held and into the bitter cold of the winter night. There he encounters a wretched, shivering derelict — wild eyed, hollow cheeked, and red bearded. (He resembles somewhat the image of Death in the first part of "Der Tod in Venedig.") This starving wretch throws him a grimace of hate and contempt and slinks away into the darkness. Detlev is struck by the insight that "we are all siblings, we creatures of restlessly suffering desire," and with sudden illumination he mumbles, "a different love is called for, a different love." And with that insight Tonio Kröger's despairing "there just is no right way" is challenged by the first gleam of a new possibility.

Indeed, the sun was rising — the sun of fame. *Buddenbrooks* was becoming a great critical and popular success. Thomas was now listed in Munich's *Who's Who,* and while he still — or again — suffered from isolation, he tried a different tune: not only the beggar is lonely, but so is the prince. And for the first time since childhood he once again felt like a prince, a prince who is seeking a princess.

He found her, looking down from the gallery of the concert hall to the parterre, where she sat in a row with her four brothers, elegant and lovely; he found her once more on a streetcar where, briskly and peremptorily, she told off the conductor; and — oh miracle of fate — he was actually finding her *again,* because years ago he had been in love with a picture, cut from a newspaper and pinned above his boyhood writing desk, of her and her brothers in harlequin costumes.[26]

She was Katia Pringsheim, daughter of rich and prominent Jewish parents, whose palatial home was one of the artistic and musical centers of Munich. Thomas, smitten, maneuvered to be properly introduced to the Pringsheims,[27] and by February 1904 he had succeeded. Katia's father, Alfred, was not enthusiastic about the new suitor — he did not wish to lose his only daughter so soon, and besides he did not think much of writers.[28] But her mother, Hedwig, a beautiful woman and accomplished hostess, appreciated Mann's writings and welcomed him into her home. He, in turn, flattered her richly in his story "Beim Propheten" (At the Prophet's, 1904), describing her as "the rich lady . . . lovely, fragrant, and luxurious" as well as intelligent, humorous, and kind. And he won her utterly for his cause.

Katia did not surrender so easily. As a little girl she had been robust and vigorous — far more so than her frail twin brother Klaus — to the extent that the five Pringsheim children were known as "the five Pringsheim boys." She received her schooling at home and became, according to Klaus, the first woman in Munich to pass the *Abitur,* the baccalaureate graduation exam from the Gymnasium;[29] and she went on to study physics at the university — a daring venture that, according to learned opinion of the day, was unsuited for women and exceeded their capacities.[30] At the time of the streetcar incident she was a student, enjoying her life, her studies, her tennis club, her brothers — she was in no hurry to get married.[31]

So Thomas, who, he wrote, was "ordinarily of a truly Indian passivity," had to develop, "in word and deed, an unbelievable initiative" which totally unsettled "the quiet and egocentric inwardness necessary for work."[32]

This was not entirely true. As before, during the Paul Ehrenberg days, Mann immediately turned experience into literature. Wishing to put his best foot forward, he wrote letters to Katia — not just carefully phrased letters of love but also letters in which he painfully tried to explain himself to her:

> I know very well that I am not the sort of man who would arouse simple, immediate, clear-cut feelings [. . .]. I do not think this should be held against me. To cause mixed feelings, "perplexity": that is — forgive me — a sign of personality.[33] [. . .] Of course I know, know it terribly well, that it is my fault if you experience toward me "a kind of awkwardness, or something" — how my lack of ease, of openness, or spontaneity, the entire nervousness, artificiality and complexity of my being renders it difficult for anyone [. . .] to come close to me [. . .]. You know what a cold, impoverished, purely creative, purely formal life I have led all these years [. . .]. A cure is possible only in one way: through good fortune, through you, my wise, sweet, kind, beloved little queen! [. . .] What I beg of you, hope for, long for, is confidence, is an unwavering alliance with me against the world, even against myself, it is something like faith, in short — it is love. Be my affirmation, my justification, my completion, my redemptrix, my — wife![34]

Yes — letters like this one eventually swayed her, won her over; and they were also promptly built into a project he had started, a novel about a lonely and crippled prince called *Königliche Hoheit* (Royal Highness, 1909).

This charming tale has been criticized for its operetta-like happy ending. It had not been planned that way. Initially, the prince, doubly isolated by his rank and by a birth injury that stunted his left arm, was merely to represent the example of a high-level loner, analogous to the artist isolated by genius. But the story takes a turn with the appearance (after some two hundred pages) of an American millionaire, Mr. Spoelmann, and his daughter Imma, a lovely creature. Imma is herself isolated by virtue of her wealth and her "colorful" background — she has an admixture of Indian blood which makes her unacceptable in American society. Spoelmann, in his gruffness and contempt for the prince, closely resembles Alfred Pringsheim; and Imma, in appearance and manner, is a duplicate of Katia, whose "Indian" blood consists of her being Jewish. And just as Katia resisted Mann's wooing, so does Imma for a long while resist the Prince. But she finally comes around. In a moving little scene she openly comments on the embarrassing — and always anxiously hidden — crippled left arm and by way of total acceptance kisses it.

There apparently occurred a similar scene between Katia and Thomas. He refers to it in a letter: "You — unforgettable figure of speech — 'showed me your books.'"[35] Katia, like her brothers, had her own library. There they could be alone, and there she finally — what? "Kissed his withered arm?" What was it he was hiding that she accepted? Could it possibly have been that heretofore, where he had loved, he had always loved his own sex? We do not know. But we do know that Katia, during their entire life together, was extraordinarily tolerant of his repetitive homoerotic infatuations.

In any case, this was now "the other love" he needed: "Do you realize," he wrote, "why we are so suited to each other? Because you are neither a bourgeoise nor an aristocrat; because, in your own way, you are something extraordinary — because you are, as I understand the word, a princess. And I — now you may laugh, but you must understand me — I who have always seen myself as a sort of prince, I have surely found in you my predestined bride and companion."[36] This love, he wrote, "is the strongest [. . .] is my first and only happy love."[37]

In October they were engaged, and in February 1905 they were married — and did they live happily ever after?

Well, yes and no. On the whole theirs would be an enduring, solid marriage, and it certainly produced an abundance of offspring: three girls and three boys, all highly complicated, gifted, and productive. But some difficulties, some misgivings were built in.

One of them was Thomas Mann's "inherited," mild but pervasive anti-Semitism. He had to make allowances for the Pringsheims, calling them "Tiergarten with true culture" (Tiergarten was a Berlin district inhabited by rich Jews) and stressing "with these people one is not aware that they are Jews; one only senses culture."[38] Which did not prevent his referring to Katia, in his own notes, as a "strange, kindly, and yet egotistical, (only) reluctantly polite little Jew-girl."[39] He badly needed to derogate where he was in awe. He claimed that the Pringsheim household reminded him of home, but in fact it was far grander than the solid but relatively simple patrician atmosphere of his home in Lübeck. And he was ambivalent about their wealth. He wrote to Heinrich, "I do not fear wealth [. . .] even now I already have more money than I know what to do with" — a bit of hostile bragging toward the still impecunious brother, but also an attempt at fending off the awareness that his finances would hardly impress the Pringsheims. What would?

He continues: "I have the feeling that the family will welcome me. I am Christian, from a good family; I have merits that these people in particular esteem highly."[40] He is trying to reassure himself, but he is wrong. Alfred Pringsheim had refused baptism, and though his wife Hedwig and the children were baptized, they were quite indifferent to such matters. And as to finances, Alfred paid for the young couple's first apartment, and supplemented their income for the next ten years. Despite this — or because of it — Thomas Mann never liked him; he was close only to his mother-in-law[41] and to Katia's twin brother, Klaus.

Klaus of course had figured in the photograph of the Pringsheim children we have mentioned earlier, the one Thomas had pinned up by his desk. In this context, Mann mentioned Klaus in a speech as "the almost equally pretty, roguish-melancholy little fellow" sitting next to Katia (*GW* 11, 523). They do look very much alike in that painting — only close attention reveals that one of the five is a girl. And during the courtship Klaus often acted as mediator and as a (sometimes blind and deaf) chaperone. He favored the marriage and maintained all of his life that it was really he who had brought it about.[42] There may be some validity to his claim. Mann's seemingly abrupt — and perhaps somewhat shaky — transition from homoeroticism to heterosexuality was surely smoothed not only by Katia's tomboyish qualities, but also by the "compliance" of the Katia-Klaus constellation with Mann's preexisting and enduring fascination with brother-sister twins, which was to reach a belated but glorious culmination in *Der Erwählte* (The Holy Sinner, 1951). (Was it in response to this fixation of his that his children Erika and Klaus, though one year apart, experienced and openly presented themselves to the public as twins?)

But Thomas Mann himself, in reflecting on André Gide's marriage to his cousin Emmanuele "despite his recognition of his [homosexual] nature," suggested another mechanism for such an apparent switch. "Is it because his heart, following a personal law, goes different ways than his sensuality, that his Eros and Sexus are strictly separated? Is it because he is reluctant to break his bridges to normalcy, to life? Or is his perception after all 'natural,' attuned to femininity, and only in higher, spiritual spheres the sensual split from the spiritual? [. . .] Even today there are thoughtful observers who [. . .] claim that true, genetic homosexuality does not exist" (*GW* 10, 719, 1929). He is writing about Gide, but he is — as always — also talking about himself.

Be this as it may. Thomas at times considered his marriage "the crowning of my life, without which everything else I may have achieved would seem worthless to me,"[43] and at other times wondered whether his "surrender to 'Life' really represented something highly moral or whether it was some sort of delinquency."[44] But in any case he knew that he was starting "a new chapter in the novel of my life, a chapter that began with a fine passion and that now must be built up with love, skill and constancy."[45]

And all seemed to go well. Following a luxurious honeymoon they settled into their comfortable apartment. Katia promptly became pregnant and changed from being a studious tomboy to becoming an exemplary mother, while Thomas wrote and gave lectures and in every way lived up to the demands of his new position in life. It was altogether the "strenge Glück" [the severe (serious? responsible? austere?) happiness] that is the conclusion of *Königliche Hoheit.*

But though he had "achieved in real life, just like a proper man," he complained to Heinrich that he longed for "a little monastic peace"; had he not just finished *Fiorenza* he would be feeling very bad,[46] and he wondered whether "a pact of loneliness with happiness," such as he was proposing in *Königliche Hoheit,* was not an impossibility (*GW* 11, 579). The adjustment to marriage did not come easily. He suffered depressions, sleeplessness, neuralgias, fatigue, weariness, and "a raving impatience" to achieve something in order to justify himself to himself.[47] Finishing *Königliche Hoheit* was an achievement that should have calmed him, but it did not vent his resentments. There had to be a safety valve.

"Wälsungenblut" (The Blood of the Walsungs, 1906) was that valve.

Thomas Mann asserted that he never invented (*erfinden*) but that, like Turgenev, Goethe, Schiller, and even Shakespeare, he used what he found (*finden*) (*GW* 10, 13–15); and he claimed that any indiscretion this might entail must lose all offensive quality since it was also — and in the first instance — directed against his own person.[48] Even so, since what he "found" were personalities of his own acquaintance or his own family, tact and caution required a certain amount of deception and camouflage. Those precautions were not always effective; and starting with the figure of Spinell in the early story "Tristan" (1903) to that of Rüdiger Schildknapp in the late novel *Doktor Faustus* (1947), Mann's use — or abuse — of living models over and over again got him into hot water. This was most flagrantly true in the case of "Wälsungenblut," where his awe and resentment of Pringsheim wealth — and his anger at his own awe — led him to particularly nasty distortions:

Late morning in an opulent household — recognizably the Pringsheim palais. Herr Aarenhold emerges from his library. (He collects precious books; Samuel Spoelmann collects glass; Alfred Pringsheim had an important Majolica collection.) Frau Aarenhold descends heavily carpeted stairs. She is small, ugly, aging, as if "parched by a foreign, hotter sun." She sports an absurd coiffure and is festooned with jewelry. She is, in short, the very cliché of a nouveau-riche, ostentatious, obnoxious Jewess — the very opposite of Mrs. Pringsheim, whose beauty and sophistication Thomas had extolled in his story "Beim Propheten." Thus Mrs. Aarenhold cannot possibly be a takeoff on Mrs. Pringsheim! Or can she? Why does she have to be "as if parched by a foreign, hotter sun"? Well — Thomas often referred to Katia as his "Princess from the Orient" (*GW* 8, 1088) — surely a foreign place with a hot sun, a place where Jews come from; says it, referring to Katia, lovingly and in appreciation of her beauty; but with this short phrase then connects Mrs. Aarenhold to Katia, makes her an older Katia, makes her Katia's mother.

Her first sentence is already bitchy, and emphasizes her preoccupation with money. She implies that their expected guest and future son-in-law will be on time for brunch because he is broke and needs a free meal. By implication, he is just a gold digger.

The Aarenholds have four children: Kunz, a Hussar with a sabre-cut cheek; Märit, a bitter old maid of twenty-eight who studies law; and the twins, Siegmund and Sieglinde.

Kunz — the very name is arch-German; sabre cuts are acquired in student dueling organizations, which usually do not admit Jews and which generally are despised by Jews. Since the Hussars hardly ever accept Jews, the Aarenholds would have had to buy Kunz's way in. They obviously are trying very hard — too hard — to act assimilated, to be German. (Katia's brother Erik briefly served in a cavalry regiment; but as a Jew he was refused a career appointment.[49]) Märit has the tell-tale Jewish nose and is dried out by studying law. (Would this have been Katia's fate, had Thomas not "saved" her from studying physics?) And Siegmund and Sieglinde? They are clearly named after the protagonists of Wagner's *Die Walküre* (1870). And what Jew would have given his children such names, except a passionate admirer of Wagner like Alfred Pringsheim, who had helped to finance Bayreuth, fought a duel in Wagner's honor, and adapted Wagner's scores for two pianos?

The twins are slender as saplings and physically immature for their nineteen years. They dress with exquisite care and wear expensive jewelry. They resemble each other closely and "they held hands continuously, not caring that both their hands tended to become moist" (*GW* 8, 381–82).

Thomas Mann always eroticized hands, and Felix Krull, in his great paean to love, would conclude that holding hands is in truth "a feast of nature's deviating from itself, a denial of the repugnance one body feels for an alien other, the manifestation of secretly all-present love" (*GW* 7, 643), and of course all the more so if these hands are sweaty! And so the twins' "continuously holding hands" is already an indication, if not an act, of incest.

The suitor, Beckerath, does arrive late, and is full of apologies. He is a government official and "of family," meaning that he is "von Beckerath," a minor aristocrat, and this is presumably the reason the Aarenholds have invited him to brunch and into their family. He is a stand-in for the real-life suitor, Thomas Mann, who, as we mentioned, made a point of the fact that he had something to offer, namely that he was a Christian and of a good family[50] and not "a gypsy in a green wagon" (*GW* 8, 279)! Now, to be "of a good family" is not as good as being "of family." A "good family" is merely a well-established middle-class family, not even minor aristocracy. But even so, while they differ in status, both Thomas Mann and von Beckerath have this to offer the Jewish newcomers, that they are Christian and from an "old" family. And so this once again imputes to the Pringsheim/Aarenholds, who are rich but neither "of family" nor even "of a good family," a pitiful eagerness to be "accepted," if not through wealth then through marriage.

At lunch Aarenhold speaks of his humble origins. Born "in some remote place in the East," he had been "a worm, a louse," but his very self-contempt had spurred him to unceasing efforts and thus had made him great. This is an echo of what the Jewish Doctor Sammet in *Königliche Hoheit* says about himself: that one is not at a disadvantage, compared to the regular and comfortable majority, if one has one more reason than the others for unusual achievement (*GW 2*, 32); and in this regard Mann identifies with the Jews.

Alfred Pringsheim was not a self-made millionaire. Like Spoelman in *Königliche Hoheit* he was "clean"; he had inherited his wealth; he was a professor of mathematics at the University of Munich, so surely he could not be the model for Aarenhold? — But his father, Rudolf Pringsheim, had come from "some remote place in the East," namely Silesia, where he had amassed a great wealth by exploiting coal mines and building railroads![51] It was he who had moved to the elegant Jewish quarter of the Tiergarten in Berlin, where he married into the equally august Dohm family; and it was here that Mann had seen the elegance and opulence he refers to as "Tiergarten." It follows that, shifting his story from Munich to Berlin, he still keeps it in the family. Thin camouflage indeed!

The twins at first do not take part in the conversation; they hold hands between their chairs and convey an intimacy to which, from the outside, there exists no access. Only occasionally does Sieglinde look at von Bekkerath's decent face with her big, black, questioning eyes, the same eyes with which Imma Spoelmann examines Prince Klaus Heinrich and the same eyes with which Katia studied Thomas Mann.

When the twins do open up, their speech is "cutting as it would be where brightness, hardness, self-defense, and vigilant wit are required for survival," and they accept Beckerath's lame replies as befitting someone "who, like his kind, does not need the weapon of wit" (*GW 8*, 388–89). Imma, in *Königliche Hoheit,* is equally sharp-tongued toward the prince; and in actuality the Pringsheim children were well known for their sharp language — they made up their own private vocabulary and called Thomas, behind his back, the "leberleidende Rittmeister" (liverish cavalry Captain)[52] and found his stiff appearance and manner a bit ludicrous. Some of their derision must have percolated through to him.

Eventually, Siegmund humbly requests Beckerath's permission to take his sister to the opera that evening, to see *Die Walküre*. Beckerath eagerly consents, only to realize that the tickets are already bought, that he is not invited to go along, that the "request" was just a snide joke on him, the outsider.

Siegmund gets ready for the opera. And now, with loving care and sensuous voyeurism, the author presents his young man in all meticulous detail: how he appears in domestic undress (pink silken drawers and socks, red morocco slippers, a quilted house coat); the gleam of his naked, yellowish body as he washes himself all over with scented water; the detailed sequence of his formal dressing, down to his cuff links and waistcoat buttons. By contrast, Sieglinde rates only one paragraph, fully clothed. When she joins him they compliment and caress and kiss each other, and "with a sweet sensuality each loved the other for their spoilt and exquisite grooming and their fragrance" (*GW* 8, 396).

They ride to the opera in their own coach, the curtains drawn for intimacy. They sit in their own loge, feed each other cognac-filled chocolates and watch, transfixed, as the other Siegmund and Sieglinde on the stage recognize that they are brother and sister and end up making love.

The twins return home as in a trance. Sieglinde visits her brother in his bedroom; he says something incoherent about Beckerath and revenge; she tries to soothe him; their caresses turn into a frantic tumult, and culminate in a sobbing.

Afterwards she asks: "'But Beckerath — what's with him now?' 'Well,' he said . . .'he ought to be grateful to us. He will lead a less trivial existence from now on'" (*GW* 8, 410).

So it ends. But this is not the original ending. According to Klaus Pringsheim, who was present, Thomas Mann one day at table turned to his father-in-law saying he needed a Hebrew word for "fraud" or "to defraud," and after some reflection Alfred Pringsheim, without questioning the purpose of the inquiry, furnished the term his son-in-law then used for Siegmund's reply to Sieglinde's question: "'But Beckerath, Gigi — What's with him now?' 'Well,' he said, 'we have beganeffed him — the goy!'"

A *ganef,* in Yiddish, is a thief, and *goy* is the contemptuous term of a Jew for a Christian. Obviously, what the twins have stolen from the "goyish" suitor, as an act of revenge for his stealing Sieglinde from Siegmund, is her virginity.

This is how the story ended originally. But Thomas Mann was a bit uneasy about it. Before sending it off to the publisher, he read the whole thing to Klaus and Mrs. Pringsheim, and they found the work "quite excellent." Klaus even felt flattered, for he recognized himself in the hero![53]

And so, with the family's blessing, Thomas Mann sent the story to the *Neue Rundschau.* It was almost completely printed by the time the editor began to take offense at the ending. Thomas consulted Heinrich,[54] who advised against any change. Thomas himself had stylistic qualms — the Yiddish word "fractured the style." Up to that point anything Jewish had only been hinted at. Perhaps the magazine article's ending should be milder, whereas the book version could retain the original words.[55]

But now came an explosion. A bookstore in Munich had received from the S. Fischer publishing house in Berlin a shipment of books which were wrapped in discarded galley proofs of "Wälsungenblut." An apprentice spotted them, recognized them for what they were, and "within hours it was whispered all through town: the author of *Buddenbrooks*, who had just married the only daughter of the well-known mathematician, Wagnerianer, and art collector Alfred Pringsheim, described in a novella the falling into sin of a Jewish pair of twins [. . .] and the pitiful part which the shamefully deceived bridegroom of the girl had to play in her family. Which twins and which family had served the author as models was patently obvious [. . .]. It was said that, revolver in hand [. . .] the raging father-in-law had forced the author to withdraw the offensive tale."

What had really happened was that Klaus alerted Thomas Mann to the brewing scandal, and Thomas immediately sent a telegram to Fischer asking that the story be withdrawn. And the *Rundschau* appeared without "Wälsungenblut."[56]

Thomas wrote to Heinrich: "Returning from [a trip] I encountered here the rumor that I had written a vehemently 'anti-Semitic (!)' novella in which I terribly compromised my wife's family [. . .]. I reviewed the novella in my mind and found that with all its innocence and independence it was not exactly suited to kill the rumor. And I must recognize that humanly, socially, I am no longer free [. . .]. I cannot quite rid myself of an [. . .] oppressive [. . .] feeling of being trapped. I am sure you are calling me a cowardly bourgeois. But it's easy for you to talk. You are absolute. I however have deigned to submit to a constitution."[57]

Katia, forever loyal, considered the matter in retrospect "much ado about nothing [. . .] the autobiographical interpretation is [. . .] on purely psychological grounds totally idiotic."[58]

No, Katia: on psychological grounds it is quite understandable, if not excusable: a palace rebellion staged by the "trapped" husband.

He felt appropriately guilty about it and reacted to this unpleasant sensation by releasing, within months, a furious self-defense, which, again by way of camouflage, seems aimed at claims of libel arising from *Buddenbrooks*, but relates far more immediately to "Wälsungenblut."

"The material a writer may use for his purpose," he protests, "may be his dailiness, may be persons closest to him and most beloved [. . .] yet there must remain for him — and for all the world — a profound difference between the reality and his creation!" Not to acknowledge this distinction is "philistinism": "On the basis of external similarities some people feel entitled to consider everything as 'true,' as journalistic reportage, gossip and sensationalist slander — and the scandal erupts [. . .]. People moan: 'So this is how he saw us? So cold, so cynically-hostile, so lacking in love?' I beg you, be quiet!"

The only weapon given the artist, he says, his only *revenge* against life-events (the emphasis is Mann's), is his creation, and his revenge will be the more vehement the more sensitive he is. Yet "nothing is more erroneous than to interpret the critical precision of his expressions as malice and hostility in the ordinary human sense" (*GW* 10, 16–21). So he goes on and on, proclaiming an innocence he himself does not quite believe in.

The novella did not appear again until 1921, in a limited deluxe edition with the amended ending.[59] Not until after Mann's death was it included in his collected works. But a French translation came out in 1941, was severely condemned by the French critics, and caused Mann much grief (*GW* 11, 557–60). By the time he lived in the United States the anti-Semitic slant of the novella became increasingly embarrassing. He issued a disclaimer in 1940, protesting: "The story contains in it no deliberate impugning of any race or people."[60] And in 1948, writing to a would-be publisher: "Wälsungenblut is a pretty outdated piece of work which in our day could give rise to misunderstandings [. . .]. I do not wish to have it reproduced."[61]

To some extent he is right. Not only was anti-Semitism — and sensitivity to it — not as harsh and acute before Hitler, but for him the point of the story lay elsewhere. It expressed his fascination with sibling incest, and his rage at having to "submit to a constitution" which involved responsibilities of tact and limited his absolute freedom as an artist.

The incest theme was quite popular — in all its permutations — during Mann's youth, in the "decadence" of the *fin de siècle*. Wagner's "barely contained passion"[62] for his sister Rosalia spooks through his early works and erupts openly in the wish-fulfilling lovemaking between Siegmund and Sieglinde. And Wotan's deeply erotic relationship with his daughter Brunhilde makes them seem like lovers, something Mann half-jokingly referred to in a letter where, having gushed about his daughter Erika's wonderful qualities, he equates her with Brunhilde.[63]

There is another emotional overlap: Little Tommy had worshipped his four-years-older brother Heinrich to the point of desiring a "brotherly experiencing of the world"[64] — as if he and Heinrich were Siamese twins. Heinrich denied any such closeness,[65] and Thomas's brotherly love turned into a rivalrous hostility that sometimes swelled into hate. "The brother problem," he once wrote, "is the true and in any case the most difficult problem of my life."[66] The open breach still lay some years in the future, but its roots were anchored in childhood. Thomas would have felt a degree of empathic satisfaction when, on stage, Alberich subjugates his brother Mime and Fasolt slays his brother Fafner.[67]

As if that were not enough, there is a further, quasi-political congruence: both Siegmund-Sieglinde couples — the Wälsungs as well as the Aarenholds — are of a race expressly "chosen and singled out by God" ("ein gottgewähltes Geschlecht"), hence lonely, hated, and vengeful. The richness of interwoven themes fitted Mann so well that he even borrowed Wagner's dramatic structure — recapitulating, mutatis mutandis in "Wälsungenblut," the first act of the *Wälkure,* event by event, scene by scene.[68]

Mann's resentment against being "trapped" in the married state erupted once more two years later in the little story "Anekdote" (Anecdote, 1908), barely five pages long: At a social gathering, the theme of longing and the sweetness of yearning is contrasted with the bitterness of actual experience. In this context someone tells the "true" story of Director Becker and his "heavenly" wife who is the idol of society: "She was worshipped by all of us but had no friends; and that was good so, for how could one be intimate with an ideal?" The apparent bliss of the Becker marriage filled everyone with an "invigorating and yearning belief in goodness." But one evening, at a dinner party, in response to the lavish praise which is again being heaped on his wife, Becker explodes. Once, just once, he must tell the truth about his wife and about the hell of his marriage — how mendacious, unloving, and indolent she is, how she deceives him with servants and laborers, and how "she doesn't even wash! She is too lazy for it. She is dirty under all her finery!" (*GW* 8, 411–15).

In contrast to the all-too-obvious roman-à-clef characters of "Wälsungenblut" and *Königliche Hoheit,* there is no obvious model for "Anekdote" (though "Becker" is only three letters short of "Beckerath"). This time Thomas seems to have written about something he had not himself experienced. Katia was anything but indolent. She was, while Thomas incubated his anecdote, in charge of the infant Erika and either pregnant with or recently delivered of their second child, Klaus; and on top of all this, she ran the household. There was simply not the slightest suspicion of her deceiving him. Becker's wife is not Katia. And yet — the bitterness of disappointment, the fury at "dirty" reality sound too heartfelt not to have some kernel of "lived" truth. Could it have been the all-too-rapid appearance of children, which shifted Katia's attention from him to the nursery and thus made her "unfaithful" to him? Or could it have been the occasional "dirty" fragrance of that nursery, offensive to Thomas's sensitive nose? We do not know.

In any case he got busy with other things. *Königliche Hoheit* needed to be completed, and demands for a position paper on "Die Lösung der Judenfrage" (The Solution of the Jewish Question, 1907) needed to be met. This gave him a chance for mending fences, protesting his philosemitism, attributing to Jews an indispensable role in European culture, extolling the physical beauty, elegance, and appeal of assimilated young Jews which "must make the notion of a mixed marriage quite tolerable for any maiden" (*GW* 13, 459–62, 1907). And as children continued to arrive, he would eventually, enamored with an infant daughter (his third), begin to feel not just like a real man, but actually like a real father. Meanwhile it was his unassailably respectable status as a middle-class paterfamilias that freed him to write his most self-revealing and most famous story, "Der Tod in Venedig."

Notes

[1] *Nb* 2 (7–14), 46. Mann's notebooks will hereafter be cited in the text.

[2] *GW* 8, 162–67. Mann's Collected Works (*GW* 1–13) will hereafter be cited in the text.

[3] Peter De Mendelssohn, *Der Zauberer: Das Leben des deutschen Schriftstellers Thomas Mann*, vol. 1, ed. Cristina Klostermann (Frankfurt am Main: S. Fischer, 1996), 574.

[4] *TM/OG*, 128.

[5] *TM/HM*, 18–19; 13 February 1901.

[6] *TM/OG*, 135–36; 22 February 1901.

[7] *Br* 1, 27; 7 March 1901.

[8] *Br* 1, 28.

[9] *Br* 3, 432.

[10] *TM/OG*, 115.

[11] *Tb* 24 November 1950.

[12] *Tb* 25 April 1934.

[13] Wolfgang Lederer, *The Kiss of the Snow Queen* (Berkeley: U of California P, 1986), 148–50.

[14] Martin Green, The Von Richthofen Sisters; The Triumphant and the Tragic Modes of Love (New York: Basic Books, 1974), 54, 63, 70.

[15] Blüher's full title is: *Die Rolle der Erotik in der männlichen Gesellschaft: Eine Theorie der menschlichen Staatsbildung nach Wesen und Wert*, 2 vols. (Jena: Diederichs, 1917, 1919).

[16] *Tb* 11 February 1919, 17 September 1919; *Br* 1, 177, 4 July 1920.

[17] *Br* 1, 214; 22 August 1924.

[18] *Tb* 28 November 1935.

[19] Klaus Mann, *André Gide and the Crisis of Modern Thought* (New York: Creative Age Press, 1943), 161–62.

[20] J. E. Rivers, *Proust and the Art of Love* (New York: Columbia University Press, 1980), 117–18.

[21] James D. Steakley, *The Homosexual Emancipation Movement in Germany* (New York: Arno Press, 1975), 21–102. Mann signed a petition against section 175 of the German penal code, which had made homosexuality a crime. In 1928, in a congratulatory statement to Magnus Hirschfeld, he declared this section, which was still being enforced, obsolete, and contributed his own text supporting the "Protest der Prominenten gegen die geplante Beibehaltung des Paragraph 175" (Protest of Prominent Persons against the Plan to Continue Section 175). See *Essays* 3, 280–82, 405, 462.

22 *Br* 1, 40; December 1903.

23 Georg Peter Landmann, *Vorträge über Stefan George* (Düsseldorf and Munich: Küpper [formerly Bondi], 1974), 141.

24 Karl Werner Böhm, *Zwischen Selbstzucht und Verlangen: Thomas Mann und das Stigma Homosexualität* (Würzburg: Königshausen & Neumann, 1991), 380.

25 Mendelssohn, *Zauberer*, 573.

26 Katia Mann, *Meine Ungeschriebenen Memoiren* (Frankfurt am Main: S. Fischer, 1974), 18–19.

27 Katia Mann, *Memoiren*, 22–23.

28 Katia Mann, *Memoiren*, 15.

29 Klaus Pringsheim, "Ein Nachtrag zu 'Wälsungenblut,'" *Neue Zürcher Zeitung* (17 December 1961). Reprinted in *Betrachtungen und Überblicke*, ed. Georg Wenzel (Berlin: Aufbau-Verlag, 1966), 4.

30 Peter Gay, *The Bourgeois Experience*, vol. 1, *Education of the Senses* (New York: Oxford UP, 1984), 221–25.

31 Katia Mann, *Memoiren*, 25.

32 *TM/HM*, 52 (27 March 1904).

33 *Br* 1, 43; May 1904.

34 *Br* 1, 45–46; June 1904.

35 *Br* 1, 56; September 1904.

36 *Br* 1, 56; September 1904.

37 *Br* 1, 53; August 1904.

38 *TM/HM*, 49 (27 February 1904).

39 Mendelssohn, *Zauberer*, 944.

40 *TM/HM*, 50–51 (27 February 1904).

41 She, in turn, liked him well enough — as long as he wrote; though she found him "ein rechter Pimperling, der nicht viel verträgt" (a delicate soul who can't stand much): Hans-Rudolf Wiedemann, *Thomas Manns Schwiegermutter Erzählt* (Lübeck: Werkstättenverlag, 1985), 8 March 1907. But she became scornful of him during the war, when he was stuck laboring on his *Betrachtungen eines Unpolitischen:* "Some have said," she wrote in a letter, "that Th.M. appears to be more fruitful in the production of children than of books. This is true to some extent, though right now, after a long while, a book of his will appear. We are actually looking forward to it with some misgivings, for it is not at all 'in his line'" (Wiedemann, 7 September, 1919).

42 Katia Mann, *Memoiren*, 26.

43 *Br* 1, 58, Fall 1904.

44 *Br* 1, 57; 30 October 1904.

45 *TM/HM*, 57 (18 February 1905).

46 *TM/HM*, 57.

47 *TM/OG*, 158 (27 February 1906).

[48] *TM/OG,* 149.

[49] Mendelssohn, *Zauberer,* 593.

[50] *TM/HM,* 51 (27 February 1904).

[51] Mendelssohn, *Zauberer,* 542.

[52] Katia Mann, *Memoiren,* 26.

[53] Pringsheim, "Nachtrag," 4.

[54] *TM/HM,* 63; 20 November 1905.

[55] *TM/HM,* 65 (5 December 1905).

[56] This, at least, is how Klaus Pringsheim remembered it, long after the fact (1961). The actual sequence of events must have been somewhat different, but would not alter the emotional significance of the episode.

[57] *TM/HM,* 67–68 (17 January 1906).

[58] Katia Mann, *Memoiren,* 68–69.

[59] *DüD* 1, 229.

[60] *DüD* 1, 220.

[61] *DüD* 1, 230.

[62] Gerhard Kaiser, "Thomas Manns *Wälsungenblut* und Richard Wagners *Ring;* Erzählen als kritische Interpretation," *TMJb* 12 (1999): 241.

[63] *Br* 3, 29; 26 March 1948.

[64] *TM/HM,* 137 (3 January 1918).

[65] *TM/HM,* 140 (5 January 1918).

[66] *TM/OG,* 184 (11 March 1917).

[67] Kaiser, "Thomas Mann's *Wälsungenblut,* 239–50.

[68] Christine Emig, "Wagner in verjüngten Proportionen; Thomas Manns Novelle *Wälsungenblut* als epische Wagner-Transkription." *TMJb* 7 (1994): 172–79.

"Death in Venice"

Clayton Koelb

Background[1]

IN THE SPRING OF 1911, when he was working on his story of the confidence man Felix Krull, Thomas Mann found himself in severe artistic difficulties. Not only was he so physically and mentally exhausted that he felt like checking into a sanatorium,[2] but he was also at a critical stage in the composition. He was uncertain as to where next to take the narrative. This turned out to be only the first of several interruptions of writing a text that remained fragmentary in the end.

This crisis was just the most recent in a series of unsatisfying, frustrating, or downright failed projects. The career of the former twenty-five-year-old prodigy who had produced the best-selling hit *Buddenbrooks* (1901), now in his mid-thirties, seemed to be in a pronounced valley. Before the problems with "Krull," Mann had given up on several other stories he had wanted to write; and the things he completed did not have the luster of his youthful productions. The play *Fiorenza* (1905) satisfied neither its author nor its intended audience, and Mann would not try his hand at drama again until the very end of his career. The novel *Königliche Hoheit* (Royal Highness, 1909), though a perfectly respectable success by most standards, did not attain to the same exalted status formerly achieved by — and now almost expected of — the author of *Buddenbrooks*.

With the "Krull" manuscript now at an impasse, it was clear that Mann needed some respite from the tension that was overwhelming him, and so he decided to take a vacation. He, together with his wife and brother Heinrich, went first to Brioni, an island on the eastern shore of the Adriatic. It was there that Mann learned of the death of Gustav Mahler, whom Mann had spoken with as recently as the occasion of the premier of Mahler's Eighth Symphony in the fall of 1910. But the Mann party decided quickly that Brioni was not a good place to remain for an entire vacation.[3] They decided to move on to Venice, where they stayed at the Hotel des Bains on the Lido from late May to early June. While in Venice, Mann wrote a short magazine article for the Viennese publication *Der Merker* on the subject of Richard Wagner.[4] He had visited the Bayreuth Festival in 1909, and this was the principal basis for his article, but certainly the death of Mahler was very much on his mind. Among the several memorable events of the holiday was a problem with the shipment of luggage that obliged the Mann group to remain longer than first intended. Another was a purely psychic event: while relaxing on the beach in front of the Hotel des Bains, Mann noticed a handsome Polish boy who made an immediate and lasting impression on him.

On his return to Munich in June, he began almost immediately to form a plan to write a story about "an aging artist's love for a young boy."[5] The troublesome manuscript of "Felix Krull" was put aside; and the new project, taking far longer than he at first imagined, completely took over his working life. In June of 1912, a full year after his return from the trip to Venice, he completed the story, and it appeared later that same year in the October and November issues of the literary periodical *Neue Rundschau*.

The Opening

Mann begins his story by confronting his protagonist, Gustav von Aschenbach, with the same problem of writer's block that had stopped Mann's progress on "Felix Krull" in the spring of 1911. Like Mann, the fictional Aschenbach lives in Munich near the great park called the English Garden, and like Mann he regularly takes long walks in the park to try to relax from the mental strain of his morning's work. Mann chose the name Gustav for his hero in honor of the recently deceased composer Gustav Mahler, though perhaps also in the back of his mind was the name of the great French novelist whom Mann admired and emulated, Gustave Flaubert. The surname Aschenbach literally means "Ashbrook," and it carries connotations of exhausted fires, of a stream gone dry, and of the aftermath of cremation. The presence of death is thus lurking on the edges of the narrative right from the beginning. Threat is also in the air in the form of an explosive political climate alluded to in the opening sentence. Mann's audience might not recognize immediately that the year cited mysteriously as "19" was in fact 1911, but they would understand that it was a recent, trouble-filled year, a year that discretion would forbid fully identifying.[6]

Aschenbach's walk takes him and the reader almost immediately into the realm of the dead. Taking a longer route than usual, the writer finds himself outside the English Garden at the edge of the cemetery, where a streetcar stop next to the cemetery's mortuary chapel offers him a convenient opportunity to get a ride back into town. Waiting for the streetcar gives Aschenbach the leisure to consider the chapel and to encounter on its steps a figure whose appearance has immediate and fatal consequences for him. The man he sees on the chapel steps is the first of several who share at least a few of a number of significant features — the traveling clothes, the hat, the red hair, the exotic face, the pale complexion, the prominent teeth — that convey a sense of strangeness and of foreboding in Aschenbach, though he cannot quite specify why. Mann would expect his audience to realize, consciously or unconsciously, that the man on the steps has some of the traits of the classical god Hermes. The wide-brimmed hat and the stick are of particular significance, for they are always part of Hermes's costume, even if he is otherwise naked. Hermes is the messenger of the gods, the one who brings powerful visions to mortals — as he does here — and also the divinity charged with the duty of conducting dead souls into the underworld. One might well expect to catch a glimpse of him on the steps of a temple dedicated to the dead. The figure also has a strong connection to another Greek divinity, the wine-god Dionysus, who was considered by the Greeks to be of foreign origin, a traveler come to the Mediterranean world from a place much like the one conjured up in Aschenbach's mind by the sight of the stranger on the steps (see below). Mann will offer much more material later in the story that will confirm this connection between the figure on the chapel steps and both the wine-bearing Dionysus and the message-bearing Hermes.

The message that this particular Hermes brings is one that will eventually conduct Aschenbach into the realm of the dead, but at the outset it appears overwhelmingly sensuous. Mann may have expected at least some members of his readership to recognize in the intense exchange of glances between the two men the possibility of a homoerotic encounter.[7] But even leaving this aside — and Aschenbach does in fact appear to leave it aside, with some embarrassment — there is no doubt that the sight of the man starts the writer's mind moving along a path toward the erotic, the exotic, and the forbidden.

Aschenbach's vision of the "marvels and terrors of the earth"[8] is very specific, though it has no name in the text. The tropical swamp and the presence of a tiger lurking behind a thicket of bamboo make it clear that the landscape must be southern Asia. While the precise spot is of no consequence now, it will acquire significance later when the "warm swamps of the Ganges delta" (53)[9] are mentioned as the origin of the pestilence that infects Venice and ultimately causes Aschenbach's death. Mann has carefully structured his story so that the deadly place where his protagonist begins his adventure (the mortuary chapel in Munich) and the deadly place that nurtures the disease that eventually kills him (the tropical swamp) come together in this visionary moment. Another warm, watery locale full of islands, the lagoon of Venice, will be the setting for some of the most important incidents later in the story.

The intensity of Aschenbach's daydream of the tropical landscape mirrors the intensity of his silent encounter with the strange man on the steps, and it is thereby tinged, very obliquely and tactfully, with homoerotic desire. There is no hint as yet of the relevance of this desire, just as there is no hint of the eventual importance of the swampy landscape, but eventually the reader will become aware of that relevance as a pattern of repeated images becomes evident in the course of the narrative. For now the story keeps its attention on Aschenbach's conscious awareness that his escapist fantasies are rooted in his case of writer's block. He understands his yearning to get away as nothing more than a reaction to the difficulties raised by his own sense of artistic perfectionism. He thus has every reason to be suspicious of his motives and to reject his wanderlust. But he does not reject it; he chooses instead to compromise enough with his unseemly longings to consider a trip to the south. He is careful to curb himself by planning a relatively modest journey no farther than somewhere in the south of Europe and certainly not "all the way to the tigers" (6).[10] Once he has taken this decision and determined to spend his evening studying maps and timetables, he notices that the figure who had first inspired his daydream of exotic travel has disappeared. The opening chapter thus ends with the curious absence of the very thing that has set the whole fatal chain of events in motion.

A Biographical Excursus

The second chapter of the story stops the action in order to fill us in on the background of the protagonist. With this leap back to events that precede the incident that opens the story, Mann signals his intention to make his tale part of the classical tradition by conforming to classical narrative norms. The first chapter is now revealed as a kind of epic opening *in medias res* on the model of Homer's *Odyssey* and Virgil's *Aeneid*. This classical element will become even clearer as the story continues and as Mann adds classical features that are more direct than this narrative device or the rather indirect allusion to Hermes in chapter 1.

As in the first paragraph of the first chapter, Mann makes free use of material taken from his own experience. In spite of the differences in age and accomplishment (Aschenbach is in his fifties and a world-famous writer; Mann was in his thirties and was not yet a Nobel laureate), the author and his creation share much — far more, in fact, than even the most diligent reader among Mann's contemporaries could know. The list of Aschenbach's great masterpieces is in fact a bitterly ironic list of Mann's relatively recent failures: *Maja,* "Ein Elender" (A Man of Misery), and "Geist und Kunst" (Intellect and Art) were all titles of projects Mann had begun in high hopes and then, at least for the time being, abandoned in frustration. Knowing this, we can appreciate more deeply just how great a distance Mann was putting between himself and Aschenbach even in the very act of looting his own experience to furnish the biography of his protagonist.

Like Mann himself and like his earlier characters Tonio Kröger and Hanno Buddenbrook, Aschenbach is the hybrid progeny of the union between a diligent bourgeois, purely German father and an artistically inclined mother with a touch of exotic foreign blood. Mann's audience would recognize the pattern, if not from Mann's earlier works then surely from Goethe's autobiographical *Dichtung und Wahrheit* (Poetry and Truth, 1811–14), in which Goethe describes his own family situation in similar terms.[11] It would seem reasonable and fitting to Mann's audience that a great artist would be born of such a mixture of the homely and the exotic, the staid and the impetuous, the bourgeois and the bohemian.

Mann builds up the picture of his hero as a martyr to his art, once again suggesting the kinship of this Gustav to Gustave Flaubert, the "martyr of style." Martyrdom is not only implicit in the references to moral courage, exertion, endurance, virtue, sacrifice, and so on that characterize the rhetoric of this chapter, but also explicit in the image of St. Sebastian that the narrator cites as the apt figuration of Aschenbach's particular sort of achievement. The depictions of the saint, shot full of arrows and yet somehow still serene and dignified, capture, we are told, the essence of an art which consists above all of "grace under pressure of pain" (9).[12] Aschenbach's life is presented as an unending struggle to keep in check the forces of ruin that threaten him on all sides. Illness and a host of other afflictions beset him from childhood on. He must do his work as an artist always in the grip of an iron discipline that offers the only defense against the constant threat of tumbling into the abyss.

Mann carefully builds up a picture of a man for whom the greatest catastrophe would be to let go of the iron grip he maintains on himself. That stern discipline is not only the condition that makes possible his work but also the essence and subject matter of that work as well. Aschenbach has won his large and appreciative audience by depicting in the heroes of his stories a heroism that is firmly based on his own ethic of endurance. We begin to see in retrospect why the vision of the tropical landscape of swamps and tigers Aschenbach experienced at the streetcar stop was something that he had to reject. He could not, ever, go "all the way to the tigers" without losing the very essence of himself. It would have meant giving way to a desire to break the bonds of his own stern regimen. Taking a short vacation somewhere on the Mediterranean, however, would apparently resist the tigers and thus be relatively safe. Or so it would seem at this early stage of the narrative.

The second chapter closes with a kind of covert classical ekphrasis (a description in a literary work of a piece of art). It is an ekphrasis because Mann was in fact offering a description of a photograph of Gustav Mahler he had found published in a periodical; it is covert because no one reading the story without a privileged access to Mann's working notes could know that he was describing the photograph. In any case, Mann's description follows the photograph very closely, including details such as the cleft in the chin, the furrowed brow, and the slightly tilted posture of the head. Aschenbach's (Mahler's) face is then transformed into a kind of living text in which the narrator reads the traces of all the writer's "imaginary mental adventures" (12).[13] The congruence of the man and his work is thus made complete.

Descensus Averno

In one of the best known passages in Book VI of Virgil's *Aeneid*, the Sibyl informs the hero that the descent into hell ("descensus averno") is rather easy; it is getting out again that presents the challenge. Aschenbach's journey into his own realm of death in chapter 3 of "Der Tod in Venedig" is also relatively easy, with only modest impediments to his progress. Getting out again, as it happens, will prove impossible.

Aschenbach, like Mann in the spring of 1911, does not set out directly for Venice. He goes instead to the eastern coast of the Adriatic, though not to a place explicitly called Brioni but to a town on the Istrian coast then called Pola (now Pula) eighty-six miles south of Trieste. Almost immediately, however, Mann's hero, like Mann himself, feels unhappy with his choice of destination and decides to sail the relatively few miles across the Adriatic to Venice. There were literary as well as biographical reasons behind Mann's decision to put his protagonist through this false start. The most important among them perhaps is that it forces Aschenbach to journey to Venice by boat across the Adriatic rather than by the more direct railway route overland south from Munich. The train trip to Trieste that Aschenbach does take is in fact hardly mentioned — it had no place in Mann's plan for the hero's journey downward. And of course a train has very little about it that could be considered classical, whereas boats can easily be accommodated to a mythic vision of the descent into hell. Boats are in fact an outright necessity for such a journey, and Mann provides an abundance of them.

The vessel that Aschenbach boards for his trip to Venice does not seem promising for a vacation cruise on the Mediterranean, but it is very well suited to a journey across the Styx into the land of the dead. It is suitably dark and gloomy, and its interior is hellishly cavernous. The official who writes Aschenbach's ticket has a skeletal look about him, with his "yellow, bony fingers" (14)[14] and he seems overly eager to book the traveler's passage. Even the hunchbacked sailor who leads Aschenbach about the vessel has a deformed and demonic presence. None of these ominous portents deters the eager traveler in the slightest.

Another portent awaits him up on deck. Here he encounters one of the most grotesque figures in any of Mann's stories, the garishly dressed and overly made up old fop who accompanies a group of young people from Pola. Aschenbach reacts to this apparition with a shudder of disgust and with a sense that his trip has now taken a decided turn toward the uncanny. His feeling of disorientation may be partly explained by the motion of the boat as it suddenly starts to pull away from the dock, but it also arises — as we will discover later — from the fact that his trip to Venice really is turning into a journey into a mythic realm on the other side of everyday reality. The old fop who disgusts the writer so thoroughly prefigures Aschenbach's future, though it is only the reader and not Aschenbach himself who will recognize the fact. When the dandified old man appears again, at the end of the crossing to Venice, he drunkenly asks Aschenbach to convey his greetings to the writer's "beloved." The sentiments are unwelcome enough, considering the source, but doubly so given that Aschenbach has no beloved and no prospect of having one. But here again future events will validate the propriety of the old man's words, ludicrous as they may appear in this context. The hero has already crossed not only the physical boundary of the Adriatic but also the spiritual boundary between the normal world and the mythic underworld where the normal rules of temporal precedence and of cause and effect no longer apply.

The geography of Venice allows Mann to stretch out further the hero's journey across the river Styx. Once landed at the docks in Venice, Aschenbach must cross the lagoon (again) to reach the barrier island of the Lido. Though he intends to do so by means of the little steamboats that ply the lagoon, chance puts him in the hands of an unscrupulous gondolier who, instead of taking Aschenbach to the steamer landing, starts to row him directly all the way to the Lido — a long and expensive trip in a gondola. That this gondolier is a version of Charon, the boatman of the river Styx in classical mythology, is an idea that occurs to Aschenbach himself as he resigns himself to letting himself be taken for this ride. "Even if you are just after my money, even if you send me to the house of Aides with a stroke of your oar from behind, you will have rowed me well," he thinks to himself (19).[15] The gondolier also bears a striking resemblance to the man on the steps of the mortuary chapel. His red hair, bared teeth, and short, turned-up nose are quite the same, and the language used to describe him ("clearly not of Italian stock" [18])[16] echoes precisely the words used of the man in Munich ("clearly not of Bavarian stock" [4]).[17] In addition to being Charon, then, he is also another version of Hermes, the conductor of souls into the underworld. All these descriptions of bared, protruding teeth also put us in mind of the human skull, the death's head. There can be little doubt now about where the writer is going.

Connected with this powerful imagery of a descent into the realm of Hades ("Aides") is the fact that Aschenbach, contrary to the habits of a lifetime, is beginning to relax. "A magic circle of indolence seemed to surround the place where he sat" (19).[18] In other circumstances this would seem a very desirable thing for a person on a holiday, but the picture painted in chapter 2 warns us clearly that relaxation is potentially very dangerous for this particular person, whose very existence has been held together by a sheer act of unrelaxed discipline. Indeed, Aschenbach is entering a world where otherwise desirable things are quite dangerous. When he tries to pay the rogue gondolier who has ferried him across the lagoon, he learns that the scoundrel has run off. He has obtained a free ride. This might be a happy accident in the ordinary world, but in the mythic realm into which Aschenbach has entered, it is quite the opposite. A soul who does not pay the ferryman Charon his fare is in for a bad time of it in Avernus.

At first nothing bad seems to happen. On the contrary, Aschenbach finds his new vacation spot entirely charming. Even more charming than the place is the fourteen-year-old Polish boy whom the traveler discovers in the lobby of the hotel, a boy who immediately begins to fascinate him. Part of this fascination, it is worth noting, is the boy's participation in the world of classical myth that is ever more prominent in Aschenbach's point of view and in the rhetoric of the narrative. The boy's face is "reminiscent of Greek statues from the noblest period of antiquity" (21),[19] and his hair is compared to that of the classical statue of the "Boy Pulling a Thorn From his Foot."

Aschenbach is struck by the cosmopolitan atmosphere of the society vacationing on the Lido, but his thoughts run less to possible common European interests of the present than to a common European heritage from the past, especially the Greco-Roman past. His voyage to Venice has been a voyage into history, as in a sense every modern trip to Venice is a step back in time. Politics, economics, and geography have conspired together to keep this extraordinary place from entering completely into the twentieth century. That is a large part of its charm. But this charm comes with a certain price, for it means that the living present is excluded in exchange for the spectral presence of a departed past. Aschenbach has deliberately chosen to take his holiday in such a place, and he is at least half-consciously aware of the darker implications of his choice. He knows perfectly well, for instance, that the Venetian gondola is "painted the sort of black ordinarily reserved for coffins" and that it "makes one think [. . .] of death itself, of biers and gloomy funerals, and of that final, silent journey" (17).[20]

But what could the beautiful Polish boy he sees in the hotel and on the beach have to do with such things? One connection of course is his classical beauty, more appropriate to dead statues than to living beings. Another is his fragility, which seems to put him at some risk of an early death: "Was he in poor health? Perhaps, for the skin of his face was white as ivory" (22).[21] "Tadzio's teeth were not a very pleasing sight. They were rather jagged and pale and had no luster of health [. . .]. He is very sensitive, he is sickly, thought Aschenbach. He will probably not live long" (29).[22] The aging writer is curiously comforted by this thought, very possibly because it permits entertaining the notion of a sort of kinship between the two of them. One may be old and the other young, but both are close to death. For all his youth and beauty, then, the enchanting boy is also a figure of the underworld and a proper inhabitant of this city of shades.

Numerous features in the text reinforce the classical atmosphere that suffuses Aschenbach's conception of the boy. Some are very direct, like the allusions to classical art mentioned above, or the quotations from Homer and Xenophon that bubble up in the writer's consciousness when he contemplates the object of his growing affection. Others are embedded in the structure of the narrative. Mann exploits a conception of antiquity familiar to his audience and to the European community at large since the time of J. J. Winckelmann, who first promulgated the notion in the middle of the eighteenth century. When Aschenbach observes the bathers on the beach "enjoying the nakedness sanctioned by the bold and easy freedom of the place" (21),[23] Mann's serenely hyperbolic language transforms modern Europeans dressed in what would be considered today quite modest bathing attire (though, indeed, the boys swam with upper bodies bare) into naked figures at home in an ancient Olympic landscape. The boy Tadzio is transformed into a classical athlete captured in stone by a brilliant Greek sculptor.

And indeed Mann takes his classical rhetoric much farther. Not only does he quote Homer, he even imitates the dactylic hexameter of Greek and Roman epic poems for passages scattered here and there in the text. It is even possible that Mann planned at first to compose the entire story in epic verses.[24] We hear echoes of the *Odyssey* and the *Aeneid* in rhythms like these: "rose up that blossom, his face, a sight unforgettably charming" (25), or "mussels and sea horses, jelly fish, crabs that ran off going sideways" (36), or "brother-god's sacred chargers, hooves beating, mounted the heavens" (41).[25] Mann may not have expected his audience to recognize consciously the metrical form of such passages, but he certainly expected them to feel the presence of the classical heritage in the familiar cadence of the epic line.

All this classical baggage (and there is much more to come) could easily have strained the narrative beyond all endurance. What makes it all fit comfortably in Mann's tale is that it belongs to the personality of the central character. It is the furniture of Aschenbach's mind.[26] Mann exploits a technique he (and many others) had learned from Gustave Flaubert called the "free indirect style," a technique whereby the narrative point of view is carefully restricted to the mind of the central character and freely delves deeply into that mind when necessary. Although the story is told always in the third person ("*he* did this and thought that"), it is constructed as if it could equally well have been told in the first person ("*I* did this and thought that").[27] It is thus not some learned external narrator who compares Tadzio to a Greek god ("lovely as a tender young god" [28])[28] and quotes Homer; it is the character himself. It is exactly the kind of thing we would expect of a person of Aschenbach's learning and literary stature, a writer who had already himself become something of a classic, and whose style "moved toward the paradigmatic, the polished and traditional, the conservative and formal, even formulaic" (12).[29]

Aschenbach remains very much the literary artist, always at least half-heartedly concerned with his art, even on his beach holiday. He does not so much participate in the beach scene as observe it, with the Polish boy nearly always at the center of his attention. There is a connection between his increasing attraction for Tadzio and his artistic calling, for he sees in the boy an embodiment of the goal of his art. He feels "the attachment that someone who produces beauty at the cost of intellectual self-sacrifice feels toward someone who naturally possesses beauty" (28).[30] That the aging writer is rationalizing his growing erotic attraction to the young man is clear, but the rationalization has it roots in the classically sanctioned link between erotic love for a person and the spiritual love of the divine principle that person represents. As his love deepens, Aschenbach will cling with ever-greater tenacity to this Platonic doctrine of the coalescence of eros with art and philosophy.

In spite of the charms of the beach and the boy playing on the beach, Aschenbach has doubts about the advisability of staying in Venice right from the start. The weather on his arrival is not pleasant, and this situation reminds him of a previous visit to Venice when a long stretch of such weather had made him so uncomfortable that he had to leave. He is not at all sure that the place is good for his health. What deters him from leaving is mostly the effort it would take. His attitude parallels his experience in the gondola crossing the lagoon: at first he protests to the gondolier to take him back; but after his half-hearted attempt proves ineffective, he simply gives in and lets events carry him along as they will. So it is with his entire stay on the Lido. Every time he makes an attempt to reassert his habitual self-discipline, events conspire somehow against it.

The most dramatic of such events is the incident that brings chapter 3 to a climax. After a trip into the city that causes Aschenbach to feel seriously ill, he makes up his mind to depart. Overwhelmed with ambivalence, he regrets his decision even as he is carrying it out, and when he learns that his luggage has been shipped to the wrong destination, it seems to him as if fate has stepped in to save him from his own resolution. Mann exploits his personal experience here in a psychologically brilliant fashion, for the misdirected luggage would in fact be no greater inconvenience to Aschenbach in another place than it is in Venice. Either way, he has no luggage. The accident provides an excuse for him to do what his heart wants, though his intellect warns against it.

The chapter closes with an image of Aschenbach, now returned to the hotel, regarding Tadzio from the high vantage point of his window, relaxed in an armchair. Upon seeing the boy and realizing that it was because of him that he had decided to return, he makes a "slow circling and lifting movement" with his arms while they were "hanging limp over the arms of his chair" (34).[31] The attitude of his arms takes us back to a detail mentioned earlier in chapter 2. An acquaintance had once said of Aschenbach that he "'always lived like this' — and the speaker closed the fingers of his left hand into a fist — 'never like this' — and he let his open hand dangle comfortably from the arm of the chair" (8).[32] The very thing that acquaintance said never happened has now happened. Aschenbach has let go.

Obsession

Aschenbach now immerses himself completely in the classical erotic fantasy that he has constructed for himself. The fourth chapter opens with trumpets blazing, featuring a Homeric image introduced with a Homeric hexameter: "The god with fiery cheeks now, naked, directed his horses, four-abreast, fire-breathing, day by day through the chambers of heaven, and his yellow curls fluttered along with the blast of the east wind" (34).[33] The allusion to the sun god Helios slides easily into an image of Tadzio, whose yellow curls so delight the besotted writer. The god's nakedness links him with the figuratively naked beachgoers upon whom he shines. The Italian Adriatic is transformed into the Greek "Pontos," and the Lido is transformed into a kind of "Elysium at the far ends of the earth" (35)[34] exempt from the cares of everyday life. The Edenic Greece of Winckelmann's pre-romantic fantasy, with its mild weather, its sunny landscapes, and its beautiful naked inhabitants, moves out of Aschenbach's memory and into his present experience. But even this lovely vision is tinged by death, for the writer's imagination places his earthly paradise in the Elysian fields, one of the precincts of the classical underworld.

The figure of Tadzio dominates the narrative more and more, with sentence after sentence devoted to a loving description of his habits, attire, moods, and looks. Aschenbach begins to think of his situation in images from Plato's *Phaedrus,* the dialog so famous for its discourse on the nature of love and for the homoeroticism with which it is saturated. He pictures himself as Socrates and the Polish boy as Phaedrus, thereby putting the noblest possible construction on his growing passion, but also thereby foregrounding the homosexual nature of his involvement.

It is crucial to the effect Mann seeks in his story that the reader should constantly be aware of the impermissible nature of Aschenbach's longing. This is not the story of just any love; it is the story of a love that is forbidden, a love that threatens the foundation of everything that Aschenbach has achieved in his career. Of course, this is not to suggest that Mann is passing some sort of negative judgment on his hero (though at times Mann's narrator may appear to do so) or that he wishes his audience to pass such a judgment. The plain fact of Mann's own homosexuality (or, to be accurate, bisexuality) warns against such a notion.[35] We are not meant to think that this is a "bad" love, but rather that, given the realities of the world Aschenbach inhabits, it is a very, very dangerous love indeed.

It is also a one-sided love, a relationship that exists primarily in Aschenbach's imagination and in the accident of regular physical proximity. The writer and the boy do not interact, do not speak to each other, do not even exchange silent greetings. On one occasion Aschenbach almost attempts to make contact with Tadzio by offering "some friendly French phrase" (39),[36] but he is so overwhelmed by nervousness that he gives up the attempt in shamefaced defeat. His shame is based in part on his lack of courage, but even more on his dawning realization that he really prefers the "licentiousness" ("Zügellosigkeit") of his fantasies to the possibility of a genuine — and far less exciting — proper acquaintance. "For it is licentiousness to be unable to wish for a salutary return to reality" (40).[37] The German word *Zügellosigkeit* derives from a metaphor of horsemanship, of "loosing the reins," that cannot be reproduced precisely in English. Mann's use of the word here plays upon the image of the horses of Helios that opens the chapter and even more relevantly upon a famous image from Plato's *Phaedrus*. Though this image is not explicitly cited in Aschenbach's imaginary *Phaedrus* earlier in chapter 4, it is one that has become part of the common currency of European thought. Plato's metaphor compares human intellect to a charioteer driving a pair of horses, one of which is a recalcitrant creature characterized primarily by its wantonness.[38] Plato's charioteer tames the wanton behavior of the troublesome horse and brings it into line; but Aschenbach has let go of the reins, letting his wanton horse run wild.

The reader, with a reader's privileged access to the hero's mind, knows much that the outside world does not. The licentious ardor burning inside Aschenbach does not yet show in a way that would be obvious to an ordinary observer. On the contrary, that ardor gets transformed by Aschenbach's artistic skill into a piece of classical prose "that soon would amaze many a reader with its purity, nobility, and surging depth of feeling" (39).[39] The contrast between the masterful control displayed in Aschenbach's prose and the utter lack of control slowly overwhelming his emotions is particularly sharp.[40] That the inner licentiousness is really in control is shown by the fact that the writer, upon completing his literary work, feels "as if his conscience were indicting him after a debauch" (39).[41] Though he cannot bring himself to exchange a single word of greeting with the boy in the real world, his adept and powerful imagination enables him to participate in a figurative intercourse with the adored body, a body that serves as a model for the classical elegance of his writing.

Aschenbach's obsession with Tadzio has become complete. The boy is the center of his life, and he regulates his existence so as to maximize his opportunities to be in the presence of his idol. He goes to bed early because there is no reason to stay up after Tadzio retires at nine. He awakens at dawn in half-eager, half-anxious expectation of Tadzio's morning appearance, and the whole world is engulfed in his classical erotic fantasy. Aschenbach experiences the sunrise not simply as the ordinary result of the earth's rotation back into the radiation of its star but as a mythic event suffused with lust. Dawn is the goddess Eos, a seducer of young men, and the pink clouds surrounding her are attending Cupids. The amorous traveler feels himself at the center of a whole universe of longing, a universe peopled with Greco-Roman gods and goddesses intent upon nothing other than sexual satisfaction. The Venetian landscape thus becomes a mirror of his mind.

In this state of mental excitement, Aschenbach sees everything in terms of his obsession. This is particularly true of Tadzio's every movement and expression, many of which he starts to interpret as signs of a reciprocated attraction. The same "free indirect style" that gives us access to Aschenbach's innermost thoughts denies us such access to the minds of other characters, so we have no direct knowledge of Tadzio's feelings. We see only the same external actions that the traveler sees, and we are left with only our own interpretations of those actions, and Aschenbach's. The latter of course may be quite mistaken and are certainly the subject of intensely wishful thinking. Such is the case with the incident that closes chapter 4, where Aschenbach witnesses a smile cross Tadzio's face and considers himself its intended recipient. The description of the smile — once again in classical images — reads into it more than one would ordinarily be able to credit, were it not for the careful preparation Mann has provided. After the magnificent description of the lust-filled sunrise and all the other mythic-erotic images that fill chapter 4, the comparison of Tadzio's smile to the "deep, beguiled, unresisting . . . coquettish smile [of Narcissus], curious and faintly pained, infatuated and infatuating" (43),[42] seems entirely appropriate, even if it is fashioned primarily out of Aschenbach's imagination.

The smile reduces the aging lover to a helpless, seething broth of emotions. Once returned to solitude, Aschenbach for the first time utters the declaration of love we knew he was longing to make. But even here, even at the highest pitch of emotional stress, the writer knows that his avowal is "impossible under these conditions, absurd, reviled, ridiculous" (44).[43] We are not allowed to forget, even in this moment of supreme intoxication, just how far out of bounds Aschenbach has let himself go.

Dissolution

The final chapter of Mann's novella takes its protagonist into utter dissolution. Indeed the English word "dissolution" almost perfectly captures the fusion of lasciviousness and ruin that Mann intended for his tale. Aschenbach's experience in Venice is a steady, ruinous process of letting go in which the protagonist, as he becomes more and more dissolute, comes closer and closer to dissolving into formlessness. Mann gives this fusion a local habitation and a name in the figure of the "Pontos," Aschenbach's beloved sea. The ocean is clearly identified in the story both as the scene of sensuous abandon (the "nakedness" of the beach society) and as the elemental "ground of all being" to which the soul returns in death. The setting in Venice, a city completely dominated by water, provides an opportunity for numerous variations on this theme. Canals, fountains, and the great lagoon separating the city from the barrier island of the Lido all provide locations for important events in the tale. The whole city is presented as a "sunken queen" in the process of nearly dissolving in the waters that surround and sustain it.

The waters of Venice are also the medium in which the fatal cholera thrives, offering a swampy environment akin to the Asiatic morasses where it originated. The disease moves quickly in this final chapter from the margins to the center of the narrative. It becomes a force in Aschenbach's life as powerful as his passion for Tadzio, and in fact it proves to be somehow mysteriously connected to that passion. Mann brilliantly arranges matters so that even the cholera participates in Aschenbach's mythic-erotic fantasy, taking on unmistakable traits of the Greek god Dionysus.

The god of intoxication arrives in Venice in the form of the cholera epidemic, following the same route ascribed to him by the playwright Euripides in the *Bacchae*.[44] The English travel agent who confirms Aschenbach's suspicions about the presence of an epidemic in Venice details its progress out of the Ganges delta, where "tigers lurk in bamboo thickets" (53),[45] across Afghanistan and Persia, and then to the cities of Mediterranean Europe. Thus, although Aschenbach has made good on his promise to himself not to go all the way to the tigers, he has reached them just the same. They have been carried to Venice on the shoulders of the god, who has now let them loose among the canals of the city.

There is a much deeper connection between Mann's story and Euripides's *Bacchae* than this itinerary.[46] The central plot of the Greek play involves the humiliation and destruction of an important personage (Pentheus, king of Thebes) by Dionysus, a god he has slighted. The manner of the king's humiliation — the god convinces him to dress as a woman in order to observe the Bacchic rites — provides a model for the humiliating and grotesque change in Aschenbach's attire. He dyes his hair, puts on heavy makeup, and dons a red tie and a colorful straw hat. He looks, in fact, very much like the horrid old fop on the steamer from Pola.

Like Pentheus, Aschenbach gets to observe before his death the forbidden orgiastic rites honoring the wine god. In a dream Aschenbach has late in his sojourn on the Lido, he casts himself in the role of a curious onlooker caught up in the midst of a Bacchic rite. The atmosphere is one of terror, frenzy, and lustful abandon, and at its center is an enormous representation of a phallus, the representation of the god's sexual power. The presence of the god is greeted by a noise characterized by "a drawn-out *uuu* sound at the end" (56),[47] a sound we recognize as the call on the beach directed to the Polish boy: "a drawn-out cry of *uuu* at the end. 'Tadziu! Tadziu!'" (28). The boy who had from the first reminded Aschenbach of a statue of a Greek god is now revealed as an incarnation of a very particular, very dangerous god, a god who takes terrible vengeance on those who have previously slighted him.[48]

The god is present on the Lido in another form as well. The guitar-playing singer who entertains the hotel guests one evening has a familiar look about him. He has a snub nose, a prominent Adam's apple and he "seemed not to be of Venetian stock" (50).[49] Thus he appears a reincarnation of that same figure who appeared first on the steps of the mortuary chapel and then in the form of the rogue gondolier. He also reprises the role of the old fop, as he lets "his tongue play lasciviously at the corner of his mouth" (50)[50] just as the old impostor on the steamer had done. As much as he is Hermes, then, this recurring figure is revealed to be also Dionysus come down to earth to take terrible vengeance on a mortal who has built his existence upon a refusal to give in to intoxicated lassitude.

The singer's performance demonstrates the close connection between the Dionysus of Mann's story and the Dionysus of Nietzsche's *Die Geburt der Tragödie* (The Birth of Tragedy, 1872). Nietzsche's conception of Greek culture as a precarious combination of Apollonian and Dionysian elements was undoubtedly a powerful influence on Mann.[51] The Nietzschean Dionysus shows himself particularly strongly in the performance of the laughing song, in which the refrain consists entirely of "a certain rhythmically structured but still very natural laughter" (52).[52] Nietzsche's Dionysus is the god not of the individual but of the group, of the denial of the *principium individuationis*. He is the god who dissolves the separate psyche into the communal, and his representation on the Greek stage was the chorus. The laughing song achieves the Dionysian result of dissolving all the onlookers, including not only the hotel guests but the employees as well, into a single mindlessly laughing chorus.

The world is dissolving around Aschenbach even as he becomes more and more dissolute. He becomes a stalker, following Tadzio around the city so as not to miss a single opportunity to be in his presence. And as he does so, the signs of cholera are everywhere, both in the reek of disinfectant all over the city and in the increasing symptoms of illness in Aschenbach himself. He is often overwhelmingly intoxicated by an amalgam of his love-sickness and his physical infection. He has long known for certain that prudence would require him to leave the city, but he cannot. Charity would require him to share the knowledge he has with the apparently unsuspecting Polish family, but he cannot. He cannot undertake any action that would cause a separation from the boy, even though all their lives are in danger.

Aschenbach's infection reaches the point that he is at times in delirium. The Bacchic dream is one delirious episode, and another is a second fantasy of Socrates and Phaedrus, yet another dream-vision fusion of high philoso-phy with yearning eroticism. The fantasy, coming as it does very near the end of the novella, represents a rhetorical climax in which Aschenbach gets to speak his mind directly. Before it begins, however, we are encouraged to consider the contrast between the writer's present low condition and his previous high achievement.[53] A part of Aschenbach's mind appears to be aware of the paradox of his present position, but that part of him does not hold the upper hand for long. He lets himself slip into his classical reverie, a dream we must admit is remarkably lucid for one in the throes of choleric delirium. The Socratic voice of the dream, musing on the relation between formal beauty and the intoxicated attraction such beauty can excite, laments that a decision to seek beauty can lead a "noble soul to horrible emotional outrages [. . .] lead him to the abyss" (61).[54]

The distinguished writer has deliberately chosen the road to the abyss, and he has done so with relatively little regret (just as Adrian Leverkühn, the hero of Mann's late novel *Doktor Faustus* [1947] will do). To be sure, he appears aware that he has humiliated himself. To be sure, he knows he has placed himself squarely in the path of death. But the danger does not seem to him too great. In his present intoxicated state, a single moment in the presence of his beautiful Tadzio is worth any risk.

And so it is that, as soon as he determines that the Polish family has packed its bags to leave Venice, Aschenbach goes down to the beach to take leave of his divine idol. He watches the boy linger on the edge of the water. As he watches, his dying imagination transforms the figure of the youth into the god he had truly become, Hermes the psychagogue, conducting the soul of the traveler to his home across the waters.

Notes

[1] Only a small part of the available background information can be provided in this short article. T. J. Reed, *Death in Venice: Making and Unmaking a Master* (New York: Twayne, 1994) provides more. See both this volume of Reed's and Clayton Koelb, ed. and trans., *Thomas Mann: Death in Venice: A New Translation, Back-grounds and Contexts, Criticism* (New York: Norton, 1994) for extensive bibliogra-phies.

[2] Hans Bürgin and Hans-Otto Mayer, *Thomas Mann: A Chronicle of His Life*, trans. Eugene Dobson (University, AL: U of Alabama P, 1969), 28.

[3] See Herbert Lehnert, "Thomas Mann's Interpretations of *Der Tod in Venedig* and Their Reliability," *Rice University Studies* 50:4 (1964), 41–60.

[4] Mann's article, "Auseinandersetzung mit Richard Wagner," appeared in the July issue of *Der Merker*. It marked a shift in Mann's attitude away from his earlier enthu-siasm for the composer toward a far less positive, far more critical position. This

coolness can also be found in the prose of Mann's hero Aschenbach, who likewise composes a brief piece on the beach in Venice).

⁵ Bürgin and Mayer, 29.

⁶ For more on the historical context of the story, see Herbert Lehnert, "Historischer Horizont und Fiktionalität in Thomas Manns 'Der Tod in Venedig,'" *Wagner, Nietzsche, Thomas Mann: Festschrift for Eckhart Heftrich* (Frankfurt am Main: Klostermann, 1993), 254–78.

⁷ See the argument to this effect in Robert Tobin, "Why is Tadzio a Boy?" in Koelb, *Death in Venice*, 207–32.

⁸ This and all English translations of "Der Tod in Venedig" in this chapter are my own, as they are taken from my translation *Death in Venice: A New Translation, Backgrounds and Contexts, Criticism* (this citation page 5). Subsequent references to this edition will given as page numbers in the text. For the convenience of the German-speaking reader, the German originals of all quotations appear in the notes; thus, for the passage just cited: "alle Wunder und Schrecken der mannigfaltigen Erde"(*GW* 8, 447).

⁹ *GW* 8, 512: "wärmesten Morästen des Ganges-Deltas."

¹⁰ *GW* 8, 449: "nicht gerade bis zu den Tigern."

¹¹ In addition to Book VI of *Dichtung und Wahrheit,* there is a well-known poem of Goethe's old age that proposes this same idea in perhaps even more forceful terms: "Vom Vater hab' ich die Statur, / Des Lebens ernstes Führen, / Vom Mütterchen die Frohnatur / Und Lust zu fabulieren" (I have my stature from my father, as well as his earnest conduct of life, but from Mommy I have my happy disposition and love of story-telling).

¹² *GW* 8, 453: "Anmut in der Qual."

¹³ *GW* 8, 457: "Spuren imaginärer und geistiger Abenteuer."

¹⁴ *GW* 8, 459: "mit gelben und knochigen Fingern."

¹⁵ *GW* 8, 466: "Selbst, wenn du es auf meine Barschaft abgesehen hast und mich hinterrücks mit einem Ruderschlage ins Haus des Aides schickst, wirst du mich gut gefahren haben."

¹⁶ *GW* 8, 465: "durchaus nicht italienschen Schlages."

¹⁷ *GW* 8, 445: "durchaus nicht bajuwarischen Schlages."

¹⁸ *GW* 8, 466: "Ein Bann der Trägheit schien auszugehen von seinem Sitz."

¹⁹ *GW* 8, 469: "erinnerte an griechische Bilderwerke aus edelster Zeit."

²⁰ *GW* 8, 464: "so eigentümlich Schwarz, wie sonst unter allen Dingen nur Särge sind [. . .] es erinnert noch mehr an den Tod selbst, an Bahre und düsteres Begängnis und letzte, schweigsame Fahrt."

²¹ *GW* 8, 470: "War er leidend? Denn die Haut seines Gesichtes stach weiß wie Elfenbein [. . .] ab."

²² *GW* 8, 479: "daß Tadzios Zähne nicht recht erfreulich waren: etwas zackig und blaß, ohne den Schmelz der Gesundheit. . . . Er ist sehr zart, er ist kränklich, dachte Aschenbach. Er wird wahrscheinlich nicht alt werden."

²³ *GW* 8, 474: "Nacktheit, die keck-behaglich die Freiheiten des Ortes genoß."

[24] See Reed, *Making and Unmaking a Master*, 86. While one cannot rule out the possibility that Mann began by writing hexameter verses, such a notion is hardly necessary to explain the presence of metrical passages in the story. Mann liked the effect of embedding verses in his prose, as he did not only here but also in his novel tetralogy *Joseph und seine Brüder* (1934–43).

[25] *GW* 8, 474: "ruhte die Blüte des Hauptes in unvergleichlichem Liebreiz"; 489: "Muscheln, Seepferdchen, Quallen und seitlich laufende Krebse"; 495: "stiegen des Bruders heilige Renner über den Erdkreis."

[26] Cf. André von Gronicka, "'Myth Plus Psychology': A Style Analysis of *Death in Venice*," *Germanic Review* 31 (1956): 191–205; rpt. in Koelb, ed. and trans., *Death in Venice*, 115–30.

[27] This technique is called "erlebte Rede" (experienced discourse) in German and is one of Mann's preferred modes of narration.

[28] *GW* 8, 478: "schön wie ein zarter Gott."

[29] *GW* 8, 456: "wandelte sich ins Mustergültig-Feststehende, Geschliffen-Herkömmliche, Erhaltende, Formelle, selbst Formelhafte."

[30] *GW* 8, 479: "die gerührte Hinneigung dessen, der sich opfernd im Geiste das Schöne zeugt, zu dem, der die Schönheit hat."

[31] *GW* 8, 486: "mit beiden schlaff über die Lehne des Sessels hinabhängenden Armen eine langsam drehende und hebende Bewegung."

[32] *GW* 8, 451: "'von jeher nur so gelebt' — und der Sprecher schloß die Finger seiner linken Hand fest zur Faust —; 'niemals so' — und er ließ die geöffnete Hand bequem von der Lehne des Sessels hängen."

[33] *GW* 8, 486: "Nun lenkte Tag für Tag der Gott mit den hitzigen Wangen nackend sein gluthauchendes Viergespann durch die Räume des Himmels und sein gelbes Gelock flatterte im zugleich ausstürmenden Ostwind."

[34] *GW* 8, 488: "elysische Land, an die Grenzen der Erde."

[35] Mann's sexual orientation has taken center stage in much recent writing about him in both the scholarly and popular press. "Der Tod in Venedig" is now even cited as the leading gay novel of all time (*USA Today*, June 7, 1999). This essay cannot devote adequate attention to the issue, important though it is. For a more thorough discussion of the story from this perspective, see Tobin, "Why is Tadzio a Boy?"; for an account of Mann's life and work primarily in terms of his homosexuality, one might consult Anthony Heilbut, *Thomas Mann: Eros and Literature* (Berkeley: U of California P, 1995), though the reader should approach this work with caution. The author's agenda is more powerful than his scholarship.

[36] *GW* 8, 493: "eine freundliche französische Phrase."

[37] *GW* 8, 494: "Denn heilsame Ernüchterung nicht wollen zu können, ist Zügellosigkeit."

[38] *The Collected Dialogues of Plato*, ed. Edith Hamilton and Huntington Cairns (New York: Bollingen/Pantheon, 1961), 499–501.

[39] *GW* 8, 493: "deren Lauterkeit, Adel und schwingende Gefühlsspannung binnen kurzem die Bewunderung vieler erregen sollte."

[40] The contrast with the essay Mann actually wrote on the beach in Venice is also significant. In this connection see Herbert Lehnert, *Thomas Mann: Fiktion, Mythos, Religion* (Stuttgart: Kohlhammer, 1965, 1968), in which it is pointed out that Mann's piece is hardly a work of classical prose. Mann's relation to the classical and neoclassical is discussed in Hans Rudolf Vaget, "Thomas Mann und die Neuklassik. 'Der Tod in Venedig' und Samuel Lublinskis Literaturauffassung," in *Stationen der Thomas Mann Forschung*, ed. Hermann Kurzke (Würzburg: Königshausen & Neumann, 1985), 41–60.

[41] *GW* 8, 493: "als ob sein Gewissen wie nach einer Ausschweifung Klage führe."

[42] *GW* 8, 498: "Jenes tiefe, bezauberte, hingezogene Lächeln [des Narziß], kokett, neugierig und leise gequält, betört und betörend."

[43] *GW* 8, 498: "unmöglich hier, absurd, verworfen, lächerlich."

[44] See Manfred Dierks, *Studien zu Mythos und Psychologie bei Thomas Mann, TMS 2* (1972). This work is excerpted and translated as "Nietzsche's *Birth of Tragedy* and Mann's *Death in Venice*" in Koelb, *Death in Venice*, 130–49.

[45] *GW* 8, 512: "in deren Bambusdickichten der Tiger kauert."

[46] Cf. Dierks, "*Birth of Tragedy* and *Death in Venice*," 133–35.

[47] *GW* 8, 516: "im gezogenen u-Ruf."

[48] Cf. A. von Gronicka, "Myth Plus Psychology," 125.

[49] *GW* 8, 507: "schien nicht venezianischen Schlages."

[50] *GW* 8, 508: "die Zunge schlüpfrig im Mundwinkel spielen zu lassen."

[51] This point has been made particularly forcefully by Dierks, op. cit.

[52] *GW* 8, 509: "ein rhythmisch irgendwie geordnetes, aber sehr natürlich behandeltes Lachen."

[53] There has been considerable disagreement among Mann scholars as to how to interpret the rhetoric of Mann's introduction to the final pseudo-Phaedrus passage. T. J. Reed, for instance ("The Art of Ambivalence," in Reed, *The Uses of Tradition* [Oxford: Clarendon Press, 1974, 1996]; rpt. in Koelb, *Death in Venice*, 150–78), reads it as open sarcasm directed at Aschenbach from an extra-textual point of view; while Dorrit Cohn ("The Second Author of Death in Venice," in *Probleme der Moderne: Studien zur deutschen Literatur von Nietzsche bis Brecht* [Tübingen: Niemeyer, 1983]; rpt. in Koelb, 178–95) would see it as evidence of a second narrative perspective embedded in the text. I take the position that it is not necessary to understand this passage as moving substantially away from the normal free indirect style of the rest of the novella. A part of Aschenbach, described as "embarrassed" in the text, sees himself fallen so low. The sarcastic voice is his own.

[54] *GW* 8, 522: "führen den Edlen vielleicht zu grauenhaften Gefühlsfrevel [. . .] führen zum Abgrund."

"Mein 'Friedrich' — das ist was Anderes": Thomas Mann's Unwritten Novel about Frederick the Great, King of Prussia

Hans-Joachim Sandberg

O N RETURNING FROM HIS FIRST VISIT to the USA, Thomas Mann found "a beautiful old book" waiting for him in Küsnacht, his Swiss refuge outside Zurich. It bore the title *Johann Müller's Briefe an seinen ältesten Freund in der Schweiz* (Johann Müller's Letters to His Oldest Friend in Switzerland) and contained the dedication: "Thomas Mann / mit guten Wünschen herzlich gedenkend / zum 6. Juni 1934 / Köln Ernst Bertram" (To Thomas Mann / with good wishes and cordially thinking of him / for the 6th June 1934 / Cologne Ernst Bertram).[1]

Müller was a historian and a contemporary of Goethe. Some of the letters, which had been published posthumously from his literary remains, testify to the high regard Müller had for Frederick II and his "most glorious deeds."[2] Müller (1752–1809) had quoted four lines of verse from one of Frederick's letters, together with some words of Christ admired by the monarch:

> La mort est un repos, mais vivre c'est agir.
> Le repos est permis, mais c'est sur les lauriers.
> Les Arts sont comme Eglé, dont le coeur n'est rendu
> Qu'à l'amant le plus tendre et le plus assidu.[3]

Words by Frederick who is the glory of humanity and my hero. In yet another place in this letter one can read: In the entire gospel by Saint John no passage is as beautiful as: "I must act as long as day prevails; night will fall when no-one can work.[4]

Mann marked the first sentence of this homage to the king with an "x." Lines of verse and the quotation from the Bible reminded the exile of a time in his own past. Thirty years earlier he had planned to write a "historical novel with the title of 'Friedrich,'"[5] because at the time he had regarded the king of Prussia as a "great" man and king. In 1739, while still crown prince, Frederick had defined his future office in his *Antimachiavell* (1740) in this manner: "The sovereign is under no circumstances an absolute ruler of his people who are under his yoke; he is instead no more than the highest of the civil servants."[6]

Mann's plan of honoring Frederick's "greatness" in the light of his merits as the "first servant"[7] of his state rested on his conviction that he was linked to the king by a relationship based on experience (*Erfahrungsverwandtschaft*).[8] He saw himself linked to the king by virtue of his work as a writer, and remarked in his notebook that he found work "always equally hard and severe whether it [was] executed in a garret or a sumptuously appointed chamber." Only "idleness" had enough awareness "to enjoy things."[9] In Mann's eyes, Frederick II was one of those exemplary figures who, because they were duty bound to achieve the "extraordinary," had never known "leisure" (*GW* 8, 451). The mission of the poet and writer and the mission of the king both demanded perseverance, diligence and patience. There could be no fame without the "ethos of perseverance."[10]

Mann saw himself as one of the king's successors, particularly in his commitment to his "categorical imperative, 'to persevere'": "to practice patience" (*GW* 11, 715–16), "to endure" (*GW* 8, 451), to "finish" (*GW* 8, 379). Unless these watchwords were observed, the struggle to produce a harmonious work would fail, and the striving for completion was condemned to failure. In his essay "Meine Arbeitsweise" (My Way of Working, 1925) Mann cites verses by Platen:

> Wie kann der Mensch, wieviel er auch vollende,
> Wie kühn er sei, sich zeigen als ein Ganzes,
> Und was er ausführt, gleicht es nicht am Ende
> Zerstreuten Blumen eines großen Kranzes?

[How can man — as much as he may complete / Or as brave as he might be, show himself as a totality. / And whatever he accomplishes, does it not resemble / The scattered flowers of a grand garland in the end?][11]

He admits that the verses always touched him; the struggle for completion may be nothing else but "fear of death." This confession only seems to contradict Mann's later remark, in a letter to Karl Kerényi of 9 September 1938, that only death was truly remarkable and pleasing, for one constantly strove and sought to finish one's work. One did not notice that one actually strove for death and the condition of being finished.[12] All striving originated in the concern that one might not be able to complete one's work.

At the beginning of the twentieth century Mann regarded Frederick II as a man who embodied the kind of heroism symbolized in the figure of St. Sebastian, a heroism that did not simply endure but one that was "active." Such heroism meant maintaining "dignity in one's fate and gracefulness in agony" ("Haltung im Schicksal, Anmut in der Qual") (*GW* 8, 453). Heroism for Mann was a position of contention, an "in spite of," a "weakness overcome"; it entailed "sensitivity."[13] Like Frederick, he too gave the name "Sans souci" to the longing for release — from the exertions demanded of a king by his office and of the writer by his commitment to his work. Both had managed to resist the temptation for repose. When the king's gaze fell from the rooms of his favorite castle onto his future resting place, he anticipated being "free of worries" there.[14] Yet he also realized that it was his very readiness to live without such freedom that had made him into the great man he was, admired by contemporaries and future generations alike. A notebook entry by Mann from the spring of 1905 relates the plan of his Friedrich novel to his own life and philosophy of life: the self is a task, concentration is in the work. But there is also nostalgia for the whole in the strong individual; the desire for the ego lives next to a desire for the world. This entry is immediately followed by one that reacts to what he considered careless writing in his brother Heinrich Mann's novel *Professor Unrat* (1905):[15] "The effortless achiever will not become great" ("Der Mühelose wird nicht groß") (*GW* 8, 1062) knows Mann's Lorenzo in his play *Fiorenza* (1905).

Having not entirely unexpectedly attained the fame he longed for with *Buddenbrooks* (1901), and being concerned to sustain that fame, Mann had in 1903 set himself the goal of exploring the phenomenon of "greatness" when he began work on *Fiorenza*. What he wanted to do was to explore election ("Erwähltheit") of those who bore the "mark on the forehead" (*GW* 8, 290). He did so in 1903 in his story "Tonio Kröger" by having the lonely poet identify with Philip II, the equally lonely king of Spain.[16] He did so again in the study "Schwere Stunde" (A Weary Hour, 1905), in which he showed Schiller measuring himself against Goethe. Schiller, with the relentless and tormenting thought of "the other" in his heart of the "radiant, active, sensuous, divinely intuitive," could not help but thinking of "*him*, in Weimar," the one he loved with a mixture of love and hatred, with "yearning enmity" ("sehnsüchtiger Feindschaft") (*GW* 8, 377, Mann's italics).

Mann explored greatness while reading for his "Friedrich," a novel about a king and a poet, a philosopher on the throne, another hero fascinated by the "phantom of glory."[17] "My youth, the fire of passion, the craving for glory, yes, not to hide anything, my curiosity, too, finally a secret instinct have driven me away from the sweet peace I savored, and the desire to see my name in the newspapers and in history has led me astray."[18] In the novel *Königliche Hoheit* (Royal Highness, 1909) the roles of prince and poet become interchangeable. After the appearance of the novel *Buddenbrooks* (1901) and the story "Tonio Kröger," Mann had been at pains to satisfy the public with works that did not fall below the level of his previous achievements. With *Fiorenza*, which turned out to be a "fiasco," he felt he had sustained "a serious defeat."[19] Fame had its price. The year 1905 marked a caesura: the marriage to Katia with a call for "dignity and love, — an austere happiness" (*GW* 2, 363), a happiness that had to be paid for with concessions seemingly detrimental to Mann's self-respect as an artist. Now that he was no longer free, he found himself obliged to withdraw the story "Wälsungen-blut" (The Blood of the Walsungs, 1905) from publication. How could he explain this step he had been forced to take — and had taken so grudg-ingly — to his older brother? He admitted that a lack of freedom oppressed him, at least in certain hours when he was visited by hypochondria.[20]

In this situation an achievement was called for that could convey the dignity appropriate to this new and self-imposed constitution. A novel about Frederick the Great could convey a form of heroism that would challenge the common view of the heroic and allow a faint reflection of the king's glory to fall on the novel's author. In a letter to Heinrich, Thomas Mann compared his intention of writing the "Friedrich" novel to his achievement of having vivified Schiller in 1905's "Schwere Stunde." He had made great-ness palpable in the Schiller study; someone had told him so. He intended to do the same now "on a grand scale" ("im Großen").[21] The plan of de-picting the Prussian king in a novel was prompted not least by the desire to secure the author's own fame.

Doubts, however, were not slow to emerge: What were the sacrifices? What sacrifices were commonly demanded in payment for fame and renown? The perspectives of Mann's teachers, Schopenhauer, Wagner, and Nietzsche did not allow him to ignore the questionable nature of the planned under-taking. Schopenhauer had called all conquerors mere predators, naming Napoleon Bonaparte.[22] Citing Schopenhauer's claim that the world's greatest phenomenon was not the conqueror but the person who could transcend the world,[23] Wagner had dismissed such heroes as depicted by Plutarch and Livy out of hand.[24] Influenced by his impressions of the Franco-Prussian War of 1870–71, Nietzsche had observed that the superiority of the Prussian king was based on a "skepticism of daring masculinity," first found in Germany "with the great Frederick." On the other hand, Nietzsche had asked the question: "is greatness even possible nowadays?"[25]

In his *Antimachiavell*, Frederick had expressed the conviction that a conqueror would never win fame.[26] Macaulay had called the crown prince's pamphlet "an edifying homily against rapacity, perfidy, arbitrary govern-ment, unjust war, in short against almost everything for which its author is now remembered among men."[27] And had he not noted that Ibsen recently had questioned greatness?[28] Mann was under no illusion. Was fame worth the cost? Did it justify the sacrifices? Was the price for achieving fame too high? Or, was fame perhaps altogether a mirage?

Mann was writing for a generation of readers who from an early age on had been made familiar with the life, deeds, and works of the king. At the end of the nineteenth century, no hero stood more in the center of instruc-tion in German schools than Frederick the Great of Prussia. After the German territories had been united in the Second German Empire of 1871, Frederick was credited not only with having had the final German unification as his distant goal, but for having indeed initiated the later union forged by Bismarck under the hegemony of the Hohenzollerns. This perception, largely uncontested in Prussia, was also increasingly popular in other parts of the German Empire during the reign of Wilhelm II. In planning the "Friedrich" project, Mann had thus chosen a subject that was assured the sympathy of the public at large and in the process was certain to enhance the reputation of its author.

It was appropriate that a "great" king should be honored by an author whose ambition was to achieve, as Mann's Schiller figure had said, "Greatness! The extraordinary! World conquest and immortality of one's name!" (*GW* 8, 376). When he resolved to write the novel, Mann had a "masterpiece" in mind that should set new standards.[29] For some time, his brother Heinrich Mann's literary works had incurred his displeasure: *Professor Unrat* had provoked him to jot down a note that he considered it "immoral" to write "one poor book after another" simply for fear of being idle,[30] and in a letter of December 1903 he had vituperated Heinrich for his style and taste.[31]

In planning to write the Frederick novel, Mann did not simply want to outdo his brother, he was also motivated by a strong desire to become a classic writer in contemporary literature, but not by idealizing the great man, as Schiller once considered doing.[32] One might handle the case of the great Frederick by emulating Nietzsche and depict "a hero human — all too human, with skepticism, with viciousness, with psychological radicalism but still positive, lyrical, from one's own perspective." Such a portrait, Thomas Mann suggested in a letter to Heinrich, had so far not been presented "at all."[33]

On 23 February 1905, Mann had returned to Munich from his honeymoon in Switzerland. He immediately began the preparatory work for his contribution to the special edition of *Simplicissimus* devoted to Schiller. Mann knew of Schiller's plan to write an epic poem on Frederick.[34] For his Schiller scene of 1905 he had read the recently published *Marbacher Schillerbuch* (1905), which contained several essays discussing Schiller's tragedy *Wallenstein* (1798–99). One of the essays, "Schiller als Kriegsmann" (Schiller as a Soldier) by Albert von Pfister mentioned the planned epic:

> Schiller had given serious thought to the idea of making the achievements of Frederick the Great the subject of an epic. He has written about it repeatedly to his friend Körner. As late as March 1790, Schiller says that he could not get the story about Frederick ["die Frideri-ciade"] out of his mind; toward the end of 1791, however, he declared that the planned epic was not a subject for him after all.[35]

Pfister's comment about the project of a "Fridericiade" — as Schiller, following the example of Voltaire's Henriade, had called it — prompted Mann

to inform himself in detail about Schiller's original plan, reading the correspondence between Schiller and Körner.[36]

Among Schiller's suggestions about an approach to the material were
reflections on historical setting and specific phases in the king's life. He
suggested that the king's spirit might be developed more poetically if one
started with an "unhappy situation."[37] The writer would thus have to demonstrate Frederick's ability to suffer greatly. What Schiller had in mind was
the king's desperate situation after the battle of Kolin and the "sad constellation" before the death of the Empress Elisabeth.[38] In his story Mann meant
to equate the king's martial enterprises with temptations, sufferings, and
defeat but also with his single-mindedness of purpose, the bright moments,
and the satisfaction experienced by a writer in wrestling with his material.

Another of Schiller's ideas focused on the course of action. Schiller had
suggested that the main story line should remain "very simple" even if individual episodes were "as complex as possible."[39] Mann's letter to Samuel
Lublinski of 6 December 1906, indicates that Schiller's reflections could be
applied to his own plan: "As far as my dream of Frederick is concerned, you
correctly insist on selection and structure. It is clear to me that the book
could never have the open form of *Buddenbrooks*."[40]

Mann's predecessor Schiller had been fully aware of the difficulties that
might arise from "the close proximity to this subject."[41] The difficulties for
Schiller's successor, by contrast, lay in his distance to it. Mann had to famil-
iarize himself with the atmosphere, the spirit and the social circumstances of
the eighteenth century. In his letter to Körner of 10 March 1789, Schiller
envisioned an epic poem of that time reflecting the period's customs, the
finest "fragrance" of its philosophy, its constitution, domesticity, and art.
Everything should be "assembled and coexist in an easy, harmonious manner."[42] Schiller's letters had information worth considering for Mann; their
content could guide the selection of sources and material.[43]

Certain core ideas for the figure of the king — and above all for the figure of the protagonist of "Der Tod in Venedig" (Death in Venice, 1912)
who measures himself against the king — were related to Schiller's treatise
Über Anmut und Würde (About Gracefulness and Dignity, 1793). In his
essay, Schiller speaks of a dignity that is "related to form and not to content." He defines it as an "example of the subordination of the sensual to the
ethical," which the law asks us to achieve despite our physical limitations.
Dignity can assure "that love does not turn into passion."[44] Goethe's account of the impact of Frederick's figure on the emergent German literature
of his time in *Dichtung und Wahrheit* (Poetry and Truth, 1811–14) also was
of decisive importance for Mann's projected novel. In Goethe's opinion
Frederick and the endeavor of the Seven Years' War had first introduced a
truly higher content into German literature.[45] In this connection Goethe
maintained that the "interior content" of the poetic object was decisive for

the beginning and end of all art, and that the "dignity of the material" ("Würde des Stoffes") is the criterion distinguishing a work of art ("Kunstwerk") from a mere artistic feat ("Kunststück").[46] Without expressly invoking Goethe's authority, Thomas Mann let his brother know that a subject that was to occupy him for years had to have a certain inherent dignity. Such dignity was a prerequisite for the creation of a "masterpiece."[47]

After reading the first volume of the king's posthumous works,[48] Goethe commented in a letter to Carl Ludwig von Knebel (1744–1834) that there was "something singularly remarkable" about the king.[49] Goethe's judgment of Frederick's personality was based on his idea of the "demonic," part of genius, especially when such a genius occupies an elevated position like Frederick or Peter the Great.[50] In Goethe's eyes, the demonic could not diminish the greatness of these figures. Schiller took a different view; he could not befriend such characters.[51] The difference in the way Goethe and Schiller looked at Frederick reflects the contrary impressions the king made on his contemporaries. In 1915, when Mann composed the essay "Friedrich und die große Koalition," he represented the king as someone influenced by the demonic. He found this idea and the repercussions it had for the king's behavior and decisions also in the literature he consulted.[52]

"Sometimes I have ambitious goals," Thomas Mann admitted to his brother Heinrich on 5 December 1905, when he casually announced his intention to write a "historical novel named 'Friedrich'": "Since I have been to Potsdam und Sanssouci twice, the figure of the king had grown on me in an exciting manner. And my latest literary encounter is Carlyle's 'Friedrich der Große' [. . .] a splendid book — even if Carlyle's idea of the heroic differs significantly from mine, as I already suggested in 'Fiorenza.'"[53]

Heinrich's reply is not preserved, but from Thomas's answer of 17 January 1906, it becomes clear that Heinrich must have expressed doubt.[54] His brother granted that his "historical instinct" was not well developed but argued that Heinrich underestimated the veracity of his image of Schiller. Thomas considered Schiller a predominantly subjective artist like Wagner. In *Fiorenza* he had been able to strike the "tone," the psychology of artistry, and that had astounded art historians. The arrogance in his undertaking was that he, the lyricist, wanted to represent greatness. Did he have experience in greatness? If he completed the novel on Frederick his merit would be having made greatness "palpable" ("fühlbar"), representing it "intimately and alive."[55] These passages from Mann's letter of 17 January 1906, reveal that his interest in Frederick II had less to do with historical correctness than with winning the competition with his older brother over literary pre-eminence.

Having learned from Nietzsche's "psychological radicalism,"[56] from the pamphlets by Brandes,[57] from Macaulay,[58] from Popper,[59] and above all from the much less famous but much more useful Paulig,[60] Mann believed himself equipped to continue the enterprise that Schiller had thought of embarking on many years before. However, the actual execution of the plan was delayed. First, Mann had to complete the novel *Königliche Hoheit*. Work on that novel gradually diverted resources from the Friedrich plan, as the collected material slowly became a treasure trove for *Königliche Hoheit*. More important was that working on the novel changed Mann's attitude toward Frederick; he began to consider the idea of a more socially oriented art. Mann's motto: "Dignity and love, — an austere happiness" ("Hoheit und Liebe, — ein strenges Glück"),[61] signaled the beginning of his farewell to the idea of "sympathy with death" ("Sympathie mit dem Tode").

This change of direction had consequences for a project in which love would have been given short shrift. Frederick's "greatness" had less to do with love than with ambition. His life was controlled by an overwhelming desire for fame, as the king's letter to Voltaire shows: "These are my [war] activities," he laments, "which I would gladly relinquish to someone else, if only this phantom called fame would not appear before me so often. In reality, all of this is a big foolishness, but a foolishness from which one has great difficulty escaping, once one has fallen for it."[62] Could the king's "foolishness," paid for dearly in three wars with heavy losses, make an acceptable topic for a novel about greatness? How would the "dignity of the material" fare in view of the questionable invasion of Silesia? Clearly, the subject was better suited for a polemical piece like Thomas Mann's wartime pamphlet, "Friedrich und die große Koalition."[63] Voltaire became Frederick's antagonist in the planned novel. While Mann shared Frederick's belief in the serious and hard-working German character and kept his identity in line with the king's, he assigned Heinrich to the company of the civilian Voltaire, a negative figure in the eyes of the Prussian king who "scorned" the French even though he enjoyed their "amusing literature."[64] Mann used this entry, dating from 1905, in his essay "Gedanken im Kriege" (Reflections in War, 1914), by which time he had already abandoned the Frederick novel. He deployed it there as a camouflaged response to Heinrich's essays "Geist und Tat" (1911) and "Voltaire — Goethe" (1910) which criticized leading German literary figures and their self-absorption; it found even Goethe wanting. One sentence from "Geist und Tat" seemed to be aimed at Thomas's *Königliche Hoheit*: "They took life as symbol for their own lofty experiences."[65] Mann cast Heinrich in the role of a civilian in the manner of Voltaire:

> Voltaire und the king: that is the great civilian and the great soldier always and forever.

> But, since we have this contrast before our eyes in national symbols, in the figures of the leading Frenchman and the German king — whose soul lives on in our souls now more then ever — the contrast gains national significance, revealing for the psychology of nations.[66]

The war and the tensions between the brothers had led Thomas into presenting the "Rousseauist" Heinrich as a "Voltairian," a type with whom he, Thomas, could identify as well. The roles became interchangeable.

Besides Schiller and Goethe, the novelist Theodor Fontane had a decisive influence on Mann's "Friedrich" project. Fontane held the Prussian king in high esteem, and Mann had recently encountered Fontane's figure Major Dubslav von Stechlin in the novel *Der Stechlin* (1897), a man who lived according to the "word and example" of the "great monarch 'comme philosophe'" and who saw the king as a "man above all who had ever achieved renown."[67] Mann's comments on Fontane's plan to write a historical novel on the "Likedeeler" — pirates of the fifteenth century with socialist ideals — in his essay "Der alte Fontane" (1910), mirror his own difficulties in executing his ambitious plan:

> Viewed calmly and with Fontane's kind of skepticism: the plan for the Likedeeler was a plan of ambition, which was recognized and discarded as such. Fontane had long been good in the art of limitation, sublime in the bourgeois sphere, had long been a secret voice as a novelist. For a few late months he dreamt of exposing what he had always been. Then, he was likely embarrassed over his vanity, found it perhaps even ridiculous to gather the old bones for the leap ahead and quietly rejected a project that was for him less new and different than he had initially thought. The case is more typical than meets the eye. His noble talents and desires had been long used for average subjects, ennobling them and raising them far beyond their sphere but recognizable as such only by the connoisseur. These talents and desires were now to reveal themselves even to the average reader when they were applied to a "worthy" object. But the stimulus of the contrast is lacking; the magic of secret artistry is missing, and a piece of work does not get done which was designed as a consequence [of his work as a whole] but proved itself superfluous in a deeper sense.[68]

What had happened to the author of the "Likedeeler" had also befallen the author of the "Friedrich" novel.

> Had the "Likedeeler" been written, we would today possess the historical novel of the highest poetical quality France possesses in "Salammbô," Belgium in "Ulenspiegel." It was not meant to be. Was the time not yet ripe? [. . .] This quiet fading of a task so new and elevated, so clearly envisioned; this quiet death of a conception of an exhilarating conception, promising immortality, makes one think.[69]

If the Frederick novel had come into existence, German literature might possibly have had a historical novel of the eighteenth century of "highest poetical quality." But the ambition to reach this goal faded with the dream.

After Mann had abandoned the Frederick plan he saw to it that the credit and "public" recognition for achieving what he had hoped for should go to a fictional doppelganger, the "author of the clear and powerful prose epic about the life of Frederick of Prussia," Gustav Aschenbach. Mann also attributed "Geist und Kunst" to him, the "passionate treatise" with the "power to categorize" and with "dialectical argumentation so impressive" that serious observers had set it next to Schiller's treatise about naive und sentimental poetry (*GW* 8, 450).

In order to preserve these projects now ground to a halt, Mann entrusted their execution to a hero modeled on the Prussian king. He instructed the narrator to establish rank: the novel about the king of Prussia was to form the brilliant beginning of the writer's career, the essay "Geist und Kunst" the crowning conclusion among the works of Aschenbach's maturity (*GW* 8, 450).

Notes

[1] *Thomas Mann an Ernst Bertram: Briefe aus den Jahren 1910–1955,* ed. Inge Jens (Pfullingen: Neske, 1960), 84, 285. June 6 was Thomas Mann's birthday. The book is in Thomas Mann's library in the Thomas Mann Archives; complete title: *Johann Müller's Briefe an seinen ältesten Freund in der Schweiz,* ed. J. H. Füßli (Zurich: Orell, Füßli und Compagnie, 1812). The recipient of the letters is Karl Viktor von Bonstetten (1745–1832).

[2] *Johann Müller's Briefe,* 197.

[3] Death is a place of rest. But to live means to act. One is permitted to rest only on one's laurels. Art is like a kiss that only the most tender and devoted lover grants to the heart.

[4] *Johann Müller's Briefe,* 26.

[5] *TM/HM,* 112.

[6] *Antimachiavell,* ed. Hans Floerke (Berlin: Deutsche Bibliothek n.d., [1925]), 103. (First published as: *Anti-Machiavel, ou Examen du Prince de Machiavel, avec des notes historiques et critiques,* à la Haye, chez Jean van Duren, Den Haag [1740]).

[7] The familiar German translation of Frederick's "domestique" or "serviteur" is "erster Diener."

[8] *GW* 9, 873. Mann's collected works (*GW* 1–13), will hereafter be cited in the text.

[9] *Nb* 2 (7–14), 148–49. On this point see Adolph Menzel's drawing in Franz Kugler, *Geschichte Friedrichs des Großen,* 5th ed. (Leipzig: Mendelssohn, 1901), 178.

[10] *GW* 12, 148. See T. J. Reed, *The Uses of Tradition* (Oxford: Oxford UP, 1996), 92–94.

[11] *Essays* 2, 242. The verses are stanza 7 from Platen's prologue to his epic poem *Die Abassiden* (1834).

[12] *Briefwechsel Thomas Mann — Karl Kerényi. Gespräch in Briefen,* ed. Karl Kerényi (Zurich: Rhein, 1960), 82.

[13] *Br* 1, 63.

[14] Friedrich R. Paulig, *Friedrich der Große, König von Preußen, Neue Beiträge zur Geschichte seines Privatlebens, seines Hofes und seiner Zeit,* 4th ed. (Frankfurt an der Oder: Paulig, 1902), 135.

[15] *Nb* 2 (7–14), 115.

[16] In 1903, while *Königliche Hoheit* was in the planning stage, Mann noted the following quotation from Pushkin as a motto for the novel: "Du bist Kaiser (Czar) — lebe allein!" (*Nb* 2 [7–14], 86).

[17] Frederick II to Voltaire on 23 December 1740, at the beginning of the first Silesian War from his camp at Herrendorf. *Briefwechsel Voltaire — Friedrich der Grosse,* ed. Hans Pleschinski (Zurich: Haffmans, 1992), 211.

[18] Frederick II to Jordan. From a source used extensively by Thomas Mann for the plan of his Frederick novel: Gustav Freytag, *Bilder aus der deutschen Vergangenheit,* vol. 4: *Aus neuer Zeit* (1740–1848); quoted here from the 30th ed. (Leipzig: Hirzel, 1913), 240.

[19] *TM/HM,* 105.

[20] *TM/HM,* 114.

[21] *TM/HM,* 117.

[22] Schopenhauer, *Paralipomena,* § 124. Arthur Schopenhauer, *Sämtliche Werke,* vol. 5, ed. Wolfgang Freiherr von Löhneysen (Stuttgart: Cotta, 1968), 287–88.

[23] Schopenhauer, *Die Welt als Wille und Vorstellung, Sämtliche Werke,* vol. 1, book 4, 490–540 (§§ 65–68). In § 64, vol. 1, 489, Schopenhauer approves of someone avenging the crime of an oppressor by murder, if one is prepared to be executed for one's deed.

[24] "Gehe man mir mit diesen großen Männern," *Richard Wagner an Mathilde Wesendonk, Tagebuchblätter und Briefe,* 1853–1871, ed. Wolfgang Golther (Berlin: Duncker, 1904), 185.

[25] *KSA* 5, 141, 147.

[26] *Antimachiavell,* 106, 109.

[27] Thomas Babington, Lord Macaulay, *Essays,* ed. Egon Friedell (Vienna: Rikola, 1924), 797. (English original: London: Longmans, Green and Co., 1889.) See Thomas Mann's notebook 9, *Nb* 2 (7–14), 153.

[28] Note for the unwritten essay "Geist und Kunst": "*Ibsen:* 'Das Große — ist es wirklich groß'" (The great — is it really great?), Hans Wysling, "'Geist und Kunst,'" *TMS* 1 (1968), 213. Ibsen, "Ballonbrief an eine schwedische Dame," Henrik Ibsen, *Sämtliche Werke in deutscher Sprache,* vol. 1, ed. Georg Brandes, Julius Elias and Paul Schlenther (Berlin: S. Fischer, 1905), 129: "Wie ein Zweifel ringt sich's los: / Ist dies Große wirklich groß?" Ibsen had contemplated Egyptian monuments with implied reference to Prussia.

[29] *TM/HM,* 113, 112.

[30] *Nb* 2 (7–14), 115.

[31] *TM/HM,* 81–88.

[32] Körner to Schiller, 14 December 1788, *Briefwechsel zwischen Schiller und Körner,* intro. Ludwig Geiger, 4 vols. (Stuttgart: Cotta, n.d. [1892]), 1: 261; Schiller to Körner, 10 March 1789, 2: 39; 28 November 1791, 2: 209.

[33] *TM/HM,* 112.

[34] Thomas Mann's claim in a letter to Max Rychner of 25 February 1955 that he did not know of Schiller's plan is a memory lapse. "Briefwechsel Thomas Mann — Max Rychner," *Blätter der Thomas Mann Gesellschaft Zürich,* vol. 7, ed. Hans Wysling. (Zurich: Thomas Mann Gesellschaft, 1967), 27, 28.

[35] Albert von Pfister, "Schiller als Kriegsmann," *Marbacher Schillerbuch: Zur hundertsten Wiederkehr von Schillers Todestag* (Stuttgart: Cotta, 1905), 65.

[36] Another work Mann consulted for the Frederick project also makes reference to Schiller's planned epic poem: Josef Popper (Lynkeus), *Voltaire: Eine Charakteranalyse, in Verbindung mit Studien zur Ästhetik, Moral und Politik* (Dresden: Carl Reißner, 1905), 15. The frontispiece has a note indicating Mann's ownership in his own hand: "Thomas Mann 1906"; the book contains numerous underlinings and marginal comments. In the section referring to Schiller's projected epic poem on the Prussian King, Mann underlined the name of his predecessor Schiller.

[37] Letter of 10 March 1789; *Briefwechsel Schiller — Körner,* 2: 40.

[38] Ibid. 2: 40.

[39] Ibid. 2: 40–41.

[40] *Br* 3, 455.

[41] "Von der so *nahen* Modernität dieses Sujets." *Briefwechsel Schiller — Körner,* 1: 263 (Schiller's emphasis).

[42] Ibid. 2: 40–41. Mann took account of these suggestions first in the novel *Königliche Hoheit.* The emphasis placed on social questions here is a first and temporary indication of the subsequent turn towards "Lebensfreundlichkeit" in Mann's ouevre. See Joachim Rickes, *Der sonderbare Rosenstock* (Frankfurt am Main: Lang 1998), esp. 232.

[43] See Anna Ruchat, *Thomas Manns Roman-Projekt über Friedrich den Grossen im Spiegel der Notizen. Editions and Interpretations* (Bonn: Bouvier, 1989), 159–67.

[44] Friedrich Schiller, *Sämtliche Werke,* eds. Gerhard Fricke and Herbert G. Göpfert, vol. 5 (Munich: Hanser, 1958–1959), 477, 482, 485.

[45] Johann Wolfgang Goethe, *Goethes Werke: Hamburger Ausgabe,* vol. 9, ed. Erich Trunz (Hamburg: Christian Wegner, 1955), 279.

[46] Ibid., 280.

[47] *TM/HM,* 115–16, 113.

[48] *Oeuvres posthumes de Fréderic II, Roi de Prusse.* Tome I: *L'histoire de mon temps* (1788).

[49] 25 October 1788 to Carl Ludwig von Knebel. In Johann Wolfgang von Goethe, *Briefe,* ed. Rudolf Bach (Munich: Hanser, 1958), 259.

[50] Goethe to Eckermann on 8 March 1831. In Thomas Mann's war pamphlet of 1914, "Gedanken im Kriege," the "Dämon" Frederick occupied the contrary position to Voltaire, the representative of "Vernunft" (*Essays* 1, 195).

[51] *Briefwechsel Schiller — Körner,* 2: 209.

[52] Admired by Carlyle, disliked by Macaulay, rejected by Popper, and excused by Freytag.

[53] *TM/HM,* 112.

[54] *TM/HM,* 113–17.

[55] *TM/HM,* 117.

[56] This expression is in Aphorism 209 of *Jenseits von Gut und Böse* (Beyond Good and Evil, 1886; Nietzsche, *KSA* 5, 140–42). It is perhaps an analogy to Brandes's concept of "Aristocratischer Radicalismus." Georg Brandes, *Menschen und Werke: Essays* (Frankfurt am Main: Rütten & Loening, 1894), 137.

[57] *Nb* 2 (7–14), 182–83.

[58] *Nb* 2 (7–14), 153.

[59] Popper, *Voltaire.*

[60] Paulig, *Friedrich der Große.* See Peter de Mendelssohn, *Der Zauberer: Das Leben des deutschen Schriftstellers Thomas Mann,* vol. 2, ed. Cristina Klostermann (Frankfurt am Main: S. Fischer, 1996), 1141.

[61] *GW* 2, 363. See also Thomas Mann's letter of 11 January 1910, to Kurt Martens (*Br* 1, 79–80).

[62] *Briefwechsel Voltaire — Friedrich,* 211. Frederick to Voltaire from his camp at Herrendorf after the invasion of Silesia on 23 December 1740.

[63] For two contrasting views on this essay, see Paul Ueding, "Thomas Mann und sein Heldenbild Friedrichs des Grossen, in *Neue Jahrbücher für das klassische Altertum, Geschichte und deutsche Literatur* 19 (1916), 416–23, and, more recently, Gerhard Kluge, "Friedrich, der König von Preußen, in Essays von Thomas und Heinrich Mann und der Bruderkonflikt," *TMJb* 12 (1999): 259–90.

[64] This opinion may be have been based on a letter of Frederick to Voltaire of 5 December 1742 in which he compares the manly Northerners with the Parisian life of joyfulness.

[65] Heinrich Mann, *Macht und Mensch: Essays* (Frankfurt am Main: Fischer Taschenbuch Verlag, 1989), 17.

[66] *Essays* 1, 195.

[67] Theodor Fontane, *Sämtliche Werke,* ed. Walter Keitel, vol. 6 (Munich: Hanser, 1964), 11. Portions of the novel had already appeared in the journal *Über Land und Meer* in 1897. For Mann's early acquaintance with *Der Stechlin* see Hans-Joachim Sandberg, "Gesegnete Mahlzeit(en): Tischgespräche im Norden," *TMJb* 15 (2002): 83–87.

[68] *Essays* 1, 140–41.

[69] *Essays* 1, 140.

Magic and Reflections: Thomas Mann's *The Magic Mountain* and His War Essays

Eva Wessell

Excellent Plans

ON 25 MARCH 1917, Thomas Mann wrote a letter to the Austrian literary historian and pacifist Paul Amann in which he reminisced about a
problem he had encountered with a particular project he had been working
on two years earlier, in 1915. The project, which had been under way since
July of 1913,[1] was a "slightly expanded short story"[2] with the title "Der
Zauberberg" (The Magic Mountain). In an earlier letter Mann had already
called it a "novel" (*DüD* 1, 455). He found himself unable to continue the
composition in 1915, he said in his letter to Amann, because the project had
threatened to become "intellectually unbearably overburdened."[3] Although
he continued to write on it intermittently,[4] it is quite certain that he put the
work down completely by January 1916 near what is today the chapter
"Hippe." Mann did not return to his project until three years later, in April
1919.[5] Still called *Der Zauberberg*, the novel was finally published in 1924,
eleven years after it had first been conceived.

By "intellectually overburdened," Mann could simply have meant that
his work had somehow attracted extraneous ideas that, while seemingly
fitting, threatened to weaken the plot or explode the form. Mann's compositions, as his first novel *Buddenbrooks* (1901) shows, always stood in close
relation to their historical time and place. The artist's special sensitivity to
life, his "seismographic awareness," the "secret alignment" of the "personal
to the factual" that enabled the artist to transform ordinary matter into
spiritual form ("Beseelung"),[6] all of these factors could help expand a theme
and make a project grow. In this case, the particular genre Mann had chosen
could also contribute to the material's growth. He remembered having
planned *Der Zauberberg* as a comedic prose work, a kind of "humoristic
complement" (*DüD* 1, 451) or "Satyrplay" (*GW* 11, 607) to the somber
and stylistically restrained novella "Der Tod in Venedig" (Death in Venice,
1912). Perhaps thinking of Dickens's novels, Mann expected the work to be
"comfortable" at the time (*DüD* 1, 451), and he called it "English-
humoristic expansive" when he thought about it later on (*GW* 11, 608). Yet

he managed to complete the novel in 1924 after all, despite its continuous growth and ample intrusions by contemporary ideas during the second work period. He acknowledged that the novel had become a "sponge," having taken in "all the experiences of the time" (*GW* 11, 395). So neither sheer volume, of whatever cause, nor the relaxed style could have been the reason why Mann had difficulties with the novel in 1915.

Some of the reflections about the porous nature of *Der Zauberberg* stem from an introduction to the novel that Mann gave at Princeton University in 1939. Here he also gave reasons why he was eventually able to pick up the work and continue with it after all: his work on the intervening "analytical-polemic work" (*GW* 11, 608), the long essay *Betrachtungen eines Unpolitischen* (Reflections of a Nonpolitical Man, 1918), had had a cleansing effect that relieved the novel project of extraneous material. At the time he began work on the essay, which would eventually extend to more than 500 pages, in November 1915, he had referred to it in more neutral terms as a "critical-essayistic" work (*DüD* 1, 630). It occupied him until April 1918 (*DüD* 1, 661).

By calling this new composition analytic and essayistic, while saying that it served to relieve his fictional project of extraneous material, Mann seems to say that non-fictional material is incompatible with fiction in a principal way. This is surprising, because Mann, who was influenced by Romantic synesthesia, Nietzsche's perspectivism, and modernist stylistic pluralism, rejected such divisions in principle.[7] Not only had he always written essays along with his fiction, he had inserted essayistic material right into a story, as the discussion about art in "Tonio Kröger" (1903) shows. *Der Zauberberg* itself has such an insert in the chapter "Strandspaziergang" (Walk by the Seashore). Yet, Mann often reflected on the different skills required for the two tasks. He equated the creation of fiction with physical work, a craft, a weaving or "braiding" of carpets,[8] or with the complex mathematical systematizing of musical composition (*GW* 11, 611). Nonfiction, by contrast, was for him "talking work" (*DüD* 1, 631). While fiction's persuasive power lay in the creation of lively images, nonfiction meant to persuade through critically distanced analysis. Both skills, however, are part of one artistic consciousness in Mann's eyes; the hand that "weaves" and the mouth that "talks" belong to one body, and the art produced shares essential features. Schopenhauer's idea of art as the sublime, as a magical *nunc stans* and a vehicle for successful detachment from the relentless Will, required that art — even essayistic prose works — be separate from the world and rely on a system of ideas and references governed by its own rules. The "intellectual" intrusions that Mann had spoken of had broken down the separation.

In his Princeton address, Mann defined the "analytic" or "essayistic" work that became *Betrachtungen* as "polemical," an aptly chosen term that defines the essayist's voice as well as the circumstance that led to *Betrachtungen* in the first place. In his letter of 25 March 1917, in which Mann relates his lack of progress on the *Zauberberg* project to Paul Amann, he says that the interruption came about "as the consequence of the war" (*DüD* 1, 457). Although the war may have been the overall cause of the interruption of his novel, it was not the conflict itself or its carnage that was directly to blame. The influx of problematic material came from a different source, one much closer to home: a non-fictional prose work that Mann himself had written during August and September of 1914, the essay "Gedanken im Kriege" (Reflections in War). The essay had appeared in the journal for German Bildungsbürger, *Neue Rundschau,* in November 1914 and was one of several war essays Mann wrote.[9] It was the controversy elicited by "Gedanken im Kriege," not the war itself, that set a series of events in motion which finally led Mann to abandon his novel a year later. Initially, he had even found useful material for his novel in the war's outbreak: in a letter to his publisher S. Fischer, Mann wrote on 22 August 1914, that the war had provided him with the "solution" for his story. Hans Castorp would leave the mountain at the beginning of the First World War and join the battle for Germany (*DüD* 1, 454).

At War

"Gedanken im Kriege" is an aggressive tract in defense of Germany's war effort in which Mann argues that the war is justified in order to defend Germany's unique culture and its right to determine its own political future. As Mann saw it, Germany's tradition had created a cultural model that was more patriarchal and organic — or, as he called it, "conservative" — than that of the liberal western democracies, especially France. This model was now threatened by Germany's adversaries who, having cast Germany in the role of a militaristic and backward nation, regarded the war as defending progress, enlightenment, and humanity. Although Mann severely chastised France and Great Britain for tearing Europe apart, setting up a bipolar order that allowed for no shades of gray, he counters in kind in "Gedanken im Kriege" by creating similar dichotomies, bundling ideas and labels conveniently with the help of such terms as "intellect" and "nature": while Germany's adversaries were rationalistic, but mediocre and cowardly, Germany embodied the creativity of nature, taste, genius, and valor (*Essays* 1, 188). This was an echo of Nietzsche's opposition between the creative man and the herd, and a reactivation of terms Mann had used since his acquaintance with Nietzsche's thought. Not even a month into the war, on 22 August 1914, Mann wrote to his publisher that the problem of "the dualism of intellect and nature," the confrontation between "civilized and demonic tendencies in man," ruled him completely and affected all his thinking and writing (*DüD* 1, 454).

While radical oppositions can invigorate art (and life), they limit options and block a more inclusive view of the world. Mann had experienced the downside of such intellectual strategies as early as 1910, when he involved himself personally in the defense of the literary critic Samuel Lublinski, who he felt had been slandered by the nonconformist critic Theodor Lessing (*Essays* 1, 112–18; 347–49). The controversy may have affected Mann's work; he planned to use the material for a story with the title "Ein Elender" (A Miserable One), which he did not write after all.[10] But even before the real-life disputation, he had found his writing impacted by confrontational positions in a work he wrote in 1907, the essay "Versuch über das Theater" (Reflections on the Theater), in which he had set out to measure the cultural significance of the stage and compare it to that of the novel. In comments regarding the essay, he not only admitted to a great difficulty keeping the categories apart, but also complained about a "dialectical condition" paralyzing him (*GW* 11, 714). A similar problem arose between 1909 and 1912, when Mann planned a sweeping evaluation of aesthetic form (with an eye on challenging Schiller's essay *Über naive und sentimentalische Dichtung,* 1796) that was to carry the title "Geist und Kunst" (Intellect and Art). Here the dialectic structure, rather than locking him in, collapsed instead, and the material went "out of control." Mann admitted in a published fragment that his "essayistic discipline" had been "insufficient" for the creation of a coherent composition (*Essays* 1, 158).

The use of the term discipline in connection with his writing reminds the reader that Mann had always regarded the creation of art as a struggle, as perseverance in the face of hardship, an ethical task similar to that of a soldier in combat. He had thus "lain in battle" with his material while writing the theater essay (*GW* 11, 714). His hero Aschenbach in "Der Tod in Venedig" was a similar combatant, one of the "moralists of achievement," a hero in the battle with the word (*GW* 8, 454). Yet while the focus in Aschenbach's case lay on the ethical dimension of this combat, wartime aligned the vocabulary with the new circumstances, sharpening the language into political rhetoric. At the end of August 1914 Mann readily agreed with an admirer that in "Der Tod in Venedig" lies "soldierly spirit" (soldatischer Geist) (*DüD* 1, 454); at the same time in "Gedanken im Kriege" he declares art to be equal to war ("mit großem Recht hat man die Kunst einen Krieg genannt") (*Essays* 1, 190). In "Gute Feldpost," Mann's next essay, he finds that the artist is linked in an allegorical relationship to the man in the trenches. The artist "lives like a soldier but not as a soldier" (*Essays* 1, 207). What was initially an ethical struggle, a battle with the self in the service of the work, is now not only turned outward, it is radicalized. Moral "achievement" becomes "moral radicalism" (*Essays* 1, 190). "Radical," from the Latin word *radix,* "root," means assuming an extreme position, be it for political change or for the status quo. The term "root" itself is telling: it shows the scope and depth of the possible impact of such a position. In the introduction to *Betrachtungen eines Unpolitischen,* where Mann surveys his completed work, trying to justify it to himself and his reader, he claims that the "foundation" of his entire existence had been affected (*GW* 12, 12).

Reflections

Mann interrupted his work on *Der Zauberberg* again in the fall of 1915 to begin writing *Betrachtungen eines Unpolitischen.* No clear signs point to a serious difficulty with his novel as yet. In October and December of 1915, already well into *Betrachtungen,* he looked ahead to a future that would bring progress on both novels, *Der Zauberberg* and *Die Bekenntnise des Hochstaplers Felix Krull* (The Confessions of Felix Krull, Confidence Man, 1954) (*DüD* 1, 456). *Betrachtungen* also progressed well. By the end of 1915 Mann had completed the text of what would become the first chapters, "Der Protest" and "Das unliterarische Land" (The Nonliterary Country); the beginning of 1916 saw him writing chapter three, "Der Zivilisationsliterat" (Civilization's Literary Man).[11]

In these early parts of *Betrachtungen,* Mann expands on the themes and dualisms he had worked up in "Gedanken im Kriege" and in the other war essays. But, mindful of his strong and acrimonious prose in those works, he had already begun in his correspondence to downplay his message with self-deprecatory comments. He now finds his war writings "purely journalistic"; they amount to "political and historical games."[12] In *Betrachtungen* itself also reigns a far more conciliatory tone, starting with attempts at justification. Mann enlists intellectual allies to shore up his ethos as a speaker and opens up with Dostoyevsky and his essay "The German Question" (1877).[13] Mann also faces personal criticism head on, quoting it in his text. He mentions "Gedanken im Kriege" and challenges the French novelist Romain Rolland's response to his war writings: Rolland had called him a "furious bull charging head down [. . .] into the matador's sword" (*GW* 12, 47).[14] Broadcasting insults like these carried risks. Although Rolland's voice was that of the enemy, he was a respected novelist whose voice carried weight. It also amounted to an admission that his war essay may not have been of the highest literary quality. But, by admitting Rolland's voice directly into his narrative, Mann creates a form of dialogue. The conversational element is enhanced by the colloquial language Rolland uses; the discourse becomes more informal and familial. The entire war is thus turned into something like a family brawl. Mann even uses the label "europäischer *Bruderzwist*" (fraternal conflict within Europe; Mann's italics) in this context, and reminds his adversary that only where there is communality, a "community of thoughts," can there be true animosity (*GW* 12, 47). This idea appears here in 1915 before Mann repeated it in a similar form in 1917 when the war had reached a stalemate (*GW* 12, 331). A field of mutuality seems to evolve, allowing for a plurality beyond the divisions. Mann recalls that Luther and Goethe had traveled to Rome (*GW* 12, 46); the verse by Molière that appears as an epigraph to the finished work, even appearing before the accompanying quotation from Goethe, strengthens the idea of an inter-European dialogue.

Zola

In the beginning of 1916, however, an event broke into Mann's routine that affected any self corrections that were under way. Mann's brother Heinrich had published an essay titled "Zola" in the November issue of the liberal-socialist journal *Die Weißen Blätter*.[15] Thomas read the essay between January and June of 1916; he marked up a borrowed copy of the journal profusely, a sure sign that he was very much engaged in the matters under discussion there.[16]

"Zola" was in a sense a continuation of two of Heinrich Mann's earlier essays, "Voltaire-Goethe" (also titled "Der Französische Geist," 1910) and "Geist und Tat" (Intellect and Action, 1911). In both essays Heinrich Mann had called for Germany's intellectuals and writers to work for political progress in a country that, in twentieth-century Europe, was still comfortable with authoritarian rule. Finding German writers and intellectuals aloof and in pursuit of abstract philosophical ideas while being absorbed by the veneration of great men, especially Goethe,[17] or — worse — colluding with the bourgeois elites and the nobility, Heinrich Mann urges in these essays that they use their talent to bring about social and political change, as French intellectuals and writers had done. Scathingly, he calls intellectuals who curry favor with the ruling caste traitors.[18] Now, in 1915, Heinrich Mann points to Émile Zola as the new model.

According to Heinrich Mann's essay, Zola's political engagement came about because Zola, incorporating naturalist and idealist-Romanticist aesthetics, held that literature and politics have one mutual interest and "goal": a nation and its people; hence, literature and politics "must penetrate one another" (einander durchdringen). Art and life respond to one another through mutually accommodating patterns. Art projects its form onto reality, and reality courts art through spontaneously organized models. The artist, and other intellectuals, can recognize these patterns and communicate them, thereby influencing and shaping events. In a message similar to that of his earlier essay "Geist and Tat," Heinrich Mann now asserts that "Intellect is the action that is performed in the service of man."[19]

Heinrich Mann not only holds up Zola as a model; his long essay traces the French novelist's life and work, pointing to a developmental arc: Zola had grown from an author purely engaged in art for art's sake to a political writer who was committed to the betterment of life for his nation. In the beginning, Zola had "despised the political trade."[20] But his early naturalistic works, such as *Thérèse Raquin* (1867), were followed by more ideologically and politically inspired novels like *La débâcle* (1892), or the "gospel of a future humanity," *Germinal* (1885).[21] Finally, Zola moved into active politics in connection with the most notorious incident of his time, the Dreyfus affair, by writing his open letter, "J'accuse" (1898). By casting Zola as a hero of a Bildungsroman, Heinrich Mann not only absolved Zola from his Romanticist beginnings, but he could also excuse his own grand-bourgeois, elitist beginnings in literature. In a way, and probably most galling to his brother Thomas, Heinrich's portrayal of Zola's development could be seen as reflecting Thomas's own path from a professed apolitical writer to the politically engaged essayist of the war essays — except that in Heinrich's eyes he engaged himself of course on the wrong and politically reckless side.

The "Zola" essay only lightly concealed that matters under discussion there had a direct relevance for Germany in 1915. Napoleon III had declared war on Prussia in 1870, causing the downfall of his empire; the French empire is thus an example for the German Empire under Wilhelm II. Zola became a model for what German intellectuals and writers ought to do, and Thomas Mann could not help but feel he was being addressed. The essay not only accused writers of having sold out to those in power, it accused them of having done so for nothing but personal ambition: to "shine and be recognized." Rather than serve, they wanted to rise to the status of "national poet."[22] While this was a stinging accusation in itself, Heinrich Mann also accused those writers of a grave lack of responsibility: Running along with the crowd, they insisted on cheering it on as their nation headed into a certain catastrophe.[23] This clearly referred to Thomas's war essays. Heinrich was one of the very few Germans at that time who foresaw the coming catastrophe.

Thomas Mann reacted to his brother's essay with a vehemence that seemed excessive when judged by his reserved standards, but was understandable. Mann understood himself as a writer who created from the core of his being, and thus he felt himself to be expressing the nation's thoughts and values. Challenging the authenticity of his being, its foundation or roots, meant challenging the authenticity of his work. The essay currently in progress thus became the platform on which Mann staged a counter-argument that resumed and exceeded the confrontational style of the war essays. Although he called it "Reflections of a Nonpolitical Man," the work was in fact entirely political. Germany's "conservatism," defended as something apolitical, was not only depicted as making intellectual and artistic freedom possible; it meant that creative freedom, both in art and life, was best protected by an administrative state legitimized by monarchical authority then in a republic where writers were constantly asked to argue politics. Such arguments addressed political concerns, and Mann openly admits that anyone defending his nation against seditious intellectuals cannot help but turn at least temporarily into a "politician" (*GW* 12, 57). That the work could be easily read as political can be seen by the eagerness with which conservative German "Bildungsbürger" appropriated it after 1918.[24]

Although Mann must have revised his original manuscript, the reader can still get an idea of the impact of "Zola" — and the consequent polarization of the essayist's voice — when examining the chapter "Der Zivilisationsliterat," which is at the juncture where the first references to the "Zola" essay appear. (Mann later dedicated a full chapter, "Gegen Recht und Wahrheit," to "Zola.") Mann's *Zivilisationsliterat* is a symbolic figure made to represent the popular democratic political values based on the European Enlightenment. By nature and persuasion he is opposed to German conservatism and its mysticism and heroic heritage. Although Mann declared the *Zivilisationsliterat* intellectually allied to France, he had also given him the label "noble" (edel) up to this point (*GW* 12, 56; Mann's italics). He still distinguished the intellectual who rises above nationalism from the mere political agitator. Just as in "Gedanken im Kriege," Mann was willing to find some fault with the German national character itself.[25] With the beginning of direct references to "Zola," however, the language grows more severe. The *Zivilisationsliterat* not only becomes a firm enemy of Germany, but Mann revokes his status as a national writer by suggesting he has lost his ability to communicate in his native language. Thinking in "French concepts" and in "antitheses," the *Zivilisationsliterat* cannot understand his country; using "French syntax and grammar," he can no longer speak for it (*GW* 12, 59–61). While Heinrich's "Zola" essay had shown the close relationship between a writer and his nation, *Betrachtungen* severs the link for Zola's villainous German counterpart. Such a move seriously polarizes the discussion and affects the entire work. Similarly strong oppositions dominate the following nine chapters: between speech and music ("Einkehr"), politics and the burgher mentality ("Bürgerlichkeit"), between the politician and the artist ("Politik"), between popular morality and virtue ("Von der Tugend"), between humanity and life ("Einiges über Menschlichkeit"), between faith and liberty ("Vom Glauben"), between and politics ("Ästhetizistische Politik"), and between intellectual tolerance and radicalism ("Ironie und Radikalismus").

And the Zauberberg?

Did Thomas Mann then simply lose his taste for enjoyment, unable or unwilling to continue with a comedic work in the midst of contentiousness? Was it that he could not rise above the dichotomies he and others had created, and that his novel threatened to turn into a tract much like *Betrachtungen* finally would? What if *Betrachtungen* had not been written, and the disputatious atmosphere of the post-"Zola" period had entered the novel? In that case, he might not have finished it at all, getting locked into a "dialectical condition" much like in "Versuch über das Theater," or his "discipline" might have failed him, much like in "Geist und Kunst." The antithetical scheme of the work itself and especially two figures, Ludovico Settembrini and the hero of the story, Hans Castorp, had the potential for becoming mouthpieces for their angry author.

Mann's comments about *Der Zauberberg* link the novel to a personal experience and to another of his works: In May and June of 1912 he had visited his wife Katia at a sanatorium for the treatment of tuberculosis in Davos, Switzerland. He was closing out his work on "Der Tod in Venedig" (published in June) at that time and, after returning initially to *Die Bekenntnisse des Hochstaplers Felix Krull,* he tells one of his correspondents in the following summer that he is now working on a new project, a "kind of countertext" to the Venice novella (*DüD* I, 451). Indeed, the main feature of "Der Tod in Venedig" is easily recognizable in the completed novel. A journey out of everyday existence leads to the protagonist's losing his previous sense of orientation through a love experience and to his physical and mental dissolution. While Aschenbach dies in the novella, the humoristic version of the story that is told in *Der Zauberberg* involves a protagonist who is not really sick and can leave the place of enchantment. Similar shifts in meaning render the later text farcical: the journey down to a luxury resort at the Lido shoreline near Venice now goes upward to an equally luxurious establishment in Davos, a hospital; the ocean turns into snow — although not entirely, as the chapter "Strandspaziergang" (Walk by the Seashore) shows —; the gondola becomes a sled or "music coffin" (*GW* 3, 907). Even insignificant details from the earlier work reappear as entries through glass doors or books that remain unread.[26] More complex is the change of the beloved from a boy to a woman, since she represents the memory of a pubescent boy in Hans Castorp's past.

The novel was meant to explore ideological oppositions. Mann gave an overview of his plan in a letter to Amann on 3 August 1915, describing how he planned to lead a young man through "intellectual oppositions" such as humanism and romanticism, progressive and reactionary thinking, health and illness, and to confront him with the tempting power of death. The experience was intended to leave no lasting mark; it was meant to be more informative than decisive (*DüD* 1, 455). In 1917 Mann, while still writing, fictionalizes the oppositions: his young man would be placed between a "latinist-talkative advocate of 'work and progress'" and a "desperate-intellectualistic reactionary figure" (*DüD* 1, 457). In the first case, he was referring to the Italian man of letters and advocate of Enlightenment values Ludovico Settembrini; in the second to a certain Pastor Bunge, a "mystic, reactionary, and champion of irrationalism." The pastor would in the later stages of the work change into the Jesuit Naphta,[27] and a Dionysian figure, Mynheer Peeperkorn, representing Nietzsche's cult of Life as a parody, would be added. The fictional arrangement of the novel avoids a final commitment. It was thus compatible with the initial part of *Betrachtungen*, with its review of values and its emphasis on mutuality, but not with the contentious and seriously ideological tract that *Betrachtungen* finally became.

Settembrini and the *Zivilisationsliterat*

The figure most affected by the "Zola" essay and Mann's reaction to it was the one who most closely resembled the *Zivilisationsliterat*, Settembrini. "Droll" (schnurrig, *GW* 12, 424) and "comical" (*DüD* 1, 495), Settembrini's role was to counter Castorp's slothful behavior and his keen interest in the married and unwholesome but attractive Clawdia Chauchat. Settembrini was indeed part of the original conception, as preserved early pages of the manuscript reveal.[28] Settembrini is a many-layered figure from the beginning: he is presented as positive when he represents the bourgeois values of work and tries to reduce Madame Chauchat's impact on Castorp; but in regard to his engagement in the politics of progress he is seen as negative. The latter feature puts him in close proximity to the *Zivilisationsliterat* of *Betrachtungen*, something Mann acknowledged when it suited him. In a diary entry of 1919 he admits that Settembrini's lectures on the virtue of politics, although not taken seriously, represent the "only morally positive momentum in the novel, opposing the fascination with death."[29] In 1920, when Mann began to move closer to supporting a republican form of government for Germany, Mann claimed that the "Civilisationsliterat" [*sic*] appeared "personally" in his novel (*DüD* 1, 461). In 1939 Mann even played with the idea that Settembrini might represent his own "voice" (Mundstück) (*GW* 11, 613).

How Mann managed to address features that the two figures shared while still keeping them apart, can be observed with reference to *Betrachtungen*, specifically the juncture following his reading of "Zola," when Mann addresses war as a means of revolution. The *Zivilsationsliterat* and Settembrini — and Zola himself — are all pacifists except when war seemed to promote political progress, in which case they all opportunistically sanctioned armed conflict. The Franco-Prussian War had brought the end of Napoleon III's empire for France; a new war would now end the Wilhelminian state. Mann quotes from "Zola" Heinrich Mann's label for the revolutionary spirit that he says drives all political activists: "determined love of humanity" (entschlossene Menschenliebe), which sometimes makes war necessary.[30] Mann points out features of language that again show the *Zivilisationsliterat's* alienation from his culture: he justifies a German defeat by reading "beaten" and "converted" as synonyms (*GW* 12, 62). A defeated Germany would thus automatically join the Western nations linguistically and ideologically.

Settembrini does not reject war either, but he remains loyal to his country despite his internationalism. While Italy's liberal intellectuals, among them the Freemasons, are said in *Betrachtungen* to be ideologically aligned with the Western democracies, Settembrini, their representative in the novel, and himself a Freemason, is a supporter of nationalism. Settembrini advocates attacking Austria because of old enmities between the two nations (*GW* 3, 222, 530). When Settembrini approves Hans Castorp's departure for the war at the end of the novel, he sends him off to fight among those of his "blood," and he himself plans to employ his literary skills to "pull his own country into battle" (*GW* 3, 989). Settembrini's internationalism, contrary to that of the *Zivilisationsliterat,* is balanced by pride in his nation. Although he speaks German "without foreign accent" (*GW* 3, 83), a sign of his internationalism, he does not downgrade his national culture but shares it with others, a testament to his loyalty to Italy. Settembrini had published an obituary for the Italian poet Giosuè Carducci in a German newspaper (*GW* 3, 85), while the *Zivilisationsliterat* glorified French writers in Germany. Settembrini does not become the *Zivilisationsliterat.*

The early chapter "Das Unliterarische Land" in *Betrachtungen* sets up a dichotomy between the literary humanism of classical Latin culture and a stubborn and silent, perhaps even morally less trustworthy, musical culture represented by Germany. The ideas draw on Schopenhauer's philosophy, which connects music with the irrationality of the Will and with pessimism. Because the *Zivilisationsliterat* sees in Germany's musical tradition a psychological and emotional block against the optimistic Enlightenment tradition of progress, he connects music with political quietism. The Settembrini figure in the novel also claims greater respect for the word, finding music "politically suspect" (similarly to Mann's apologetic stance in the early parts of *Betrachtungen*) (cf. *GW* 12, 50–51 with 3, 160, 62). Yet he also confesses to be a sincere admirer of music. Settembrini is, of course, Italian, and a close relationship to music is a national trait. Music, like war, can be something positive in the context of a national culture. When Settembrini encounters the cousins attending a concert, he justifies their listening pleasure by calling it — together with beer and tobacco! — in tune with the "national mood" of their country (*GW* 3, 159). Again, Settembrini's approach is balanced while the *Zivilisationsliterat* wants to end Germany's special relationship with music altogether ("Finis musicae," *GW* 12, 39). Settembrini can accept music more readily, because despite its difference from verbal reasoning, music is built on form. Music proceeds in linear order; it follows the pulse of time; it measures it out and can thus initiate action in a similar way as rhetoric can. By allowing for music's role in culture, although with the strong warning that it must be accompanied by language lest it become "dangerous" (*GW* 3, 161), Settembrini again rejects a monolithic view of the world and remains a multi-dimensional character.

Hans Castorp and Germany

Unlike the Settembrini figure, which has much in common with the *Zivilisationsliterat* in *Betrachtungen,* Hans Castorp, the central character in the story, is not as vulnerable to distortion by polemics because he has no complement in *Betrachtungen.* Or, does he? What could quite easily distort the figure of Castorp is his representative status. Castorp was initially conceived as a contrast figure to the artist Aschenbach and might have been no more than an ordinary citizen, simple but appealing (*GW* 3, 9). But almost from the beginning Mann spoke of his novel as something readable, something with "many-layered intentions" (*DüD* 1, 452). Pointing to his novel as being pedagogical and political (*DüD* 1, 455, 57), Mann suggests early on that Castorp's fate might exceed the limited dimension of a private person: Castorp began to represent Germany itself. After the publication of *Der Zauberberg* in 1924, Mann discussed his figure with a journalist. He stressed Castorp's unwillingness to commit to a firm ideological position and called him "profoundly" German.[31] Mann may refer to Germany's location in the center of the European continent, but he had defended both political and aesthetic nonalignment as the essential German characteristic in all his war essays. Late in *Betrachtungen* Mann admits that the day had come for him when it became clear that a given orientation implied a certain political attitude, at least latently. "Nobody" could avoid addressing this political correlate, especially not in such circumstances as wartime[32] Was Hans Castorp, or could he have become, that political correlative? Perhaps not. Castorp's intellectual independence in the novel is guaranteed by the wit and cleverness with which he resists all his educators. This was in accordance with Mann's plan of 1915, in which he states that he wants Castorp's education to be "more informative [. . .] than decisive" (*DüD* 1, 455). And later, when Mann wrote the chapter "Schnee" in 1923, he had Castorp's insights into the inner workings of human understanding and morality remain inconclusive and without consequence. This might not have been the case in 1916, had Mann gone forward with the novel: at that point he might have been tempted to use his novel to present a political agenda or vision.

The chapter "Schnee" has Hans Castorp, on skis, undertaking the climbing of a mountain where (encouraged by some port, not beer) he has a dream about an Arcadian settlement filled with young and happy people. But he also finds a temple in its center where witches kill and devour children. The dream shows the beautiful and the horrid coexisting. Castorp concludes that these two radical expressions of his vision belong together and must be kept in balance. What he has seen validates his conviction that the "other half" always needs keeping in mind: life and death, spirit and nature, health and sickness; in the middle is where man, "Homo Dei," has his place (*GW* 3, 684–86).

But the temple Castorp views is located within the community, not next to it, suggesting that the beautiful and the horrid do not simply coexist but may form a whole. Such ideas suggest a form of synthesis. Castorp concludes as much when he asks himself if perhaps the young people were so polite and friendly to one another *because* of the horror in their midst? (*GW* 3, 684–85, my emphasis). They had created their community through transcendence, by mastering the contradictions ("der Mensch ist der Herr der Gegensätze," *GW* 3, 685). Mann himself had thought early on of ways to move beyond divisions by forging a kind of synthesis. In his second war essay, "Brief an die Zeitung 'Svenska Dagbladet'" (April/May 1915), he had suggested a "synthesis of power and intellect" (Macht und Geist) (*Essays* 1, 274). By that he meant the fusion of the Wilhelminian empire with the nationalist spirit of 1813, when Napoleon was defeated in the Battle of Nations in Leipzig, and the revolutionary fervor of 1848. In *Betrachtungen* Mann later played with the idea of a Romantic republic he called a "people's state" (Volksstaat) (*GW* 12, 245, 272) where innovation would enhance tradition, and where the monarchy would be retained as a "corrective force" (*GW* 12, 260).

To infuse his novel with a message, to let it culminate in a vision for Germany must have been tempting. Mann had expressed a general disappointment in the content of his production already in 1913, barely into the writing of *Der Zauberberg*.[33] It was a worry that did not leave him; it intensified after the war.[34] The tale of the amicable Hans Castorp, a young man, fond of good food, leisure, detachment, and involved with married women, who whiled away his time in a foreign country, could not compete with the nationalistic tales his brother had discovered in Zola's works. Such feelings may explain Mann's later tendency to agree with people who elevated Hans Castorp to a quester hero or called the *Zauberberg* an "initiation story" or a Bildungsroman in the great tradition of Goethe's *Wilhelm Meister* (1795–96).[35] As late as 1925 Mann still thought that his novel should have ended with the chapter "Schnee" (*DüD* 1, 509), perhaps because it at least suggested the possibility of a positive message, balancing the mood of decadence in the novel.

Mann's feelings that his novel might lack weight were probably compounded by the fear that it would send a negative message. He admitted in fearful moments that his "peculiar Bildungsroman" did not point to a way out of the decline (*DüD* 1, 465). The lack of commitment, the humorous treatment of modern society's intellectual conflicts, might have been interpreted not as a sign of tolerance but as nihilistic. Mann admitted as much in the earliest stages of the writing when he called the mood permeating his novel "humoristic-nihilistic" (*DüD* 1, 455). Yet he does not use the term nihilistic in its generally accepted meaning as the denial of all objective truths but rather as the acceptance of all in tolerance. Modernist and indebted to Nietzsche's perspectivism, Mann's form of nihilism transcends divisions without erasing them but also without falling prey to relativism. The human mind, as Hans Castorp concludes in his own personal visit to the mountain, can rise above the dualities and the conflicts and manage the interplay of all with the help of "goodness and love" (*GW* 3, 686). But the question mark Mann puts at the end of his novel, and Castorp's slide into a silent "contrariness" (Widerspenstigkeit) (*GW* 3, 715) rather than seeking to moderate his educators' increasingly severe and finally deadly altercations, also raise doubt about such a hopeful turn.

Yet the unresolved conflicts, the juxtaposition of ideas, and the lack of a definite message made the novel a success. Mann had not allowed contemporary events, anger, or frustration, to change his plan: to present a humorous account of Germany's tradition of nonalignment. Hans Castorp refused to become indoctrinated by his teachers; he remained loyal to Schubert's melancholy song. Yet the novel's ending, where Castorp is depicted singing that song in the trenches of the First World War also questions the legitimacy of this attachment and its value for the future. As the boot of the young Castorp grinds the hand of a fallen comrade into the mud in that scene, as a "fountain of soil, fire, iron, lead, and torn humanity" spews into the air (*GW* 3, 993), the reader cannot help but read the novel as an indictment of war itself and anyone who promoted war, including Thomas Mann, the writer of the war essays. Does *Der Zauberberg* then contain a message after all? Is the book an anti-war novel? Mann does not commit himself. The battlefield scene on the final pages of the novel — a human foot crushing a human hand, two bodies "mingled and vanished" (*GW* 3, 993) — presents images that resemble the kind of disintegration of order Mann had claimed to have experienced in his struggles to write essays before and during the war: compulsive absorption in divisive "dialectical" thinking (*GW* 11, 714) and "furious partisanship" (*GW* 12, 11) had defeated all hope for a balanced, coherent, and meaningful composition. That included *Die Betrachtungen eines Unpolitischen*, which Mann called, after he had finished it in 1918, a mere "volume," hesitating even to give it the label "work" or "book" (*GW* 12, 9), although he had filled over five hundred pages with his writing. But when *Der Zauberberg* appeared in 1924, still true to its original conception, it signaled that the long essay had been successful after all. It had made the novel possible.

Notes

[1] *DüD* 1, 451. The three volumes of *Dichter über ihre Dichtungen* will hereafter be documented in the text with the abbreviation *DüD*, volume, and page number. For literature on *Der Zauberberg* see: *A Companion to Thomas Mann's "The Magic Mountain,"* ed. Stephen D. Dowden (Columbia, SC: Camden House, 1999); Hans Wysling, "Der Zauberberg," *Thomas-Mann-Handbuch*, ed. Helmut Koopmann

(Stuttgart: Kröner, 1990), 397–422; *Thomas Mann's Magic Mountain,* ed. Harold Bloom (New York: Chelsea House, 1986).

[2] *GW* 11, 606–7. Mann's collected works (*GW* 1–13) will hereafter be cited in the text.

[3] "Und die Betrachtungen muß ich nur deshalb schreiben, weil infolge des Krieges der Roman sonst intellektuell unerträglich überlastet worden wäre" (*DüD* 1, 457). Mann's letters to Amann are translated in *Thomas Mann: Letters to Paul Amann 1915–1952,* ed. Herbert Wegener, trans. Richard and Clara Winston (Middletown: Wesleyan UP, 1960).

[4] Compare entries in Mann's notebooks 9 and 10 (*Nb* 7–14) and see Herbert Lehnert, "Anmerkungen zur Entstehungsgeschichte von Thomas Manns 'Bekenntnisse des Hochstaplers Felix Krull,' 'Der Zauberberg' and 'Betrachtungen eines Unpolitischen,'" *Deutsche Vierteljahresschrift für Literaturwissenschaft und Geistesgeschichte* 38 (1964): 267–72; Heinz Sauereßig, "Die Entstehung des Romans 'Der Zauberberg,'" *Besichtigung des Zauberbergs,* ed. Heinz Sauereßig (Biberach: Wege und Gestalten, 1974), 5–53.

[5] *Tb* 8 April 1919.

[6] *Tb* 3 March 1920; *GW* 12, 80; *Essays* 1, 40–41. Mann's *Essays* (1–6) will hereafter be cited in the text. Cf. also *GW* 11, 385: "Man gibt das Persönlichste und ist überrascht, das Nationale getroffen zu haben. Man gibt das Nationalste — und siehe, man hat das Allgemeine und Menschliche getroffen."

[7] See *Essays* 1, 21–24; *GW* 13, 519–20 and Stephen D. Dowden, *Sympathy with the Abyss: A Study in the Novel of German Modernism: Kafka, Broch, Musil, Thomas Mann* (Tübingen: Niemeyer, 1986), esp. 1–16. See also Richard Exner, "Roman und Essay by Thomas Mann: Probleme und Beispiele," *Schweizer Monatshefte* 24 (1964–65): 243–45.

[8] *DüD* 1, 455. The English term "playwright" for an author of stage works, derived from the Old English *wyrhta* or *wryhta,* meaning worker or maker, captures this idea well.

[9] The others are "Gute Feldpost" (Good News from the Front, 1914), "Friedrich und die große Koalition" (Frederick and the Great Coalition, 1915), and an editorial piece for a Swedish newspaper in response to a questionnaire, "Brief an die Zeitung 'Svenska Dagbladet,' Stockholm," 1915.

[10] There is a reference to "Ein Elender" in "Der Tod in Venedig" (*GW* 8, 455).

[11] For the genesis of the essay see Hermann Kurzke, "Betrachtungen eines Unpolitischen," 681–84, and Hermann Kurzke, "Die politische Essayistik," 696–706, both in the *Thomas-Mann-Handbook,* ed. Helmut Koopmann (Stuttgart: Kröner, 1990); and Hermann Kurzke, "Die Quellen der 'Betrachtungen eines Unpolitischen.' Ein Zwischenbericht," *TMS* 7 (1987), 291–310. See the list of Mann's works for the English translation.

[12] *Br.* 1, 113, 117.

[13] Cf. Ülker Gökberk, "War as Mentor: Thomas Mann and Germanness," *A Companion to Thomas Mann's* "The Magic Mountain," ed. Stephen D. Dowden (Columbia, SC: Camden House, 1999), esp. 63–65.

[14] Rolland had published a collection of antiwar essays under the titel *Au-dessus de la mêlée* in 1915, which Mann had read. See also T. J. Reed, *Thomas Mann. The Uses of Tradition,* 2nd. ed. (Oxford: Clarendon, 1996), 189–90.

[15] Heinrich Mann republished "Zola" in his essay collection *Macht und Mensch* (Munich: Kurt Wolff Verlag, 1919), 35–131. An edited version, missing some of the sharp comments Thomas could have read as directed against him, appeared in 1931 and was republished in Heinrich Mann, *Essays* (Berlin: Aufbau-Verlag; Hamburg: Claassen, 1960), 154–240. Citations here follow the original version as printed in *Macht und Mensch.*

[16] Mann borrowed the journal from Heinrich Mann's lawyer Maximilian Brantl; cf. Mann's letters of 31 December 1915 and 18 June 1916 (*Br.* 1, 124, 127).

[17] Heinrich Mann meant first of all his brother's admiration for Goethe. In the background is Nietzsche's verdict "Das *Ziel der Menschheit* kann nicht am Ende liegen, sondern nur *in ihren höchsten Exemplaren*" (Nietzsche's emphasis). Friedrich Nietzsche, "Vom Nutzen und Nachteil der Historie," No. 9 (The Use and Abuse of History, 1874), *KSA* I, 317.

[18] "Ein Intellectueller, der sich an die Herrenkaste heranmacht, begeht Verrat am Geist." Heinrich Mann, "Geist und Tat," *Essays,* 14.

[19] "Geist ist die Tat, die für den Menschen geschieht." Heinrich Mann, "Zola," 98; cf. "Geist and Tat," 14.

[20] "In seinen Anfängen hat er das politische Handwerk verachtet" (Heinrich Mann, "Zola," 98).

[21] Heinrich Mann, "Zola," 88.

[22] "Aber ihr seid nicht zu dienen da, sondern zu glänzen und aufzufallen [. . .] Durch Streberei Nationaldichter werden für ein halbes Menschenalter, wenn der Atem solange aushält" (Heinrich Mann, "Zola," 114–15).

[23] Heinrich Mann, "Zola," 115.

[24] In November 1920 the University of Bonn awarded Thomas Mann an honorary doctorate, pointing mostly to *Buddenbrooks.* But praise for *Betrachtungen eines Unpolitischen* and Mann's special contribution to the political enlightenment of the youth abound. Cf. Paul Egon Hübinger, *Thomas Mann, die Universität und die Zeitgeschichte. Drei Kapitel deutscher Vergangenheit aus dem Leben des Dichters 1905–1955* (Munich: Oldenbourg, 1974).

[25] Cf. *Essays* 1, 204–5 with *GW* 12, 58.

[26] For a detailed comparison of the two texts see T. J. Reed, "*Der Zauberberg.* Zeitenwandel and Bedeutungswandel 1012–1924," *Besichtigung des Zauberbergs,* ed. Heinz Sauereßig (Biberach: Wege und Gestalten, 1974), 84–89.

[27] *Tb* 14, 16, 17 April 1919 and 2 May 1919.

[28] The manuscript pages are now at Yale University. They are printed and annotated in *The Yale Zauberberg-Manuscript. Rejected Sheets once Part of Thomas Mann's Novel,* ed. James F. White, *TMS* 4 (1980); Hans Wißkirchen, "'Ich glaube an den Fortschritt, gewiß.' Quellenkritische Untersuchungen zu Thomas Mann's Settembrini-Figur," *Das Zauberberg-Symposium 1994 in Davos,* ed. Thomas Sprecher. *TMS*

11 (1994), 81–115. See also Mann's statement: Settembrini belonged to the "original conception" (*DüD* 1, 495).

[29] *Tb* 14 November 1919.

[30] Cf. *GW* 12, 63, with "Zola," 96.

[31] "Sobald Settembrini in ihn dringt, geht er, nicht ohne Schalkhaftigkeit, der Entscheidung aus dem Wege. Diese Haltung scheint mir der Zwischenstellung Deutschlands zu entsprechen — und in sofern ist etwas zutiefst Deutsches in Hans Castorp" (*DüD* 1, 506). See also Christian Gloystein, *"Mit mir aber ist es was anderes." Die Ausnahmestellung Hans Castorps in Thomas Manns Roman "Der Zauberberg"* (Würzburg: Königshausen & Neumann, 2001).

[32] "Es kam der Tag, wo sich erwies, daß einer bestimmten seelisch-geistigen Verfassung eben doch eine bestimmte politische Haltung latent innewohnt oder von weitem entspricht, die einzunehmen unter Weltumständen wie den gegenwärtigen niemand umhin kann" (*GW* 12, 425).

[33] *TM/HM*, 166–67. Heinrich and Thomas Mann's letters are translated in *Letters of Heinrich and Thomas Mann, 1900–1949*, ed. Hans Wysling, trans. Don Reneau with add. trans. Richard and Clara Winston (Berkeley: U of California P, 1998).

[34] In September 1918 he found that the work reflected a "moribund Romanticism" but also said "yes to life" (Todesromantik plus Lebensja) (*DüD* 1, 459), but in October the diary shows Mann concerned about "the ending" of the novel, which he had planned to be the outbreak of the war in 1914 (Tb 14 October 1918; *DüD* 1, 454). In 1921, he agonized over *Der Zauberberg's* political relevance and lack of life-affirming message (*DüD* 1, 465).

[35] *GW* 11, 615; *DüD* 1, 470, 72. In 1922 Mann called Hans Castorp his "Wilhelm Meisterchen" (*DüD* 1, 471).

Thomas Mann's "Autobiographical" Stories

Helmut Koopmann

"ALL OF IT IS AUTOBIOGRAPHY."[1] Thomas Mann made this claim in the foreword to his late essay collection *Altes und Neues* (Old and New, 1953).[2] It applies to all of his work. Yet it is significant that Mann never embarked upon a more extensive autobiography than he did in his two essays "Lebensabriss" (Sketch of my Life, 1930) and *Die Entstehung des Doktor Faustus* (The Story of a Novel: The Genesis of Doctor Faustus, 1949). In 1950, in the lecture "Meine Zeit" (My Time), he told us quite clearly why: "It is true, I have been asked occasionally to tell my life's story, to make *one* book out of the many for which I have used my life as rootstock. But, I have given in to such suggestions only occasionally by telling friends, or myself, of the origin of this or that piece of work. Perhaps, I don't love my life sufficiently to be an autobiographer" (*Essays* 6, 160, Mann's italics).

Why did Mann believe he was not suited to write autobiographies, when he had constantly used his life as material for his texts? He explained it in the same context, speaking of "his life" in the third person: "The production of a lifetime, from its beginning to the approaching end, had been the result of an anxious desire to make amends, of a craving for cleansing and justification" (*Essays* 11, 302). This wish is of an arch Protestant nature. In Thomas Mann's eyes his life needed justification. Mann was a person who carried with him the awareness, if subliminally, that his life was questionable and not progressing as it should. His was not an unchristian life, but it was flawed enough to burden him with the awareness that it might be wanting; insights like these might even have included feelings of sinfulness. If we take these sentences seriously, not only Mann's essayistic work but his entire oeuvre must be considered autobiographical in the sense that it seeks some form of justification. Mann never put any obstacles in the way of his readers, should they wish to discover in his works their author and his problems: his self, his experiences, and his problematic relationship with the world — and with himself.

Even though Mann consistently talked about himself in his works, he did not like to do so expressively. "I ask you," he said in the lecture "My Time" quoted above, "not to forget that I am saying all this in order to explain my objection to writing autobiography, I mean my reluctance to use my life directly as object of my writing and lecturing" (*Essays* 6, 161). As a result, he wrote about himself in his early years, but only through deflecting his wishes, hopes, and anxieties on fictional characters and depositing them into imagined stories, thus camouflaging what was personal. Starting around 1910, he began to depict the historical period in which he had lived and which he had shared with others. But the veil of this "historical" representation is so thin that the author's contours shimmer continuously through its weave. The reader recognizes with ease that Thomas Mann is writing about himself, yet pretending to write about other people, events, and objects.

Mann wrote in 1913 in a foreword to an autobiographical fragment by the novelist Erich von Mendelssohn, something that turned out to be crucial for the understanding of his own work:

> "Love of oneself," said an author whose name I do not remember — it was a clever author, that much is certain — "love of oneself is always the beginning of a fictionalized existence." Love of oneself, one may add, is also the beginning of all autobiography. The drive to fixate one's life, to show how one became what one is, to celebrate one's life experience in a literary text — and thereby passionately to engage the sympathy of present and future readers — is based on the same lively self image that, according to this author, not only turns life into a novel on a subjective level, but elevates it objectively to an interesting and meaningful one. The result is not mere "conceit" but something powerful, more profound, and more productive.[3]

The author whose name Thomas Mann could not remember was Oscar Wilde. By quoting from memory, he changed a *bon mot* from one of Wilde's plays. Wilde's original wording has a different meaning: "To love oneself is the beginning of a lifelong romance."[4]

No one would deny Mann a vivacious love of self. But how can such a love of self be reconciled with his reluctance to compose autobiographies directly, a reluctance explained by a need for amends? In Mann's view writing about oneself can only be justified if one's life becomes "objectively" interesting and meaningful, if the ego outgrows the confines of its private existence by representing something universal. In the foreword to Mendelssohn's fragment, Mann had tried to explain why the autobiographical piece by the young writer who had died so early had attained such universal meaning.

Mann's remarks as quoted above help us to understand some seemingly autobiographical narratives where Mann depicts himself, his inclinations, wishes, difficulties and fears, but where the character seems to exceed a mere self portrait. There is a tension in all of Mann's work: on the one hand, there is the strong desire to talk about himself, an internal need to confess and to externalize his personal experience — perhaps a craving to liberate himself through writing about his life's events. On the other hand, there is an aversion to direct autobiographical confessions, a resistance to reporting too narrowly on his immediate self. This aversion endures despite Mann's ability to distance himself from his own ego and even to criticize it. What is autobiographical in his writings is always connected to the time-period in which he lived, while, conversely, this time-period, its outside world, is always mirrored in his very personal experience. This is not only true of his late works but also of his early novels and stories.

Despite this general reluctance, Mann occasionally took "material" for his narratives from his own life. "Wie Jappe und Do Escobar sich prügelten" (The Fight Between Jappe and Do Escobar) is one of several such "autobiographical" stories. Bearing the subtitle "Novelle," it appeared first in the journal *Süddeutsche Monatshefte* in 1911. Mann included it in his story collection *Das Wunderkind: Novellen* (The Infant Prodigy, 1914). It appeared again in 1922 in the first volume of *Novellen* contained in Mann's first set of *Collected Works*, which he himself assembled. Mann did not distinguish clearly between "Erzählung" (story) and "Novelle" (novella) in his early years. Various other designations for stories appear in his works: "Skizze" (Sketch), "Studie," "Anekdote," "Idylle," "Legende," "Geschichte" (History), "Kurzgeschichte" (short story). During his early career, the designation "Novelle" prevails. Given the title, the reader might expect an "extraordinary, unheard-of event" as Goethe had defined the novella,[5] perhaps the report of a duel, but the event turns out to be a fight between two fifteen-year-olds.

One of the combatants, Jappe, comes from the German middle class, the other, Do Escobar, is an "exotic stranger" (*GW* 8, 429) who leads a "disorderly but idyllic existence." The altercation had happened accidentally. "When strolling past each other," the boys had perhaps "merely touched each other's shoulders" and had, in their fixation on honor, "made a *casus belli* of the event" (*GW* 8, 430). The reader does not learn of the exact motivation for the struggle, but may assume that a girl, the object of both boys' desire, was to blame. While the circumstances sink into oblivion, the duel itself becomes a serious matter because of the formalities governing such encounters. Readers of "Tonio Kröger" (1903) know the referee: he is the ballet-master Knaak from Hamburg who instructs youngsters of better society in dance and manners. Knaak's "relationship with militant and decidedly manly young people" (*GW* 8, 435) is a difficult one. He is not part of a group that now relies on his judgment. While in the center of events, he remains a suspicious figure; his authority is questionable.

The fistfight is narrated phase by phase as the "mobile Southerner" meets the "German bear" (*GW* 8, 440). The latter wins, and the conflict ends in a honorable manner. The entire adventure comes to a close when no one volunteers for additional combat and dance-and-manner-master Knaak bows out as well, claiming that he has enjoyed his share of beatings in his own past. The affair of honor, having ended in mere play, is over, and the story ends as well. The "mobile Southerner," Do Escobar, is left without serious injury, though bleeding.

Fights are no rarity in Thomas Mann's novellas. "Der Weg zum Friedhof" (The Way to the Churchyard, 1900) and "Gladius Dei" (1902) tell of physical altercations; a duel with pistols occurs in *Der Zauberberg* (The Magic Mountain, 1924); the same novel tells of comic challenges among a group of Polish inhabitants of the sanatorium. Turn-of-the-twentieth-century literature abounds with stories about duels, especially in works by Arthur Schnitzler. Characteristic for Mann's representation of such fights is the spectators' interest and their commentary. The confrontations are also often between unequal opponents. In "Wie Jappe und Do Escobar sich prügelten," a Spaniard meets up with a German; in "Der Weg zum Friedhof" an old grumbler and a young, virile cyclist have a shouting match; a monk and a factotum of an art-gallery confront each other in "Gladius Dei." "Mario und der Zauberer" (Mario and the Magician, 1930) contains a fight as well; in "Tobias Mindernickel" (1898) a dog is killed, while in "Wälsungenblut" (Blood of the Walsungs, 1906) jealousy is fought out by subtler means. These stories merely approximate Goethe's definition of the novella genre, but they certainly narrate unusual events; they also satisfy a requirement of Mann's that they be situated within society and reflect its concerns. While still solidifying his position in the literary world in his early years, Mann presented unusual events because such stories were expected.

But could Mann succeed by narrating a boxing match among a pair of fifteen-year-old boys? The fight itself scarcely occupies more than two of the seventeen pages. What then could possibly be the subject of the remaining fifteen? At stake are not events but ambiance, modes of characterization, the author's memories. Part of the story also relates what happened before the fight and gives the narrator's impressions. Although he relates the two opponents' perspective sympathetically, he also treats them with ironic distance. Characters, clothes, and attitudes appear in naturalistic detail, especially when it comes to the unpleasant but indispensable dance instructor. Given the meticulous and comedic narration of the attendant circumstances, the reader can assume that the fight is not the real subject of the story, but rather a vehicle to depict atmosphere. "Atmosphere" was the subject of Mann's very first story "Vision" (1893), and it is also of much interest in *Der Zauberberg*. The duel between Settembrini and Naphta occurs in a section called "Die große Gereiztheit" (The Great Irritation). "Jappe" conjures up a picturesque painting of a summer vacation at the seaside resort of Travemünde. The novel *Buddenbrooks* (1901) tells of Hanno's deep enjoyment of his holidays in that coastal resort, of the happy days of enchantment both for the character and his author, who is now the author and narrator of "Wie Jappe und Do Escobar sich prügelten."

More autobiographical features can be found. One character, more important by far than the two boys engaged in their fight, is Johnny Bishop. Johnny is introduced in the first sentence of the narrative and appears again in its last. As a precursor of Tadzio in "Der Tod in Venedig" (Death in Venice, 1912) and as a remembrance of Hanno Buddenbrook, Johnny Bishop is endowed with the androgynous beauty that fascinates the narrator more than all the action he could possibly observe. Johnny, lying stark naked beside the narrator on the beach, smiles amiably and engagingly with his pretty, blue, friendly, and mocking girl's eyes.[6] When he is dressed, he wears his outfits with unaffected grace, elegantly attired as a "foreigner or part-foreigner" tends to be (*GW* 8, 427). (The elegant deity will be the god Hermes later on in Mann's work.) But tucked away in this description lies the key to the real identity of the person down there in the sand: "a gaunt little amor" lay there "with his arms raised, his handsome, elongated English head with soft blond curls resting in his hands" (*GW* 8, 428). Alleged to be the story of a duel, this tale is in reality a love story. The narrator's love for Johnny Bishop furnishes the autobiographical substrate from which the story draws its charm. The descriptive detail conjured up for Johnny Bishop becomes a genuine declaration of love, but everything else remains playful pretense. The reader learns that Johnny wears his blue cap on a "handsome little head," that his "long and lean feet are in flat shoes made of fine white leather." Johnny also knows how to sing lustful songs; in his childlike way he is well informed, speaking in a "lovely accent" (*GW* 8, 439). Johnny, the beautiful stranger, the divine youth endowed with Hermes-like attributes, serves as a counter to the two brawling boys. As a foreigner, he also provides a contrast to the ballet instructor who, in turn, is a complete inversion of the "manly youth," an adult whose presence among the adolescents is not quite appropriate. The dance-master, "brown, handsome and fat, especially around the hips" (*GW* 8, 435), carries homoerotic features, and the tender relationship between the homoerotically enamored narrator and handsome Johnny Bishop thus is contrasted to the homosexuality of the older man who is rumored to have a wife and children in Hamburg (*GW* 8, 436).

This story is autobiographical because it is grounded in homoeroticism: it contains the confession of love for a boy. This confession is hidden in a fictional story, but by being hidden there, it does some revealing of its own. The irony imbedded in the style, the serene aloofness of the narrator are directed toward the author himself. By employing these devices, Mann distances himself from the memory of an emotional involvement, from a magical attraction that a beautiful boy had once exerted on him. (The model was a schoolmate of Mann's, John Eckhoff, who was born in Manchester, England.)[7] Mann did not hide his disposition, but he was aware that it ran counter to the accepted morality of his age. That knowledge must have been a constant burden to him.

The story has a psychological dimension. It explores "premature puberty" (frühreife Jugend) (*GW* 8, 433), the interactions among adolescents. It does so in an ironic manner, to be sure, but convincingly. Even more convincingly realized in the story is an insight that Mann would later use more broadly in "Mario und der Zauberer": opponents, their differences not withstanding, share a common basis, resembling one another in astonishing ways. Although in "Jappe," one person is a drifter and the other a *bon vivant*, both stand apart from the other members of their youthful society (*GW* 8, 430). While both are recognized by people as "men of the world" as they promenade in the park, neither belongs to the affluent bourgeoisie commonly at home there. Both are the kind of people who "went to bed late, frequented taverns, loitered on Breite Straße, chased girls, and performed gymnastics in a reckless manner." In short, they were "dandies" (Kavaliere) (*GW* 8, 430). What these two characters have in common is obviously more than what separates them, and the duel takes place among "brothers." This is an old theme of Mann's from the antagonistic brothers Buddenbrook to the story "Die vertauschten Köpfe" (The Transposed Heads, 1940). Here too there is an autobiographical substrate: Mann's conflict with his brother Heinrich.

Is this just an autobiographical narrative then? Wherever Mann describes his own experiences, whenever he depicts something of himself, the outside world and contemporary history are close at hand. It is not merely the idyllic world of Hanno Buddenbrook that resurfaces in "Jappe"; the reader becomes a witness to the crises looming in European politics since 1905/6. Although the story brings up no specific events and depicts no gathering clouds, it reflects those moods and mood changes that are precursors of crisis: characters from different nations fight with their fists for the sake of honor in this story, with a detached Johnny the Brit between them. Such an atmosphere of crisis is later narrated in thorough detail in *Der Zauberberg* and again in *Doktor Faustus* (1947); in both novels, written after the events, occur predictions, made in an earlier fictional time, of terrible fates that were about to grip the world.

In January of 1909, two years before writing "Wie Jappe und Do Escobar sich prügelten," Mann had published an "autobiographical" story in a Viennese newspaper: "Das Eisenbahnunglück" (The Railway Accident). It was reprinted in the story collection *Der kleine Herr Friedemann und andere Novellen* (Little Herr Friedemann and other Novellas) in the same year. Again, the title seems to suggest that the reader can expect the account of an unusual event and not much more. Indeed, the narrator reports a railroad journey from Munich to Dresden in a sleeper-car that suddenly ended in the collision of two trains. But, contrary to expectations, no real catastrophe results here; there is serious material damage, but the passengers remain unhurt. The report of the accident — more a short story than a novella —

serves merely as a vehicle for a humorous and ironic incident involving a journey. It is an ironic story about the author himself.

Mann actually was involved in a train collision, making the story in principle autobiographical, but it is autobiographical in a more profound sense. One of the themes Mann explored throughout his life and career was the question of the artist's role, his status as a cultural representative. Here surfaces Mann's trademark motif of self-directed and double-layered irony. The narrator speaks in the first person singular, appearing to be concerned only with himself. He confesses that from time to time he enjoys a journey as an "artist and virtuoso," adding that "one makes a representation, one appears on stage, one shows oneself to the cheering people; it is no accident that one is a subject of Wilhelm II" (*GW* 8, 416). While the speaker is clearly chastising himself, the irony of the story also targets the emperor, who is guilty of the same urge to show off. The story is thus able to expose some of the false pretenses that reign in Germany in the first decade of the twentieth century. The railroad accident, which involves much irony, shows the government to be incompetent. The train's conductor, of whom it is said that he "is the state," the "father, authority, and security," cannot prevent the accident (*GW* 8, 417). The credibility of the self-styled public facade of the Wilhelminian empire is again cast into doubt by such incidences as the appearance of a "gentleman" (Herr) who has "a monocle in his eye," with "pointed" facial expressions and a mustache "defiantly raised" — all of which gives the corners of his mouth and his chin a "contemptuous and strong-willed appearance" (*GW* 8, 418). The description of this gentleman could have been modeled after a caricature common in the derisive journal *Simplicissimus*. Of course, both representatives of the Wilhelminian empire lose their martial attitude after the accident, but the reader is provided with a glance behind the scenes of the Reich.

"Herr und Hund" (A Man and his Dog, 1919), another "autobiographical" tale, does not quite fit the format of a novella. The story's length of almost one hundred pages moves it outside the general norm, and Mann's subtitle, "An Idyll," indicates that the story should not be counted among the customary novella fare. This is not the first time that Mann, an enthusiastic friend of canines, has presented incidents from the life of a dog. In the early story "Tobias Mindernickel" (1898), he explored the soul of a dog; *Königliche Hoheit* (Royal Highness, 1909) contains another such description. Cervantes's and E. T. A. Hoffmann's dog stories may have served him as models.

Although narrated with epic expansion, nothing exciting happens in "Herr und Hund." The focus of the author is on rendering scenes from a dog's life with serenity and irony. Mann apparently had internalized the statement of Schopenhauer that "the task of the novelist is not to report big events but to make little ones interesting,"[8] and here he followed that advice.

The first-person narrator tells of strolling with his dog, depicting the surroundings in detail. The descriptions are interspersed with common-sense
wisdom, presented with much irony, yet never taking center stage, and the
story has hardly any progression or momentum of its own. What it presents
instead is an image of life in which the world itself and world history are
rendered ironically.

For Bauschan, the dog, the hunting of rabbits and ducks is exciting, and
that excitement is narrated while the narrator himself continues "merely
observing" (*GW* 8, 590). It is an idyllic world that Mann offers to his readers: it includes the warm narrative tone, the descriptions of animals and
nature, and the ironic distance maintained by the narrator who is sheltered
by his bourgeois life, as he maintains a serene superiority despite ongoing
events. The story was written in the spring and summer of 1918 with the
First World War still raging. An idyll in such severely troubled times, one
might ask? The answer is yes: the story is meant to be read as a counter-
image, as the narrative of a world still unbroken.

Shortly before writing "Herr und Hund," Mann had finished his enormous essay *Betrachtungen eines Unpolitischen* (Reflections of a Nonpolitical
Man, 1918), which was concerned only too directly with the events of the
time and their intellectual consequences for Germany and for Mann himself.
He had often composed such counter-balancing works: after *Buddenbrooks*,
a novel of the bourgeoisie, he had written *Königliche Hoheit*, a novel of the
nobility; after *Der Zauberberg*, a novel of a more contemporary era, he began
Joseph und seine Brüder (Joseph and his Brothers, 1934–43), a novel of
mythical times. The story of the dog Bauschan pretends that the war had
mostly bypassed the gates of a certain villa in a Munich suburb. Its author
seemed to be living in a late bourgeois world that had long ended. Is it then
only Thomas Mann the conservative writer at work here?

Perhaps, but the narrator is aware that he is only playing with his surroundings. Mann justified the writing of the story as training for new tasks
(*GW* 13, 161). But in a unique way, the story does bear witness to the
troubled times. It deliberately omits what the author and his contemporary
German readers knew only too well: the horrors of a still-ongoing war and
its certain and impending loss for Germany. Bauschan's is an artificial world,
closed to all evil. Telling the dog's story against such a harrowing background is ironic but also profoundly humane. Bauschan's idyllic world is
vivid, folksy, and unshakable. As such it not only opposes the real world
outside, but it can also offer hope.

In October of 1918, following "Herr und Hund," Mann wrote a small
verse epic, "Der Gesang vom Kindchen" (Song of the Newborn). In a way
it can be counted among his autobiographical narratives. The piece was
published in the journal *Der neue Merkur* in 1919 and was printed in the
same year in book form, together with "Herr und Hund." The poem's subti-

tle is "Idylle," like that of the preceding piece. This time the idyll is a lyrical experiment in hexameter. What apparently appealed to Mann was the attempt to apply language in a way that was new to him. The poem begins with the questions "Am I a poet? Have I been one at times?" The answer is at first "I do not know" (*GW* 8, 1068), but later the question is answered in the affirmative. The occasion was the birth of Mann's youngest daughter, Elisabeth. Telling of the new addition to his life and family, and of the baptism of the child offered Mann opportunities for reflections on greater subjects, on "being and becoming" (Sein und Werden), and thus the work becomes an "expression" of his "very own life" (*GW* 8, 1072). The poem also recounts family history, thereby telling not only of the newborn child but of the others as well. While the representation of the author's paternal sentiments is most intimate, the intimacy is meant to express "the humane applying to all."[9]

Mann put much effort into writing these verses. At one point he noted in his diary, "I am afraid that some passages may turn too prosaic, but I want to avoid the verses becoming separate and closed off in themselves."[10] He read Mörike's "Idylle vom Bodensee" (Idyll of Lake Constance, 1846)[11] during the composition in order to become more sensitive to the rhythm of the hexameter and to a fictional dialogue with a child who cannot answer. When the dialogue turns into a monologue, as Mann addresses himself rather than the child, he glances into a mirror: the verses reflect solid bourgeois principles regarding marriage, love, and family. This creates a world unrealistically harmonious, but a setting quite suitable for the tradition of the verse epic. Mann read Goethe's epic *Hermann und Dorothea* (1797) for its uplifting effect on his mood, and called it the "lofty example that I had before my eyes when improvising my poem" (*GW* 11, 588).

The reader, however, is not meant to read this idyll as a representation of an undisturbed middle-class world. The reference to *Hermann und Dorothea* in Mann's commentary "Über den 'Gesang vom Kindchen'" (About the Song of the Child, 1921) points to the background of revolutionary events and war that both poems share. The child in Mann's poem was conceived in monstrous times; it grew up in the midst of hunger and want caused by an enemy blockade (*GW* 8, 1078). As a consequence, the girl carries a "fiery mark" on her body, a "stigma of war" (*GW* 8, 1079). Her godfather, a war veteran, is still ailing with injuries. All of it confirms that she, indeed, is a "child of troubled times" (*GW* 8, 1096). Here again, the intimate and private story cannot be separated from the period's history; the events of the world are mirrored in the domestic sphere.

Yet the poem remains an idyll. Mann called both idylls, "Herr und Hund" and "Gesang vom Kindchen," "products of a deep desire for tranquility, peace, serenity and humaneness," a need stemming from a "desire for the persistent, untouchable, ahistorical, holy." He also claims to have taken the idyll form and the use of hexameter seriously (*GW* 11, 588), although it must be said that when an author takes his texts too seriously, they tend to become parodistic. The idylls of the child and dog have that in common, but it is a feature shared by the other "autobiographical" narratives too. In all these stories, narcissistic tendencies, still in the background, lead to a form of self-stylization as in the novella "Der Tod in Venedig." There, the self-stylization is better camouflaged; in the more directly "autobiographical" stories, the self-stylization became a more difficult task; hidden in the style and by irony. Thus the environment of the family idyll is parodistic, a game the author plays with his wife and children. Faulty verses are meant to be read for their comical content against this background.

Following the idylls about a dog and a child, Mann composed "Unordnung und frühes Leid" (Disorder and Early Sorrow), a family idyll. The story was written quickly in the spring of 1925 and appeared in the journal *Neue Rundschau* in June of that year, after the publication of *Der Zauberberg* and before Mann began his work on the Joseph novels. The setting is the house of a certain Professor Cornelius, where, much as in the other idylls, little happens: the adult children of the house are preparing for a party that will include their much younger siblings. Little Lorchen's participation generates the early sorrow mentioned in the title; she has fallen in love with one of the adult guests. The narrative depicting the afternoon and evening in the professor's house is almost unconcerned with the events. The young people's gathering is presented from the ironically distanced point of view of the academic historian Cornelius — who can easily be recognized as a portrait of the author himself. The work is rather lightweight. Even though the background music in the story can be identified as songs fashionable during the inflationary period after the First World War, this backdrop is not taken seriously. The skillful but fraudulent purchase of eggs, and other "crazy difficulties of the economy" such as wildly climbing prices for groceries, appear as grotesque components of daily life rather than as lethal threats or reasons for lamentation (*GW* 8, 622). Discontent with the order of things breaks through only once, when Professor Cornelius reflects on his profession. He knows that "professors of history do not love history while it happens but only afterwards." They "hate the present upheaval because they recognize it as lawless, disjointed and impudent, in a word as 'unhistorical.' Their heart belongs to the coherent, pious, and historical past" (*GW* 8, 626). Here speaks the conservative Thomas Mann, who cannot derive joy from the present state of the world. Some of the lawlessness and perversion of the time encroaches on and threatens the ambience prepared by the older children; their dance is somewhat like a dance on a volcano. But Cornelius does not want to take note of it, and the participants do not see it at all. The historical changes, no matter how extraordinary, are underemphasized. Yet the characters are vividly drawn, lending the story elegance and spirit — with a little portion of escapism tucked in between the lines.

Mann described "Unordnung und frühes Leid" in 1926 as a postlude to *Der Zauberberg,* produced for the *Neue Rundschau* quickly and with a light hand. The journal, Mann explains, needed something like a novella, "a story of revolutionary times told by someone who is not a revolutionary, but who knows the times and, after experiencing Valmy, does not claim that everything will remain unchanged."[12] At the end of his short essay about the story, he maintains that only what is written "exactly and thoroughly is genuinely entertaining" (*GW* 11, 622). In *Buddenbrooks* the story of the family does not mirror world history. Here the historical background seems bizarre, couched as it is in desperate economic circumstances. Perhaps it is difficult for someone not inclined toward revolutionary activities to take control of revolutionary times in his art.

Mann's "autobiographical" narratives provide insight into his life, but they were not written for biography's sake, nor are the life experiences they contain mere artistic material. All of the stories confirm Mann's own statement: "I believe that by telling about myself I give voice to the community and to my time. Without such belief, I might as well stop undergoing the trouble of producing anything."[13] Thomas Mann always understood and legitimized his life and his writing by claiming a representative role. Occasionally he acted surprised when he was faced with such a role: "One expresses the most personal things and finds with surprise that one has hit upon national significance. One expresses what is most national, and, behold, one has hit upon what is general and human — hit upon it with more certainty than if one had started out with a program of internationalism."[14] These comments appear in Man's speech "Lübeck als geistige Lebensform" (Lübeck as an Intellectual Form of Life) of 1926, not long after "Unordnung und frühes Leid." Given these lines, Mann must have meant that his "autobiographical" narratives should be read as autobiography, but that they should also be read as images of the "times," where, from an ironic and humorous distance, the narrator tells about an occurrence from his author's life.

Notes

[1] *GW* 11, 695. Mann's collected works (*GW* 1–13) will hereafter be cited in the text.

[2] This collection did not appear in English in this form.

[3] "'Liebe zu sich selbst' hat, ich weiß nicht mehr welcher Autor gesagt — es war ein geistreicher Autor, soviel ist sicher — 'Liebe zu sich selbst ist immer der Anfang eines romanhaften Lebens.' Liebe zu sich selbst, so kann man hinzufügen, ist auch der Anfang aller Autobiogrphic. Denn der Trieb eines Menschen, sein Leben zu fixieren, sein Werden aufzuzeigen, sein Schicksal literarisch zu feiern und die Teilnahme der

Mit- und Nachwelt leidenschaftlich dafür in Anspruch zu nehmen, hat dieselbe ungewöhnliche Lebhaftigkeit des Ichgefühls zur Voraussetzung, die, nach jenem Autor, ein Leben nicht nur subjektiv zum Roman zu stempeln, sondern auch objektiv ins Interessante and Bedeutende zu heben vermag. Das ist etwas Stärkeres, Tieferes and Produktiveres als 'Selbstgefälligkeit'" (*GW* 10, 559).

[4] The mistranslation Mann had read was "Self-love is the beginning of a lifelong novel." See Hans Wysling, *Narzissmus und illusionäre Existenzform: Zu den Bekenntnissen des Hochstaplers Felix Krull*, TMS 5 (1982), 324, note 14. The false translation from *An Ideal Husband* (1895) is from Franz Blei, *In Memoriam Oscar Wilde* (Leipzig: Insel, 1904), 75.

[5] Eine "unerhörte sich ereignete Begebenheit." Goethe to Eckermann, 25 January 1827.

[6] ". . . mit seinen hübschen blauen zugleich freundlich und spöttisch lächelnden Mädchenaugen" (*GW* 8, 427).

[7] Peter de Mendelssohn, *Der Zauberer: Das Leben des deutschen Schriftstellers Thomas Mann*, vol. 1, ed. Cristina Klostermann (Frankfurt am Main: S. Fischer, 1996), 214.

[8] Arthur Schopenhauer, *Sämtliche Werke*, ed. Wolfgang Freiherr von Löhneysen, vol. 5 (Stuttgart: Cotta, 1968), 519.

[9] "Das Allgemeinste und Menschliche" (*Tb* 10 January 1919).

[10] *Tb* 2 January 1919.

[11] *Tb* 27 December 1918.

[12] *GW* 11, 621. Under the date 20 September 1792, Goethe recorded in his *Campagne in Frankreich 1792* (1822) his comment to some Prussian officers on the evening of the lethal encounter between canons at Valmy: "From here and from today a new epoch of world history is beginning; and you can say that you have participated." The cannonade of Valmy indeed was the turning point of the wars against revolutionary France in 1792. It is doubtful that Goethe really uttered these words at that time, but Mann must have taken for granted that he did.

[13] "In mir lebt der Glaube, dass ich nur von mir zu erzählen brauche, um auch der Zeit, der Allgemeinheit die Zunge zu lösen, und ohne diesen Glauben könnte ich mich der Mühen des Produzierens entschlagen" (*GW* 11, 571).

[14] "Man gibt das Persönlichste und ist überrascht, das Nationale getroffen zu haben. Man gibt das Nationalste — und siehe, man hat das Allgemeine und Menschliche getroffen — mit viel mehr Sicherheit getroffen, als wenn man sich den Internationalismus programmatisch vorgesetzt hätte" (*GW* 11, 385).

Joseph and His Brothers

Peter Pütz

THE FOUR PARTS OF the Joseph novels appeared between 1933 and 1943. Thomas Mann wrote the first three volumes in Munich and Switzerland; he completed the last in the United States, in exile. The entire work was published in 1948 under the title *Joseph und seine Brüder* (Joseph and His Brothers). In contrast to the novel *Doktor Faustus* (1947), the grand composition of nearly two thousand printed pages does not owe its existence to plans conceived long ago but to a chance event: an invitation to contribute something written to a collection of pictures the painter Hermann Ebers planned to dedicate to the biblical stories of Joseph.

Mann's main source for the novels is the Book of Genesis, especially chapters twenty-one to thirty, covering the period from the birth of Isaac, Jacob's father, to the death of Joseph.[1] In a wider sense, however, the story relies on the entire biblical narrative, especially if one takes the many typological references between the Old and the New Testament into account. One example will suffice for many: Joseph spends three days in the well; Jesus spends as much time in his tomb. The covered time in the novels stretches even further. If one considers both prologues, the "Höllenfahrt" (Descent into Hell) preceding the first novel and "In oberen Rängen" (In the Upper Levels) at the beginning of the last, then the narrative includes the entire biblical history of humankind, from the time of creation and Lucifer's rebellion to Thomas Mann's own time. This does not only involve contemporary social and economic events, as we find in the parallel between Roosevelt's New Deal and Joseph's actions as the "provider," but the novels also comment on the anti-Semitism rampant in Germany at the time, countered in the Joseph novels with a dignified image of the Jewish people. While the narrated time in *Buddenbrooks* (1901) covers little more than forty years, in *Der Zauberberg* (The Magic Mountain, 1924) only seven, time in the Joseph novels reaches back into an immeasurable pre-history when there was nothing on earth, because the earth did not yet exist. Time is in effect plumbed in these novels, whereby the plumbing device vanishes in fathomless depths. The idea that space and time, as well as being and appearance, may be interchangeable marks the representational style of the entire tetralogy. Everything in this work is fluid to such a degree that in the beginning not even God has coalesced into solid form. God seems to prefer to vanish into an undefined "One" (German: man) rather than risk being addressed. God's ontological status is still one of becoming and not yet of being.

"Höllenfahrt"

When the narrator contemplates his enterprise in the prologue preceding the four novels, especially his planned treatment of time and temporality, he is preparing to enter the "well of the past" (Brunnen der Vergangenheit).[2] The very first sentence demonstrates the interchangeability of spatial and temporal dimensions. The narrator's "descent into the well" not only makes reference to Joseph's descent, but foreshadows in a much wider sense the duality of time and space in the novels, their propensity for sudden reversals that move along the action and plot. The downward motion, however, never terminates in a final plunge but serves as prerequisite for a new elevation. Joseph is not the first who is tossed into the pit; in a larger context the same has already happened to his father Jaakob (Jacob). The flight from familiar places to distant and unknown regions drives him far away from the land of his fathers into a quasi underworld before he will be uplifted again. His son Joseph also finds himself in such a region. After his rescue, he lives in Egypt, in his tribe's view another underworld. An ascent follows in the house of Potiphar before a new variant of the cycle is initiated by Potiphar's wife: this time, it is a prison from which the captive is retrieved. He is elevated to the court of Pharao (Pharaoh) and chosen for the highest position in the land, directly under Pharao himself. After this point, there will be no more plunges, but the exalted himself will raise father and brothers from the depths of want. Their descendants will remain in Egypt but must suffer subjugation later, until the Exodus again lifts them up — but all this already lies beyond the story's scope.

The recurrences of "descents" and "ascents" not only determine the narrative progression in these novels but also control such central themes as the inseparable nature of the upper and lower spheres, heaven and hell. Polar opposites as well as complements, these oppositions bring forth everything on earth, while all oppositions are in turn produced on earth by humankind, liquefying the boundaries between the here and the beyond.

The disintegration of laws and norms that were once binding characterize a principle feature of modernity[3] where even contradictions no longer offer reliable orientations. Epistemological perspectivism, Nietzsche's legacy, makes everything, even the seemingly discordant, tend to blend into the other: ascent and descent, the earthly and the transcendental, the divine and the human. Theories and theorems all give way to the fractional and the temporal; all are invaded by their opposites. This is how the "descent into hell," into the "well of the past" (*GW* 4, 9) can be a climb into heaven at the same time, where not only the "past" is explored but also the future. Because where the relentless reoccurrence of ascent and descent dominates, the will-be contains the has-been, and the impending contains the foregone. The mythic transmutation of time leads to an exchangeability of time's dimensions: the spatial transitions of up and down correspond to the temporal division of present and past, of already and still to come.

Boundaries are not only permeable in space and time, in the now and then, but also in the relations between generations. When the discussion turns to Joseph, the son of Jaakob and the moribund Rahel (Rachel), the character contours of Jaakob, his father, even those of his grandfather and other ancestors seem to melt into one another, so that all the figures become interchangeable. The identity of Joseph's natural father in fact becomes meaningless; the progeny, as any mythical figure, is only imaginable as a link in the chain of his predecessors. The chain loops back into the unfathomable and at the same time up into the immeasurable: from one generation to the next, from past bearers of the blessing to the future ones. No one can decide who emigrated from Ur of the Chaldees, whether it was Abraham, Isaak, or Jaakob, all of them men, lured away. Each of them changed in his new environment, but precisely in this manner, they again come to resemble one another. Their restlessness is existential; the roaming search for their God is innate to the nomadic shepherd tribes. These fictional characters lack all individuality; they do not even conform to familiar mythical patterns.

The reader's gaze reaches from Joseph and his ancestors into the most distant origins, from the rise of civilization (the art of writing, the cultivation of grain, agriculture and animal husbandry), all the back way to the Garden of Eden and to the dawn of humankind. The metaphor for this evolution is the landscape of sand dunes, always moving and yet always the same. Whenever the narrator constructs oppositions or contrapositions, he does so only for the purpose of dissolving them, letting positions leak back into one another. How the interweaving of opposites can culminate in a complete inversion is evident in this example out of "Höllenfahrt": God creates the universe in order to give shape and soul to chaos. Spirit in turn confronts the soul, eager to pronounce the soul's cohabitation with matter as foible. Yet spirit's negativity will not prevail. Tired of playing the undertaker, spirit ceases to deny the world (like Schopenhauer), but accepts it in loving and ironic-humorous fashion.[4]

It is not difficult to imagine that Mann expected a similar achievement from his art. The narrator therefore operates in binary oppositions, but he also operates in what might be called a "half this, but also half that" mode. Most of the time he offers at least two interpretations, often from two different perspectives. This corresponds to Mann's method of motivation: playful confrontation of contrasting views rather than adherence to strict causality. In the Joseph novels, however, this method is substantially expanded when not only two but more reasons are put into play, as is the case in the discussion of Joseph's chastity (*GW* 5, 1133–35). Seven motives surround the biblical account with ever new perspectives. This manner of writing prevents the totality of life from falling victim to restrictive and reductive limits.[5]

Most verdicts meet the mark only partially, something the text admits or even stresses through the use of terms like "perhaps" or "controversial." Motivations do not pretend to fix meaning but constitute mere open propositions. Guessing has priority over knowledge, especially in the case of those parts lacking secure biblical foundations or other sources. In such cases, bold hypotheses often abound, as when the angels discuss the creation of humans. Mann has his angels regard man's creation with a jaundiced eye, perhaps with envy, and has them ask: "What is man, o Lord, that you think of him?" (*GW* 4, 47). When God requests that the angels bow to Adam and pay him respect, the majority follows God's order, albeit reluctantly. Semael (Lucifer), however, refuses to obey, precipitating his fall from grace. In a theologically bold construction, the narrator links the fall of the angel of light with the creation of humankind, so that humans become the measure for the angels' continued company with God or for their transformation into demons. The anthropocentric view in this exegesis is unorthodox; it stands outside Judeo-Christian tradition and belongs to classical antiquity, marking an era during which humans were the measure of all things. Man as the yardstick, even for the beings nearest to God, points here, as early as in the prologue "Höllenfahrt," to a fundamental tendency in the entire tetralogy, a tendency that is often quoted: "den Mythos ins Humane umzufunktionieren" (to convert myth to human and humane functions).[6]

The journey into the well turns into a descent into hell because the narrator plunges into the deepest precipice of time. Although time is produced by the narrator, the depth he encounters causes him to make contact with death, for time travel means the departure from the prison of individuality, meaning death. By breaking through the confinement of his limited self, the narrator enters into a more general, symbolic, and mythic sphere. Again, the temporal levels are intertwined: The past related in the epic preterit, in narrative time, presents a bygone world which we ourselves will enter one day, and to which the epic preterit will then be applied. The narrative act conjures up the mythical past and celebrates the commemoration of its return in the present time. While Schopenhauer's philosophy stands behind the idea of the escape from the prison of individuality, the notion of an eternal recurrence brings Nietzsche into the foreground. Pessimism and asceticism lead to the dissolution of individuality, but from there to broader connections. The myth of Thanatos is replaced by the myth of universal life, where the individual is merely a link in a chain, and the narrative act accomplishes the ordered reoccurrence of people, ideas, and events. All of the narrative strategies of shifting spheres, permeable borders, fluidity, and transmutation serve the same principle. They are all tools of a narrative dialectic — although without idealism's move to a higher level or synthesis. Here, oppositions are not leveled but dissolved. This act applies even to the principle of repetition and its counterpart, change: Both move toward one another and penetrate each other until the moment of fusion. Repetition is unthinkable without modification, from the slightest shift to an inverse design. The complete antithesis is always constructed with reference to the has-been, even if the has-been is inverted like a mirror. As Semael turns away from his God because of the creation of humankind, he simultaneously confirms God's plan of creation: in order to give to earthlings the freedom to choose evil, they need a representative of evil to seduce them: Satan's resistance to God's design serves to bring about its completion. The constant in this conceptual and narrative strategy is the sliding plane placed between repetition and variation, between confirmation and inversion.

Die Geschichten Jaakobs (1933)

The first novel of the tetralogy contains a long and significant dialogue between Jaakob and Joseph, which ends in the image of nature: "The moon, gleaming in a pure radiance that transfigured her materiality, had moved along on her high journey as they were talking; the stars' positions had silently changed according to the laws of their hour. The night cast peace, mystery, and a future far beyond."[7] We have become familiar with the spatial elasticity among the elements above ("moon," "stars," "high journey") and below, on earth, where the partners of the dialogue are standing. Their meeting place, the well, even points to a further depth. Up in the heavens there is movement ("journey," "changed"), while down here on earth father and son converse in quiet assembly. We are also accustomed to the connection between time and space or, better, to their interdependence, here expressed in "location" and "hour." One is consolidated and changed with the help of the other.

What marks the narrative of the Joseph novels most distinctively is the coloration and pitch of its style. In earlier writings by Mann, we almost never find landscapes or skies drawn in clear contours. As a rule, contours are blurred by reservations and limitations, leaving the setting in perpetual twilight. The Buddenbrook family, for instance, is never seen under a crisp blue sky; the brimming colors of summer appear pale and shaded. When lilac fragrance whisks through the garden of the declining merchant family, it mixes with the odors streaming from the syrup factory nearby. By contrast, in the natural setting quoted earlier the heavenly lights glimmer in "pure" radiance, changing the moon with her crude substance into an ethereal being. The night thus becomes the personification of a goddess weaving at the loom of fate, concerned with "peace" on earth, the "secret" of divine awe, and a "future far beyond." If the last word of the sentence quoted at the beginning of the discussion of *Geschichten Jaakobs* had read "voraus" (ahead) rather than "hinaus" (beyond), it would have located the distant event in a strictly temporal way. "Hinaus" is semantically close to "hinweg" (away) and "hinauf" (upward); its meaning is more spatial. The night mediates between the "now" and the "then," between the here and there, and between the above and below.

Rhythm and timbre of the chosen words often approximate the pitch of lyrical speech. Echoes of the Old Testament — especially the Song of Songs, praising the beauty of the lovers in glowing and chaste images — partially account for this impression. When the characters of the novels speak, metaphors and formulations are akin to the language of the Old Covenant or at least to that of its descendants. Some sentences, especially from Jaakob, sound almost Yiddish in their unique syntax. Jaakob has the tendency to switch the verb from its customary position ending the sentence, to an earlier location in the sentence: "als Esau kam an die Furt," rather than, "als Esau an die Furt kam," or "daß ich hätte mögen" and "wie ich hätte müssen" (*GW* 4, 165). In the latter case, auxiliary verb and modal are altered. The modal is no longer a participle ("gemocht hätte"; "gemußt hätte") but an infinitive ("mögen"; "müssen"). This artful and cautious imitation of Old Testament language and of Yiddish speech also serves to reenact the mythic past through art.

Jaakob himself becomes a mythic poet, not only through linguistic form but also through what is spoken. We become acquainted with Jaakob mainly through his stories and through his thoughts. Among the stories that are told or cited by Jaakob himself are the events surrounding him and his brother Esau: the deception of the father, the theft of the blessing, Jaakob's flight and his service in Laban's household, his relation to both daughters of Laban, the wedding and the circumstances connected with Rahel and the twelve sons. At the beginning of the second volume of the tetralogy, *Die Geschichten Jaakobs*, Jaakob is the old father with Joseph at his side. All the other stories are recovered from the past. While the reader is well informed about the historical period — Abraham's origins go back to Egypt's Twelfth Dynasty (1991–1785 B.C.E.) — the generations of Abraham's tribe drift in time, so that figures and events overlap and seem to collapse into one another. Abraham's and Isaak's stories and those of their wives Sarah and Rebecca approximate each other to such a degree they are virtually fused. The sequence of historical events blurs in the recurrent omnipresence of the myth. Every one of the patriarchs shapes his existence according to the mythic patterns of his forerunner, so that every succession grows into a conscious or half conscious *imitatio*. Yet it is not even certain that Jaakob is Abraham's direct descendant; even father-son relationships disappear in the mist of the eternal sameness where all boundaries dissolve into transitions.

What alone lends cohesion to the generations of this tribe of herdsmen is their common faith in the one and only God who developed into Yahweh from a more demonic than divine war and weather spirit — or, *was* developed. But this too remains an open question.

Jaakob appears to us in his stories and in the stories of his forefathers. He reveals himself through a powerful mind and through the universal tendency of his thought and action as evidenced by his ability to forge relationships between what appears unrelated and diffuse. Jaakob's mythopoetic practice rests on his ability to show through comparisons, reflections, and inversions how repetition works as the fundamental principle of myth. Thus Jaakob works tirelessly to find analogies between himself and his ancestors and tries to uncover eternal truths in generational patterns.

Through this process Jaakob pays homage to the only One, his God, the One to whom no other and nothing else can be compared. Hence, in Jaakob's eyes, no other sin exceeds the sin of idolatry. Jaakob's mind circles restlessly around the uncertain contours of the divine being who resists all attempts to be goaded into form. In this respect he follows in the footsteps of his forefathers, presaging the Second Commandment of the decalogue: "Thou shalt not make unto thee any graven image, or any likeness of any thing that is in heaven above, or that is in the earth beneath, or that is in the water under the earth" (Exod. 20:4). The deity's sensory or, worse, material actualization in a fixed and solid representation would make this God susceptible to limitless variety and endless duplication. Tribes and individuals would create different images, pleasing only to themselves, and would then worship such images. Thousands of divergent forms, mere idols to the Israelites, would eclipse the only One. The abstract idea alone could warrant the survival of the principle of monotheism and further its success over the heathen worship of surrounding neighbors and their cultures. The second commandment on Moses's tablets is therefore the necessary consequence of the first but also its compelling pre-condition: "Thou shalt have no other gods before me" (Exod. 20:3). Such inversion, in this case that of cause and effect, is also evident in the repeating and inverting narrative patterns in the Joseph novels.

The novels' relationship to the biblical sources rests on a scheme of imitation and deviation, of repetition and variation. At times, the narrative follows the patterns of the Old Testament; at other times, the temporal sequence of its story strays from tradition.[8] The inversion serves mainly to emphasize the idea of a mythic recurrence which not only permits but demands that biblical events become inverted, and that later events precede those of earlier times. The narrator even fancies himself in competition with his sources, exhibiting impressive numerical skills as he pushes his own more reliable dates. Thus, he "corrects" the biblical time span when he has Jaakob remain with Laban for twenty-five years, appearing quite certain about it.

The tendency of the enlightened mind to cast doubt on traditional truths, to analyze them and to set them right, carries the appearance of destroying myth. Yet all counting and calculating, all deriving and justifying serves only to confirm the mythic patterns. When the narrator — with his constant "yes" and "but" — meticulously checks and interprets possible motivations of his characters, he does alter certain details, but overall he confirms the traditional story line by joining mythology with psychology.[9] The apparent sagacity of author and narrator, ironic and humorous throughout, aims at reaffirming the validity of myth; the message from above is thus supported by the artist's labor from below. While the myth of the Old Testament was a gift of revelation, Yahweh offering Abraham and his descendants a distinguishing covenant, the analysis of such an occurrence by the human narrator's humorous psychology confirms the mythic bond linking the above and the below. The psychological analysis, playfully countering and confirming the biblical myth, corresponds to Gotthold Ephraim Lessing's *Erziehung des Menschengeschlechts* (Education of Humanity, 1780): God's words in the Old and New Testament prepare mankind for an increasing autonomy of thought. Without God's assistance, reason alone could not have gained the knowledge that it had. But, reason will eventually probe revealed truths and verify what both Testaments have witnessed in advance. Lessing calls this third level of humanity "the time of a new eternal gospel."[10]

Goethe's drama *Iphigenie auf Tauris* (Iphigenia on Tauris, 1787) takes the decisive step toward eliminating the line between the human and the divine. Shortly before the desperate Iphigenia recalls the Song of the Fates, she implores the gods: "Save me / And save your image in my soul!" (Rettet mich / Und rettet euer Bild in meiner Seele!) (4.5, 1716–17). A faithful person of antiquity or Christian provenance would question the arrogance behind this plea, the assumption that heavenly inhabitants may have an interest in the image a human being might carry in her soul. Those would be the reservations of a god-fearing person, including a Greek from the mythic age of the House of Atreus. Goethe has his Iphigenia fall back to that mythic era when, soon afterwards, she pays tribute to the atavistic gods of fate. Barely resisting the temptation, Iphigenia recognizes that gods do indeed care about the "images" (Bilder) humans have created in their souls, that gods depend on them and may even be identical to them. The pious will read blasphemy in this; but for the author of *Iphigenie*, the most noble form of humanity has revealed itself. Gods exists only as images in the souls of humankind, and humans need gods in order to compare themselves with the aim of their perfection. The fervor of Iphigenia's supplication rises from a consummate fear, for herself no less than for the gods, the two fears being indistinguishable. In the Joseph novels, Abraham "thinks out" his deity (hervordenken) (*GW* 4, 426–28); here, too, the difference between God's real and imagined existence has lost its meaning. When Orestes finally returns home with his living sister rather than with the noble image of the goddess, Goethe has already prefigured Mann's call "to convert myth to humane functions." As the many displacements and inversions in the tetralogy (even Jaakob and Esau, Lea and Rahel are interchanged) follow the mythical principle of repetition, the limits between literary traditions, between classicism (Lessing, Goethe) and modernism (Schopenhauer, Nietzsche) become fluid.

Der Junge Joseph (1934)

Boundaries vanish and transitions become obscured in the second volume of the tetralogy as well. Jaakob's seventeen-year-old son Joseph is very handsome, intelligent, and verbal. His pleasant personality does not only charm his father but later also Potiphar's wife. His brothers however, with the exception of Benjamin, consider him an intolerable rascal (*GW* 4, 393) and a conceited brat. But even their hatred is nothing but an expression of fondness, wrapped in fierce rejection. Joseph's relationship with his grown brothers rests on arrogance on his part and on the envy of his brothers. But here again, the alternatives remain cloudy: what is the first and initiating element, envy or arrogance? The relationship between cause and effect slips away in the giving and taking, thus becoming reciprocal.

Joseph has a special fondness for the moon; he likes to bathe in its luminous glow. The moon is a symbol of beauty, wisdom, and letters; all of it reserved for Joseph alone. Already in his first appearance at the beginning of *Die Geschichten Jaakobs,* we see Joseph in a near convulsive rapture over the moon's bewitching radiance. He is called up by his father, admonished for his nakedness, and warned about the depth of the well — anticipating the recurrent theme of descent and ascent. Joseph's cultic devotion to the moon is the consequence of his favored idea of the propinquity of body and soul, of beauty and wisdom. Body and soul support one another in Joseph's eyes; neither can subsist without the other, and the moon functions as metaphor confirming Joseph's own existence. Worthy of his veneration are correspondences that serve as medium or affirmation of his *egodicy,* the justification of his self. In this sense, the divine is an *analogon* in the Greek sense of *prepón,* that which is befitting and complimentary for humankind. Here, as in the idea of *kalogathia,* which joins beauty with moral or intellectual virtue, we find another parallel with classicism: Joseph believes that the power of the carefully chosen, fitting word — even the written one — can create reality, while his father puts exclusive faith in oral tradition. Jaakob's son thus anticipates a written document that later will be associated with Moses as the assumed author of the Pentateuch. Joseph is prepared from his earliest days for his future in Egypt where literacy forms the very basis of civilization.

Joseph's most important teacher, therefore, is not his father but Eliezer, who instructs him in speech and writing, initiating him into the history and the stories of his tribe. Repeatedly Eliezer and Joseph discuss Abraham's covenant with the one and only God while employing a dialectical form of reasoning, again breaking down the boundaries between the mortal and the divine. Once more the question is proffered whether the ancient father had found his God or had invented him (*erfunden* or *gefunden*), and the concept of generative thinking (Hervordenken) becomes the vehicle for the mediation between objectivity and the participation of the subject. This does not mean that Abraham has invented his God in a reversal of the relationship between creator and creature; the "hervor" merely signals that the idea of God has substance supporting it, even if only potentially. Yet God's potentiality is not apparent; it may be buried deep beneath the surface, requiring effort to discover and develop it. Not yet real, God needs man to retrieve him from afar or from the depths in order to render him real. The relationship between God and man corresponds to the relationship of *dynamis* and *energeia* (the potential and the actual) in Aristotle or to the identity between creator and creation in Spinoza's philosophy.

As God's existence depends on man, so does his way of being. Only a person who considers himself noteworthy can measure what he demands of himself by a divine model and expect the best and the highest. Only a unique figure, not a multitude of idols, can satisfy such expectations. Such an anthropocentric figure is also not limited to righteousness; he can be cruel and his punishments destructive. While this God blesses and destroys as the one and unique, he also represents the aggregate in the sense of Nietzsche's "Jenseits von Gut und Böse" (Beyond Good and Evil, 1886). Another logical distinction vanishes: this time the contrast between God's singularity and his totality. A God who embodies the sum of all things suggests a being not befitting any single character or image; hence no characteristic stories can be told of him.

The biblical plot offers much more narrative material for representing humans and their families. This is especially true in the case of Jaakob and his sons. The narrator not only investigates Joseph but also his brothers; he explores their interests, feelings, and motivations, ferreting out their mixed incentives. After Joseph had revealed his offensive dreams — one to his brother Benjamin, another to the sons of Leah, and the final one to all in the presence of his father, Jaakob — the ten envious sons become enraged and plot revenge. But the brothers' resolve is not unanimous and determined; doubt and scruples suffuse the plans and motivations. The sentiments are most confused when Joseph is thrashed and beaten: fury, mixed with remnants of affection for the envied and still beloved rascal; the stimulating effect of physical contact during the beating and dragging to the well, especially with Reuben who wants to prevent the worst; and, above all, the fear of the father's curse. Joseph, too, shares in the range of emotions: from fear and self-pity to an affectionate understanding for the hostile brothers. It becomes clear to Joseph that he had provoked them, had driven them to the cruel deed by his pretentious ambitions. He had indeed recognized much earlier that he had elicited their hostility with his stylized idiosyncrasy, yet he had felt incapable of avoiding it. He had perceived himself under a higher command, destined for a great future through the changes and repetitions of elevation and deprivation. Thus the propitious feeling that his confinement in the well was not life's last stage also enriched the medley of Joseph's feelings.

The same confused sentiments control the brothers even after the assault. Reuben suffers most from pangs of conscience, and he reproaches himself as he imagines Joseph's certain death. The idea of having to convey the bad news of the favorite son's demise to the father haunts him no less, and he therefore contemplates Joseph's rescue in order to regain his lost right of the first born. The later sale of Joseph creates animosity among the brothers; those who had participated in the sale had failed to inform the absent Reuben. When all ten brothers finally join in the solemn oath never to speak a word about Joseph's fate, the degree of their knowledge is quite different, causing a weakening of the oath. The parsing of the varied psychological aspects of emotions sets mental certainties in flux, all in the spirit of "living uncertainty" (lebendiger Ungenauigkeit) (*GW* 5, 1483). The text constantly offers a variety of motivations; together they confirm the totality of life in Nietzsche's sense and resist determining concepts, theses, or theories.

The resistance against determinations extends to the typological relationship between the Old and the New Testaments, however in such a way that the typological analogies become subject to the novel's variability, as contrast or as complement. While the brothers are negotiating the price for Joseph with the Ismaelites (Ishmeelites), Juda initially asks for thirty pieces of silver. The amount corresponds to the sum Judas will receive for the betrayal of Jesus. When the buyers reject this amount as too high and finally agree to the amount of twenty pieces of silver, the price mentioned in Genesis 37:28, the difference between the initial demand and the final price serves to separate Joseph from the Son of Man, at least to a degree. Such playful typology distinguishes the mythic-poetical process from the natural model. While the monotony of eternal recurrence rules the natural world, art offers tension between repetition and variation. Repetition that allows for change is a more dignified form of *imitatio*. Especially small incidences like the shift from thirty to twenty pieces of silver show both the analogies and the variations between distant yet connected events: Joseph appears as the precursor of Christ, but not entirely. It is characteristic for this variable form of typology that Joseph saves his people by becoming their provider in the end, but that the divine blessing is not bestowed on him. The dialectic of the novel alters the conventional mode of thinking; it does not distinguish between identity and variation: everything is always the same and, at the same time, every-thing is not the same. Boundaries between concepts finally become so fluid that even contrasts usually considered solid are caught up in the uncertainty.

Joseph in Ägypten (1936)

Joseph moves on with the Ismaelites, having been bought as a slave. Yet despite such lowly status he regards himself as the chosen figure located in the center of the action and on the right path. Hence he does not attempt to make contact with his father, although this would have been quite possi-ble. Joseph sees the hands of a higher power engaged in his rescue, his sale, and his journey to Egypt. The structure of flexibility informs also the third volume of the tetralogy: this time as a fluctuating play between freedom and fate, self-determination and divine guidance. More and more the traveler assures himself that not only his plunge into the well but also his subsequent rescue was willed by him and blessed from above.

While with the Ismaelites, Joseph again encounters the peculiar stranger whom he had met earlier on the way to his brothers. Again the tension between the "once before" and the "once again" appears; the motif of recurrence informs the structure of the novel. The mysterious companion is a kind of angel and at the same time a Hermes figure endowed with a nota-ble role in Mann's entire oeuvre ("Der Tod in Venedig" [Death in Venice, 1913]; Der Zauberberg [The Magic Mountain, 1924] and Felix Krull, 1954). Hermes, as the messenger of the gods, is the mediator between above and below; he can also function as the God of peddlers and thieves (who practice merely different forms of exchange, and the stranger is there-fore not squeamish about matters of personal property). Mainly, however, the stranger fills the shoes of Hermes Psychopompos, the leader of souls to the underworld. Joseph himself is bound for the underworld, which for his ancestors was synonymous with Egypt. The companion reveals on the jour-ney that he had acted as a guard during Joseph's stay in the well. The revela-tion makes reference to myth while confirming the connection between the underworld and Egypt.

In Egypt, Joseph experiences the spectacular contrast between the stun-ning wealth of the kingdom and the humble conditions in his home country, between the uncorrupted vigor of the Israeli tribe and the decadence of a late culture, between the rural world of the nomadic desert tribe and the highly civilized urban world. Despite his reservations about the strange encounter, Joseph recognizes with some fascination that he and his family are not alone, that other nations populate the earth, each regarding its way of life from its own perspective, and measuring and valuing things quite differently. Such perspectivism in the reading of the world (again, Mann follows Nietzsche) pleases Joseph. With awe and admiration he stands in front of the pyramids and the sand-blown sphinx; both are symbols of unfathomable mystery to him. But Joseph does not only notice differences between the Israelite and the Egyptian people, he has a keen eye for contrasts within the kingdom: between rich and poor, between the ruling and the oppressed. He recognizes the sharp economic and social disparities characterizing Egypt's urban population, by far exceeding the gap between master and slave in the country of his origin.

The Ismaelites sell Joseph to the house of Peteprè (Potiphar), the head of which, having been destined for a high court position, had been castrated. Peteprè's affections were meant for the Pharao alone and not to be squandered on dynastic ambitions. The condition of her husband is one explanation for the infatuation of Peteprè's wife Mut-em-enet with Joseph early on in the text. Even before she appears in the novel, psychologizing preparations for her heedless passion begin. The narrator collects a wealth of causes and motivations designed to explain Mut-em-enet's apparent wild desire and to lighten the guilt attributed to her by a long tradition. The psychologizing serves as a means to humanize her; Bible and Koran only report her one lascivious line ("And it came to pass after these things, that his master's wife cast her eyes upon Joseph; and she said, Lie with me." [Gen. 39:7]; "His master's wife attempted to seduce him. She bolted the door and said: 'Come!'" [*The Koran*, Sure 12:2]). But neither tradition knows her name. In Mann's novel, by contrast, she not only receives a name but flowers into a magnificent character: beautiful, intelligent, drawn with the finest psychological differentiation. When Joseph sees Mut-em-enet for the first time, her delightful white arm and the cloudy dimples of her cheeks receive full attention, but then the third section ends with the line: "eine verhängnisvolle Person" (a fateful person) (*GW* 4, 816). Mut-em-enet will become fateful also for Joseph, in a sinister as well as in a positive way. Like his brothers, she will become a new dynamic force for the continuous up and down in Joseph's life and in the story.

Whatever happens to Joseph adheres to the mythic patterns of succession and imitation — in the progression of his own life but also in relation to the life of his ancestors. Everything happens within the dialectic of voluntary action and external influences (the brothers, Mut-em-enet) but also through guidance from above. When Joseph follows the pattern of Jaakob's life, his succession seems almost compulsive, yet it is willed as well. Jaakob's flight from home, from the wrath of his brother Esau, is matched by Joseph's abduction and the fury of his brothers, and both times the journey proceeds to the underworld. This pattern of imitation holds in Egypt as well. As Jaakob served Laban seven years for the hand of Rahel, so must the son spend seven years climbing the ladder of service in Peteprè's house. Some of the analogies are proscribed by the sources; others are added by the novelist in order to strengthen the density of the web of mythical reenactments. The repetitions are not mere copies; shifts are possible. They lead to variations, expansions, and heightened variants. Joseph does not serve in the fields watching the flock like his father but serves with rising prestige in a noble household. He will not remain a shepherd and tent-dweller but will take over the highest position in Egypt next to the Pharao.

During Joseph's ascent in his master's service, Peteprè's emasculation again plays a significant role because of the consequences it yields. Joseph, having discovered the fact, makes cunning use of his knowledge. A gardener at the time, he is engaged in fertilizing bisexual blossoms on a tree with the help of a special tool, when he encounters Peteprè who is walking in his garden. Joseph's well-thought-out speech explaining his activity, turns into a hymn downplaying the mere physical aspect of sexual union. Joseph praises the artificial and artistic manipulation of all that is chosen to multiply and to live on. He denies the fundamental separation of the sexes and vociferously supports — with allusions to the virgin birth (typology with reference to Mary) — a universal monism, questioning the strict polarity between the male and female sex. This, of course, provides balm for the soul of his master who finds himself — in all his damaged personhood — for the first time confirmed and appreciated. Joseph demonstrates the superiority of the creative mind over the baseness of sexual coupling. Now even the barriers between the sexes are set adrift, much as the barriers between the "up and down," the "downward and upward," the divine and the human. The song of praise in favor of an artificially arranged insemination also reaches to the realm of art; art is separated from animalistic, ordinary life. This abrogation of sexual boundaries in a general sense may have been a positive idea taken from Thomas Mann's own life experience.

After Joseph speaks to Potiphar, he steadily moves ahead in the Pharao's service: from gardener to reader, to personal valet, and finally to master of the full estate. Joseph makes himself more and more indispensable; he uses all his ambition to become superior to everyone, except to the highest, his God. Through his alliance with Him, Joseph gains the almost superhuman strength that helps him to achieve his goal. Again, as in the case of his forefathers, it remains undecided if God exists independently of man, or if he is the result of "Abrahams Gottesdenken" (*GW* 4, 131). The German possessive in the word "Gottes" is ambiguous: On the one hand, it suggests "thinking of God" (Denken an Gott; or: seiner gedenken), on the other hand, the "creation of God through thinking" (das Erdenken Gottes). That is why we read in the chapter "How Abraham discovered God" that Abraham had thought God into existence ("hervorgedacht") (*GW* 4, 426–28). But God is not pure fiction either. What can really be called "pure" in this novel? "Hervorgedacht," a form of "Hervordenken," is not the same as "Ausdenken" (imagining); rather, it cancels the basic separation between objectivity and creative subjectivity. "Hervordenken" mediates between oppositions without settling for one or the other. Again, one might think of Iphigenia or of Kant's philosophy, which links the thing in itself inseparably with the form that consciousness gives. Joseph's relationship with his God is analogous to Kant's epistemology: Joseph needs his God as an ally in order to gauge his own level of perfection.

The theme of coherence in seemingly discordant matters appears not only in connection with fundamental questions of ontology, epistemology, and religion, but also with concrete physical details, where the bridging of oppositions becomes especially telling. The extensive descriptions of Mut-em-enet's body and face, often repeated, focus especially on the contradiction between the strict gaze of her eyes and her seductive, curved mouth. It seems as if her eyes were ruled by her super-ego, her mouth by contrast forced to expose the libido of her Id. A long battle will be fought before the lower part defeats the upper. In this conflict, pomegranates play a significant role: their wealth of deep red seeds signals fertility, yet pomegranates are also given as burial offerings to the dead. Here, an emblematic detail covers the dual poles of Eros and Thanatos.

The continuously reenacted principle of movement and disintegration of seemingly definite concepts takes on special significance when the narrator feigns extreme precision while clarifying and justifying matters. In the case of Joseph's chastity, the narrator offers proof, listing seven pieces of evidence in meticulous detail. Joseph's motivations could not have been explored more thoroughly, and yet, doubt seems to remain. The number seven in Thomas Mann's oeuvre is a mythic code, not an exact measure; it expands what can be counted to the infinite and into uncertainty. Hans Castorp's seven-year sojourn on the Magic Mountain is much more than an exact phase measurable by a calendar. His stay leads into the timeless space of eternal *nunc stans*. Joseph's seven reasons could be reduced to only one, his awareness of being chosen, or they could be multiplied endlessly. There is at least one more potential reason omitted by the narrator but suggested to the reader: Joseph's premonition that the passionate Mut-em-enet must be driven into madness to open a new path into the pit for him, and with it — through revenge and punishment — a new and even more glorious ascent. Without Mut-em-enet's twisting of the facts — if she did fully twist them — there would have been no audience with the Pharao; Joseph had to fall before he could be raised again. Had he instead succumbed to temptation, the consequences would have been immeasurable. Fear of the unmanageable could be a ninth reason; more could be added. Seven reasons could easily turn into seventy, as many as there were chairs lined up in the dining room on the Magic Mountain.

Joseph's path leads next into jail, and this time the former steward of the Pharao, a fellow prisoner, assumes the role of the mediating Hermes figure. Joseph stands in front of Egypt's ruler at thirty, ready to interpret the

Pharao's disturbing dreams about the seven "fatfleshed" and the seven "leanfleshed" cows and of the seven rank and good and the seven thin ears of corn (Gen. 41:1–7). This encounter with the Pharao, not limited to the mere interpretation of dreams, becomes the apex of Joseph's life, or are we to say, of his life's design. All that follows from now on evolves rather than develops; there is no further fall and therefore no further elevation.

The dialogue between Joseph and the Pharao follows the maieutic pattern of Socratic arguments: both men take turns at the interpretation of the dream. Joseph puts causes and results of his own interpretation piece by piece into the Pharao's mouth, and Pharao, eager for the knowledge, formulates the findings. This procedure naturally strengthens the credibility of what is said and heard. Similar maneuvers guide Joseph's appointment to the highest stewardship. Deviating from the Old Testament, where Pharao simply awards the office, Joseph himself now participates in his elevation, employing both clever and complaisant rhetoric. This does not escape the Pharao's astute mother who casts mocking glances toward the man who labored effectively for his advantage. Drawing conclusions from Pharao's dreams, Joseph can recommend precautions, making his appointment as a steward a necessary result of the intelligence and foresight he has demonstrated.

As the lines between reader, prophet, and advisor become fluid, the identities between Joseph and Pharao, the dreamer, fade. Joseph grows more and more into a medium, and Pharao gains insight by learning to recognize his own thoughts. The chapter with the apodictic title, "Pharao Prophesizes," seems to invert the roles of dreamer and interpreter in opposition to the biblical narrative. But as often in these novels, the inversion only functions as a move to eradicate distinctions: before Pharao can "prophesy" at all, Joseph must obtain Pharao's trust and willingness to speak with his own clever rhetoric. Joseph establishes a comfort zone for his partner, removing not only barriers between the men but also between "yes" and "no" (cf. *GW* 5, 1429). The conversation ceases to be a discussion, and moves on to reciprocal erotic harmony. To recast Pharao's beliefs in his own image, Joseph leads him through a series of philosophical and theological discussions, well-spun stories about Jaakob, and on toward a convergence of the minds that allows for no more "but" and only a consenting "Amen." Joseph and Pharao are immersed in a sphere of universal correspondences where distinctions, even oppositions, lose all significance.

Joseph mediates between himself and Pharao but also between the Pharao and the world of his father and forefathers, including the God Yaweh, who had been "thought" by them into existence (hervorgedacht) (*GW* 4, 426). He mediates between his forefathers' way of producing God through thought ("Gottesdenken"; *GW* 4, 131) and the rapidly changing conceptions of Pharao's own beliefs in the divine. Stimulated by the growing intimacy with the Israelite, Pharao moves toward Joseph's faith in a sole and imageless God until he no longer venerates Egypt's supreme deity (Amun-Ra) as the sun in the sky, but instead as the spiritualized creator of beings in a heaven. As the sun-god Aton, the deity is no longer limited to a single phenomenon, no matter how lifegiving, but becomes the principle of all phenomena. The young Pharao calls himself "Akhnaton" (serviceable to Aton) in his honor, and, in an ecstatic hymn to his new spiritual God, he speaks of him as "father" and of himself as "son" "sent down" from heaven, whereby "all will be one in the light and in love, as the father and [he] are one" (*GW* 5, 1469). In this accentuation, Pharao himself not only approaches the God of the Old Testament but also the God of the New Testament, where the son is the father's issue but also identical with him. The narrator lets the Egyptian metaphysician join in the play with biblical typologies.

The many and still similar forms of shifts, of dissolution and transitions, are altogether shadings of the novels' structural principle of a mutual penetration and a reciprocal exaltation. By this principle, the encounter between Joseph and the Pharao becomes an enormous enhancement for both participants: for Joseph it leads to the promotion to the second highest office in the land, for the Pharao to the ecstatic vision of his new God. But the same principle had been at work in the covenant of Joseph's ancestors with their highest God: the chosen people are ennobled and their God, too, ascends to his full stature. A covenant ("Bund") is reciprocal. Even Joseph's hostile brothers are bound to him, affecting his advancement in the long run, and they will later profit from the deed themselves. The same force controls all levels of interaction, be they dialogues, performances, or the love of God or man.

One might call this mutual penetration and exaltation poeticized eroticism. Within the content of the novels, Eros rules as well. Whatever benefits Joseph comes as a gift, courtesy of his comely body and the love others have for it. Even when the brothers trounce him and drag him to the well, they sense the physical attraction. Yet Joseph's effect is not limited to the external; his inner qualities weigh in, his brilliant reasoning, his psychological insight, and the power of his erudition — again, seemingly separate spheres commingle. While two closely related gods, Eros and Thanatos, reign over the *Zauberberg*, in the end only Thanatos remains. In the Joseph novels, however, Eros wields the wand until the very end: Joseph will caress his brothers' hands. One of Eros's qualities is humor. More than irony, humor suffers, or even celebrates, ambiguities in all their apparent melding and invasions. The Joseph novels, more than any other works by Thomas Mann, contain the highest level of such poetized eroticism: in the form of love of self, love of the world, and the love of God.

Joseph der Ernährer (1943)

The tight sequence of descent and ascent (the structure, incidentally, of picaresque novels) no longer rules in volume four of the tetralogy. The undulating narrative structure gives way to a smooth linear one. Agitation crops up at the reunion of the family, but it affects father and brothers more than the former castaway. The reader feels that a turbulent stream, now swollen to a river, has reached the sea and spends itself in calm detachment. Only the story of Juda and Thamar in the fifth chapter, when Thamar inserts herself into the line of the carriers of the blessing, recalls the earlier form. Other movements, upward or downward, like the seven rich and seven lean years, are controlled by Joseph's actions: Joseph, the prophet and interpreter of dreams, overcomes the looming crisis with far-reaching precautions. He orders the construction of huge warehouses and silos and appoints innumerable attendants and supervisors, so that the surplus will be overseen and equitably divided.

Since the appearance of *Joseph der Ernährer*, critics and interpreters have pointed out that Mann put much into the novel that he owed to experience and values acquired in his exile in the United States. The ethnic variety of Mann's host country is echoed in the multinational Egypt, open to everything foreign. Akhnaton not only renews and spiritualizes the image of his God; he also opens his country to the outside world more than any of his predecessors had done. Similarities between Joseph's policies and Franklin Delano Roosevelt's reform of the American social system, the New Deal, have often been discussed. In the novel, Joseph counsels Pharao on how to manage supplies in lean years: "Distribute to the weak and poor but sell to the powerful and wealthy." Moreover, Joseph advises to charge the wealthy more than the customary price, so that "wealth will be humbled" (*GW* 5, 1473). Roosevelt's social policies are alluded to when the advisor recommends easing the burden of the needy, while advocating that the wealthy pay. Mann respected Roosevelt perhaps more than any other statesman, not only as victor in the Second World War but also as social reformer.

Joseph's far-sighted planning also profits the members of his family. His economic arrangements link the socio-political sphere with the private, as the starving brothers are drawn to the Pharao's court. They arrive in order to provide for themselves and their kin, initially without Benjamin, something Joseph finds in need of correcting. What follows is a cagey probe into the origin and motivations of the travelers, the demand that the brothers return home with the exception of one hostage, the incriminating story about the priceless goblet in the sac of grain, and finally the anagnoresis: the brothers recognize their brother. Jaakob, having discovered that Joseph is still alive, starts out a year later with the entire clan of nearly seventy people to meet his lost son and to settle in Egypt. The tearful reunion between Jaakob and

Joseph confirms that the father has kept his love for Rahel's son. It also clarifies Jaakob's intent not to bestow the blessing of the first born on Joseph and with it the leadership of Israel. Reuben and the next two brothers in line are ruled out for different transgressions, and since Jaakob is forced by the iron rule of birth order, it is Juda, the fourth son, who will be the chosen one. The one driven by Astarte, the Phoenician goddess of fertility and love, the one who in his advanced age is still consumed by the lust of the flesh, becomes the bearer of the blessing according to the Bible — and not Joseph. Jaakob and Joseph, and perhaps the reader, share a certain amount of melancholy, but as the giver of the blessing is tied to his law, so is the narrator bound by his sources. Joseph will, despite his exceptional position and extraordinary exaltation, remain a transitory figure in the history of his tribe. He and his descendants will not determine his people's destiny. Joseph's elevation is only secular, not spiritual. His life bears obvious signs of the fantastic, and the entire opus reads much like a grand fairy tale. The future of the chosen people will be different; Joseph's story belongs to its history but only as an interlude.

Reminiscent of a fairy tale is also the unsettled way the Joseph figure is portrayed. Despite the narrative effort devoted to him, despite Joseph's central role in the story and his conspicuous assets and talents, Joseph never quite gains solid contours (in contrast to Jaakob, Rahel, or Mut-em-enet). The reason lies in the priority of function over personality: Joseph is not meant to have defined characteristics. He represents the principle of mediation, of the leveling of boundaries. As a narrative figure, Joseph thus approximates the narrative structure itself, which treats him as he himself conducts his thoughts and actions. Other characters do not share this trait, least of all the brothers, who are each locked into certain types. Joseph and the narrator always move within a field of tension where certitude confronts its erosion, making playful mediation possible. The protagonist is an artist figure, not only because he directs his life artistically, but also because he represents the artistic principle governing the story as a whole: universal transitoriness.

While the opening of the tetralogy commences with a far-reaching prelude, the last of the novels begins with a "Vorspiel in den oberen Rängen" (Prologue in the Upper Levels). In the first prelude, "Höllenfahrt," the narrator glances into the heavens and reports the angels' reaction to God's plan of creation and especially his intent to create human kind. Now there is again talk of the Kingdom of God, and at the center stands the Most High who is still called the impersonal "One" (German: man). This designation corresponds to the Israelites' idea of the divine as indeterminate and imageless; it also establishes an affinity with Aristotelian philosophy, according to which raw matter must first acquire form in order to become reality. As it was in the case of Abraham's "creative thinking," God, when still alone, is in the state of pure potentiality and needs actualization in form so that "One" can become Yahweh. In the "Upper Levels" the devil assumes the function of stimulating the undetermined One to create man. Evil will gain a foothold in the world while God, facing man, will reach awareness and contour. Man can thus be called the "product of God's curiosity toward himself" (das Produkt von Gottes Neugier nach sich selbst) (*GW* 5, 1283). The principle of mutual penetration and exaltation, then, existed before the time of creation: God reaches his potential through the creative act, and the devil gets the space to work his designs.

When looking at the theological reflections in the earlier chapter "Descent into Hell," a sharp divergence, even a contradiction, becomes apparent. The angels, gazing at man and prompted to genuflect in front of him, part ways in choosing good or evil. In "Joseph der Ernährer," however, Lucifer sins prior to creation. The devil now no longer regards the new creatures with envy and resentment but accepts them as necessary in the completion of the universe. Yet the spirit of narration would be belied if contradictions had the final word. What appears to be a reversal from one prelude to the next once again harmonizes and completes oppositions within the narrative.

The emphasis has merely shifted: The devil's fundamental enmity toward God and man turns into an all-embracing friendship among everyone. Together, the preludes represent the polar opposites structuring the complete narrative in idea and representation: the first stands for separation and opposition, the second for the work of mutuality and bonding.

Notes

[1] Among the sources of the Joseph novels are, besides the biblical texts, the *Koran,* archaic Persian lyric poetry, and numerous historiographic, psychological, philosophic and theological reference texts. Cf. Herbert Lehnert, "Thomas Manns Vorstudien zur *Joseph*-Tetralogy," *Schillerjahrbuch* 7 (1963): 458–520; Herbert Lehnert, "Thomas Manns Josephstudien 1927–1939," *Schillerjahrbuch* 10 (1966): 378–404.

[2] *GW* 4, 9. Mann's collected works (*GW* 1–13) will hereafter be cited in the text.

[3] On the "fusion of traditionalism and modernism," cf. Eckhard Heftrich, *Geträumte Taten: Joseph und seine Brüder*" (Frankfurt am Main: Klostermann, 1993), 31–33.

[4] Käthe Hamburger, *Der Humor bei Thomas Mann: Zum Joseph-Roman* (Munich: Nymphenburger Verlagshandlung, 1965).

[5] Peter Pütz, "Die Verwirklichung durch 'lebendige Ungenauigkeit': 'Joseph' von den Quellen zum Roman," *Thomas Mann und seine Quellen,* ed. Eckhard Heftrich and Helmut Koopmann (Frankfurt am Main: Klostermann, 1991), 173–88.

[6] In a letter to Karl Kerényi, February 18, 1941. *Thomas Mann — Karl Kerényi: Gespräch in Briefen* (Zurich: Rhein-Verlag, 1960), 98. Mann found this phrasing in

a letter by Ernst Bloch, dated June 23, 1940. Cf. Manfred Dierks, *Studien zu Mythos and Psychologie bei Thomas Mann, TMS* 2 (1972), 260.

[7] "Der Mond, schimmernd von reinem Licht, das seine Stofflichkeit verklärte, hatte die hohe Reise fortgesetzt, während sie sprachen, der Sterne Ort sich still gewandelt nach dem Gesetz ihrer Stunde. Die Nacht wob Friede, Geheimnis und Zukunft weit hinaus" (*GW* 4, 120).

[8] Gerhard Von Rad, "Biblische Joseph-Erzählung und 'Joseph-Roman,'" *Neue Rundschau* 76 (1965): 546–59.

[9] Dierks, *Studien zu Mythos und Psychologie.*

[10] "Sie wird gewiss kommen, die Zeit eines *neuen ewigen Evangeliums,* die uns selbst in den Elementarbüchern des Neuen Bundes versprochen wird" (italics by Lessing). Gotthold Ephraim Lessing, "Die Erziehung des Menschengeschlechts," ed. Helmut Göbel, *Werke,* vol. 8, ed. Herbert G. Göpfert (Munich: Hanser, 1970–1979), 508.

Lotte in Weimar

Werner Frizen

Charlotte Kestner

IN THE FALL OF 1816, a matron, well into her sixties and accompanied by her grown daughter, set out on a journey from Hanover to Weimar in order to visit her sister. During her stay of a few weeks in Weimar, she also had lunch with Goethe; soon after this she departed for her hometown, as unnoticed as when she had arrived. Her visit has left few traces in intellectual history. It would have completely vanished from memory had the visitor not been a certain Hofrätin Kestner, who, forty-four years earlier as Lotte Buff, had been the object of the young Goethe's passion. As such she was one of the external and internal causes responsible for the first bestseller in German literature, *Die Leiden des jungen Werthers* (1774). However, the reappearance of the former beloved and muse seems to have done little to impress the elderly gentleman, now a famous writer and Minister of State. With two unremarkable entries in the *Annalen* (1830) and in his diary, Goethe saved himself and the world any further commentary: "Hofrätin Kestner aus Hannover," reports the one, "Mittags Ridels und Mad. Kästner [*sic*] von Hannover," reads the second.[1]

These laconic notations, however, were not the seed from which Thomas Mann developed the "bookworthy event"[2] of his novel *Lotte in Weimar* (The Beloved Returns, 1939). The material had already been treated by someone else when Thomas Mann first laid eyes on it, and it had been treated in such a way that the novelist's instincts were aroused. In March 1935, when Thomas Mann decided to embark on his "Arbeitsplan Goethe-Lotte Kestner,"[3] he remembered, probably not for the first time, Felix A. Theilhaber's book, *Goethe. Sexus und Eros* (1929). In Theilhaber's book, this "Vorfallenheit," as Mann's Goethe calls the event of Lotte's visit (*GW* 2, 685), appears to have been a psychological fine-tuned idea or even as an "unheard of event" ready-made for the author Thomas Mann looking for inspiration. Theilhaber quotes the story of the reunion of Goethe and Charlotte Kestner as written by a certain Ludwig Häberlin in the nineteenth century. In this form it is already a suitable nucleus for a novella:

H. E. R. Belani (Ludwig Häberlin) narrates in his book, *Goethe und sein Liebesleben:* On a beautiful day in May in 1816, the elderly *Charlotte Buff, Kestner's wife,* appeared in Weimar (the immortal beloved of [Goethe's] Wetzlar Werther years). Charlotte is asked to the table and appears in noticeably youthful attire, namely in a white dress with red ribbons, the same kind she had worn forty-four years earlier when Goethe had seen her for the first time.

He himself had long forgotten this detail, and when Charlotte finally reminded him of it, he admitted openly that he did not remember this circumstance at all.

Charlotte, who would have felt flattered had the now world-famous man confessed his earlier passion once more, passion she had met with reluctance then, felt hurt by this reserved attitude and returned home earlier than intended, let down in her expectations. Even the memory of her had become inconsequential to him (Theilhaber's emphasis).[4]

The novelist Ludwig Häberlin (1784–1858) had transformed the episode into a pointed anecdote, seriously distorting the historic events. At first, Mann was inspired by Häberlin's story. Mann's Charlotte, too, is motivated by twisted purposes when she sets out on her journey into the province of her youth (*GW* 2, 389). Later, in a daydream, immediately following her arrival in Weimar, she candidly admits to herself that repressed desires had motivated her. As a result, everything else, especially the visit with her sister and brother-in-law, becomes only a pretext for her craving to see the beloved of her youth. Indeed, in the dream scene at the end of the novel, Mann's Charlotte even calls the journey "a school girl's prank" (Schulmädchenstreich, *GW* 2, 757).

The fictive Charlotte Kestner is concerned only with the urgent question of who, within the "Reigen," the dance of Goethe's beloved, is the essential, the immortal, or, in Riemer's superlative, "the utmost beloved one" (die Geliebteste, *GW* 2, 471–72). In her jealousy, she raises the claim to be more dear to the master than the other servile women who have circled him. More specifically, Mann wants to show the Hofrätin suffering from the competition with Friederike Brion, Goethe's earlier beloved from the Sesenheim period of 1770–71. In the writings of a few Goethe biographers, especially in an essay by Eduard von Bülow, who was, like his fellow Young German writers, critical of Goethe,[5] Mann had read that Friederike should be considered the Ur-image of all of Goethe's lovers. She alone represented the type of "Mädchen aus dem Volk" Goethe preferred erotically; she was the Ur-form of all his abandoned favorites. Friederike Brion is also marked as the most favored among Goethe's loves in the popular Goethe biography by Albert Bielschowsky, which Mann consulted regularly.[6] Bielschowsky slips into the language of saintly legend when he glorifies the literary afterlife of the girl Friederike, forsaken by Goethe:

> The more noble and uncorrupted Friederike's nature appeared, and the more she suffered and had suffered in silence, the more her image became shrouded in the poet's eye with the glory of the Madonna. From the two figures of Mary in *Götz* and *Clavigo,* she [Friederike] slowly mounts the heavenly steps to the transfiguration of Gretchen at the conclusion of *Faust.*[7]

In her wishful fantasy to be adored like the Madonna in front of whose niche in the "cathedral of humanity" the multitudes congregate (*GW* 2, 473), Mann's Charlotte demands a similar apotheosis in literary history — as if the historical Lotte had known of the future misdirection of her own reputation. But she is concerned with more than her possession of Goethe; she wants to partake in the Gretchen figure, as Mann's notes for the novel show, and thereby partake in the immortality of fame. Herein lies the cause for her exhibitionist attempt to come to the aid of literary history as best she can in order to secure her own role in the cult of Goethe and to justify her life's story in the face of history:

> Charlotte hates Friederike jealously and is glad to have her in the grave, the poor victim; she has done a better job with herself as a victim and has been smarter . . . Terrifying, however, if the people were to discover this in time and were to topple, destroy, dismiss her, tear her from her niche, from his side. (Mann's emphasis)[8]

Despite having been "moved" by Theilhaber's quotation of Häberlin's rather garish rendering of the late reunion,[9] Mann begins to adjust the accents surrounding the figure of Lotte by reducing the elements of caricature and stripping away Häberlin's offensive showmanship. Charlotte Kestner ceases to be the silly goose that Häberlin had presented and the diarist Goethe had wanted to dismiss. Mann's Charlotte undertakes a journey as so many other characters in his work: she slips out of the familiar form of her existence and enters unexpected dimensions. Having barely arrived in Weimar, and before she encounters her past, Lotte lingers dreamily in fantasies, reactivating the buried images of her youth. As Castorp in his dream of Hippe, she calls forth the Ur-event of her life: her passion for the young Goethe — suppressed as it was, merely climaxing in a kiss. Now, as an elderly woman, she has come to Weimar to find closure for her passion. In Mann's novel, Charlotte Kestner not only embarks on a journey covering space, she travels through time, into the depths of her being, and she experiences an awakening in the process.

To see her visit in therapeutic terms may sound exaggerated, but the matron experiences how it feels to be cured of illusions, even though the experience occurs late in her life. Indeed, the curious constellation of characters to whom Charlotte grants an audience in the hotel Elephant makes for a parody of the psychoanalytic situation: she who had come to heal her broken heart is now besieged by visitors who find themselves in the same dilemma she had faced in times past, being victims of the "great man." These people are obtaining balm for their psychic wounds, and they compel Charlotte to assume the role of an untiring conversationalist and a crafty midwife for the delivery of their traumata. When Mann has her call this activity "study of the soul" (*GW* 2, 389), he transfers psychology and psychoanalysis into a "Biedermeier" atmosphere. The character Riemer, based on the actual figure of Goethe's aide and scribe, by contrast, prefers the analogy of a confessional, as Lady Kestner is pushed into the role of a "super confessor" (Großpoenitentiarius) (*GW* 2, 444), unable to do justice to other troubled souls as she struggles to alleviate her own afflictions. In a few hours, a small story of disillusionment will have run its course: Charlotte, the heroine, will have to acquire a virtue that has become the emblem for the older Goethe, "Entsagung" (renunciation).

Rose Cuzzle

All of Charlotte's visitors orbit, in thoughts and aspirations, like planets around Goethe, the central star and gravitational center of Weimar. But by visiting Charlotte, the great man's courtiers attend a plain burgher who has just arrived among them. And while the great man is constantly discussed, about two-thirds of the novel pass before he is finally at hand and is allowed to speak for himself.

A figure who does not exist in historical accounts in the form depicted in Mann's novel, Rose Cuzzle, opens the progression of characters that climaxes in the epiphany of the Olympian's arrival. In a comic prelude, and with strapping vivaciousness, she opens up central themes of the novel, which will be modulated to minor key by the representation of other victims in Goethe's Weimar.

Although the British woman has no historical or literary model, she is neither ahistorical nor entirely fictional. Mann had found the idea for her character in Goethe's conversations: Charlotte von Schiller tells Fritz von Stein about a Count Reiß-Köstritz who has the fancy of sketching all the learned men who will sit for him. Only Goethe and Schiller had refused him.[10] With her comical hunt for luminaries, Rose Cuzzle parodies fame and the halo of prominence,[11] and Mann, with unmasked delight, makes fun here of sensationalist reporting and celebrity stalking. The analogy to the photo journalism of the 1920s and 1930s, to the relentless hunt by whirling reporters oblivious to the choice of object they pursue, is obvious. A passage in Theilhaber's study encouraged Mann to relate the fashions of Goethe's day to his own experience. People then went to Weimar much like people in his day traveled to boxing matches, to cycling races, to Mont Blanc, to the pyramids, or to Niagara Falls.[12]

An additional model for Rose Cuzzle was the American journalist Marcus Aurelius Goodrich, who interviewed Thomas Mann in Paris in 1926 and amazed him with his Anglo-Saxon immediacy, his monumental boyish cheerfulness. The interviewee took the journalist's impulsiveness as a refreshment of the first order: "And [he] sat himself down and starts talking and laughing with his fervent Anglo-Saxon boyish modulations — he is too glad and he would so *very* much like to know — and asked *questions*. . . . And eruptions of glowing admiration for the smallest of answers" (Mann's emphasis).[13] The outlandish journalist, whose directness and disrespect Mann considered typically American, was one step ahead of his later literary incarnation, Miss Rose Cuzzle, as the American journalist managed to come face to face with the object of his admiration. The fictive British lady, as well as the historical Count Reiß-Köstritz, had to console themselves with substitutes. This is a tongue-in-cheek reminder that a Rose Cuzzle may hunt down a Castlereagh, a Metternich, a Talleyrand, and may draw all kinds of possible celebrities on her canvas (*GW* 2, 399) but not the One, Goethe. The task of portraying him, even if only as a reflection in a distorting mirror, may fall to no one else but to Thomas Mann himself.

The adroit traveler embodies the prototype of the Weimar pilgrim in satirical form. In the 1820s, "Athens on the Ilm" had become a place of pilgrimage. To visit Weimar, to admire Weimar celebrities and to consume Weimar "Bildung" were essential activities performed in Europe, especially for the British.[14] "It's crowded with Englishmen in Weimar," wrote no less a man than Herzog Carl August von Sachsen-Weimar-Eisenach to Goethe's friend Knebel on 23 September 1797. In this way Rose Cuzzle represents an entire class of foreign Weimar pilgrims. She connects, in comedic shorthand, Weimar as intellectual capital with other centers of intellectual and political history: Miss Cuzzle had sketched Napoleon under arrest, she was present at the Congress of Vienna when the crowns of Europe divided up the spoils, and the leading minds of idealism had become her targets in Berlin. Thus, she unites war and peace, "Dichten und Denken," intellect and action in her sketch pad — and all that "in die Breite gezerrt," in sensationalist expansion rather than in any refined manner.

Riemer

Friedrich Wilhelm Riemer, the second character to appear in the procession of orbiting planets, is a historical figure. It is with him the coquettish comedy begins to shift toward tragedy. The historical Riemer (1774–1845), part of Goethe's household for years, had been the tutor of Goethe's thirteen-year-old son August. Riemer had mainly functioned as aide and scribe, tirelessly performing antiquarian, scientific, and bibliographical research. He had rendered stylistic, grammatical, and metric council; he had assisted as reader and editor of Goethe's works. Goethe had chosen Riemer along with Eckermann as executor of his papers. Riemer published his observations, experiences, and conversations in his *Mitteilungen über Goethe*, which served as a significant source of information for Mann.[15] In the setting of the story, Riemer had left Goethe's residence; he had taken a position as a teacher at the Weimar Gymnasium in 1812 and had married.

Anyone who tries to find Mann's morbid, complaining, suffering, and grudge-carrying figure in Riemer's own *Mitteilungen* looks in vain. Riemer's Goethe memoirs, like those of Johann Peter Eckermann, the other famulus in Goethe's circle, are written with extreme devotion; they are a testimonial to Riemer's admiration for Goethe and his loyalty toward him; the apologetic character of Riemer's narrative more than once skirts the embarrassing. The Riemer of Mann's novel is a different person. Mann selects the traits that betray Riemer as a grudging victim and brings them into focus. In order to sharpen the image of a self-effacing character, he overlays Riemer's portrait with traits of Eckermann, who more aptly represents the self-sacrificing amanuensis. Whenever the historical Riemer cannot muster the necessary humility, Eckermann steps in, a willing substitute commonly linked with Riemer in tradition. Mann blends these two characters because his goal is not to draw Riemer realistically but to show a type: the disciple who gives up his life's aspirations for the master's sake, rendering the "noble ministration of love" (*GW* 2, 405) in an imitation of Christ. Eckermann, who himself described his relationship with Goethe as one of student to master, would have been a closer match for the self-effacing type Mann wanted to portray, but the *getreue Eckart*, as Goethe called Eckermann in a letter to Zelter of 14 December 1830, did not start his duty in Goethe's service until seven years later, in 1823. In order to avoid a sharp anachronism in a novel not short of anachronisms, Riemer becomes the novel's ersatz Eckermann. Riemer represents what Mann calls in his conceptual notes for the novel a "prelude of the Eckermann melancholy, pulled into the circle and exploited."[16] A marginal note in Mann's copy of Theilhaber's Goethe-book says the same with cutting brevity: "Victim, like Kleist."[17]

To substitute Riemer as ersatz victim was suggested by a psychoanalytic study about Eckermann by Eduard Hitschmann.[18] Mann not only owned a copy; the essay shows signs of heavy use. Eckermann, according to Hitschmann, lived his life only for Goethe and to a much greater extent than Riemer. For Goethe's sake, Eckermann had foregone domestic bliss, a career, and the acquisition of wealth. Love for his bride and for Goethe were caught in competition for years — and the love for Goethe won out. The psychoanalyst draws a picture of Eckermann as a feminine, frightened, infantile, passive, dependent, and also physically disadvantaged man, and he diagnosed him as a person who compensated his aggrieved narcissism by believing to be chosen and by an underhanded use of power. The psychiatrist notices an especially exaggerated ability for identification, resulting from a deficient ego formation: Eckermann, whom the poet Heinrich Heine labeled a "Goethe-Papagei" (Goethe-parrot) had so much identified with Goethe's interests that he had become a model in the craft of imitation ("Original der Unoriginalität").[19] Eckermann had imitated Goethe's mannerisms of speech, referred to Goethe and himself in the plural, as if they were similar, and had experienced mental transubstantiation in his dreams, with Goethe as the active partner. In short, Goethe was for Eckermann both father figure and an idealized ego materialized.[20]

In the psychoanalytic description of the ascetic, self-sacrificing disciple, Mann could recognize a figure only too familiar to him as a son of the *fin de siècle:* Nietzsche, the one who not only had destroyed the myth of classicism's "stille Größe," but who had also brought the psychological substrate of the seemingly selfless mode of conduct into the light of analytic reasoning, and with it had pulled out the rug from under formal ethics. Nietzsche's man of resentment is the model for the submissive-reactive Riemer/ Eckermann.[21] This type of personality is for Nietzsche the incarnation of the modern decadent *par excellence,* the ascetic who in all his weakness is nonetheless directed by the Will to Power. Hitschmann's diagnosis of Eckermann was easily applicable to Nietzsche's analysis of decadence.

Mann used Riemer's financial difficulties, his unappealing physique (as depicted in the portrayal by J. Schmeller, which was Thomas Mann's model for Riemer's appearance), his bad temper,[22] his grumpy discontentment, his irritability, his suffering in the hell of teaching duties, his bad humor, his envy of the aristocratic form of Goethe's life to depict the dominant features of a resentful person in the Nietzschean mold. It is not without a provocative edge when Riemer, the first person in the novel allowed to speak about the father figure, does so from the perspective of his *ressentiment.* Of all the images ("Bilder") placed into the reader's view, the first self-contained portrayal of Goethe is constructed from a position of impotence: Goethe and Riemer are polar opposites when regarded as ideal types: creative man and reactive scholar confront each other; Riemer's activity as philologist and antiquarian merely amounts to a substitute creativity. And the famulus not only *is* a victim, he acts like one. Riemer is permanently engaged in the self-reflexive observation of his relationship to "greatness." He has abandoned himself to the creative man of action in an ambivalent love-hate relationship. His mechanism for overcoming the humiliation inflicted by Goethe's superiority and for the restoration of his pride is moral outrage. In an imaginary act of revenge — as Nietzsche teaches — the famulus takes advantage of the creative and active person; he disparages him in private in an attempt to degrade him in his own mind.[23]

It is also the great jealous "other," the sentimental opposite in Jena, Schiller, who speaks through the pouting mask of Riemer. As far back as in "Schwere Stunde" (A Weary Hour, 1905), Mann had portrayed Schiller as looking up to Goethe, the "other," the man of unconscious creativity. We know that the historical Schiller had imagined himself in the patricidal role of Brutus: "He [Goethe] has awakened in me a completely strange mixture of hatred and love, not unlike that which Brutus and Cassius must have felt toward Caesar."[24]

A character like Mann's Riemer fits in with the conception of the novel; another victim meets up with Charlotte. Two "accomplices in misery" (*GW* 2, 456) would loosen each other's tongues: one person would stir up introspection in the other, while avoiding criticizing the genius openly in any fundamental way. Charlotte usurps Goethe's motto in this oversized dialogue: "Compare yourself; recognize what you are."[25] She consistently proffers the perspective of the burgher, honed by life, to Riemer, the pretentious poet and inferior rival of the great man. Using this contrasting partnership of victimhood, Mann can now tap the reservoir of his Goethe essays of the 1920s, revitalize objections and disinclinations toward the nation's idol, while simultaneously smoothing harsher edges.

Adele Schopenhauer

The philosophical and heroic chatter of the characters, which only too often turns mythical, deteriorates into popular gossip with the entrance of Adele Schopenhauer, as Weimar is not only the Athens of the intellectual elite but also a pit of rumors. While Riemer had focused in on Goethe's psychological makeup, applying different viewpoints, even malicious ones, it had always been the Olympian of whom he spoke. The sister of the philosopher Arthur Schopenhauer, Adele, often carries on about the same topics as her brother, but she does it from the perspective of a day-to-day association with greatness. Chapter 4, therefore, contributes crucial material for the deconstruction of the great Goethe, much as chapter 3 has already done.

Regardless how the real Adele Schopenhauer appeared to her contemporaries, — some treasured her benevolence, cordiality, intellect, and artistic talent, others her inner beauty — literary and philosophical history have painted this often less than fortunate woman as a proverbial spinster and bluestocking. Such a picture was just what Mann needed. Though only nineteen years old at the time of the novel's action, the precocious friend of Ottilie von Pogwisch must play the role of a gossip, always ready to disseminate the latest hearsay. Adele's high-strung emotionalism charges up the narrative when she describes her beloved Ottilie; her exuberant personality surfaces in the eloquent and impulsive manner in which she discusses different subjects in her conversation with Charlotte.

The gifts of the historical Adele Schopenhauer, a lively imagination combined with writing talent, make her apt to "conjure up the narrative past," to use the phrase of Mann's epic narrator ("Beschwörer des Imperfekt," *GW* 10, 349). Still, as a literary character Adele must put aside her personal feelings, her dreams and disappointments, far more than the historical figure had to. While Adele serves as a narrative medium, she must also become a rounded character. Unlike the fictional Riemer, who as a literary-aesthetic "essayist" can fit the theoretical mold of *ressentiment,* the historical Adele Schopenhauer, a storyteller, must fit into the smaller scope of the familial life in Goethe's house and the private life of contemporary Weimar. To some extent Mann uses her views, especially her emotionally charged nationalism, but he alters and reshapes her opinions to fit his plans.

In contrast to the other conversationalists, Adele is not herself a victim of the great man. Her lack of literary success saves her from Goethe's envy and his tendency to cut down his competitors: she does not have the literary stature of a Lenz, a Kleist, a Hölderlin. She merely suffers from Goethe's mockery of poetically inclined women. But her function is to *narrate* the lot of two victims of greatness: August von Goethe's and Ottilie von Pogwisch's. Only indirectly does the fictional Adele succumb to Goethe, to the artistic ambience of Weimar where life was lived according to the rules of literature. Even in her youth, life had assumed a fictional dimension; life in her mother's salon appeared to be fictitious, if not fictional. Thus it is in the mode of fiction that she experiences the love story of Ottilie von Pogwisch and Ferdinand Heinke, her novel's Prussian Prince of Light, vicariously and with her heroine. Her self-realization occurs in literature. Cocooned in an aesthetic sphere, she fails to experience the authentic drama of life; she only co-exists, co-experiences, and co-loves. Because she substitutes narration for life, Adele Schopenhauer is a victim of literature and of nature.

Mann avoids letting the encounter between the youthful matriarch Charlotte and the matronly young gossip Adele — who, to make matters worse, speaks in a colloquial Saxon accent — descend into the farcical by opening the curtain to an interior drama.[26] In this drama, more is at stake than love alone. Two aesthetic and political principles confront each other: those of reactionary thinking and of progress. And as in the *Der Zauberberg* (The Magic Mountain, 1924), the discussion of polar opposites leads to confusion. Polarities and their erosion are already part of the constellation of characters: Lotte, the passionate mother (*GW* 2, 448), practically life itself, encounters the barren Adele, the embodiment of the *belles arts* as it was understood in the Biedermeier period of the novel's action. The sister of the philosopher of the negation of life, herself merely skirting it, stands at the edge of life's stage, similarly to certain characters of decadence from Mann's early works, such as the little Herr Friedemann or Detlev Spinell. Both of these characters fail in their attempt to harmonize art and life.

Mann's favored antithesis of intellect and nature did not have to be invented here; it already lay in waiting. But as a figure of renunciation, Adele Schopenhauer also points to characters from Goethe's late prose works and to Goethe himself, the real and fictional alike. Even as a nineteen-year-old woman, Adele illustrates the element of sexual resignation (Goethe as lover of Marianne von Willemer, Minna Herzlieb, Ulrike von Levetzow). However, the parallel is not so simple. Adele, though removed from life's plenty, soberly tattles the scandalous news from the household of the prince of poets ("Dichterfürst") to the burgher women unaccustomed to such lively candor — all the scandals, the erotic irregularities, the unseemly pastimes.

Above all, Adele stands intellectually and artistically at the height of her time, despite the narrator's grotesque brush-strokes. Goethe — and this is the point of contention between the young and old — closes himself off from the Romantic movement, the aesthetic modernism of his time. Goethe regards the nationalistic patriotism of the wars of liberation from the position of political abstinence, if not from outright contempt. Asked by Charlotte Kestner why Goethe approached the new literature with reserve, Miss Schopenhauer has only one response: "Thou shalt have no other gods before me" (*GW* 2, 490). The salient difference is packaged into Old Testament myth. Inflexibility, stagnation, and historical regression indicate a pre-enlightenment, mythical mode of thinking. The youth of 1816, however, pay homage to "the new gods": to the Gespenster-Hoffmann, the "pious Cornelius" (*GW* 2, 490) and to pan-German nationalism. Goethe's symbolic conservatism, in turn, labels these objects of worship reactionary. The children of the new life, as they call themselves, are according to Goethe looking backwards; they reactivate Catholic medievalism and oppose Napoleon's unification of Europe.

August von Goethe

"Story of a Minor Character" (Geschichte einer Nebenperson) is the subtitle of Wilhelm Bode's biography of Goethe's son August, which served as a principal source for Mann.[27] August, everywhere else a minor character, has been allowed to become a major one only in Adele's narrative, which she calls a "Novelle" (*GW* 2, 558). As the novella is encased in the text of the novel. The story of the son is encased in the six chapters that provide the frame for Goethe's appearance. The way Mann's narrative encloses the story of the son mirrors the way the father had encased the son in his life. But even in the novel's two chapters dedicated to the son, the son's "pseudo-life"[28] only serves as a foil for the life of others; he is not the object of the narration. He is no more than the third member of a triangle in Adele Schopenhauer's narrative (together with Ottilie and Ferdinand Heinke), and his life is spent in the role of professional son filling in for the father as needed.

August von Goethe is, in Mann's novel as in history, a victim of his great father. Even on his tombstone at the Cestius pyramid in Rome (where the father himself wished to be buried), August von Goethe is called "Goethe filius," as if he had never gained a separate identity, and as if being Goethe's son were indeed "the principal function of his life" (*GW* 2, 552). Driven to estrangement from himself emotionally and intellectually by the domestic dictator, he now acts, lives, and thinks as a substitute for the father, and the fictional August reflects his historical model. The real August had tried to break the bonds only at the conclusion of his life when, shortly before his death, he composed the verse "I don't want to be led by a children's harness / as I used to be"[29] — as he travels through Italy in place of and in the footprints of his father.

Departing from his main source on August, Bode's biography, Mann augments the erotic complications between father and "daughter," Goethe's future daughter-in-law. Mann does not miss out on the opportunity to transfer the motif of "Doppelliebe" shared by father and son to the "Doppelexistenz" (*GW* 2, 500) of Ottilie. Ottilie plays a double game; she is a fanatical nationalist while connected to the house of Goethe who is anti-Romantic and anti-nationalist. The double love is a motif that Goethe himself had repeatedly put to use in his works (in *Die Wahlverwandtschaften* [Elective Affinities, 1809] and in *Wilhelm Meisters Wanderjahre*, 1829), and which in *Lotte in Weimar* hints at an inverse Oedipal relationship: The son does not challenge the father for his mother, but the father challenges the son for his daughter-in-law. According to an article by the journalist Eberhard Buchner[30] that Mann clipped in his research for the novel, Goethe was the more active part in this relationship. In reality Goethe warmed up to his daughter-in-law only long after her wedding. The biographer Bielschowsky holds that Ottilie, by contrast, married the father in the son.[31] However the relationships may have been weighted, Ottilie von Pogwisch gets drawn into the dance of the immortal beloved as much as Charlotte Kestner herself. The narcissistic Goethe lives out this relationship in his imagination and translates it into his work. Ottilie, therefore, belongs (for Buchner) to the feminine type, which Goethe, according to *Dichtung und Wahrheit* (Poetry and Truth, 1811–14),[32] assembles into a Venus figure from various women. In the novel, Goethe's female type is called "Persönchen" (little person). While the father tries to make himself younger by those he chooses to love and then limits that fantasy by self-denial or renunciation (in his works), far sadder circumstances rule the melancholy and depression of the son. August von Goethe is not permitted to ripen into a personality; his entire being is made up of dependency and transference, an imitation of the paternal archetype without individual variation. Ottilie, too, falls victim to this vexation when August von Goethe acts "in his name" (*GW* 2, 502), in the name of the father that is, and the father appears to her as the son or in the son.

The story of the son involves the story of the father in more than one way. Underlying the father-son play in the house of Goethe is the father-son play in the house of Thomas Mann. Not that Mann had enlarged his ego at the expense of his son, as Goethe did when he exploited August. Still, he had repeatedly met his oldest son Klaus with the kind of frostiness the fictional Riemer diagnoses as a characteristic trait he sees in Goethe. Klaus resembles August in the failure of his attempt to escape the father's shadow, an attempt that failed even in Klaus Mann's own account: "People regard me *as the son*," he wrote.[33] Overwhelmed by the powerful super-ego of the "Zauberer," Klaus passes through serious depressions: "He [the father] conquers wherever he appears [. . .]. Will I *ever* escape his shadow?" (Emphasis by Klaus Mann). Klaus asked this question in his diary on 30 March 1938; he was thirty-one years old.[34] Despite several withdrawal treatments, Klaus Mann succeeded as poorly as August von Goethe in overcoming his drug dependency, and the "sickness unto death" (die Krankheit zum Tode) began to control him. The entire tragedy of the father-son relationship between the Manns is contained in two corresponding diary notations, each entered without awareness of the other. While the son ponders: "Great men really should have no sons," the father considers (referring less to his greatness than to his homosexuality): "Someone like me 'should,' of course, not bring children into this world."[35]

August von Goethe, the "hero" of Adele's story, acts as a substitute for someone else, not only in everyday life but also in love and war, and he does so by overwhelmingly unheroic means. It is easy for his rival in the story, Ferdinand Heinke, an epic Germanic hero and Siegfried figure, to overcome August's weak ego. As so often in Mann's novel, a triangular relationship develops, in which an antagonist, interfering more passively than actively, pushes his way into a relationship (a quadrangle if the elder Goethe mixes in, and a pentangle if the yearning Adele Schopenhauer is included on the sidelines — relationships more involved and confusing than even the relationships Goethe develops in his *Wahlverwandtschaften*). The Heinke counter plot that dominates the novel lacks almost all historical foundation while August's sad story is well documented. Yet the gossipy manner in which the story of Heinke was augmented by nineteenth-century biographers invited imaginative augmentation, "Genaumachen" (to make precise) as Mann called it in regard to his Joseph novels. Bode briefly mentions the rifleman from the Corps Lützow, who, seriously wounded, hides in the park, is discovered by two fantasizing girls, hidden from the enemy under personal risk, and nursed back to health by the two angels of mercy who promptly fall in love with their blond hero, defender of the fatherland.

The Heinke story offered Mann the opportunity to use the viewpoint of two sentimental girls to elevate a trivial yarn to the more weighty level of a fairy tale. At the same time, the account allowed for a chance to confront mythic fantasy with the banality of the bourgeois world. The patriotic fairy tale owes its existence to lax historiography by Bode. Heinke did not belong to the riflemen of the Corps Lützow, he was not wounded in Weimar, and there was no daring and romantic rescue. Rather, Premierleutnant Heinke, originally belonging to Gneisenau's staff but since July 1813 aide-de-camp of Major Anton von Kleist, was ordered to Weimar to prepare quarters. He knew Weimar, and he knew Christiane Vulpius from Halle and Lauchstädt; she too had cast an eye on him. Ottilie von Pogwisch and Adele Schopenhauer had met the soldier in a civilian and uneventful way on the sixteenth of November in Ottilie's mother's salon and had carried on an intense social relationship with him, often *en trois*.

Why this quite prosaic story has turned into a legend in biographies of the Goethe circle remains unclear. Two life stories seem to overlap — Heinke's and that of the Lützow rifleman Theodor Körner (whom Heinke is reported to have resembled). Körner, a Romantic poet famous during the nineteenth century, had in fact been wounded in June 1813 under circumstances that Bode describes, became lost and lay helpless in a forest.[36]

The conflict between illusion and reality governs Adele's story; another conflict is that of intellect and action, *vita contemplativa* and *vita activa*. Both are closely related and condense in the figures of Goethe and Napoleon, Goethe representing the *vita contemplativa* and Napoleon the *vita activa*. The conjunction of the poetic and political stars of the time, Goethe (Hafis) and Napoleon (Timur),[37] was the historical feature overshadowing the commonplace chatter about greatness among Lotte's visitors. Both antithetical "imperators," Goethe, whom the story depicts as the "dictator of Weimar" and Napoleon, "the mind that brings order to the world" (*GW* 2, 511), lend Adele's story weight and contour, so that the history of the period can be reflected.

Between 1936 and 1939, as Thomas Mann composed his novel, history and politics provided several imperial figures with pseudo-mythic qualities — among them Adolf Hitler. *Lotte in Weimar* addresses the danger of the imperial person, active or contemplative. Mann foregrounds but de-mythologizes the poet Goethe, while the other mythic hero, Napoleon, hovers in the background. Napoleon's name may elicit the idea of apocalypse;[38] in 1938 the question for the author would be what the world might still expect of Hitler. The banished novelist Mann looks from his exile at the dictator Napoleon and at the great colleague, Goethe, asking: what will happen when someone who usurps greatness reaches into history?

Goethe

"Goethe! No smaller mind than yours paints you or describes you." This admiring line was written by Johann Kaspar Lavater beneath an oil painting

by Johann Daniel Bager that Lavater owned. It was a portrait of the young
Goethe painted in 1773. Mann was only too familiar with both the picture
and the dedication by the preacher and author,[39] and he himself took up the
challenge of portraying Goethe when he was sixty, after having avoided
doing so at forty[40] when he had planned "Der Tod in Venedig" (Death in
Venice, 1912). Lavater, with the rhetorical exuberance of his emphatic age,
wanted to capture the signature and cult of genius in the Goethe portraits
of young Goethe:

> Who is there who could deny this face — GENIUS. And genius, *com-*
> *plete,* true genius, *without heart* — is, as will be proven elsewhere —
> *nonsense* — because not *towering intellect alone, not imagination alone,*
> not *both together* make for *genius — love! Love! Love* is the soul *of genius.*
> (Emphasis Lavater's)[41]

While Lavater makes Goethe a phenotype of inspired revelation, Mann's fictionalized portrait is a collage built from his readings. Mann's Goethe is constructed out of quotations, a method lacking originality. Nearly everything
in this portrait, Goethe's very being, his manners, his facial expressions, his
gestures comes from the descriptions of Goethe's admirers — and dispar-
agers. This Goethe portrait is a product of the Goethe reception through the
ages. While Lavater had described the bold and vivacious genius as neither
harsh nor stiff, Mann describes his Goethe as the old, sclerotic excellency,
the rigid courtier, the lover who has betrayed his love. The nature of the
novel itself signifies a historical change: it portends a farewell to Lavater's
idea of genius, a farewell to a conception of art that pretends to be in arbitrary control of its material.

In reality, Goethe's dinner party on 25 September 1816, was a small,
intimate affair. August von Goethe, Charlotte Kestner with her daughter
Clara, and the Ridels were the only guests. Mann convenes a large reception
instead. He gives the event a formal edge, creating an affair of state inappropriate to the event itself and to the middle-class standing of the visitors.
Indeed, the various collections of Goethe's conversations frequently contain
reports of such formal receptions by his Excellency, the Minister of State.
Those affairs were run as well-designed rituals, especially during the last
decade of Goethe's life. Mann combines these numerous accounts, rear-
ranging, blending, condensing their content into one narrative. He typifies
the formality of Goethe's conduct and goes beyond the specificity of the
historical visit by the ladies Kestner.

As a result, the dinner party in chapter 8 becomes a portrait of the official Goethe: the young genius has turned bureaucrat. A different, more
intimate portrait of the great Goethe, yet one no less critical, had already
appeared in chapter 7. The reader is allowed to look behind the scenes and
into the inner world of the creator of *West-östlicher Divan* (1819) — before

the official Goethe could stage the show of his reception. The uneasy guests at the more formal dinner party lack that advantage. Yet their prolonged wait at the start of chapter 8, and the let-down when Goethe finally appears, are paralleled in the retardation the reader has experienced reading chapters 1 to 6. In both cases, an immense tension has built up, a keen anticipation of the principal character's appearance. In contrast, when at the beginning of chapter 7 the interior monologue presents Goethe himself, the reader is scarcely up to enduring the step from the sublime to the all-too-human, as the mythical figure, the idol of the Weimar court of muses, the hero of the Weimarans, appears, lying in bed, reflecting on his morning erection, washing himself, and shuffling across his bedroom in his robe. The meaning of this grand deflation can only be understood against the background of imperial Germany's fanatic Goethe-cult, in which the historical Goethe was aggrandized and turned into a majestic phantom — a myth-making endeavor that the revered author himself had only too often supported.

Literary history and criticism know many images of Goethe: the brilliant and the divine, the heroic, the wise, and the genius in the art of life. Mann puts none of these on view. His Goethe is modern — in the emphatic sense in which the period around the turn of the last century called itself modern. He upholds his intent to modernize Goethe in the face of his most important sources, which he consulted every day. There was Albert Bielschowsky's *Goethe,* highly popular during the German imperial period, a present from his mother to the then-thirty-year-old. The book promoted the elevation of Goethe to Olympian status, made him a gloriously youthful Apollo figure.[42] Mann's diary during the period of preparation for the novel reflects a "peculiar resistance" to saintly legends of this kind,[43] with their groveling, flattering interpretations and embellishments. The Goethe myth needed to be rectified.[44] Mann's Goethe is sunny and cheerful, but only immediately after waking up (see *GW* 2, 617), when he is still surrounded by his dreams and not yet taxed by the psychopathologies of daily life. In broad daylight, he shows little radiance and charm; he is cold, even sinister.

Mann's move to counter the exaggerated and embellished Goethe portrait was coached above all by a psychoanalyst: Felix Aaron Theilhaber.[45] Theilhaber did not belong to the psychoanalytic movement proper, but he did use its vocabulary and practice the analytic method. He opposes the popular "bildungsbürgerliche" Goethe biography by claiming that Goethe inherited a degenerated gene pool;[46] he also pointed to Goethe's sexual neuroses. Goethe's sexual inhibition, his fear of women, the many incidences of his taking flight, appear to the psychologist as a tragedy of an abnormal psychic inheritance. Theilhaber calls the chapter in which he develops these ideas "Tantalus' Geschlecht" (Tantalus's Lineage), using the family's curse in Goethe's *Iphigenie auf Tauris* (1787) as a fictional parallel and confirmation. The particular genetic inheritance of his family rescued Goethe himself from mediocrity, but the creative potential was exhausted in the son and grandchildren. For Theilhaber, Goethe's achievements in life and art seem wrested from these adverse conditions, so that life and art appear precariously balanced. Mann expressed Theilhaber's view by quoting the bitter and proud Xenion from Goethe's posthumous papers as a leitmotif in the seventh chapter of the novel: "'Wohl kamst du durch; so ging es allenfalls.' / Mach's einer nach und breche nicht den Hals."[47]

Mann also reaches back past the adulatory Goethe literature to the Goethe criticism of early Romanticism and Young Germany. Next to Novalis's derision of Goethe's lack of interest in Romanticism stand Ludwig Börne's attacks on the tyrant of Weimar.[48] Börne had made Goethe, the impeding social force (*GW* 9, 357), the bulwark against liberty, into the king of the bourgeoisie ("Bürgerkönig") — a designation that was, in the days of the *juste milieu,* not without wit: "Goethe was king neither of the common minds nor of the distinguished ones, but of 'bourgeois souls.'"[49] The image of Goethe as king is more than a *bon mot* for Börne. He did not expose the despotism of Goethe's personality alone but also the despotism of his art. Börne hailed the day of "tyrant" Goethe's death as the birthday of freedom.[50] Mann uses this view by having Adele Schopenhauer stress Goethe's dictatorial streak in his reign over the domain of art (*GW* 2, 485).

The metaphor of the majestic Goethe hides a problem that had, more urgently since 1933, become personal for Thomas Mann. The problem reads like this: can the artist claim and achieve social leadership? It is Riemer, the theoretician and pedant, who contemplates the personality and effect of the creative person: "This right of royalty, what is it? One speaks of personality" (*GW* 2, 427). "Persönlichkeit," a key word in Goethe's world, marks the point where Mann's glass bead game with tradition (the subject of Hermann Hesse's novel) turns political. A charismatic personality, a messianic savior for Germany, was exactly what the conservative middle class and the Weimar elite had been looking for. The playwright and novelist Gerhart Hauptmann appeared to many to be the promised one. Hauptmann indeed impersonated King Goethe. The "Nationalschriftsteller" of the Weimar Republic combed his hair à la Goethe, acted like Goethe, imitated Goethe's works, and admired himself in the role of the Prince of Poets. The national Hauptmann cult peaked in 1932. This was not only the year that ended the Weimar Republic, it was also the centennial of Goethe's death and the seventieth birthday of the then-ruling "Nationalschriftsteller" Hauptmann.[51]

To embrace Goethe was not easy for the National Socialists. Nietzsche, Wagner, Liszt — those men "appeared" to be the proper guardians of the Third Reich's grail. But National Socialism's founding text, Alfred Rosenberg's *Mythos des zwanzigsten Jahrhunderts* (1930), had little use for the Weimar skeptic, the admirer of Napoleon, and the ironic deflator of German nationalism.[52] It took the National Socialists some time and a number of detours, before the clarion call from the extreme right could thunder: "He is ours!" The anniversary of Goethe's death proved to be the fitting moment for his enrollment in the party, the hometown Weimar having been a center of National Socialism for some time (*GW* 13, 71), and the brown shirts carrying the majority of votes in the state of Thüringen.[53]

One of the speakers at the national memorial celebration honoring the hundredth anniversary of Goethe's death was Julius Petersen, professor of German literature at the University of Berlin who, at the time, dominated the field of university studies in German. In his speech in the Weimar auditorium, he constructed a sweeping deification of the poet in which the images of god and Goethe merge — and not only metaphorically. Looking at the tomb where the sarcophagi of Goethe and Schiller rest beside those of the duke's family, he cried out to the audience with biblical pathos: "Put off thy shoes from off thy feet, for the place whereon thou standest is holy ground" (Exod. 3:5). In 1932, the anniversary of Goethe's death fell during Holy Week, and Petersen, the mighty manager of literature, demanded "to change the way we keep time and to set the markers of centuries not following the birth of Christ, but according to his [Goethe's] death." Petersen succeeded where Rosenberg had failed: to proclaim Goethe as the Messiah and simultaneously to fit him into a brown shirt. Together with the savior Hitler, Goethe is called upon to form the unholy alliance in whose spirit the German nation would return to health:

> Today, this nation, trampled on and humiliated, surrounds this sanctuary of his resting place [. . .] but, filled with the eternal knowledge of an everlasting new becoming [. . .]. In the growth and development of her greatest, the nation of Goethe sees the image of her still limited self, in the immortality of his being the guarantee of her own endurance, in his faith in life the leader and companion for a tireless striving.[54]

In Petersen's audience, among the cultural elite of the dying Weimar Republic, we also find Thomas Mann. His face most likely did not betray what he thought of Petersen's deification of the artist, of the "Gleichschaltung" (alignment) of Mann's aristocratic poet.[55] Known is only his laconic and ironic commentary:

> I listened to the speech of Professor Julius Petersen, the Germanist and literary historian of the University of Berlin. The most pleasant part was the musical performance of the Thomaner from Leipzig [. . .]. I enjoyed their singing more than the entire speech. (*GW* 13, 73)

It might appear that Mann had done too much in order to protect his Goethe from membership in the National Socialist Party and had gone too far in humanizing the divine myth, so far that in exposing the poet's darker side he might have obscured the luster of the Goethe image. This would be a serious misreading and simplification. Despite all his skepticism, Mann never ceased to admire the great colleague. He even assigns his own self-doubt to his fictional Goethe, revealing the contrastive, even contradictory views he held toward Goethe's greatness. He has Goethe muse in the interior monologue of chapter 7: "Could it be that dear love ["die liebe Liebe"] is composed of nothing but impurities, the brightest light is composed of darkness, a possibility that I never wanted to admit? Nothing darker than light? Could Newton be right after all?" (*GW* 2, 636). That Mann lets his Goethe figure even contemplate such a thought seems a paradox. At no time would the historical Goethe have entertained friendly thoughts toward Newton, much less granted validity to Newton's findings. Goethe had struggled with savage tenacity against Newton's theory of light, against the assertion that light is composed of all the colors of the spectrum: "Nothing is darker than light" read the provocation raised by Newton's theory; even the darkest color has a part in it. The historical Goethe rejected such ideas for theological reasons: pure light, god's revelation, must not contain impurities.

Thomas Mann wants his reader to see his Goethe in the way Newton understood light: colors, shades of light, impurities make up bright white light. Similarly the shades in Goethe's character and the incongruities of his love-life coalesce and form his creative greatness. Greatness for Thomas Mann paradoxically cannot be without impurities. Thus in symbolic terms, it would be wrong to see the light of greatness without the shadows in Mann's image of Goethe. His is a modernized Goethe; Mann pares down the Goethe myth without destroying it. The task of art is not to evade the dark side of existence, but to enlighten and to serve culture.

Repeated Reflections

What experience has Charlotte the traveler collected on her journey into the land of her youth? Despite the return to comedy in the last chapter of the novel, despite the resolution through a *deus ex machina* of a plot with tragic potential, the Hofrätin has experienced a consummate story of lost illusions. The character of Charlotte functions as a medium providing the reader with insight into an artistic world, in a loving as well as in a destructive manner. The appearances of the actors on this stage allow for ever new and ever varying reflections on the question: is the great man, the creative personality, a public disaster?

With Rose Cuzzle, the question is approached from a humorous perspective and in the manner of a prelude. The British lady, modeled after an American, has, in all her impudent naiveté, not the slightest apprehension when facing the sublimities of political and cultural life. She represents the popular perspective of the people in the crowd who gather in front of the hotel Zum Elephanten, to snatch a glimpse of their idol's halo. As a traveling artist — today we would say *paparazzo* — she chases sensation and unintentionally downgrades celebrity to caricature.

Riemer destroys Charlotte's hope of the most beloved for a prayer niche in the temple of humanity. Gone are the days of confidence, when the poets of the "Geniezeit," even Goethe himself, expected the old man now living at the Frauenplan in Weimar to grow into a Messiah and redeemer. Goethe's metaphor of the fly, willing partner in being hooked by poison and paralyzed, serves as metaphor for Riemer's own existence: the *famulus* and the son have sacrificed their souls in the service of greatness.

August von Goethe, "Goethe filius," has fully absorbed the father's will. He lives a life of unmitigated imitation, wears his father's mask and "represents" his father's myth.

Looking at Ferdinand Heinke, we can observe the *process* of myth formation. The figure of the blond Siegfried takes on heroic traits because he too serves as a screen for fictional dreams and hopes. Nationalist hysteria and erotic ecstasy produce their myth. The formation of the modern idol is presented in a consistently modern way: the Prince of Light does not deliver on the expectations of his enthusiasts but abandons them to their dreams of a fulfilled life.

And Goethe? Bielschowsky's Goethe, the star of educated German "Bildungsbürger," the myth of the German cultural tradition, is unmasked. Lotte, before she comes to Weimar, lives the expectations of a nineteenth-century reader of Bielschowsky. Thomas Mann might have at one time been such a reader. He had also venerated Goethe like Bielschowsky and his Lotte do. But in *Lotte in Weimar,* his Goethe pays a steep price while still remaining the symbol of the sovereign in the realm of intellect and art. The historical Goethe had played the role of the national poet, both because he had wanted it and because it was handed to him by the world. But Goethe's role in the novel is different. Like Lotte and the other participants in the dance around him, he had become a sacrifice: "They sacrificed to the gods, and in the end the god himself was the sacrifice" (*GW* 2, 763). This Goethe hides his innermost self from the sensationalist world "under stiff and clever masks" (*GW* 13, 168). The mask has become a requirement for the ethical achievement of the work, but the work has consumed the happiness that life and love could have granted.

Notes

[1] "Hofrätin Kestner from Hanover." "At noon [meaning for lunch] Ridels and Madame Kästner from Hanover." Johann Wolfgang von Goethe, *Goethes Sämtliche Werke,* 45 vols. (Munich/Berlin: Propyläen, 1909–1923), vol. 28, 343 (*PA*); *Goethes Sämtliche Werke,* 15 vols. (Berlin, Leipzig: Tempel, 1909–1910, vol. 15, 273 (*TA*). See also Thomas Mann, *Tb* 6 January 1937.

[2] *GW* 2, 375. Mann's collected works (*GW* 1–13) will hereafter be cited in the text.

[3] Thomas Mann, *Tb* 19 November 1933.

[4] "*H. E. R. Belani (Ludwig Häberlin)* erzählt in seinem Buch 'Goethe und sein Liebesleben': 'An einem schönen Maientage 1816 erschien die alte *Charlotte Buff, die Frau Kestners* in Weimar (also die unsterbliche Geliebte seiner Wetzlarer Wertherzeit). Charlotte ward natürlich zur Tafel geladen und erschien dabei in auffallend jugendlicher Toilette, nämlich in einem weißen Kleide mit roten Schleifen, wie sie an dem Tage getragen, wo Goethe sie vor vierundvierzig Jahren zum ersten Male gesehen.

'Er seinerseits hat dies längst vergessen, und als Charlotte ihn endlich darauf aufmerksam machte, gestand er offen, daß er sich dieses Umstandes auch nicht im mindesten mehr erinnere.

'Charlotte, welche sich, nachdem Goethe ein weltberühmter Mann geworden, geschmeichelt gefühlt haben würde, wenn er die Leidenschaft, die er früher für sie gehegt und gegen welche sie sich damals so ablehnend verhalten, jetzt abermals laut bekannt hätte, fühlte sich durch sein zurückhaltendes Wesen verletzt und kehrte, in ihren Erwartungen schmerzlich getäuscht, eher in die Heimat zurück als sie ursprünglich beabsichtigt hatte. Selbst die Erinnerung an sie war ihm gleichgültig geworden.'" Quoted from Felix Aaron Theilhaber, *Goethe: Sexus und Eros* (Berlin: Horen, 1929), 288–89.

[5] See Herbert Lehnert, "Dauer und Wechsel der Autorität. 'Lotte in Weimar' als Werk des Exils." *Internationales Thomas-Mann-Kolloquium 1986 in Lübeck, TMS 7* (1987), 39–41.

[6] Albert Bielschowsky, *Goethe: Sein Leben und seine Werke.* 2 vols. (Munich: Beck, 1905).

[7] "Je edler und reiner die Natur Friederikens war und je mehr sie still duldete und geduldet hatte, um so mehr umzog sich dem Dichter ihr Bild mit einer Madonnenglorie. Von den beiden Marien im Götz und Clavigo steigt sie allmählich zu der himmlischen Verklärung im Gretchen des Faustabschlusses empor" (Bielschowsky, *Goethe*, 1, 138).

[8] "Charlotte haßt Friederike eifersüchtig und ist froh sie im Grabe zu wissen, das arme Opfer, sie hat sich als Opfer besser gehalten und es klüger gemacht. . . . Entsetzlich allerdings, wenn das Volk es mit der Zeit entdecken wird und sie stürzte, vernichtete, absetzte, aus der Nische, von seiner Seite risse. From Thomas Mann's notes to *Lotte in Weimar,* Thomas Mann Archive Zurich (Mp. XI 14/39).

[9] *Tb*, 23 March 1935.

[10] *Goethes Gespräche,* ed. Woldemar Freiherr von Biedermann, vol. 1 (Leipzig: Biedermann, 1889–1891), 250; see also Helga Collet, *Das Konvolut zu Thomas Manns Roman "Lotte in Weimar." Eine Untersuchung* (M.A. Thesis, Kingston, 1971), 95.

[11] Eckhard Heftrich, "Lotte in Weimar," *Thomas-Mann-Handbuch,* ed. Helmut Koopmann (Stuttgart: Kröner, 1990, 1995), 431.

[12] Theilhaber, *Goethe: Sexus und Eros,* 240.

[13] *GW* 11, 43–44; see also Gerhard Lange, *Struktur- und Quellenuntersuchungen zu "Lotte in Weimar"* (Bayreuth: Tasso, 1954, 1970), 60.

[14] Ludwig Geiger, *Goethe und die Seinen: Quellenmäßige Darstellungen über Goethes Haus* (Leipzig: Voigtländer, 1908), 246–47.

[15] Friedrich Wilhelm Riemer, *Mitteilungen über Goethe: Auf Grund der Ausgabe von 1841 und des handschriftlichen Nachlasses,* ed. Arthur Pollmer (Leipzig: Insel, 1921).

[16] A "Vorspiel der Eckermann-Melancholie. In den Kreis gezogen u. ausgenutzt" (Mann's underlining). In Mann's notes to *Lotte in Weimar* in the Thomas Mann Archive in Zurich (Mp. XI 14/16; see also Wilhelm Bode, *Goethes Sohn* (Berlin: Mittler and Son, 1918), 73–75.

[17] In Mann's copy of Theilhaber, *Goethe,* 293, in the Thomas Mann Archive, Zurich.

[18] Eduard Hitschmann, "Johann Peter Eckermann. Eine psychoanalytisch-biographische Studie," *Psychoanalytische Bewegung* 5 (Vienna: Internationaler psychoanalytischer Verlag, 1933), 1–30.

[19] Hitschmann, "Eckermann," 11.

[20] Hitschmann, "Eckermann," 23.

[21] Bernhard Blume, *Thomas Mann und Goethe* (Bern: Francke, 1949), 113.

[22] "Böse Laune"; Goethe to Riemer, 19 May 1809. Johann Wolfgang von Goethe, *Goethes Werke,* edited at the request of Großherzogin Sophie von Sachsen, 133 vols. (Weimar: Böhlaus Nachfolger, 1887–1918), IV 20, 333. [*WA*]

[23] Nietzsche, *KSA* 5, 369–70.

[24] *Goethe's Gespräche* contains reports from others, as here from Schiller. *Goethes Gespräche,* ed. Flodoard Freiherr von Biedermann, vol. 1 (Leipzig: Biedermann, 1909–1911), 163; Gerhard Lange, *Struktur- und Quellenuntersuchungen,* 65–66.

[25] "Vergleiche dich! Erkenne, was du bist!" Goethe, *TA* 5, 335.

[26] Heftrich, "*Lotte in Weimar,*" 437: "Innendrama."

[27] Bode, *Goethes Sohn.*

[28] "Scheinleben"; K. R. Eissler, *Goethe: Eine psychoanalytische Studie: 1775–1786,* vol. 2 (Munich: Deutscher Taschenbuch Verlag, 1987), 1439.

[29] "Ich will nicht mehr am Gängelbande / Wie sonst geleitet sein." Bode, *Goethes Sohn,* 386.

[30] Among the material for *Lotte in Weimar* in the Thomas Mann Archives in Zurich, Switzerland (Mat. 5/30), there is an undated newspaper clipping with Eberhard Buchner's article: "Goethes Sohn August" (from: *Berliner Illustrirte Zeitung,* 21 December 1930, Nr. 51, 2305–7).

[31] Bielschowsky, *Goethe,* 2, 482.

[32] Goethe, *Dichtung und Wahrheit,* Dritter Teil, 13. Buch, *TA* XII, 176. Goethe explained in his autobiography that he acted like a painter who assembled a Venus figure from various images when he drew up his Lotte in *Die Leiden des jungen Werthers* with the help of features belonging to contemporary women of beauty.

[33] Klaus Mann, *Kind dieser Zeit* (Munich: Nymphenburger Verlagshandlung, 1965), 260.

[34] "Er [der Vater] siegt, wo er hinkommt [. . .]. Werde ich *je* aus seinem Schatten heraustreten." Klaus Mann, *Tagebücher 1938–1939*, ed. Joachim Heimannsberg (Munich: Spangenberg, 1990), 31.

[35] "Große Männer sollten doch wohl keine Söhne haben." Klaus Mann, *Tagebücher 1938–1939*, 31; "Jemand wie ich 'sollte' selbstverständlich keine Kinder in die Welt setzen" (*Tb* 20 September 1918).

[36] See Körner's poem *Abschied vom Leben*.

[37] Goethe played with a mask under the name of the Persian poet Hafis in his lyric cycle *West-östlicher Divan* (1819). In the same work he alluded to Napoleon in a poem called "Der Winter und Timur." Timur was a Mongolian conquerer also known as Tamerlane.

[38] See *GW* 2, 535 and Riemer, 302.

[39] See Hans Wahl, *Goethe im Bildnis* (Leipzig: Insel, 1930), 5.

[40] *DüD* 2, 456.

[41] Wahl, *Goethe*, 18.

[42] See Bielschowsky, 1, X.

[43] *Tb*, 6 November 1936.

[44] *DüD* 2, 454.

[45] Theilhaber, *Goethe: Sexus und Eros*.

[46] See Siefken, *Ideal der Deutschheit*, 230–33.

[47] Goethe, *TA*, 3, 257: "'You made it through; it barely worked'"; / May others do the same without breaking their necks.

[48] See also Theilhaber, *Goethe: Sexus und Eros,* 297.

[49] Leo Schidrowitz, *Der unbegabte Goethe. Die Anti-Goethe-Kritik aus der Goethe-Zeit mit zeitgenössischen Karikaturen* (Basel/Leipzig/Wien: Zinnen, 1932), 200. Leo Schidrowitz was a lyric poet and publisher in Vienna who collected "complainer, reductionists and hairsplitters" and gave them a chance to speak. His goal was to destroy the "literary critics' fairy tale of the pampered, blissful Goethe" (Schidrowitz, 3) — an intent that suited Thomas Mann.

[50] Mann, "Zur Jüdischen Frage" (Thomas Mann and the Jews, 1921), *Essays* 2, 89.

[51] See "Der Briefwechsel zwischen Thomas Mann und Gerhart Hauptmann. 'Mit Hauptmann verband mich eine Art von Freundschaft.' Teil I: Einführung. Briefe 1912–1924," ed. Hans Wysling and Cornelia Bernini. *TMJb* 6 (1993): 245–82.

[52] Robert Mandelkow, *Goethe in Deutschland: Rezeptionsgeschichte eines Klassikers,* vol. 2 (Munich: Beck, 1980, 1989), 78–79.

[53] See Thomas Neumann, "Fast ein Frühstück bei Goethe. Thomas Mann über die Goethe-Woche in Weimar." *TMJb* 10 (1997): 238.

[54] Julius Petersen, "Erdentage und Ewigkeit. Rede bei der Reichsgedächtnisfeier am 22. März 1932," *Drei Goethe-Reden* (Leipzig: Insel, 1942), 7, 11.

[55] The word "Gleichschaltung," literally meaning (electrical) switching everything toward the same level, relates to the takeover of public, semi-public, and private organizations by the National Socialists in 1933.

Thomas Mann's Late Politics

Manfred Dierks

The Relationship with the Public: The Representative

THE EXISTENTIAL PROBLEM of the young Thomas Mann was his feeling of isolation, the loneliness of the narcissist who cannot develop deeper relationships with other human beings. Freud discusses this condition as the inability to love an object. In Mann's early work he developed a veritable ideology around this problem, stylizing his inability to extend empathy to other human beings as a conflict of "Art and Life." However, after Mann had written *Buddenbrooks* (1901), and after this novel had been well received by the reading public, the author had new experiences that proved helpful: a successful series of public readings from his works, the first of which took place in the spring of 1903 in Berlin. His performance was impressive; he immediately won control over the audience in the hall, and there was strong applause. The experience of this success became a fundamental asset for him as an artist. He had learned that he was able to connect with living human beings.

Mann must have noticed soon that here lay the most intense relationship with other human beings he would ever achieve. Because of this realization, he loved to perform, and constantly sought opportunities for performances that would recreate the situation: He, up there on the platform, the listening audience down in the hall — a mutual exchange between artistic achievement and grateful applause. Anyone who is familiar with such settings recognizes the erotic elements in this kind of event (something Freud showed convincingly in "Massenpsychologie und Ich-Analyse" [Group Psychology and the Analysis of the Ego, 1921]).

Before the spring 1903 reading, the contact between Mann and his reading public had been an anonymous one. Now, however, it became a living one: now his audience had faces and bodies. Yet it remained a relationship drastically different from any "normal" exchange between human beings. The exchange between a performer and his public always implies a physical separation of the parties. During the moment of contact, a space separates the artist on the podium from the audience, a gap that cannot be bridged physically (Mann himself would later even call it a "chasm" (Kluft). Yet the gap was conquered, and the public readings made Mann ask three questions: What was it that had overcome the gap? What kind of relationship had established itself between him and his audience? And what exactly was it that governed his relationship with the people in the hall? Mann soon found an answer, calling the power at work "representation" (Stellvertretung). From his elevated position he represented (repräsentiert) the very existence of his listeners, their worries, hopes, destinies. His artistic works thus depicted the experience of his readers in symbolic terms. This could explain the great success of *Buddenbrooks;* contemporary readers had found themselves in the book. As plausible as the idea of art producing symbols of the spirit of the time may be, it became something uniquely personal to Mann when he combined it with a strange and megalomaniac fantasy: that he was a prince. Infantile day dreams, narrated directly, recur also in Mann's work in new forms.[1]

In 1903, the princely fantasy and the idea of representation fuse in the plan for the novel *Königliche Hoheit* (Royal Highness, 1909). Mann explains this fusion in a letter to a reader who seems to have complained about Mann's aloofness:

> Nobody can be closer to me than a reader of "Tonio Kröger." If you found me uncommunicative as a person, the reason may be that a person loses his taste for personal communication when he becomes accustomed to express himself symbolically, that is in works of art. This person then leads a representative existence similar to that of a prince.[2]

Here we have the basic pattern for Mann's relationship with his public. The representative assumes an eminent position ("similar to that of a prince"), while the people whom he represents, and who recognize themselves in his artistic symbols, are down below, separated from him. The basic pattern is frequently mirrored and enriched by similar concepts Mann found in Wagner's and Nietzsche's works.[3] At core it remained unchanged.

In 1910 and 1911 this pattern entered into Mann's fictional work for the first time, in the early text portions of *Bekenntnisse des Hochstaplers Felix Krull* (Fragment 1922; "First Part," 1954; remained incomplete). The novel is a self-parody: Krull is a self-critical alter-ego of Mann. The scene of Krull's first visit to the theater serves as an initiation into the world of deception. On stage, occupying an elevated and glorified sphere, the star of an operetta gives his performance while simultaneously acting out the longings of the audience — their "ideals of the heart" (*GW* 7, 287) — in the shadows down below. The scene in the novel contains an allusion to Plato's Allegory of the Cave: the ideas are presented up in the light while the deprived multitude remains down in the shadows, staring up at the perfect symbols of its confined existence. This is the relationship between the artist and his public, between the symbolic representative and the represented. Thomas Mann's self-criticism enters here, casting suspicion on art, as he had learned it from Nietzsche's critique of Wagner. Art creates illusion and thus must be fraudulent; the artist is not what he seems to be. When Krull visits the shining star in his dressing room after the curtain has come down, the artist displays a torso with purulent pimples and a cheesy, sallow complexion — the actual shape of this shining illusionist and deceiver. "What is it," Krull asks himself, that brings this insipid person to pursuing such "nightly glorification of himself"? The desire to please! Behind this desire lies an "inexpressible power, indescribable in its appalling sweetness." And when the artist offers the joy of living to the desiring multitudes and the crowd satisfies his need for applause, does that not lead to mutual satisfaction, an erotic meeting of two desires? (*GW* 7, 295). "Erotic meeting" in the original German is "hochzeitliche Begegnung," literally a "nuptial" encounter.

Already in his first experience with art's charming magic (Gefälligkeitszauber) (*GW* 7, 295), Krull himself notices that Eros is involved. This experience was probably Mann's own: he felt a sensual tie that connected him to his audience when he performed publicly in lectures and readings from his works. He explained the phenomenon to himself with the help of Schopenhauer's philosophy. This is evidenced by a special word the narrator uses in the novella "Der Tod in Venedig" (Death in Venice, 1912).

"Der Tod in Venedig" was written in 1911, just after the earliest *Krull* manuscript was abandoned. The novella's protagonist, Gustav von Aschenbach, is conceived as a representative. The narrator explains the success of Aschenbach's works by their ability to be representative:

> In order for a significant product of the mind to create a response that is both broad and deep, a secret relationship, even agreement must exist between the personal destiny of its originator and the destiny of his generation. People do not know why they make a work of art famous. They are really far removed from critical expertise when they mean to discover hundreds of merits in order to justify their great concern. But the real reason for their applause is something imponderable: it is empathy [Sympathie]. (*GW* 8, 452)

This empathy is explained: contemporary people "recognized" themselves in Aschenbach's works; they found themselves "confirmed, elevated, celebrated [besungen] by it" (*GW* 8, 454).

But is such an explanation sufficient? Every publisher would object. There ought to be a foundation for this *secret* agreement between the lot of the author and that of his generation. What Mann meant by the German word "Sympathie" can be understood in the context of Schopenhauer's "Practical Metaphysics." Schopenhauer's general metaphysics holds that the individual's perception of himself as a self-contained entity is an intellectual self-deception. Schopenhauer claims that it is merely the functioning of the mind that causes human beings to see the phenomena of the world in individual forms. Without this self-deception, in true reality, everything is identical with everything else and contained in the metaphysical Will without distinction. Individuation means enclosure and, hence, separation. There exists however a condition under which the human intellect is liberated from the principle of individuation, and that is empathy. Empathy can occur in three forms: sympathy (Mitleid), sexual love, and magic.[4] In practice, Schopenhauer holds, when beings are connected in the metaphysical condition of empathy, their physical segregation vanishes — such a "hochzeitliche Begegnung" (nuptial encounter) can be felt as an erotic or a magic one. Mann, having structured the world for his own purpose — as well as for some of his novels — according to Schopenhauer's philosophy, always turns to "practical metaphysics" in Schopenhauer's sense in order to understand psychic phenomena not easily explained by psychoanalysis. We will discuss this tendency again on the occasion of "Mario und der Zauberer" (Mario and the Magician, 1930).

Representation and Politics: The Educator of the People

After the fall of the monarchy, the dream of being a prince was over. Another image for the relationship with the public was needed, one compatible with democracy. Still, at the occasion of Gerhart Hauptmann's sixtieth birthday, Mann indefatigably tried the formula "King of the Republic" (*GW* 11, 812), but even that artful definition turned out to be unsalvageable. It had become evident to Mann that the general population mattered more than his reading public. As early as in "Der Tod in Venedig" he had "the contemporary generation" in his sight (*GW* 8, 452). To do justice to the "republic of internal reality" (Republik der inneren Tatsache) (*GW* 11, 823), representation had to be defined in political terms. The fantasy of high rank, of Prince Carl (as in "Kinderspiele" [Children's Play, 1904], *GW* 11, 328), had to be democratized, but the sense of eminence needed to remain in order to satisfy Mann existentially.

The modification in the manner of representation can be understood with the help of a curious passage contained in the foreword to the speech "Von deutscher Republik" (Of German Republic, 1922), the speech by which Mann, surprising for many, had declared himself in support of the republic. As a consequence, he had been accused of desertion, of having betrayed his positions as expressed in *Betrachtungen eines Unpolitischen* (Reflections on a Nonpolitical Man, 1918). He denied that reproach with a strange argument that has often been criticized: "I do not know of any change of mind. Perhaps I have changed my thoughts, but not my intent

(Sinn). Thoughts are always means to an end, instruments in the service of intent. I say that even if it sounds sophistic." And now, he continued, it was important "to maintain a solid intent during changing times" (*GW* 11, 809).

He had only changed instruments or thoughts, then, but what was the "solid intent" (bleibende Sinn) that governed the changed thought processes? He called it: "deutsche Menschlichkeit" (German humanity) (*GW* 11, 810). "Deutsche Menschlichkeit" belongs to a pre-political sphere and can be touched by political change only superficially, never in substance. The choice of the term "deutsche Menschlichkeit" shows how deeply the idea of representation is rooted in Mann's mind. In a commentary to *Königliche Hoheit* of 1910, he claims representation: "I believe that I only need to talk about myself in order to express the language of the time and the voice of the public" (*GW* 11, 571). In "Der Tod in Venedig" this belief is raised to the level of Schopenhauer's practical metaphysics as empathy, connecting the writer with the contemporary generation, the public (*GW* 8, 452). Now, in 1922, the bond that links him and the German public is not merely his own humane attitude but Mann calls it "deutsche Menschlichkeit." And, where does the idea of "deutsche Menschlichkeit" get its luster for Mann? Where does the source of prominence rest for the elevated representative on the podium? Mann borrows it from Goethe, the "Dichterfürst" (Prince of Poets).

Beginning with the year 1922 — the year in which Thomas Mann transformed himself into a democrat — we witness a new construction of the bridge that links the writer and the multitude through representation. Prince Carl wears a democratic mask from now on — he becomes *Nationaldichter* and educator of his people. The author of *Joseph und seine Brüder* (Joseph and his Brothers, 1926–43) himself rises to become Joseph the Provider in intellectual terms. In essays such as "Goethes Laufbahn als Schriftsteller" (Goethe's Career as a Writer) and "Goethe als Repräsentant des bürgerlichen Zeitalters" (Goethe as Representative of the Bourgeois Age) — both written in 1932 when Germany celebrated the one-hundredth anniversary of Goethe's death — Mann makes it very clear that he leans on Goethe, compares himself with him, even places himself on the same level with him.

By managing to succeed in writing himself into kinship with Goethe, Mann would gain two advantages: being elevated to a level of importance similar to Goethe's, and achieving an official legitimization as preceptor of the German people. Granted, Mann constructed his parallels with the superfather (Übervater) of the German bourgeoisie self-critically, leaving his self-portrait ambivalent, yet he nevertheless did it in a way that could not be misread. His public in Germany, and the worldwide audience he addressed from exile, confirmed him in this role. His function as representative increased at the same time: after 1933 he no longer represented the Weimar Republic alone; instead, his audience recognized him as the representative of German intellectuals in exile in the West; he became a symbol of the "good German."

Mann's educational ideas and directives addressed to the German people were guided by his defensive stance against the rising and, later, established fascism. They warned of a "false" romanticism, of a relapse into nationalism; they tried to establish psychoanalysis as the historically correct form of Romanticism, and they sided with social democracy. Mann had to work hard in order to hold on to the authorities that had sustained him up till then: Nietzsche, Wagner, Bachofen, Schopenhauer; all of them having one foot in the "wrong" camp, being invoked by the National Socialists as well. Goethe offered a better opportunity as a guarantor of "deutsche Menschlichkeit." Even though the Nazis could cite Goethe as a German cultural monument, the man from Weimar was a far less questionable figure than the Romanticists from Schopenhauer to Nietzsche. In the case of Goethe, there was no doubt that he was representative and had greatness; kinship with him was the most comfortable.

Mann's identification with Goethe is a construction, a kind of arrogating play with myths. Mann was aware of this because it was in these years that he was writing the novel of his mythical confidence man, Joseph, and then the confessions of the confidence man Felix Krull. Mann's mutation into a kin of Goethe becomes the foil that enables the corresponding mutation into a democrat and an educator of his people. The mutation is both instructive for Mann's psychology and fundamental for the understanding of his political development. No such kinship existed before the composition of *Betrachtungen eines Unpolitischen*. Then, Mann had described his position toward Goethe quite correctly: he felt closer to Schiller, the intellectual, who stands distant from nature, the Schiller who is forced to seek the warmth of life because he does not "possess" it. Mann did identify with Goethe occasionally even then, but the relevant passages are of minor weight. This principal position does not change with *Betrachtungen* — the many Goethe quotations only serve him as ammunition in his trench warfare. But it does change with "Goethe und Tolstoi" (1921, 1925, 1932) when Goethe becomes a model for republicans. The new emerging foe, fascism, partly motivated that change.[5] Mann's two Goethe lectures, delivered during the centennial of Goethe's death in 1932, concluded his move toward Goethe.

I will forego discussion of the many grounds by which Mann "proves" the relationship — for example that they both had a similar work ethic (*GW* 11, 305) or harbored "sympathy with death" (Sympathie mit dem Tode) (*GW* 11, 324). These passages over-stylize traits common to a writer, or they generalize an isolated quote. Mann molds his Goethe into a value-free ironic writer and into an indifferent egotist (*GW* 11, 316) like himself.

Regarding Mann's political attitude, one might ask the question: How can a writer break away from narcissistic isolation and join his nation? How or in what way can he communicate with the public? The answer is: by his *educational effect*. In his speech "Goethes Laufbahn als Schriftsteller," Mann explicates this effect in a passage that once more recalls the surprising experience of the young author who suddenly discovers that a greater public is interested in the products of his loneliness.[6] Thomas Mann speaks of Goethe, but he also means himself:

> Goethe was an educator par excellence. Proof is in the two great monuments of his life: *Faust* and *Wilhelm Meister*. The novel, especially, shows how the autobiographical, confessional, self-constructing impetus objectifies itself, turns outward toward society, even to statesmanship, and thus becomes educational. Neither the urge, nor a calling [Berufung] for education, have their origin in a harmonious self, but rather in the author's problematic nature, in his disharmony, in the difficulty, the burning distress, the struggle with himself. The educational mission of the writer must be defined by his readiness to confess inner problems; it is a calling to transform unusual experiences into representative ones that are capable of expressing what is common to all mankind. "True symbolism," Goethe says, "occurs where the specific becomes representative of the general." The creative mind is capable of producing such symbolism: an individual speaks with his own charms and limitations. But in expressing himself he becomes — unintentionally — the voice of the general public. Not that he makes pronouncements of general validity, but the import of what he says grows unexpectedly and assumes new meaning. (*GW* 9, 340)

Mann connected these discoveries with his early and surprising experiences: that *Buddenbrooks* had so soon reached a broad public, and that the lecturer up on his podium could generate such intense alliance with his listeners down below. The experience had meant for him a deliverance from the iron cage of self-referentiality; what had been personal in origin had, surprisingly, attained importance for many. No wonder that Mann named and explained this event using the quasi-metaphysical term: empathy (Sympathie). Speaking of Goethe (but meaning also himself) he uses a metaphysical and religious word for this unexplainable deliverance, "grace":

> Grace, when it partakes in a work [. . .], endows it with the potential of unintentionally and unknowingly representing the inner destinies of the many — not in the sense that average or normal destinies will be represented. Rather the representation may or even ought to be extraordinary, coming from suffering, or may be even sick. (*GW* 9, 340)

The promise of deliverance from self-referentiality is not fully plausible: the writer, as a person, always remains separate from his public; the lecturer on the podium is excluded from his audience. But in a certain way both writer and audience are in alignment with one another, as separate as they may be otherwise. This is what unexplainable grace does. This belief is the basis for Mann's idea of an educational mission for the writer. It is hardly democratic; it is rather aristocratic pretentiousness. Mann continues in "Goethe's Laufbahn als Schriftsteller":

> The writer can be defined as the educator who himself is educated in the most unusual way. His education is always accompanied by a struggle with himself. The inner and the outer world are intertwined; the self wrestles with itself and with the world. When an educator, assuming he is perfect enough, merely conveys information, the result is only an empty drill [leere Schulmeisterei]. Wrestling with the *larger self, the nation,* however, and thereby correcting and transcending the personal sphere and establishing solidarity with one's social environment, with the people — how much more dedication is required for such an engagement than the howling affirmation of self and the nation commonly practiced by jingoist patriots. This kind of solidarity expresses itself often by holding oneself distant from one's nation, often severely criticizing it — as we have experienced it in the words and judgment of great Germans, especially Goethe and Nietzsche. (*GW* 9, 341, my emphasis)

In this educational idea of Mann's we have the new "democratic" formulation of the relationship between a writer and his public, or the "Royal Highness" and his subjects. The relationship functions by way of an analogy: as the writer has to wrestle with himself in order to attain his form, so he wrestles with the nation in the attempt to shape it. This is the basis of all politics for him. Since the highness is no longer royal, the analogy of writing and politics suggests equality and democracy, but the psychological substance, the emotion that underlies Mann's view of politics, is certainly not democratic. In it the "nation" is not an equal partner but rather, employing terms from psychology, the nation remains a subject (Untertan). Even more precisely formulated, the nation grows into the role of the writer's extended self. This is not a metaphorical relationship. Rather Mann describes — honestly and precisely as usual in such matters — the consciousness of a narcissistic person who cannot recognize or acknowledge an other — neither a person nor a nation — in his or its own right, and within the other's limits. If a narcissist establishes a relationship with an object, the object appears to him as an extension of his self. This is exactly what the *larger self, the nation* means to Mann (*GW* 9, 341).[7] This is no perfect way to attain to democratic convictions. But perhaps it serves as an adequate reaction to what Goethe had been calling the "demands of the day" (Forderungen des Tages).

Humanistic Politics: Applications

The underlying psychology of Mann's relationship with the "crowd," with the public, with the nation cannot be adequately understood in political terms. Rather, this relationship is rooted in a deeper layer of his personality. This layer, in turn, becomes the basis for Mann's political thinking. As a consequence, Mann's thinking will always show a tendency toward authoritarianism. Mann is not the only one so affected, and the psychic relationship should not be appraised in ethical terms. The history of Western democracies knows sufficient "Royal Highnesses" with authoritarian tendencies. Most were eventually forced to recognize the equality of all under their respective constitutions and accept political pluralism. What degree of democratic convictions motivated their actions is not a political question; what matters is whether or not their actions were beneficial for democracy. Thomas Mann made important concessions to democratic rule after 1922, and he did much for the Weimar Republic. Motivated by practical considerations, he understood that democracy was the form of the body politic suitable for the contemporary German nation and for the future of humanity. His public pronouncements in the political realm, however, remain abstract, and his political semantics lack concrete, empirical roots. What he demanded of the good writer in 1924 characterizes his own political efforts: "Sensitivity toward what the future needs" (*GW* 11, 355).

Mann defines the republic as the unity of state and culture (*GW* 11, 854); he had denied the possibility of such a union until 1922, but thereafter such an assertion became the general line in his overall argument. As educator of the people, culture was his concern. The directions he began giving, starting in 1922, spell out Germany's future cultural needs: Wagner appears as a dynamic psychologist and Nietzsche as overcoming Romanticism. Mann advises against the mystical matriarchy of Bachofen (while still studying Bachofen in private). Freud is to be preferred over Carl Gustav Jung, and Goethe is presented as a European and world citizen. Mann plied his educational craft in speeches, essays, and in many occasional writings such as book reviews or book promotions. He soon aimed his program at the rising National Socialism and its bourgeois support from the right. Mann had to deny private sympathies in this process; examples are Bachofen or Carl Gustav Jung.

Working along these lines Mann came to accept socialism, which he saw as humanizing materialism. "Socialism," he wrote in February of 1933 in an open letter, "is nothing other than the duty-bound decision to stop surrendering one's mind to celestial fantasies in the face of social and collective needs, but to side with those who want to lend significance to the earth — human significance. In this sense I am a *socialist*"(*GW* 12, 681; italics by Mann). Five years earlier Mann had argued that the well-being of Germany depended on Karl Marx reading Friedrich Hölderlin, which, he felt, was actually happening (*GW* 12, 649). Mann's socialism has little to do with Marxism, though; it is aligned with the humanism of the progressive bourgeoisie and its desire to preserve its own cultural values for the future.

Mann's republican career progressed steadily after 1922. Though opposed by the rightist camp, he soon came to represent the German republic inside and outside Germany. He attended conferences in Paris and Warsaw, addressed P.E.N.-Congresses; he became a founding member in the section "Dichtkunst" (approximately: Artistic Writing) of the Prussian Academy of the Arts with rights to elect new members. Applause engulfed him in assemblies. In a way he still remained a "Royal Highness" or, formulated in the compromise he had found for Gerhart Hauptmann, he was "the King of the Republic" (*GW* 11, 812). Yet he also felt ambivalent about his role. The story "Mario und der Zauberer" is an account of this ambivalence.

"Mario und der Zauberer": A False Nobility

In the summer of 1926 Thomas Mann spent two weeks of his vacation in the popular Italian seaside resort of Forte dei Marmi. Italian fascism had seen a complete victory at home that year; it was becoming successful abroad as well. The country was ubiquitously aware of the fascist "revolution" and of Mussolini's theatrical appearances — both, without a doubt, permeated the atmosphere in Forte dei Marmi — and it is likely that Mann experienced at least the salient events occurring in the story. In August of 1929, he apparently remembered the incident and composed the work. The Great Depression was to start only three months later, and National Socialist agitation was on the rise.

The first person narrator in "Mario und der Zauberer" tells of a family vacation in Torre di Venere. It happens during the high summer season; the village and the beach are filled with families from Florentine and Roman society; the tense atmosphere is saturated with the national reawakening of the Italian people. This is when Cavaliere Cipolla, a hunch-backed magician and charlatan, puts on his star-performance on an elevated stage set up as a classroom, right down to the blackboard (*GW* 8, 673). After performing juggling tricks and mathematical games, Cipolla commences with experiments of "transferring his will" to members of the audience (Willensaufnötigung) (*GW* 8, 696). Against his own will a boy sticks out his tongue, another is punished with colic for his resistance. With a cracking whip the cripple controls the scene; time and time again he fires up his magic power with intoxicating drink. Slowly it becomes apparent that this magician is really an unusually strong hypnotist who augments his experiments by playing with his audience's free will. The principle is always the same: either Cippola forces his will on someone else and that person draws the predicted card, or Cippola himself surrenders his will and accepts the public's collective one, finding a needle hidden by the audience. The narrator slowly perceives that there is a current flowing "from organism to organism in an unexplained manner" (*GW* 8, 690) and thus recognizes the metaphysical quality of the events. Those events are rooted in the occult: "ambiguously unclean and not to be unraveled" (zweideutig-unsauber und unentwirrbar). At the end, Cipolla exceeds his limits. He ventures too deeply into one man's emotional integrity, revealing his secret love. When he taunts the young man, the youth shoots him.

The novella must be read on several levels. As a representation of contemporary history, "Mario und der Zauberer" can be understood as an allegory of fascism. The novella demonstrates the interplay of "Volk and Führer" (people and leader) (*GW* 8, 691); it shows the loss of freedom of the individual will; and, finally, it defines the end of the game as the point when the "Führer" violates the emotional integrity of other human beings.

On a secondary level, the story serves to put the artist Thomas Mann under suspicion. Mann recognizes the constellation "writer and public" in the relationship of "Volk und Führer," as it had occupied him since his novella "Tonio Kröger" (1903). This time Cipolla is meant to demonstrate that constellation. Mann was called "Zauberer" (magician) by members of his family; the name also carried an allusion to the "old magician" from Bayreuth, Richard Wagner. Nietzsche had used Wagner in order to exemplify his critique of the modern artist: he called him a deceiver, an actor, a demagogue, a false priest. Much of this Mann had applied to himself; this kind of self-criticism now fed "Mario und der Zauberer."

The novella depicts the principal configuration that characterizes the relationship between the author and his public: the writer ("Royal Highness," "educator") on the podium, the audience ("people," "multitudes," "nation") down below. What connects the two realms is mysterious. It is not corporeal because the writer remains physically isolated. What is it then that is bridging the gap between the two spheres? "Representation" was Mann's early answer: the writer, his life, and his destiny have symbolic value that relates to everyone. But how does representation come about? In "Der Tod in Venedig" the answer had been: by empathy (*GW* 8, 452). Schopenhauer's practical metaphysics is at work: a magic current passes below the individuals in their state of individuation; it connects the writer with the "multitude," the "nation," subliminally. The uncompleted novel *Felix Krull* contains a parody of this metaphysical relationship. In the scene of Krull's visit to the theater, the actor Müller-Rosé beguiles the public because he plays to the ideals of their hearts on stage (*GW* 7, 287). Müller-Rosé demonstrates the "magic charm of art" (*GW* 7, 295), but soon, Krull, entering Müller-Rosé's dressing room, learns how questionable the effect of such performance is. Although dubious, the relationship between Müller-Rosé and his audience is nevertheless magical. It is "a power" (eine Kraft) (*GW* 7, 290) that connects him with the people in the hall.

The same scenario linking author and public appears both in *Krull* and in "Mario." Mann's self-criticism, which underlies this imagery in both texts (exposing the questionable circumstances), is essentially the same as in

"Tonio Kröger." Dubious or not, Cipolla is meant to represent the artist and is thus a partial alter-ego of Mann himself: he, too, has the hunchback and is excluded from "life" as was little Herr Friedemann. Like other artist characters in Mann's work, Cipolla is dependent on his "achievement" (Leistung); therefore he stresses the hardship caused by his act (*GW* 8, 692). Yet he is able "to control himself" (*GW* 8, 678). We hear the same of Mann, the educator of the people, who finds his pedagogy in self-correction and endurance, calling it wrestling with the nation as an extended self (*GW* 9, 341). It is similar in Cipolla's case: the audience grows into his extended self, and only then is the magician able to control the crowd with his hypnotic power, assuming the position of a "ruler" (*GW* 8, 694).

From the beginning of his performance it is the extension of Cipolla's self that constitutes the core of his achievement:

> He kept talking [. . .]. It was part of his style that he immediately set out to bridge the gap between the podium and the audience in the hall. The bantering with the young fisherman had done that, and also the fact that he came down to the representatives of the public after having compelled them to enter the stage. He looked for a personal touch. (*GW* 8, 681)

At this point, the current between Cipolla and the multitude is free to flow because they have joined. It was obviously important to Thomas Mann to explain this phenomenon. He does it by way of Schopenhauer's practical metaphysics, using passages from the philosopher's "Versuch über Geistersehn und was damit zusammenhängt" ("Essays on Spiritism and Related Subjects," 1851). As in the narrator's explanation in "Der Tod in Venedig" (*GW* 8, 452), there is empathy involved, magically traversing the boundaries of individual consciousness.[8] The "blind execution of complicated actions" (by the audience) is explained by "a direction which passes in an unexplained manner from organism to organism" (*GW* 8, 690). We also take part in the reverse: Cipolla is to search for a hidden item and is guided by the will of the community. The current moves in an opposite direction, and the artist reaffirms it, talking constantly. It is now he whose will has been switched off. He now acts out the passive part, executing the unspoken desire of the community, a desire that has been hanging in the air. Yet he has not changed. He is the same person who exercised his own will before and was in control. The ability, he says, to give up one's will, to become a tool, to obey in a complete and unconditional manner is merely the opposite of the capacity to control. Together they constitute one principle, one indestructible unit. He who knows how to obey also knows how to command, and the same is true in reverse; one notion is buried in the other, as people and leader ("Volk und Führer") are enclosed in one another. However, the achievement, the severe and exacting achievement, is Cipolla's. He is the leader and agent in whom will becomes obedience and obedience will. His person is the place of origin for both, and, as a consequence, his performance makes him weary (*GW* 8, 691–92).

Initially, this account gives a "practical-metaphysical" explanation of the bond between Cipolla and the people in the hall, but it also encompasses the relationship between writer and public, as Mann understood it.[9] Mann then translates this relationship, using Goethe as his model, into the constellation "educator-nation." He is guided by what Schopenhauer calls "Sympathie," the ability to grasp the magic current flowing beneath all individual consciousness, thus recognizing the metaphysical oneness among beings. In Schopenhauer's view, only few people possess such ability, and Mann obviously means Cipolla to be one of them. He can exercise the Will as well as practice obedience to it; his person embraces both. Mann, likewise, claims to belong to the group when he says, "I need only to tell of myself in order to lend words to my time, to the general public: this is my belief" (*GW* 11, 571). When Cipolla asserts that the task is hard on him, he resembles Tonio Kröger, who laments: "I live between two worlds [that of burgher and artist]; I am at home in neither and suffer weariness as a consequence" (*GW* 8, 337).

A yet different reading of this psychology between an artist and his public is delicate indeed; it is a psychology of fascism cast in Schopenhauer's terms. The nucleus is contained in the cry of German crowds during the reign of National Socialism: "Führer befiehl, wir folgen dir" (Führer give orders, we will follow). The underlying ideological assumption of this collective clamor is the belief that the leader represents the will of the people and that his will can shape the masses. The construction of a resemblance between fascist leader and humanistic writer and educator of a nation in "Mario und der Zauberer" is consistent with Mann's later polemicism in the essay "Bruder Hitler" (English title: "A Brother," 1939). The essay proposes that the failed artist Hitler and the Nobel Prize winner Thomas Mann have something in common. It is not the best they share, but it is in the inescapable cultural bond that Mann recognizes himself. But he also recognizes his "uncomfortable and shameful brother" in it (*GW* 12, 849).

Mann always knew that he was not who he said he was. In 1912 the writer Gustav von Aschenbach in "Der Tod in Venedig" abdicates his role with these words:

> The masterly pretension of our style is foolish and a lie [. . .]; the confidence the masses have in us is most ridiculous; education of the people and of the young by artistic means is a precarious undertaking that should be prohibited. For how should he be fit to be an educator who has a natural, innate and incorrigible direction toward the abyss? (*GW* 8, 522)

"Mario" is an echo of Aschenbach's insight. In the story of the magician, Mann ironizes his own idea of the educational mission a writer has and places it under suspicion. The "Royal Highness" has deteriorated into the false nobility of the Cavaliere Cipolla. However, this is merely one side of the ambivalence Mann apparently felt. At the end of "Bruder Hitler" he defines his insight into the similarities between himself and the failed artist Hitler as "expressions of self-contempt of art which, in the end, does not want to be taken literally" (*GW* 12, 852). Similarly, we need to read the self-contempt in "Mario" in political terms as well. Mann, the democrat, places himself under suspicion for his enduring, incorrigible tendency toward aspiring to a position of preeminence. But here too he does not want to be taken quite so literally.

Late Politics:
Sensitivity for the Future and its Needs

Thomas Mann's political attitude is principally the same as his ideas about the relationship between the artist and his public, between the writer and the times in which he lives. These relationships can be seen as ambivalent. In his fictional writings Mann plays with this ambivalence: the artist can be an educator or a deceiver. In his political writings he stresses the positive side, advocating democracy in the role of preceptor.

Mann had formulated his concept of the artist's educational mission in 1932 in his speeches about Goethe. A year later he was forced into exile, and he reacted with deep shock. "Fear to lose my senses," he wrote in his diary while staying at a Swiss hotel in March 1933.[10] For a variety of reasons, Mann abstained from political utterances during the first three years in exile; he did not fight the National Socialists directly. In February 1936, however, he made his break with National Socialist Germany by way of an open letter to the *Neue Zürcher Zeitung*. In the fall of 1938, Mann and his family moved to the United States, where he soon became a leader of German exiles in the West. A great number of his statements now addressed the war, the problems of exile, Germany itself, and a future world order. Mann's political program at this point was based on two principles: 1) the republic of the future must be a *social* democracy and 2) the basis of all political action should be motivated by a new interest in humanity, a "New Humanism." This new humanism would replace metaphysics, using a pathos that is religious but in a humane or secular way.

Such an educational mission informs Mann's own pathos. But he continued to apply the suspicious irony with which he treated his artist figures in the novella "Das Gesetz" (Thou Shalt Have No Other Gods Before Me, 1943). "Das Gesetz" narrates the origin of the Ten Commandments, depicting Moses as an artist. Mann's Moses educates his people, the Israelites, artistically. Moses "aspired to his father's blood [meaning the tribe of his father] as the sculptor aspires to an unshaped block" (*GW* 8, 810). But

Mann's Moses is as questionable as Mann's artist characters used to be. Although Moses is a "chosen one" (Erwählter) (*GW* 8, 856), he is also a murderer, and having become aware that destroying life can be "delicious" (*GW* 8, 808), he recognizes that murder must be prohibited for that very reason. Moses shares the hubris of the creative artist; he cannot distinguish between his own desire and that of his god (*GW* 8, 824). When Mann's Moses claims personal greatness and feels that he is chosen (*GW* 8, 856), we have another metamorphosis of "Prinz Carl" and "Royal Highness." Moses commits adultery too, although he calls it something else. Altogether, he is a very questionable artistic educator. However, in the end, there are the Ten Commandments; the form and spirit of the people of Israel are secured for all time to come.

In the fall of 1943, Mann delivered a lecture in the Library of Congress titled "The War and the Future." In it he develops his idea of a future social democracy, and communists of both East and West Germany would later quote his words: "I cannot but see something superstitious and childish — the basic foolishness of our era — in the panic the bourgeois world attaches to the word communism, the scare from which fascism has benefited (*GW* 12, 934). The sentence immediately preceding reads: "You see that I cannot see the human ideal in a socialism that lets equality completely supersede liberty. I believe that I am [therefore] protected from the suspicion of being a champion of communism" (*GW* 12, 934). In fact, the remainder of the speech shows that Thomas Mann thought of socialist and communist elements in a future humane world order, elements, however, that had roots in the waning Middle Ages.[11] Mann's vision of an economic future included ideas of communal ownership, the progressive leveling of class differences, the right to employment, and a general obligation to contribute one's labor (*GW* 12, 935). In his speech "Deutschland und die Deutschen" (Germany and the Germans, 1945), he claimed his own version of world citizenship as the model for a global social reform.

This speech, presented three weeks after the capitulation of the German forces, was an eminently political act in itself. Facing the moral catastrophe that the images of the liberated concentration camps had spread across the globe, this historical analysis of the German soul and intellect is a bid not to condemn Germany but to understand the country in a clinical sense. The speech describes the "German character" — as Mann saw it — as ambivalent: "The evil Germany that is the good Germany that went astray, the good Germany in misfortune, in guilt and downfall" (*GW* 11, 1146).[12] With it Mann appealed to the only hope still available to him and to Germany: divine grace (*GW* 11, 1148).

Democracy from Above

We have pursued the road Thomas Mann took from the "unpolitical" author of *Betrachtungen eines Unpolitischen* to the public speaker in the Library of Congress who, as politician in exile, discusses the culpability of the Germans for their political disaster. We pursued his development on the psychological level because there lies the foundation for his political utterances. As intelligent and helpful as Mann's political pronouncements often were, they are derivative: Mann was always primarily concerned with his own problem as an artist, the relationship of the writer to his public. Since this public freed him from isolation — "I need only to tell of myself in order to lend words to my time, to the general public" (*GW* 11, 571) — he spoke of "Gnade" (grace) (*GW* 9, 340). The relationship was always asymmetrical; it brought with it the potential megalomania of "Royal Highness," and no matter how democratic Mann's language seemed to have become, that element was still part of it. Yet one cannot deny Mann's ethical achievement. He pursued political ideas for the benefit of many, even though they ran counter to his innermost desires.

The retention of the element contained in "Royal Highness" is nowhere more obvious than in the definition of democracy Mann provided in 1943 in his speech "Schicksal und Aufgabe" or "The War and the Future":

> I understand democracy not so much as a demand for equality from *below,* but as goodness, justice and empathy from *above.* I do not consider it democratic when Mr. Smith or Little Mr. Johnson taps Beethoven on his shoulder and cries out: "How are you, old man!" That is not democracy but a lack of tact and a failure to understand social distance. But when Beethoven sings: "Be embraced, millions, this kiss is for the whole world!," *that* is democracy. For he could have said, "I am a great genius and unique, while the people are a mob; I am much too delicate to embrace them." Instead, he calls all of them his brothers and the children of one heavenly father whom he shares. That is democracy in its highest form." (*GW* 12, 933; Mann's emphasis)

In 1943, we still hear the voice of the "Royal Highness." It descends from *above.*

Notes

[1] *GW* 11, 328. In "Kinderspiele" (Children's Play) playing Prince Carl is presented as autobiography, in *Bekenntnisse des Hochstaplers Felix Krull* (*GW* 7, 272–73) as fiction. In *Königliche Hoheit* a prince is the protagonist; in *Joseph und seine Brüder* Joseph becomes Viceroy of Egypt; in *Der Erwählte* Gregorius becomes the Pope; in "Das Gesetz" Moses becomes the leader of his tribe; and finally in *Krull,* Krull becomes a Marquis. Mann's collected works (*GW* 1–13) will hereafter be cited in the text.

[2] *Br.* 1, 40 (5 December 1903).

[3] See Wagner's essay "Publikum und Popularität" (Public and Popularity, 1878), in which he says that a true artist breaks through the intellectually distorted surface of things and enables the public to see things new again; that is the true "popularity" of art (Richard Wagner, *Gesammelte Schriften und Dichtungen,* vol. 10 [Leipzig: E. W. Fritzsch, 1887–88], esp. 87–90). Related to this is Wagner's later idea that the artist is something like a priest who raises the monstrance to the congregation from an elevated position (see *GW* 9, 366) as, for instance, Raphael or Beethoven in the tradition of the "poetic priest" Jesus Christ in "Religion und Kunst" (Religion and Art, 1880), Wagner, *Gesammelte Werke,* vol. 10, 217, 247, 250. See also Nietzsche's critique of Wagner for just this attitude, especially in his late essay "Was bedeuten asketische Ideale" in *Die Genealogie der Moral* (On the Genealogy of Morals, 1887), *KSA* 5, 344–46.

[4] Arthur Schopenhauer, *Sämtliche Werke,* ed. Wolfgang Freiherr von Löhneysen, vol. 2 (Stuttgart: Cotta, 1968), 771.

[5] See Herbert Lehnert and Eva Wessell, *Nihilismus der Menschenfreundlichkeit: Thomas Manns "Wandlung" und sein Essay Goethe und Tolstoi, TMS* 9 (1991).

[6] In essence Mann had said this before in "Goethe und Tolstoi." See Lehnert and Wessell, *Nihilismus,* especially 167–72.

[7] My argument uses concepts of the school of "self psychology" represented by Heinz Kohut, Ernest S. Wolf, and others. Mann's case is one of self-object relation. It can be demonstrated by his diary entry of 15 July 1935, reacting to the news of the death of the friend of his youth and early days, Otto Grautoff: "Now, the death of the companion of years of my boyhood that were full of suffering and laughter touches me with sadness, but coldly. I cannot but feel that he merely belonged to my life, and it was clumsy of him to desire to be something in his own right." For a self-psychological view of Thomas Mann see Manfred Dierks, "Doctor Faustus and Recent Theories of Narcissism: New Perspectives," *Thomas Mann's "Doctor Faustus,"* ed. Herbert Lehnert and Peter Pfeiffer (Columbia SC: Camden House, 1991), 33–54. For an introduction to self psychology see Ernest S. Wolf: *Treating the Self: Elements of Clinical Self Psychology* (New York/London: The Guilford Press, 1988) and Heinz Kohut, *The Analysis of the Self* (New York: International UP, 1971).

[8] Cf. Arthur Schopenhauer, *Sämtliche Werke,* vol. 4 (Parerga und Paralipomena I), 318, 364–65 and *GW* 8, 691–693. See Manfred Dierks, "Die Aktualität der positivistischen Methode — am Beispiel Thomas Mann," *Orbis Litterarum,* 33 (1978): 158–82.

[9] In German critical language this connection is subsumed under "Produktionsästhetik" in contrast to "Rezeptionsästhetik." "Produktionsästhetik" includes theories of the conditions of writing. "Rezeptionsästhetik" is similar to reader response theory.

[10] *Tb* 18 March 1933.

[11] The source for this view is mainly Friedrich Eicken, *Geschichte und System der mittelalterlichen Weltanschauung* (Stuttgart: Cotta, 1887), which Mann had read for *Der Zauberberg.* See Mann's diary of April 1919 and Hans Wißkirchen, *Zeitgeschichte im Roman: Zu Thomas Manns Zauberberg und Doktor Faustus, TMS* 6 (1986), especially 68–75.

[12] "Das böse Deutschland, das ist das fehlgegangene gute, das gute im Unglück, in Schuld und Untergang."

"German" Music and German Catastrophe: A Re-Reading of *Doktor Faustus*

Hans Rudolf Vaget

ARGUABLY THOMAS MANN'S most self-conscious "German" book, *Doktor Faustus* (1947) was actually written in California, where Mann had gone to live in 1942. But as seems to be the rule with exiles, the geographical distance merely compounded the emotional involvement with the country that he had left behind in 1933, making this, as he repeatedly confessed, his most radically autobiographical novel as well as his most unsparing reckoning with Germany's past. The following analysis will proceed from the historical context that gave birth to the conception of *Doktor Faustus* to the novel's sophisticated design. The central sections will address crucial issues of representation: the composer as Faust and the life and works of Leverkühn. The concluding section considers the question of the intellectual debt Mann's novel owes to the theory and practice of modern music. In a brief epilogue I offer some observations from a contemporary perspective about the position of *Doktor Faustus* in the debate about the "German catastrophe"[1] and about its historical significance.

Historical Context

When Mann began to write *Doktor Faustus* on 23 May 1943 — Serenus Zeitblom, the fictitious narrator, begins to write the story of his recently deceased friend, the composer Adrian Leverkühn, on precisely the same day — the world was in the midst of the "most destructive and barbaric war" in recorded history,[2] a war precipitated by Mann's native country. Early in 1943, a decisive turning point was reached, and after the German surrender at Stalingrad on 2 February 1943, the writing was on the wall for everyone to see. A few weeks earlier, at Casablanca, the Western allies had set the unconditional surrender of Germany as the ultimate goal of the war. This meant, among other things, that in the eyes of the outside world there was no oppositional "other Germany"; that there existed only one Germany; and that that single Germany would be held accountable for the evil perpetrated, supposedly, in the name of its people. This was a position that Mann himself had come to embrace, slowly and reluctantly, in the course of his tireless efforts to convince America, ever since coming to the United States in 1938, of the necessity of going to war and ridding the world of Nazism.[3]

Soon after the start of the war on 1 September 1939, American intellectuals and German émigrés had begun to debate the vexing question of the origins of National Socialism. Perhaps the most audible voice to emerge was that of Peter Viereck, who traced the "metapolitics" of Nazism back to German Romanticism and identified a composer, Richard Wagner, as the most influential figure and the chief inspiration for Adolf Hitler.[4] Mann was directly drawn into the debate because in an article in *Common Sense,* Viereck had referred to him as an admirer and defender of Wagner.[5] In response, Mann conceded that Wagner's work, his essays as well as his operas, was "the exact spiritual forerunner of the 'metapolitical' movement" that was terrorizing the entire world.[6] However, he tempered his indictment of Wagner by objecting to Viereck's lack of nuance and to his insensitivity to the greatness of Wagner's work[7] — an indication among many others that Mann's emotional attachment to Wagner remained strong and unbroken. Explaining such basic ambivalence about Wagner, he wrote to a friend that he was capable of writing one thing about him today, and quite a different thing tomorrow.[8] He might have said the same about Germany, which remained a tormenting enigma to him, as it did to the rest of the world not because it was evil, but because it was at the same time good. This meant that there is but *one* Germany, not two, not a good and evil; that Hitler was no accident; and that Hitler could never have come to power but for certain psychological prerequisites that must be sought deeper down than in inflation, unemployment, capitalism, and political intrigue.[9] This is perhaps the clearest blueprint we have for the historiographical project that was to become *Doktor Faustus.*

Five years later — Germany had just been defeated and the first half of *Doktor Faustus* had been completed — Mann made the same point in an address at the Library of Congress titled "Germany and the Germans." On that occasion he added a crucial nuance of fundamental importance to *Doktor Faustus:* "evil Germany is merely good Germany gone astray."[10] The barbarism to which Germany had reverted when it embraced National Socialism was not to be attributed to an evil essence endemic to German culture. Rather, it was to be viewed as the result of a process of perversion — of going astray on a monstrous scale. *Doktor Faustus,* Mann's "Deutschland-Roman," was to lay bare the hidden motivation of Germany's perversion and thus to offer an explanation of how and why Germany went astray. Implicit in the notion of "Germany gone astray" is, of course, the eventual possibility of Germany recovering a civilized form of life.

In the immediate aftermath of the war, this crucial nuance was overlooked, as intellectuals were preoccupied with the question of Germany's guilt, raised most forthrightly by the philosopher Karl Jaspers and by a group of Protestant clergymen.[11] By the time *Doktor Faustus* was published in Germany in 1948, Mann was widely perceived as a vocal proponent of "Kollektivschuld," making every German share the enormous guilt incurred by Nazi Germany. There was some evidence that appeared to suggest precisely that. In 1945, Mann, in reaction to the liberation of Buchenwald, had published a brief article in *The Nation* in which he declared that "our disgrace is bared to the eyes of the world." He spoke "our shame," observing presciently that "everything German" will be affected and tainted by the discovery of these crimes.[12] When Mann's thoughts appeared in German newspapers, they were sometimes given the misleading heading "Thomas Mann über die deutsche Schuld" (Thomas Mann on German Guilt).[13] But this title is inauthentic, for the original piece (*GW* 12, 951–53) is entitled simply *Die Lager* (The Camps). However, the damage had been done, and it was compounded when it was discovered that Mann had incorporated the substance of his article into chapter 46 of *Doktor Faustus*. Taking their cue from Mann's use of the Faust myth in its original articulation, in which Faust is sent to hell, most German reviewers and commentators read the novel as a wholesale indictment of German culture and therefore, with differing degrees of respect, rejected the book.[14]

In Germany today, *Doktor Faustus* is still widely viewed as Mann's most controversial and unpalatable book. Critics object to what they perceive to be its condemnation of German culture, and they question the grounds on which the novel purports to make its case. *Doktor Faustus* implies — and this is perhaps its most provocative aspect — that Germany took the road to barbarism not, as the humanistic cliché about the ennobling power of art would have it, despite its love and idolatry of music, but rather because of it. This poses yet another question: Does the novel in fact imply a final condemnation of music — "the most German of arts,"[15] — or, for that matter, of Germany?

Looking at *Doktor Faustus* today, we can leave behind the emotional arguments about Mann's views of German history that dominated the discussion during the Cold War, when Germany was divided into two ideologically opposed states, harboring very different readings of their common antecedent, and can take a fresh look at Mann's novel, focus on what lies at the heart of the book, and consider the transcendent issue of the fateful concatenation of art and politics. Mann chose to tell a particular part of German history in terms of "German" music. The personal and objective justification for this striking narrative strategy will be clarified below, but let it be said at the outset that the highly imaginative and professional musical encoding of the pre-history of the "German catastrophe" may be regarded as the novel's most original and conspicuously modernist feature.

Without wanting unduly to press the matter, we may liken Mann's novel about "German" music to Siegfried Kracauer's attempt in *From Caligari to*

Hitler (1947), undertaken at approximately the same time, to read German cinema of the pre-Hitler era as a harbinger of Germany's embrace of fascism. The differences are striking. Kracauer turned to popular culture and used the tools of the social sciences to uncover in Weimar cinema a collective susceptibility to Hitlerism, while Mann examined high culture and invented musical works by a fictitious German composer who starts out as a post-Wagnerian impressionist and becomes the pioneer of the Schönbergian system of twelve-tone composition in order to throw into relief the mentality that foreshadows Hitler. But both projects, *Doktor Faustus* and *From Caligari to Hitler,* share one fundamental belief: that National Socialism is prefigured in the cultural texts of the preceding period and that, properly read, these texts yield unique clues about the thinking that propelled Germany toward catastrophe.

Design and Structure

Doktor Faustus is Mann's most ambitious novel in thematic as well as structural terms. Several patterns are here interwoven to create a hybrid narrative that proceeds on two distinct though connected time lines. At its core this is yet another portrait of the artist, such as those Mann produced earlier in his career with "Tonio Kröger" (1903) and "Der Tod in Venedig" (Death in Venice, 1912), two of his most successful works.[16] But *Doktor Faustus* actually harks back, at least structurally, to an even earlier story of 1896, "Der Wille zum Glück" (The Will to Happiness),[17] which presents the short life of a painter as told by one of his schoolmates. The same constellation serves as the basic design of the novel, which may thus be viewed as an amplification of the model employed in "Der Wille zum Glück." Thematically too, *Doktor Faustus* reaches back to Mann's early years, and more precisely to 1904, shortly before his marriage.[18]

Mann especially amplified the role of the narrator, Dr. Serenus Zeitblom, by allotting him considerably more space to reflect on the difficulty of undertaking the biography of Leverkühn at that historical moment. This biography — the novel's first time line — requires roughly two years, from 23 May 1943, to the end of the war in the spring of 1945. In these passages, usually at the beginnings of chapters,[19] we are offered reflections on the course of the war and on German history from Zeitblom's perspective, the perspective, that is, of a classicist who has been forced into early retirement from his teaching position at a Gymnasium. Drawn as a representative of what came to be known as "inner emigration," Zeitblom provides an increasingly gloomy view of the fate of Germany. He often sounds like Mann himself — a Mann who would have remained in Germany and survived, of course — and he is treated with a good measure of irony.

The novel's second time line extends from Leverkühn's birth in 1885 to his mental collapse in 1930. It comprises the story of an exceptionally gifted individual who becomes a divinity student only to turn to musical composition under the guidance of his musical mentor, the American-born Wendell Kretzschmar. As he comes face to face with the creative impasse that late Romantic music reached in the early years of the twentieth century, Leverkühn strikes a kind of Faustian bargain by enlisting demonic aid in order to achieve a creative breakthrough and assure for himself — and by implication for "German" music — artistic leadership and cultural hegemony. His creativity receives a demonic boost when he deliberately infects himself with syphilis. This and a number of other biographical details are adapted from the life of Friedrich Nietzsche, who exerted a profound formative influence on Mann. Along with the Faust myth, the life of Nietzsche provides a complementary biographical model for the construction of Leverkühn.[20] In the event, he does achieve a revolutionary breakthrough to a new method of composition, but at the price of his soul. After twenty-four years of inspired musical creation he goes to hell when he lapses into insanity. His last work, a large-scale symphonic cantata, set on a theme from the old sixteenth-century *Faustbuch:* "Denn ich sterbe als ein böser und guter Christ" (For I die as a bad and as a good Christian) (*GW* 6, 646) — reveals to everyone the hidden Faustian program of his life. An epilogue summarizes the remainder of Leverkühn's life in a mental institution; his death occurs on 25 August 1940.

These two narrative strands form the solid foundation of the novel's structure. They combine, however, to create a third, more sweeping historical perspective that extends back to the Middle Ages and brings into view certain basic elements of the culture that eventually produced a Leverkühn. As may be expected, this proved to be the most contentious aspect of the novel. Mann's probing into the cultural memory of the Germans is embodied in the antithetical figures of Kumpf and Schleppfuß, two of Leverkühn's professors at the university of Halle, and, throughout the novel, in the many discursive passages that reflect the preoccupation of both Zeitblom and Leverkühn with the age of Luther and Dürer. But Mann probes the past even more deeply — this becomes critically important — by constructing the elaborate montage that is Kaisersaschern, Zeitblom's birthplace and the town in which Leverkühn grows up. Its importance is signaled in different ways, none more conclusively than by the repeated assertion that Leverkühn's music is "Musik von Kaisersaschern" (*GW* 6, 113). As if to emphasize the centrality of this imagined community, Mann placed it in the geographic center of Germany, in "Deutschlands Mitten" (*GW* 6, 308) — echoing the very words with which Wagner in *Die Meistersinger* (1867) had highlighted the geographical and spiritual centrality of Nuremberg in his own attempt to answer the question "What is German?"[21]

Like Germany itself, Kaisersaschern is spiritually shaped by both Protestantism, which is Leverkühn's religious affiliation, and by Catholicism, which is Zeitblom's. It is also home to a small Jewish community, but we learn nothing about its fate. Perhaps the most emblematic function of Kaisersaschern is suggested by its very name. The kaiser in question, whose ashes are said to be preserved in the town's cathedral, is Otto the Third (980–1002). (In reality, Otto the Third lies buried in Aachen, Aix la Chapelle.) Not generally recognized as an outstanding figure, Otto the Third was assigned a key historical role in the work of the historian whom Mann named as his chief authority: Erich von Kahler.[22] Following Kahler, Mann presents Kaiser Otto as the paradigmatic embodiment of two competing and sometimes conflicting inclinations that create a constant tension between the specifically German and the distinctly European elements in the psychic makeup of Germans, between the lure of the national and the universal in their intellectual heritage. As we shall see, this tension is fundamental to Mann's conception both of Leverkühn and of Germany. As for Mann's composer, we are told with conspicuous emphasis: "Not in vain was he the son of the town in which Otto III lay buried" (*GW* 6, 220). Kaisersaschern thus encapsulates the "geistige Lebensform"[23] — the spiritual way of life — that Mann viewed as paradigmatic of Germany as a whole.

Two further features of the design of *Doktor Faustus* must also be kept in mind. First, in the historical time-scheme of the novel, the coming to power of Hitler and his Third Reich have been deliberately omitted. The narrative of Leverkühn's life stops, as we have seen, in 1930, and Zeitblom's commentary on the war starts when the end of the Third Reich is already in sight. This suggests that whatever relationship is intended between Leverkühn's music and National Socialism, it cannot be that of historical parallel or symbolic equivalence. Rather, the operative notions are those of anticipation and foreshadowing. The intellectual climate and spiritual condition of Leverkühn's Germany anticipate Germany's turn to barbarism; and the spirit in which Leverkühn's music is conceived foreshadows the spirit of National Socialism. In the novel itself, this anticipatory relationship between Leverkühn's lifetime and the Third Reich is underlined by the allusion to the Biblical dictum "daß, wer da Wind säet, Sturm ernten wird" (*GW* 6, 50) — he who sows the wind shall reap the whirlwind. Second, Mann's use of a fictitious narrator postulates the existence of a second, omniscient narrator who manipulates Zeitblom by ironizing and frequently outwitting him. Thus, on numerous occasions, we are made aware of the limitations of Zeitblom's historical, musical, and moral understanding. Behind the back of the ostensibly authoritative narrator, much goes on that lies beyond his horizon and moral imagination and thus belongs to the confidential communication between the omniscient narrator and the reader. This marks a significant gap between the voice of the inner emigration and that of the real emigration.

The Composer as Faust

Like all other authors of Faust works, Mann too transformed the Faust myth by adapting it to his needs. What led him to construe his modern Faust as a composer? And what, exactly, is "Faustian" about Leverkühn? In Mann's mind, these two questions were closely connected, as we know from "Deutschland und die Deutschen," his Library of Congress address on "Germany and the Germans."[24] While commenting approvingly on the aptness of the Faust myth to Germany, he underlined one essential lacuna: it was a grave error on the part of the legend, he observed, to have no links to music, for if Faust is to be "representative of the German soul" — he would have to be a musician.[25] Even as he spoke, Mann was "correcting" that historical error by fashioning his own version of the Faust myth as the life of a German "Tonsetzer."[26]

Many of the reservations raised by critics in Germany concerned precisely this amalgamation of German history with the Faust myth, which seemed to imply that the reversal of "good" Germany to "evil" Germany was brought about through devilish cunning ("Teufelslist") (*GW* 11, 1146). Indeed, Mann himself had observed that "whenever arrogance of the mind mates with an archaic disposition of the soul" (*GW* 11, 1131), the devil reigns. But Mann's invocation of the Faust myth as a metaphor for historical processes is by no means so fanciful a device as it may seem to later generations of readers steeped in Marxist notions of history. In fact, as the political scientist Herfried Münkler has recently reminded us, there existed in twentieth-century political philosophy from Max Weber to Friedrich Meinecke a tradition of thinking that politics *eo ipso* amounted to a pact with demonic forces. That tradition would regard the pact with the devil as a "basic figuration of political action."[27] Mann knew Max Weber and admired him;[28] his conception of history as a realm in which demonic forces are at work can thus hardly be characterized as arbitrary or outlandish. But even critics well disposed toward Mann[29] complained that his Faustian reading of history obfuscated the true causes of the German catastrophe by focusing excessively on the psychology and mentality of its protagonists. Looking for political analysis, but finding "merely" psychological diagnosis, Mann's German critics would dismiss the novel as a contribution to their vaunted *Vergangenheitsbewältigung* — the coming to terms with Germany's past. Mann's failing was generally located in his focus on music, when what he should have written was a novel about economics and social processes. Ironically, it seems that Mann anticipated such criticism, for he incorporated into the novel a determined defense of his psychological reading of the German past by having Zeitblom explain that for a nation such as Germany the decisive motivating factor is not political but psychological.[30]

One has to wonder, though, whether critics would have dismissed Mann's conception of history had they been able to see that the novel articulates anything but an unequivocal condemnation of Leverkühn, or, for that matter, of Germany. On close inspection, Mann's revision of the Faust myth displays a profound ambivalence. On the surface, the novel appears to ignore Goethe's optimistic variation on the same theme and to vindicate the uncompromising verdict of the old chapbook: having led a "damnable life" Doctor Faustus suffers a "deserved death" and eternal damnation.[31] One must bear in mind, however, that it is the fictitious narrator who fashions our picture of Leverkühn as a modern Faust figure. Zeitblom sees his world and humanistic values crumbling around him; it is therefore not out of character for him to apply an apocalyptic reading to everything he writes about. In the same pessimistic vein, he foregrounds Leverkühn's cryptic remark that Beethoven's Ninth Symphony should be revoked (*GW* 6, 634), and with it all the lofty ideals of Weimar and Viennese Classicism. This is also a man who struggles to come to terms with his bad conscience over floating with the nationalist tide at the time of the First World War, and whose sons grew up to be ardent Nazis. Creating the figure of Zeitblom, Mann owned up to the feverishly nationalist stance he himself had taken in 1914.[32] It thus seems perfectly plausible that a profoundly disoriented humanist such as Zeitblom would view the sixteenth-century version of the Faust myth to be the only appropriate one for the time in which he lives.

But let us remember that behind Zeitblom a different narrator is at work who seems to be fully aware that any Faust work written in the twentieth century entails a critical reflection on the epoch-making Goethean position concerning the redeemability of Faust.[33] And indeed, several features of Mann's emplotment of the Faust story do point to the possibility of grace and redemption.

To begin with, there is the matter of the identity of the two female figures in the background: the shadowy woman who goes by the name of Esmeralda — the prostitute from whom Leverkühn receives the allegedly genius-inducing infection[34] — and the mysterious Madame Tolna, Leverkühn's generous benefactor and the discreet facilitator of his career. True to character, Zeitblom never acknowledges their identity, and it is left to the omniscient narrator, in the manner of the Wagnerian orchestra, to signal to the reader that Madame Tolna is the former "Esmeralda."[35] The significance of her secret identity can hardly be overstated. It seems to suggest that Leverkühn, like Goethe's Faust, acts out of love at least once in his life when, spurning "Esmeralda's" warnings, he chooses her for his fateful sexual union. Even Zeitblom admits that this is a true act of love (*GW* 6, 200). That love remains an inalienable source of inspiration to Leverkühn, even though his pact stipulates, as in the old *Faustbuch*, that he may not love — "Du darfst nicht lieben" — which is to say, love insofar as it warms: "Liebe ist dir verboten, insofern sie wärmt" (*GW* 6, 331–32). To Leverkühn, as to his creator, that truly "warming" love would be same-sex love. Thus when Leverkühn consents to an affair with the violinist Rudi Schwerdtfeger, it is a violation of the pact and spells Rudi's death. Likewise, Leverkühn's last love, that for his little nephew, Nepomuk, also proves fatal. Yet outside and beyond Leverkühn's immediate sphere, another form of love exists. Its existence is clearly acknowledged, however obliquely, by a five-note musical motif that denotes "Esmeralda"[36] in Leverkühn's major compositions and, even after his death, by the presence of "Esmeralda" at his burial (*GW* 6, 676) — still veiled and unrecognized by Zeitblom. As in Goethe's scheme for Faust's redemption, human love proves to be the pledge of divine love, which is to say of grace.

Leverkühn, well trained in Divinity, is of course fully aware of the redemptive power of love. Since he is forbidden its experience, he resorts to a cunning, characteristically self-conscious strategy: he projects his existential desire for love and redemption upon his work. At the conclusion of his hallucinatory conversation with the devil, that is, with himself, he gives an intimation of his own desperate hope for redemption when he reminds himself that the work of art itself has to do with love: "Aber man sagt ja, Werk habe selbst mit Liebe zu tun" (*GW* 6, 332). Henceforth we are given few but sufficient indications that Leverkühn's compositions are indeed veiled pleas for redemption. From his setting of Klopstock's *Die Frühlingsfeyer*, which is the first composition he undertakes after the confrontation with the devil, and which is said to be a work seeking grace in praising creation (*GW* 6, 353), to his penultimate work, the oratorio *Apocalipsis cum figuris*, which Zeitblom interprets as "a desperate prayer for a soul" (*GW* 6, 501), that is, for grace — redemption is the chief theological agenda of his entire compositional output. It is only logical, then, that his culminating symphonic cantata, *Dr. Fausti Weheklag*, should conclude softly, humbly, and hauntingly on the high G of a cello — a transparent cipher of "Gnade" (grace) which, in effect, cancels Zeitblom's earlier reading of the program of the cantata as presenting the idea of salvation as itself a temptation (*GW* 6, 650) — as a temptation to be resisted.

Mann's novel — that much should be clear — is anything but the high-handed condemnation of German culture that it has often been made out to be. Woven into Zeitblom's narrative of Leverkühn's Faustian life and deserved damnation is a pervasive subtext on the theme of grace, spun behind the narrator's back by the omniscient narrator as part of a comprehensive strategy of equivocation — a subtext that serves to undermine the apparent finality of Leverkühn's damnation and keep open the possibility of his redemption.

When Mann explained why his Faust figure had to be a musician, he invoked, as we have seen, the criterion of representativeness: If Faust is to be representative of the German soul, he must be musical. To the author of the sixteenth-century *Faustbuch* or even to Goethe, such an argument would have made no sense whatsoever, since in their day the status of music in German culture was unexceptional. But Mann's historical vantage point was not theirs. Born into a culture in which, beginning with Romanticism, music was firmly established at the top of the hierarchy of the arts, and in which, throughout the nineteenth century, music was theorized as the most profound expression of Germanness itself, he felt not only justified but compelled to re-conceptualize Faust as a musical genius.

Mann himself had fully shared in the idolization of music as the most German of the arts and as the epitome of "Deutschtum." Writing in 1917 about the national art of the Germans and citing the examples of Schubert's *Die Winterreise* (1827) and Wagner's *Der Ring des Nibelungen* (1854–74) he argued that, more than literature and politics, music has the power to unite and conjoin the national community at a time of crisis and upheaval.[37] In his massive wartime essay, *Betrachtungen eines Unpolitischen* (Confessions of a Nonpolitical Man, 1918), part intellectual autobiography, part analysis of German culture, Mann argues the German case against the Western democracies by underlining the uniqueness of Germany's music-centered culture. As he then saw it, the war had been waged for Germany's right to be different from the Western democracies, and to preserve a culture in which music rather than politics would rule. Deceiving himself, along with the great majority of German intellectuals, about the aggressive character of Germany's "holy" war of self-defense, Mann was as yet unable to see what he would later come to realize only slowly and painfully — that his idolatry of music and his patriotic pride in the international success of Wagner[38] merely masked a collectively shared pretense to cultural hegemony that turned out to be the harbinger of hegemonic designs of a quite different order and scale.

This shift of perspective was brought about by political developments. When in 1922 Mann declared his support for the embattled Weimar Republic,[39] he became a target of denunciations by his former nationalist conservative allies, such as the composer Hans Pfitzner and his partisans. Their opposition to the Weimar Republic translated easily into support of the budding, soon to mushroom Hitler movement. As soon as Hitler had assumed power, an opportunistic alliance of Wagnerians and local Nazi functionaries accused Mann — in the name of "Richard Wagner's Own City of Munich" — of having defamed Wagner, the "great German musical genius."[40] That attack was provoked by Mann's commemorative speech on the occasion of the fiftieth anniversary of Wagner's death — a brilliant homage to Wagner in the transnational spirit of Baudelaire and Nietzsche — and was masterminded by Hans Pfitzner and Hans Knappertsbusch. They had neither forgotten nor forgiven Mann's abandonment of the nationalist position of his *Betrachtungen*.[41] Mann himself viewed this shameful attack as an act of national excommunication.[42] It caused him to go into exile and to break with

Germany forever; when he returned to Europe in 1952 he chose Switzerland, not Germany, as his final abode and resting place. Here, then, was a flagrant and symptomatic case of a musical discourse with far-reaching political repercussions. In a novel that probes the hidden nexus of "German" music and German history, the traumatic events of 1933 had to have a weighty impact on its conception and genesis. Proof that the Wagner affair of 1933 was still very much on his mind during the composition of *Doktor Faustus* may be gleaned from Mann's famous open letter of 7 September 1945 to Walter von Molo, who had appealed to him to return to Germany as a "good physician" and to help heal the wounds. Mann rejected the idea, reminding everyone rather pointedly of the illiterate and murderous campaign against his Wagner essay by the Munich Wagnerians.[43]

Actually, Mann had been sensitized to the increasing political instrumentalization of music long before 1933, as he had witnessed in 1923 how Hitler was received by Houston Stewart Chamberlain and Winifred Wagner, the guardians of the Wagnerian Grail, how he was proclaimed the future savior of Germany, and how in 1924 the Bayreuth Wagner Festival, the first after the war, was turned into a lovefest by the enemies of the Weimar Republic from the Right. By the time he wrote the extraordinary chapter on music in *Der Zauberberg* (The Magic Mountain, 1924), Mann felt sufficiently sobered about the German idolatry of music to be able to have one of its protagonists famously declare music to be "politically suspect" (*GW* 3, 162) and to warn darkly that the profound enchantment of the soul provoked by romantic music from Schubert to Wagner may have sinister consequences in the political sphere; it is "Seelenzauber mit finsteren Konsequenzen" (*GW* 3, 907). Precisely this — the probing of the sinister political consequences of Germany's allegedly nonpolitical cult of music — became the chief project of *Doktor Faustus*. By the time the overall conception of the novel took shape in Mann's mind he was convinced that "German" music and German history were indeed interdependent, and, as he had put it somewhat cryptically in an essay of 1920, that Germany represented the self-realization ("Verwirklichung") of her music (*GW* 12, 603). Mann thus came to believe that a deep analysis of "German" music and of the spirit in which it was conceived, and received, would yield important keys to the understanding of German history.

The Life and Works of Adrian Leverkühn

We may now turn to the pivotal figure of Leverkühn, who owes his very existence to the belief that music provides a lens more powerful than any other for deciphering the hidden script of modern German history and for revealing the mechanism by which something "good" could turn into something "evil." How, precisely, is the figure of Leverkühn constructed? What motivates him to compose those works of which we are given such detailed and knowledgeable descriptions? How, finally, does Leverkühn's music illuminate the dark road that Germany followed in the twentieth century?

If Leverkühn's music is music of Kaisersaschern, by the logic of the novel's design it must also be music in the spirit of Otto the Third — which is to say, music that is at the same time national and transnational, German and universal. Leverkühn's compositions do indeed move between these two poles. In the early years, under the guidance of his cosmopolitan teacher, Kretzschmar, Leverkühn moves in the direction of a transnational conception of music. He immerses himself in Debussy and Ravel and turns to stylistic models that are as un-Wagnerian as possible (*GW* 6, 218). His first opera, *Love's Labour's Lost,* uses Shakespeare's English rather than a German translation and is written in the international idiom of Neoclassicism. His second opera, which takes the epitome of a great sinner — Pope Gregory the Great — as its subject, bears an unmistakable musical resemblance to Stravinsky's *L'histoire du soldat* (1918). Among his other early works are settings of Dante, Blake, and Verlaine. To this point, it can hardly be said that Leverkühn is destined to be the standard-bearer of a distinctly "German" music.

However, these early works represent but one side of Leverkühn's creative potential. Quite a different side comes into view in chapter 22, the novel's theoretical centerpiece, when he realizes that the art he practices has reached a crossroads: the compositional possibilities of the inherited, post-Wagnerian idiom seem exhausted, leaving parody the only option. In a country that looks to music as its flagship, the specter of musical sterility, and with it the decline of the entire culture, looms large. In this regard, Leverkühn merely echoes the widespread fear, shared by musicians from Pfitzner to Schönberg, that their great musical tradition may indeed have exhausted itself. Paradoxically, it is the return to a strict, self-imposed order that promises new creative freedom, and Leverkühn is ready to submit to radical principles of organization in order to move beyond the impasse. Fearing the end of German culture, he is ready, and has the audacity, to opt for barbarism (*GW* 6, 324).

In the Hegelian fashion of Mann's musical advisor, Theodor W. Adorno, Zeitblom theorizes Leverkühn's regression as a "dialectical reversal" (*GW* 6, 253). But Mann proves to be a more astute psychologist than either Adorno or Hegel. Behind the narrator's back, Leverkühn's decision to regress in order to break through is interpreted as an act of withdrawal — inward and backward. By leaving Munich and moving to Pfeiffering, where he lives in monastic isolation, Leverkühn recedes into his Germanness. When he then travels to Italy, he carries with him even more "Kaisersaschern" than usual. Facing the impending impasse, Leverkühn turns his thoughts to the great German tradition of absolute music. What made it great and gave it its universal appeal? It was Beethoven's decision, he reasons, to elevate the development section of the sonata form to the central event of musical discourse. Brahms continued and expanded this practice by subjecting the organization of the musical material to the principle of developing variation, which Leverkühn considers to be a "Residuum" (*GW* 6, 254) of earlier musical practice. Such self-imposed order and limitation had yielded an unheard-of freedom of subjective expression and, most importantly, it had led to Germany's musical hegemony. What Leverkühn concludes from this carries a certain grim logic: the most promising way out of the impasse lies in the re-establishment of order, and a radicalized form of order at that. The archaic ideal of the "strict style," he determines, is to be extended to comprise the entire composition: there shall no longer be any free notes; music will be cleansed of all ornamentation; composition will be governed by "complete organization" (*GW* 6, 255).

In chapter 22, Leverkühn is well on his way to that new strict style. He has come to realize that dissonances must be left unresolved, and he has begun to experiment, in the manner of Robert Schumann and Alban Berg,[44] with secretly coded musical figures that permeate the entire composition. Thus, in his setting of Brentano poems, Esmeralda — h-e-a-e-es (in English notation: B-E-A-E-E-flat). Here, then, for the first time, the strictly regulated permutations of a musical figure determine the organization of the entire composition. By this time, Leverkühn already carries the disease; the demonic boost to his creativity is showing its efficacy.

Leverkühn begins to emerge as the emphatically "deutsche Tonsetzer" of the novel's subtitle only in chapter 22. As he withdraws from the world and becomes preoccupied with the German musical heritage, he seems to reflect larger collective trends such as Germany's political isolation and growing nationalism prior to 1914 and Germany's quest for a place in the sun. His withdrawal, however, serves the very specific purpose of preparing himself for the great breakthrough that will project his music onto the rest of the world. The collective mind-set of Germany in 1914 might very well be described in precisely the same expansionist terms. Germany too desired the status of a world power commensurate with its cultural achievements. Kaisersaschern wants to become a world city (*GW* 6, 409) is Leverkühn's apt comment on the outbreak of war in 1914. The note of skepticism in this remark cannot quite conceal the fact that, as a musical artist, he is pursuing a similarly hegemonic goal.

Much of what we are told about the motivation behind Leverkühn's Faustian ambition to march at the head of the musical avant-garde resonates with later developments in Germany. His desire to eliminate from the musical work any and all non-thematic elements in order to realize his ideal of total organization suggests that Leverkühn's music figures as the spiritual and psychological staging ground for excesses of organization and control of a much more sinister sort.

In chapter 25, the "devil" appears to Leverkühn not to propose, but merely to clarify the terms of the Faustian pact into which he entered when he insisted on receiving the genius-inducing infection from Esmeralda. Historically, by that time, meaningful musical composition has become so forbidding that the temptation to turn to demonic powers is felt to be irresistible. Still, while Leverkühn may think that he is concerned only with the future of music, it is made clear here that he is driven by other, less innocuous desires. The inner voice he takes for the "devil" spells it out quite unambiguously: "You will lead, you will beat the march of the future" (*GW* 6, 324). Once the breakthrough is achieved, musical hegemony, so ardently pursued with Faustian hubris, will be his. It is impossible not to assume that Mann was thinking here of Arnold Schönberg's much quoted remark that his own dodecaphonic method of composition would ensure the domination of "German" music "for another hundred years."[45]

Be that as it may, we have reached here the most advanced point in Mann's thinking about the ambiguity inherent in the notion of "German" music. In his *Betrachtungen eines Unpolitischen,* and for some time thereafter, Mann held an uncritical view of what had become a commonplace: that great music produced by German composers was universal; that "German" music spoke to all the world in the sense of Beethoven's Ninth Symphony: "diesen Kuss der ganzen Welt." The work of Wagner was the most recent and perhaps strongest proof of this. By the time of *Doktor Faustus,* however, history had taught Mann that the pretense to universality harbored within it a potentially aggressive mentality.[46] In due course, this nationalistic habit of mind induced most Germans to believe that the perceived hegemony of "German" music somehow justified and even legitimized Germany's effort to achieve comparable political hegemony. This sort of reasoning found its most influential articulation in the work of Houston Stewart Chamberlain and was fundamental to the Nazi *Weltanschauung.*

Given the hegemonic designs of Leverkühn's project, it would not be unreasonable to expect in his music a growing display of nationalism. But no such tendency is discernable. If his *Apocalipsis* and *Dr. Fausti Weheklag* were intended to be read as prelude to the German catastrophe, the trajectory of Leverkühn's oeuvre would have had to point clearly in the direction of the cultural agenda of National Socialism. This is not the case. On the contrary, in the Third Reich Leverkühn's music would most assuredly have been labeled as "Kultur-Bolschewismus" (*GW* 6, 515). How then can his work be read as a prefiguration of Germany's road to barbarism, if it is diametrically opposed to all Nazi notions of healthy "German" music?

We must bear in mind here that Leverkühn's early work was conceived in a distinctly cosmopolitan spirit and that this cosmopolitan potential is as much a part of "Kaisersaschern" as is its nationalist dimension. Leverkühn's Faustian ambition to revolutionize music entails a renunciation of his earlier, benign universalism. At the same time, it represents a perversion of the notion of universalism, since it aims single-mindedly at domination and hegemony. Leverkühn is well aware of this deformation of his heritage and begins to strive for a non-hegemonic universality that would be expressive of a European Germany, rather than a Germanized Europe (*GW* 6, 229). It is true that his culminating works are drawn from two eminently German sources, Albrecht Dürer and the Faust myth. Yet both compositions rise above narrow notions of Germanness: the oratorio is a setting of biblical texts illustrated by Dürer; the cantata, stylistically, harks back to Monteverdi and links Faust to Orpheus (*GW* 6, 644–47). Moreover, the oratorio seems in part modeled on Berlioz's *Requiem* (1837), the cantata on the same composer's *La Damnation de Faust* (1846). It is on account of this transnational orientation, designed to subvert the nationalism of his Faustian striving, that Leverkühn's final composition may be seen as "a liberating work" (ein Werk der Befreiung) (*GW* 6, 644). Music is to be liberated from its latent nationalism; it is to become a spiritually less burdened, psychologically less tortured form of art — an art that will again be on a first-name basis with mankind (*GW* 6, 429).

This reading of Leverkühn's work fully accords with Mann's comment on German nationalism in a lecture delivered at the Library of Congress in October 1943, soon after he had begun writing the novel. The monstrous German attempt at the "subjugation of the world" (Weltunterwerfung), he observed, is nothing but a "distorted and unfortunate expression of a universalism that is innate in the German character" (*GW* 12, 929). It was the desire for power and domination — first in music, then in politics — that corrupted that universalism. And looking beyond Hitler's Reich, he expressed his belief that German universalism would again find a way to its old place of honor and contribute to the spiritual enrichment of the world, provided the Germans forswear any thought of world conquest.[47] Leverkühn's life and work exemplify this triadic schema.

Intellectual Properties: Schönberg, Adorno

Doktor Faustus is furnished with a number of elaborate paratexts. Aside from the title and subtitle, the novel comes with a somber epigraph quoting Dante's *Inferno*, a six-page Epilogue, and — from its 1951 printing — a significant "Author's Note." This last was occasioned by the bizarre charge of plagiarism raised in a letter to the editor of *The Saturday Review of Literature* (1 January 1948) by Arnold Schönberg who, before he had actually read the book, objected to what he alleged was Mann's characterization of his twelve-tone technique as the work of the devil.[48] To accommodate the irate composer, with whom he had been on perfectly cordial terms,[49] Mann wrote a brief statement in which he explained what should have been obvious to all who cared, that the method of composition presented in chapter 22 and attributed to a fictitious composer is in truth the intellectual property — "das geistige Eigentum" (*GW* 6, 677) — of Arnold Schönberg. Superfluous as this appendix may appear to us today, it documents the extraordinary historical authenticity of Mann's novel about "German" music and the deeply controversial nature of his indictment of German culture. Mann did manage to assuage Schönberg's pain, but Schönberg died before he was able to publish a statement signaling their reconciliation.[50]

A considerably more urgent question concerns the role played in the shaping of the novel by the philosopher, sociologist, and composer Theodor W. Adorno. A passionate Wagnerian all his life, Mann was not nearly as conversant with the technical and philosophical aspects of the music of Schönberg and Berg as it may seem; that he speaks of these matters with astonishing authority in *Doktor Faustus* is almost entirely due to assistance from Adorno, who had studied with Alban Berg. But here the question of intellectual property never became an issue because Mann acknowledged and paid tribute to Adorno in *Die Entstehung des Doktor Faustus* (The Story of a Novel: The Genesis of Doctor Faustus) published in 1949 (*GW* 11, 171–76, 245–49, 293–94). Adorno indicated that he was satisfied with Mann's characterization of their collaboration.[51] What is in fact problematic is something entirely different: the relationship between the form of Mann's novel and the compositional principles of dodecaphonic music. Or, putting it in more general terms, the relationship between this novel about the invention of modern music and the larger project of literary modernism.[52]

Mann met Adorno, a fellow exile in Los Angeles, in July 1943, at the time when the novel's first six chapters had just been completed. Adorno proved to be a godsend, since he was without a doubt the most intellectually compelling advocate of the so-called Second Viennese School (Schönberg, Berg, and Webern). He directed Mann's musical reading; he elucidated Beethoven's "late style," a crucial point of reference in Leverkühn's musical pedigree; and he gave Mann the still unpublished manuscript of his authoritative *Die Philosophie der neuen Musik* (1949). Later, having completed chapter 33, Mann submitted the entire manuscript of his work in progress to Adorno with a request for comment and criticism. By that time, Adorno, Mann's junior by almost thirty years, had become the author's "genuine Privy Councilor" (wirkliche Geheime Rat) (*GW* 11, 293) in all matters concerning modern music. Mann relied on Adorno's suggestions particularly when inventing the late works of Leverkühn and attempting to describe them as plausibly as possible. One of the most striking features of *Dr Fausti Weheklag* — the fact that the entire composition is derived from the basic twelve-tone row which sets Faustus's statement: "Denn ich sterbe als ein böser und ein guter Christ" — was Adorno's idea.

The nature and extent of this collaboration constitute a unique occurrence in Mann's entire career, and he felt honor-bound to pay tribute to his "Privy Councilor" in the most generous terms.[53] But before the publication of *Die Entstehung des Doktor Faustus*, he bowed to pressure from members of his family, who feared that he was about to hide his light under a bushel, and excised parts of the chapter on Adorno, thereby minimizing the extent of Adorno's contribution. It thus transpires that while Adorno had a role in the novel's genesis greater than Mann saw fit to admit, he can in no way be considered a co-author of *Doktor Faustus*, as has frequently been contended. Commentators who foreground Adorno's part usually do so with a particular agenda in mind. They make far-reaching claims for a structural homology between the novel and the compositional principles of dodecaphonic music, based on the assumption that Adorno's prestige as a rigorous modernist would clear the Wagnerian mists that attach to Mann's work as a whole and strengthen the modernist credentials of *Doktor Faustus*.[54] In recent years this line of reasoning has met with increasing skepticism.[55] From a musicological perspective, the case for Adorno's impact on the novel's design does not look any better; at least two readers whose musical authority is beyond question, Carl Dahlhaus and Klaus Kropfinger, have argued convincingly that Mann's novel simply cannot be made to fit any dodecaphonic paradigm, and that it rather adheres to Wagnerian principles of composition.[56]

And indeed, there is a great deal of evidence suggesting that the philosopher's role, indispensable though Adorno himself had become to Mann, was strictly ancillary. To begin with, Adorno came upon the scene when not all but most of the basic decisions about the design of the novel had been made. As we know from Mann's diaries, their collaboration proceeded on a collision course, to the point that they actually clashed over the philosophical purport of Leverkühn's last work. Adorno objected that Mann's presentation of the ending of the *Weheklag* sounded too positive and that he lessened Leverkühn's despair; it should not sound as though this arch-sinner had grace and forgiveness already in his pocket.[57] To Adorno any suggestion of a spiritual consolation was anathema. Mann thus agreed to revise the passage in question, and both later stated that they had found a compromise.[58] But the text tells a different story: Mann subverted Adorno's demand for unequivocal negation — "die Gewalt bestimmter Negation" — as the only permissible gesture, and retained the Kierkegaardian formula of "hope beyond hopelessness" (*GW* 6, 651), thereby maintaining an undeniable glimmer of grace.

They also differed in their understanding of history. In current historiographical terminology, Adorno, with his Hegelian belief in the primacy of objective laws of historical development, would have to be labeled a "structuralist," whereas Mann, a dyed-in-the-wool Nietzschean, who believed in the sovereignty of the great individual, would have to be categorized an "intentionalist." Nor did the two men see the nexus of music and history in the same light. As a theorist of music, Adorno, like Schönberg and Leverkühn in his middle period, was basically a nationalist; he considered it a foregone conclusion that one particular paradigm, which happened to be "German," was the only one and only legitimate paradigm entitled to hegemony in the world of modern music. Far from offering a solution to the conundrum of "German" music, then, Adorno must have appeared to Mann very much as part of the problem that is diagnosed in *Doktor Faustus*. This may be the reason that he chose to give the devil, at one stage of Leverkühn's conversation with him, the appearance of the musical philosopher. No one but Adorno could be meant when the devil changes his appearance into that of a respectable gentleman wearing a white collar, a bow-tie, and spectacles rimmed in horn atop his hooked nose. As if this were not enough, we are further told that Leverkühn's partner is an "Intelligenzler," an intellectual who writes about music for vulgar newspapers, and who is himself a composer, "in so far as thinking allows him to be creative" (*GW* 6, 317).

Doktor Faustus Today

It has become customary in German historiography to refer to the rise of Nazism, the war, and the Holocaust that followed in its wake as the "German catastrophe" — a term given currency by a book of that title published in 1946 by the venerable liberal historian, Friedrich Meinecke. An octogenarian at the time, Meinecke challenged future German historians and intellectuals to elucidate the causes, immediate and long-term, of that unprecedented and puzzling disaster.[59] Whether that challenge has as yet been met remains an open question. More than half a century later, another eminent historian, Heinrich August Winkler, concluded that Germany, with but one exception, had failed to accomplish the task that Meinecke had set forth. That exception, for Winkler, is Thomas Mann.[60] But neither German historiographers nor the phalanx of the German Mann industry seem as yet ready to accept Winkler's remarkably perspicacious assessment.

Winkler's generous acknowledgment of Mann's achievement nonetheless requires modification. Read as an attempt to scrutinize the antecedents of the German catastrophe, *Doktor Faustus* must in one crucial respect be deemed deficient. Mann's otherwise admirable record of speaking up for the Jews and for Israel notwithstanding, the Germany of this novel, amazingly enough, is a Germany without anti-Semitism.[61] This is all the more surprising since German musical culture in particular had been openly impregnated with anti-Semitism ever since Wagner. Add to this the presence in *Doktor Faustus* of several Jewish characters (Kunigunde Rosenstiel, Dr. Chaim Breisacher, Saul Fitelberg) who are negatively drawn and nowhere balanced by positive Jewish figures; add also the silence about the Jewish victims in

Zeitblom's commentary on Buchenwald in chapter 46; and the diagnosis of a serious shortcoming seems unavoidable.

And yet, all things considered, today more so than at any time since its first appearance, *Doktor Faustus* stands out among the countless attempts by German authors to meet Meinecke's challenge. Read in light of the landmark "Historians' debate" of 1986 and the various subsequent debates in Germany about the past that won't go away, and in light of the changes in the country's intellectual atmosphere after the fall of the wall, Mann's novel of 1947, to this day, powerfully resonates with critical issues for which the general public in Germany needed to be sensitized over a much longer period of time than he ever suspected. Long before the "Historians' debate," Mann confronted the Germans with the painful truth that National Socialism was not totally alien to them; that Nazism was not without roots in their nature as a people; that it was prefigured in the traits of their great men; and that it was not brought about by a small elite of perpetrators but rather by hundreds of thousands of Germans (*GW* 6, 639). The most painful truth articulated by Zeitblom — that the ignominy of the crimes committed would affect the perception of "alles Deutschtum," including its distinguished intellectual and cultural tradition (*GW* 6, 638) — remains even today one of the most contested assertions about the roots and ramifications of the Holocaust. This is especially true of the world outside Germany, where fascination with the sinister spectacle of Nazi Germany shows no signs of abating.

Mann mapped the terrain for Germany's long-delayed and then sputtering attempts to come to terms with the past — its *Vergangenheitsbewälti-gung*. He did so by examining the cultural achievement of which the Germans were most proud: "German" music — at a time when Germany's vaunted "Kultur" was generally considered to be irrelevant to any exploration of the mentality that had made Hitler and National Socialism possible. By drawing attention to the hidden nexus of music and history, culture and politics, Mann was far ahead of the professional historians. *Doktor Faustus* is easily the most profound interrogation of German cultural identity that German literature has produced. In this extraordinary portrait of an artist and portrait of an age, Thomas Mann courageously shines critical light upon German attitudes and beliefs that he had earlier both accepted and espoused. In particular he divests German music, which he loved to the end, of its alleged innocence and ostensible irrelevance to political currents. In so doing he created what is at once an autobiographical novel of exemplary forthrightness and a historical document of an import that still appears to be growing with time.

Notes

[1] The reference is to Friedrich Meinecke, *Die deutsche Katastrophe: Betrachtungen und Erinnerungen* (Wiesbaden: Brockhaus, 1946, 1955).

[2] Ian Kershaw, *Hitler: 1936–1945 Nemesis* (New York: W. W. Norton, 2000), 288.

[3] *The Coming Victory of Democracy*, trans. Agnes E. Meyer (New York: Knopf, 1938). Mann went on a fifteen-city tour of the United States with this speech in the spring of 1938. The original text: "Vom kommenden Sieg der Demokratie," *GW* 11, 910–941. Mann's collected works (*GW* 1–13) will hereafter be cited in the text.

[4] See Peter Viereck, *Metapolitics: From the Romantics to Hitler* (New York: Knopf, 1941). The book proved to be an academic bestseller; a third edition, subtitled "The Roots of the Nazi Mind," appeared in 1965.

[5] Peter Viereck, "Hitler and Wagner," *Common Sense* 8 (November 1939): 3–6.

[6] *Essays* 5, 81. Thomas Mann, "Zu Wagners Verteidigung. Brief an den Herausgeber des 'Common Sense,'" *Essays* 5, 75–82.

[7] *Essays* 5, 78, 80–81.

[8] *TM/AM*, 18 February 1942, 372.

[9] *Essays* 5, 80–81.

[10] "Das böse Deutschland, das ist das fehlgegangene gute" (*Essays* 5, 279).

[11] See Aleida Assmann, Ute Frevert, *Geschichtsvergessenheit — Geschichtsversessenheit: Vom Umgang mit deutschen Vergangenheiten nach 1945* (Stuttgart: Deutsche Verlagsanstalt, 1999), 84–96, 123–28.

[12] *The Nation*, 160, 12 May 1945, 535. Original German text: *Essays* 6, 11–13.

[13] For instance in the *Bayerische Landeszeitung*, 18 May 1945, 3.

[14] It would seem that Assmann, too, has joined the chorus of those critics who reject Mann's reckoning with Germany in *Doctor Faustus*. But she is surely in error when she argues, on much too narrow a basis of textual evidence, that Mann, as an émigré from Germany and as a "frischgebackene[r] US-Bürger," simply accepted and interiorized the American perspective on the collective guilt of the Germans. See Assmann/Frevert, 118–23.

[15] Thomas Mann, *Die Entstehung des Doktor Faustus: Roman eines Romans* (The Story of a Novel: The Genesis of Doctor Faustus, 1949) (*GW* 11, 227).

[16] For some insightful comments on the thematic connections between *Doktor Faustus* and "Der Tod in Venedig," see T. J. Reed, *Thomas Mann: The Uses of Tradition*, Second ed. (Oxford: Clarendon Press, 1996), 360–402, esp. 382–84.

[17] Thomas Mann, "Der Wille zum Glück" (*GW* 8, 43–61). See also *Six Early Stories*, trans. and ed. Peter Constantine with an introduction by Burton Pike (Los Angeles: Sun & Moon Press, 1997), 75–97.

[18] Two entries in Mann's notebook 7, dated 1904, consider an episode either to be included in an unwritten social novel "Maja" or to be treated separately as a novella: an artist afflicted with syphilis is in love with a chaste girl, and kills himself before the wedding; he sells his soul to the devil and the syphilitic poison enables him to create

wonderful works of genius. He ends in paralysis. *Nb* 2 (7–14), 107, 121–22. Mann mentions a notebook entry in *Entstehung des Doktor Faustus* (*GW* 11, 155), dating it erroneously 1901.

[19] Chapters 1, 5, 21, 26, 33, 43, 46.

[20] Shortly after the completion of the novel, Mann wrote a critical companion piece — a reconsideration of Nietzsche's philosophy in light of recent history: "Nietzsches Philosophie im Lichte unserer Erfahrung" (*GW* 9, 675–712). Cf. also Erkme Joseph, "Nietzsche im 'Doktor Faustus,'" in *"und was werden die Deutschen sagen?" Thomas Manns Roman "Doktor Faustus,"* ed. Hans Wisskirchen and Thomas Sprecher (Lübeck: Verlag Dräger-Druck, 1997), 61–112.

[21] In strikingly oblique fashion, Mann pays further homage to Wagner in chapter 16 of *Doctor Faustus,* in which Leverkühn describes, without identifying it, a particularly beautiful composition; it is the prelude to act 3 of *Die Meistersinger von Nürnberg* (1867). For an insightful analysis of that passage and its structural ramifications, see Steven P. Scher, *Verbal Music in German Literature* (New Haven: Yale UP, 1968), 106–42.

[22] Mann viewed Kahler's *Der deutsche Charakter in der Geschichte Europas* (Zurich: Europa Verlag, 1937) as the "standard psychological study of Germanness" and identified it as a source for his own novelistic study of Germanness. See "Erich von Kahler" (*GW* 10, 502–6) and my "Erich Kahler, Thomas Mann und Deutschland. Eine Miszelle zum 'Doktor Faustus,'" *Ethik und Ästhetik: Festschrift für Wolfgang Wittkowski,* ed. Richard Fischer (Frankfurt am Main: Peter Lang, 1995), 509–18.

[23] "Lübeck als geistige Lebensform," *Essays* 3, 16–38.

[24] "Deutschland und die Deutschen," *Essays* 5, 260–81. The English translation, as Mann read it, is found in Thomas Mann, *Addresses Delivered at the Library of Congress, 1942–1949* (Washington, DC: Library of Congress, 1963).

[25] *Essays* 5, 265.

[26] The word "Tonsetzer," meaning composer, conjures up a specifically German discourse on music as it alludes to Wackenroder, Beethoven, Carl Maria von Weber, and to Pfitzner, who all seem to have preferred the German terminology.

[27] Herfried Münkler, "Wo der Teufel seine Hand im Spiel hat. Thomas Manns Deutung der deutschen Geschichte des 20. Jahrhunderts," in *Thomas Mann: Doktor Faustus 1947–1997,* ed. Werner Röcke (Bern: Peter Lang, 2001), 89–107, 102.

[28] Cf. Harvey Goldman, *Max Weber and Thomas Mann: Calling and the Shaping of the Self* (Berkeley: U of California P, 1991).

[29] Cf. Ernst Fischer, "'Doktor Faustus' und die deutsche Katastrophe. Eine Auseinandersetzung mit Thomas Mann," in Ernst Fischer, *Kunst und Menschheit: Essays* (Vienna: Globus Verlag, 1949), 37–97; Käte Hamburger, "Anachronistische Symbolik. Fragen an Thomas Manns Faustus-Roman," in *Thomas Mann: Wege der Forschung,* ed. Helmut Koopmann (Darmstadt: Wissenschaftliche Buchgesellschaft, 1975), 384–413. For a comprehensive critical survey of the literature on *Doctor Faustus,* see John F. Fetzer, *Changing Perceptions of Thomas Mann's "Doctor Faustus"* (Columbia, SC: Camden House, 1996); see also my "Fünfzig Jahre Leiden an Deutschland: Thomas Manns 'Doktor Faustus' im Lichte unserer Erfahrung," in

Thomas Mann: Doktor Faustus 1947–1997, ed. Werner Röcke (Bern: Peter Lang), 11–34.

[30] "Das Seelische [ist] immer das Primäre und eigentlich Motivierende" (*GW* 6, 408).

[31] As the title of the chapbook's anonymous translation, Marlowe's source, puts it: *The Historie of the Damnable Life and Deserved Death of Doctor John Faustus,* ed. William Rose (South Bend, IN: Notre Dame Press, 1963).

[32] His as yet untranslated article *Gedanken im Kriege* (*Essays* 1, 188–205), written during the first weeks of the war, is but the most strident of Mann's comments at the time.

[33] On one occasion (26 September 1953), Mann himself flatly denied that his novel had anything to do with Goethe: *DüD* 3, 279. This is one of many statements of Mann on his own works that do not hold up under close scrutiny.

[34] The superstition that syphilis will under certain propitious circumstances induce genius had had some currency before; with the discovery of penicillin in 1928, a cure for the disease was discovered. Mann was, of course, aware of this. Leverkühn's gamble to bet on the alleged connection between syphilis and creativity is presented as an example of the spontaneous acts of irrationalism for which the people of Kaisersaschern are said to have a particular propensity. For the representation of Leverkühn's syphilis, Mann studied, aside from Nietzsche, the cases of two composers: Robert Schumann and Hugo Wolf.

[35] In a brilliant piece of literary detective work, Victor A. Oswald established that identity convincingly as early as 1948; see his "The Enigma of Madame Tolna," Germanic Review 23 (1948): 249–53.

[36] For an explanation, see the section "The Life and Works of Leverkühn" below.

[37] See "Musik in München" (1917), in *Im Schatten Wagners: Thomas Mann über Richard Wagner. Texte und Zeugnisse,* ed. by Hans Rudolf Vaget (Frankfurt am Main: Fischer Taschenbuch, 1999), 62–63. Hereafter quoted as *Im Schatten Wagners.* Cf. Celia Applegate, "What is German Music? Reflections on the Role of Art in the Creation of a Nation," *German Studies Review* 15 (1992): 21–32. Applegate shows that Mann's argument about the role of music in the life of the nation has deep roots in nineteenth-century discourses on music.

[38] See Mann's remembrance of Wagner performed during an outdoor concert in Rome in *Betrachtungen eines Unpolitischen* (*GW* 12, 80–81). In a telling autobiographical detail, Leverkühn, too, attends the open-air concerts at Rome's Piazza Colonna (*GW* 6, 291).

[39] For an analysis of the context in which Mann reached that decision, see Herbert Lehnert, Eva Wessell, *Nihilismus der Menschenfreundlichkeit: Thomas Manns "Wandlung" und sein Essay "Goethe und Tolstoi,"* TMS 9 (1991).

[40] *Im Schatten Wagners,* 232–34.

[41] For a more detailed account of this entire story, see my "The Wagner Celebration of 1933 and the 'National Excommunication' of Thomas Mann," *Wagner* 16 (1995): 51–60; cf. also *Im Schatten Wagners,* 229–61, 326–28.

[42] *Im Schatten Wagners,* 260.

[43] *Im Schatten Wagners,* 261.

[44] Cf. Egon Schwarz, "Adrian Leverkühn und Alban Berg," *Modern Language Notes* 102 (1987): 663–67.

[45] Cf. Willi Reich, *Arnold Schönberg der konservative Revolutionär* (Munich: DTV, 1974), 139; Alexander L. Ringer, *Arnold Schönberg: The Composer as Jew* (Oxford: Oxford UP, 1990), 18, 165.

[46] For an elaboration of this argument, see my "National and Universal: Thomas Mann and the Paradox of 'German' Music," in *Music and German National Identity,* ed. Celia Applegate and Pamela M. Potter (Chicago: U of Chicago P, 2002), 155–77.

[47] *Essays* 5, 229.

[48] The text of Schönberg's letter as well as Mann's response has been reprinted in the appendix of Patrick Carnegy's valuable *Faust as Musician: A Study of Thomas Mann's Novel "Doctor Faustus"* (New York: New Directions, 1973).

[49] As can be gleaned from Mann's diaries, he would meet Schönberg informally at various social gatherings in the German exile community of Los Angeles. On the occasion of Mann's seventieth birthday, Schönberg composed a canon in his honor with a very friendly dedication.

[50] For the complete documentation of the Mann-Schönberg affair, see Bernhold Schmid, "Neues zum 'Doktor Faustus'-Streit zwischen Arnold Schönberg und Thomas Mann," *Augsburger Jahrbuch für Musikwissenschaft* 6 (1989): 149–79; 7 (1990), 177–92.

[51] Adorno did so in his essay, "Zu einem Portrait Thomas Manns," *Neue Rundschau* 73 (1962): 320–27.

[52] I have examined this question in greater detail in "Mann, Joyce, Wagner: The Question of Modernism in 'Doctor Faustus,'" in *Thomas Mann's "Doctor Faustus": A Novel at the Margin of Modernism,* ed. Herbert Lehnert and Peter C. Pfeiffer (Columbia, SC: Camden House, 1991), 167–91.

[53] As a small but touching token of Mann's gratitude he has Kretzschmar use Adorno's middle name, "Wiesengrund" (*GW* 6, 75), to accentuate and illustrate a particularly moving moment in the concluding passage of Beethoven's Opus 111, the very work that Adorno had analyzed for him.

[54] See for example Rolf-Günter Renner, "Die Modernität Thomas Manns," in *Die literarische Moderne in Europa,* ed. Hans Joachim Piechotta et al. (Opladen: West-deutscher Verlag, 1994), 398–415.

[55] See especially the comprehensive re-examination of the Adorno-*Doctor Faustus* matter by Rolf Tiedemann, the editor of Adorno's collected works, "'Mitdichtende Einfühlung.' Adornos Beiträge zum "Doktor Faustus' — noch einmal," *Frankfurter Adorno Blätter* 1 (1992): 9–33.

[56] Carl Dahlhaus, "Fiktive Zwölftonmusik: Thomas Mann und Theodor Adorno," *Jahrbuch 1982: Deutsche Akademie für Sprache und Dichtung* (Heidelberg: Lothar Stiehm Verlag, 1982), 33–49; Klaus Kropfinger, "'Montage' und 'Composition' im 'Faustus' — Literarische Zwölftontechnik oder Leitmotivik?" in *Thomas Mann: Doktor Faustus 1947–1997,* ed. Werner Röcke (Bern: Peter Lang, 2001), 345–66.

[57] Adorno, "Zu einem Porträt Thomas Manns," 325; *GW* 11, 294.

[58] Adorno, "Zu einem Porträt Thomas Manns," 326–27; *GW* 11, 294.

[59] Friedrich Meinecke, *Die deutsche Katastrophe: Betrachtungen und Erinnerungen* (Wiesbaden: Brockhaus, 1946, 1955), 5.

[60] Heinrich August Winkler, *Der lange Weg nach Westen* (Munich: Deutscher Taschenbuchverlag, 2000), vol. 2, 112–13. Cf. also, even though she does not specifically deal with *Doctor Faustus,* Ernestine Schlant, *The Language of Silence: West German Literature and the Holocaust* (New York: Routledge, 1999).

[61] See Ruth Klüger, "Thomas Manns jüdische Gestalten," in R. Klüger, *Katastrophen: Über deutsche Literatur* (Göttingen: Wallstein, 1994), 39–58.

The Gaze of Love, Longing, and Desire in Thomas Mann's "The Transposed Heads" and "The Black Swan"

Jens Rieckmann

IN DIARY ENTRIES OF 1950, the year in which Thomas Mann encountered his last love, the nineteen-year-old waiter Franz Westermeier, a year in which he also was smitten by the sight of a number of other young men,[1] Mann repeatedly links gazing at the face or the body of a youth and the emotional experience of falling in love (*Tb* 19 July, 15 August, 25 August 1950).[2] In yet another diary entry, however, he questions this connection. Commenting on his last encounter with Westermeier in August 1950, he writes that his love for the "excitant" (Erreger) (*Tb* 11 July 1950) involved an extreme liking, an attachment from the bottom of his heart (*Tb* 15 August 1950). Yet he asks himself if the source of his fascination with Westermeier was not primarily his enchanted sensual perception rather than his heart (*Tb* 15 August 1950). The same uncertainty surfaces when Mann comments on his travels, which are always partly undertaken in the hope of "amorous adventures" (*Tb* 28 August 1950). He records either his gratitude or his disappointment when the trips offered — or failed to offer — something "for the heart" (*Tb* 3 July 1950) or a "gift for the eye" (*Tb* 29 August 1950). Mann's personal experience of gazing covertly and erotically at faces and bodies, together with his reflections on the significance of this, shaped his understanding of love as strongly as his reading of Schopenhauer's "Metaphysik der Geschlechtsliebe" (The Metaphysics of Sexual Love),[3] Plato, Freud, Nietzsche, and Plutarch.

Two of the last stories in Thomas Mann's oeuvre, "Die vertauschten Köpfe" (The Transposed Heads), written in the early part of 1940 and "Die Betrogene" (The Black Swan), written from 1952 to 1953, are centered on the problem of love and the "secret of the erotic" (*Tb* 19 August 1950). One may indeed go so far as to claim that, in a condensed form, these two texts sum up Mann's thoughts on the relationship between love and sensuality, the "heart" and the "eye." Both stories are as significant as Mann's other reflections on the thematic of love, sensuality, and metaphysics, such as the chapters "Walpurgisnacht" and "Forschungen" in *Der Zauberberg* (The

Magic Mountain, 1924), or the chapters on Potiphar's wife, Mut-em-enet, in *Joseph in Ägypten* (Joseph in Egypt, 1936) to name just two examples.

Mann's comments on "Die vertauschten Köpfe" do not seem to bear out this significance. At times he seems to dismiss the story, which he subtitled "Eine indische Legende" (A Legend of India), as nothing but a rather superfluous digression (*Tb* 27 February 1940) undertaken primarily to postpone the resumption of the Joseph tetralogy.[4] At other times he speaks of his fondness for the anecdote that contains the nucleus of his narrative. He had first come across the story of Sita and her two husbands in 1935 in the essay "Die Geschichte vom indischen König mit dem Leichnam" (The King and the Corpse) by the Indologist Heinrich Zimmer.[5] He was reminded of it when, in November 1939, he read "Die indische Weltmutter" (The Indian Mother of the World, 1939), also by Zimmer.[6] In his book and in the earlier essay, Zimmer had retold the story "Kathasaritsagara" (The Transposed Male Heads) from the *Vetalapancavimshati*.[7] What attracted Mann to the story was "die Hindu-Mischung aus Sinnlichkeit und Metaphysik, die Identitäts-Wirrnis, [. . .] das Liebes- und Persönlichkeitsproblem."[8] These themes and motifs of sensuality and metaphysics, entangled identities, the problem of love and individuality are central to Mann's oeuvre. Another, almost subconscious reason for postponing the immediate resumption of work on the *Joseph* novels, was Mann's fascination with Goethe's *Paria* poems.[9] In his Goethe novel *Lotte in Weimar,* which he completed in the fall of 1939, Mann alludes to the second part of this poetic trilogy. It shares with "Die vertauschten Köpfe" the motifs of decapitation, the exchange of bodies and heads, seduction and imaginary adultery. Although Mann claimed that "Die vertauschten Köpfe" was nothing more than a metaphysical jest,[10] this tale as well as "Die Betrogene" continue a preoccupation with themes and motifs that runs through Mann's life and career as a writer.

"Die Betrogene," written in 1952–53, tells a story of deception. The fifty-year-old Rosalie von Tümmler, deeply regretting the onset of her menopause, falls in love with Ken Keaton, the twenty-four-year-old American tutor of her son. Shortly thereafter menstruation seems to set in again. It turns out, however, that what she thinks of as a miracle wrought in her by nature,[11] is actually a symptom of a malignant growth that is spreading from the ovaries. The story is based upon Katia Mann's reminiscences of an elderly aristocratic woman who suffered a similar fate (*Tb* 6 April 1952). In "Rückkehr" (Return), an essay published in 1954, Mann writes that he was immediately captivated by the cruel "Natur-Dämonie," which he saw as the essence of the anecdote related to him by Katia (*GW* 11, 529). In addition, personal reasons played an essential role in his resolve to amplify the story and to fashion it into the heterosexually coded, radically autobiographical confession of his homoerotic attractions to young men such as the seventeen-year-old Klaus Heuser, whom Mann encountered when he was fifty-two years old; hence the — for Mann — atypical choice of Düsseldorf, Heuser's hometown, as the setting for the story.[12]

In both texts the gaze is foregrounded, as the following few examples will show. In "Die vertauschten Köpfe," Schridaman falls in love with Sita while gazing at her bathing naked in the river Goldfly. After gazing at Nanda's body, Sita closes her eyes while she is having sex with Schridaman and imagines that it is Nanda who is in bed with her. Gazing at Nanda's back, spinal column and shoulder-blades (*GW* 8, 744), Schridaman makes the fateful decision to enter the shrine of Kâlî.[13] Sita's and Schridaman's son Samadhi is soon known as Andhaka, the little blind one (*GW* 8, 795). Although beautiful himself, his defective eyesight makes it impossible for him to gaze at beauty.

In "Die Betrogene" Rosalie von Tümmler first takes an interest in Ken Keaton when she gazes at his body, particularly at his broad shoulders, long legs and narrow hips (*GW* 8, 895). Confessing her passion for him to herself, she says: "I have cast my eye upon him like a man who casts his eye on the young woman of his choice" (*GW* 8, 901–2). And when Anna, her daughter, attempts to persuade Rosalie to dismiss Ken or to move away, Anna argues that if she were unable to see Keaton ("mit Hilfe des Nicht-mehr-Sehens"; *GW* 8, 918), Rosalie would forget him. In the following I will cite some passages in which the gaze is foregrounded and try to analyze the passages' significance. I will primarily refer to passages in which the gaze is male and directed towards the female body as is the case with Schridaman and Nanda in "Die vertauschten Köpfe," occasionally to passages in which the subject of the gaze is female and its object the male body, as with Sita in "Die vertauschten Köpfe," but especially with Rosalie von Tümmler in "Die Betrogene," and also to passages in which both subject and object of the gaze are male as is the case with Schridaman and Nanda in "Die vertauschten Köpfe."

There are only two instances of a male's gaze at a female body in "Die vertauschten Köpfe" and none in "Die Betrogene." This is hardly accidental. Mann felt that supreme beauty is male rather than female, "that the admiration engendered by the 'divine young man' surpasses all feminine [beauty] by far and that it creates a longing comparable with *nothing* in this world."[14] Nevertheless, the two instances of the male gazing at the female in "Die vertauschten Köpfe" are of great significance. The first occurs toward the beginning of the story, when the two friends, Schridaman and Nanda, traveling together on business, stop at the bathing place of the goddess Kâlî and catch sight of Sita, paying her tribute to the deity: "Open your eyes," Nanda whispers to Schridaman, "it's worth the trouble. She does not see us, but we are seeing her" (*GW* 8, 725). These words signal a markedly voyeuristic scene, its eroticism heightened by Sita's unawareness of being gazed at. The sexual excitation caused by gazing at Sita's naked virginal body is indicated by the reddish tint in Schridaman's eyes (*GW* 8, 726). That the red eyes signify erotic interest becomes fully evident as the story progresses. Sita, in her confrontation with the goddess Kâlî, recalls that before her sexual awakening the sight of a young man's chest, arms or legs never caused her eyes to redden (*GW* 8, 759). When the three protagonists embark on their journey to the home of Sita's parents, the erotic tension that has arisen among them is signaled by their bloodshot eyes (*GW* 8, 744). With the same bloodshot eyes Schridaman gazes at the terrifying yet spellbinding image of Kâlî shortly before he severs his head from his body (*GW* 8, 746). I shall return to these instances later.

Of the two voyeurs at the stream Goldfly, Schridaman, more intellectual and reflective than his naïve friend Nanda, is both aroused by the sight of the naked girl and also conscious of the forbidden nature of their surreptitious observation of her. In order to assuage his pangs of guilt he attempts to transform his purely physical sensations at the sight of Sita into a spiritual, quasi-religious experience, calling it "blessed" (*GW* 8, 728). Or, to put it into terms I quoted earlier from Mann's diary, Schridaman tries to substitute a gift to the "heart" for the gift to the "eye." After Sita's departure, he embarks upon a long lecture addressed both to himself and to the earthy Nanda; for Nanda had talked coarsely of Sita's fetching bottom and had pointed out that a captivating body binds us to the world of desire and delights, entangling us deeply in the constraints of Samsâra (*GW* 8, 729).[15]

In his lecture, Schridaman strives to convince himself, and to a lesser extent Nanda, that the corporeal is a symbol of the transcendent. Arguing that in Sita the goddess Schakti (Kâlî) revealed herself to them, he asserts that the female body, in whatever shape — child, virgin, mother, or gray-haired woman — is but a vessel of the goddess. He further criticizes Nanda for failing to recognize that the intoxication caused by the captivating image not only infatuates but is, at the same time, an exaltation which leads to truth and freedom: "For so it is, that which enchains us also liberates us, and exaltation links sensual beauty and spirit" (*GW* 8, 732). On the basis of this Platonic thought Schridaman concludes that in the sexual act, and here Schopenhauer supplies the necessary ammunition, we are released from the delusion of individuality: "Just as beauty and spirit are joined in the moment of exaltation, so are life and death in love!" (*GW* 8, 734). The loss of self in death and in the sexual act is already foreshadowed at the moment of gazing at the body of another. "Is there a more blissful state," Schridaman asks rhetorically, "than to lose oneself in such an image and to exist only in it?" (*GW* 8, 728).

Once again we are reminded of Mann's state of mind in 1950. The love for Westermeier and the many gifts for the eye received during the travels of that summer, particularly that of a young Argentinean on the tennis courts, eagerly gazed at from Mann's room in a hotel in St. Moritz, brought him to a sense of loss of self (*Tb* 12 August 1950). It culminated in the "proximity of the desire to die," because Mann could "no longer bear the longing for the 'heavenly boy'" — and he was "not thinking particularly of this [the young Argentinean] one" (*Tb* 6 August 1950). The generalization Mann employs establishes the connection to Schridaman's exhortation: just as Sita's body is transformed into a vessel for the goddess in Schridaman's disquisition on love, the Argentinean boy is for Mann one of many embodiments of the "nebulously inconceivable, intangible" beauty of young males that he believed to be the foundation and inspiration of his art (*Tb* 6 August 1950).

Neither the narrator, who is obviously a reader of Schopenhauer, nor the more prosaic Nanda share Schridaman's flights of fancy. The narrator declares quite laconically that it was only physical desire that had made Sita's body appear to Schridaman so beautiful and worthy of being worshipped (*GW* 8, 789). In other words, he is the victim of what Schopenhauer terms the "delusive ecstasy," the unique delusion of love,[16] a means that nature employs for the sole end of procreation. Recapitulating Schopenhauer's ideas on the metaphysics of sexual love, the narrator argues that the magic of Maya, life's fundamental illusion and deception, is particularly evident in the desire of one single being for another; in fact, this is the essence of all the deception that entices man to the perpetuation of life (*GW* 8, 789). The foundation, then, on which love rests, is desire itself, not the desired object. Hence the lover fears nothing more than being disillusioned, and longs to continue in a state of intoxication (*GW* 8, 789–90).[17]

In keeping with this theory of love, Schridaman refuses to see Sita with Nanda's unilluded eyes. For Nanda, Sita is no goddess but quite an ordinary, though exceptionally pretty, thing who lives as others do, grinds the corn, cooks the porridge, and spins the wool (*GW* 8, 739). Similarly, Sita, whose desire transforms Nanda into Vishnu, who descended to earth in Krishna's form[18] (*GW* 8, 762), does not pay any heed to Kâlî's sobering words:

> It is ridiculous what you have made out of this Nanda in your curiosity. He is in all his aspects entirely ordinary. I have sons by the millions running about with such arms and legs, but you make a Gandharva out of him![19]

Rosalie von Tümmler in "Die Betrogene" similarly refuses her daughter Anna's advice to look at Ken Keaton not in the transfiguring light of her love but in plain daylight, for love, Anna believes, casts a false and entirely misleading light on its object. Rosalie's refusal is clearly motivated by fear of losing her state of delusion and desire, of seeing Keaton for what he is, an attractive but average young man (*GW* 8, 913). In Schopenhauerian terms all three are "dupes of the species." Their "sexual impulse [. . .] knows how to assume very skillfully the mask of an objective admiration."[20] Once again we are reminded of Mann's fascination with the young Argentinean. As long as he observes him from a distance, aware only of his body, his enthusiasm for him, transfigured by his "erotic interest," knows no bounds; as soon as he sees him close-up in the dining room, in plain daylight so to speak, the "tennis-god" turns out to be a young man of average looks, "the glowworm on the flat hand. Illusion! Illusion!" (*Tb* 6 August 1950).

These reflections on the nature of love also inform the second part of "Die vertauschten Köpfe," after Schridaman and Nanda have severed their heads from their bodies in the temple of Kâlî. Ordered by Kâlî to refit the severed heads onto the bodies, Sita, in her haste, attaches the head of her husband Schridaman to Nanda's body and vice versa, a Freudian slip, which at least temporarily satiates her longing for Nanda's body. Similarly, Schridaman, who had always admired his friend's body, delights in his new shape. Yet, at the same time, he is filled with sadness: for him, Nanda's body, the longed for Other, is no longer the object of his gaze and longing. The narrator's comments at this point indicate that Schridaman's experience is an illustration of a general law: the possession of one's object of desire results in a diminished love for that object (*GW* 8, 793).

The realization that possession of the desired cannot slake longing ulti-mately motivates the suicide of the three protagonists. Married to Shrida-man, Sita had desired Nanda's body; once she has effected the exchange of bodies and heads, her bliss is short-lived. In the arms of the man with Schridaman's head and Nanda's body she longs for the man with Nanda's head and Schridaman's body. As long as Schridaman and Nanda are alive, Sita can find neither peace nor satisfaction, because, as Schridaman puts it, the one who is present in her arms will always awake in her the longing for the absent object of her desire (*GW* 8, 802). The conviction that love in-heres in longing and not in possession is shared not only by the three pro-tagonists and the narrator, but also by their creator, and accounts in part for Mann's never acting on his homoerotic desires.

There is, however, a further dimension to the idea that longing can never be satisfied in this life, a dimension which also forms the basis of Freud's *Das Unbehagen in der Kultur* (Civilization and Its Discontents, 1930). Commenting on Schridaman's and Sita's ephemeral happiness after the exchange of bodies and heads, the narrator explores the limitations social order, the law, religion, and moral conventions set on our longing (*GW* 8, 785). These barriers play a role in both our texts. In "Die vertauschten Köpfe," the three protagonists, for a brief moment, consider the possibility of polyandry, which might temporarily solve Sita's conundrum of longing for Schridaman's body with Nanda's head while possessing Nanda's body with Schridaman's head. All three, however, reject this option: Schridaman rejects it because polyandry is unthinkable among superior beings; Nanda, because their social standing excludes polyandry and promiscuity; and Sita, because of her belief in the honor and pride of civilized human beings, a belief to be upheld despite all weakness and chaos of the flesh (*GW* 8, 802–3).

Similar barriers are encountered by Rosalie von Tümmler in "Die Betrogene." Rosalie tries to persuade her daughter Anna and herself that new political liberties in post-Wilhelminian Germany have led to a relaxation of moral standards, allowing her to defy conventions. Yet she admits, at least to herself, that Anna, who represents the voice of reason, is right: sexual desires such as hers are inconsistent with her moral convictions. These convictions are ultimately grounded in the bourgeois values of the nineteenth century, and she therefore tries, at least temporarily, to integrate the Goethean idea of "Entsagung" (renunciation) into her concept of happiness (*GW* 8, 931–32).

Yet, on a deeper level still, the narrator contends that apart from the legal, moral, conventional, and religious barriers that have been erected in the course of civilization, it is the very nature of longing that makes its satisfaction impossible. Longing knows no bounds; it is inherently insatiable. It can only find satisfaction beyond the threshold of life, in a "paradise" where the allowed and the forbidden become one (*GW* 8, 785–86). Hence the longing for death Mann expressed in his 1950 diary, hence Sita's hope that death's fiery bed will unite "us three" (*GW* 8, 804), hence the mythologized setting of the brief union between Rosalie von Tümmler and Ken Keaton in Hades and their emergence from the underworld on the Elysian fields.[21] Once again we are reminded of Schopenhauer's assertion that the longing and pain of love are "the sighs of the spirit of the species," which are in this life "imprisoned in the narrow breast of a mortal [which] can find no expression for the intimation of infinite rapture or infinite pain with which it is filled."[22]

The second instance in which the subject of the gaze is male and its object female involves Schridaman and his attraction for his wife Sita. Here too, love and possession are at odds with one another. Married for six months and certain of Sita's imaginary adultery with Nanda (*GW* 8, 748), Schridaman cuts off his own head. From the narrator's discourse on the nature of love, we can infer that Schridaman is already disillusioned with the object of his longing. In this instance as well the narrator closely follows Schopenhauer's line of argumentation. Since, according to Schopenhauer, love is nothing more than the "satisfaction of the sexual impulse," every lover, once the object of his desire is attained and with it the will of the species, "will experience an extraordinary disillusionment."[23] Psychologically speaking then, the motivation for Schridaman's desire to end his life seems obvious, and the words he addresses to the goddess shortly before he severs his head from his body — "let me enter again into you through the gate of the womb that I lose this self and am no longer Schridaman, for whom all desire is muddled, because it is not he who gives it" (*GW* 8, 748) — seem to confirm this interpretation.

Such a reading, however, ignores the transference of Schridaman's desire from Sita's body to that of Nanda, a transference that probably took place before the three set out on their journey and that marks the third aspect of our discussion here: that in which both subject and object of the gaze are male. Already at the beginning of the story, the relationship between Schridaman and Nanda, unlike in body and mind, is one of mutual attraction, an attraction that, although tinged with homoeroticism, is not of a sexual nature. During the journey this has changed. As I already mentioned above, all three participants in the journey are erotically aroused, as indicated by their bloodshot eyes. A seemingly insignificant detail, Schridaman's avoidance of gazing at Nanda's neck (*GW* 8, 744), is a telling sign. Nanda's neck, after all, is the repeated erotic focal point when Sita gazes at Nanda (*GW* 8, 744; 749; 753). When Rosalie von Tümmler finally comes into bodily contact with Ken Keaton, it is his neck that she embraces ("with a sigh from her innermost depths Rosalie flung her arms around the boy's neck" *GW* 8, 945). The move to avoid looking at this particular part of Nanda's body signals a sexual interest that Schridaman tries to repress. His lament then, "all desire is muddled" for him, has a much broader meaning than he himself is aware of. The neck as the focal point of the erotically charged gaze seems to belong to Mann's personal erotic fixations. Westermeier's otherwise pleasing physique was marred by a stocky neck (*Tb* 9 July; 13 July 1950). Years earlier, while working on *Der Zauberberg*, Mann had jotted down in his notebook: "Erotic predilections: neck (related to the concept nakedness) and arms."[24] The sexual nature of Schridaman's interest in Nanda is further underlined by the singling out of certain parts of Nanda's body: the naked back, spinal column, and shoulder blades, parts Schridaman tries to ignore "completely" (*GW* 8, 744). Yet he is fascinated by them and admits that moving away from the line of vision would not be the "right thing" to do (*GW* 8, 744). The fixation on these particular parts of the body is markedly different from the far more general description of Nanda's body given by the narrator at the beginning of the story. There, the narrator mentions features that Schridaman finds attractive merely because they are different from his own: Nanda's dark complexion, his muscular arms, his well-shaped body, his pleasant beardless face and his laughing black eyes (*GW* 8, 714). Focusing the gaze on one part of the body, the naked back, eroticizes it and emphasizes its corporeality. Baumgart has pointed out that the segmenting of the body, making the isolated part serve as a sign for the whole, is an erotic strategy that Mann employs throughout his writings.[25]

It is in this state of sexual disorientation that Schridaman enters the temple. He first perceives "visions of life in the flesh." These Schopenhauerian visions reveal life in its most disconsolate aspects, consisting of "passions, anger, illusion, desire, envy, and despair [. . .] hunger, thirst, old age, sorrow, and death," fed and perpetuated by "the sweet, hot stream of blood" (*GW* 8, 746), Schopenhauer's Will. Schridaman internalizes these visions, can internalize them at this point because for him "all desire is muddled," that is, he lacks the will to perpetuate life through procreation. Under the spell of this vision, Schridaman is confronted with the image of the goddess Kâlî. We recall that when Schridaman first saw Sita, whose deliciously curved hips made a spacious pelvic cavity and indicated her potential fertility, he thought her to be a revelation of the goddess in her "sweetest shape" (*GW* 8, 733). In other words, Sita then revealed one aspect of this bifurcated goddess, who in Indian mythology is both the "all-life-giving one" and the "all-devouring one" (Allgebärerin, Allverschlingerin) (*GW* 8, 733). Now, given Schridaman's changed psychic disposition, the goddess Kâlî appears to him in her most terrible aspect. The shift in narration from authorial to figural at this point signals that it is Schridaman's gaze that transforms the image of Kâlî into the horrifying vision of woman as a destructive force, a force demanding the sacrifice of Schridaman's manhood and the annihilation of his self. Thus the male gaze can perceive woman, goddess or human, as both angelic and demonic, as life-giving and life-destroying, a dichotomous view that had gained prominence in much of late nineteenth and early twentieth-century art. The view here is prefigured in such Mannian fictional characters as Gabriele Klöterjahn in "Tristan" (1903) and Gerda von Rinnlingen in "Der kleine Herr Friedemann" (Little Herr Friedemann, 1897). Still, this clichéd view is somewhat corrected in "Die vertauschten Köpfe." When the goddess appears to Sita after Schridaman's and Nanda's sacrificial deaths, she is thoroughly demythologized and transformed into a practical, commonsensical woman.

Although the self confessed incarnation of disorder, the goddess insists upon order, particularly the inviolate nature of the institution of marriage (*GW* 8, 764). And yet, when Sita in her partially unconscious desire to possess both Schridaman and Nanda effects the exchange of bodies and heads, it is again woman who sets in motion events that ultimately lead to the death of all three protagonists. With this in mind, the story might be interpreted as somewhat misogynistic. Implicitly the text seems to suggest that the tale of Schridaman and Nanda — for it is as much their story as Sita's — would have had a "happier" ending had the goddess not interfered, that is if Schridaman's and Nanda's "longing to become one in death" had been realized.[26] In restoring the two friends to life, the goddess, who rejects the Schopenhauerian view that life is an infectious disease, communicating itself through sexual desire from one generation to the next (*GW* 8, 758), returns them to the suffering of insatiable longing.

Some critics have suggested that the story ends on a note of reconciliation, that in the figure of Sita's son Samadhi — the name implies balance — Thomas Mann had finally resolved the tension between spirit and life.[27] In *Betrachtungen eines Unpolitischen* (Reflections of a Nonpolitical Man, 1918), Mann had characterized this tension as an erotic one and had added: "Therefore there is no union between the two, only the short-lived, intoxicating illusion of union, an eternal tension without resolution" (*GW* 12, 561). In Sita's son Samadhi, physical beauty and intellectual gifts seem indeed harmonized, but his gifts only qualify him for the rather lowly, passive, and certainly not creative position of reader to the king of Benares.[28] Peter Szondi ignores the fact that the narrator repeatedly emphasizes that Samadhi's given name is soon replaced by Andhaka, "the little blind one" (Blindling) (*GW* 8, 795, 799, 806). The boy's myopia makes it impossible for him to perceive beauty and thus spares him the conflicts Schridaman, Nanda, and Sita experienced.[29] It does, however, also draw him away from the sensual and the physical into a sterile existence. Ultimately the reader is not left with an image of a life in which mind and body are reconciled but rather with that of an impoverished life. We last see Samadhi/Andhaka reading from holy and profane texts holding the book very close to his glimmering eyes (*GW* 8, 897), hardly an image of what the narrator calls the "world's goal of union between mind and beauty, of perfection" (*GW* 8, 793).

Reconciliation is, however, the note on which "Die Betrogene" ends. Upon first hearing the story of the Munich aristocrat on which he based his last story, Mann's creative imagination immediately seized upon two possible endings: either death or suicide of the deceived woman as a rebellion against nature or renunciation and the peace of the grave (*Tb* 6 April 1952). Ultimately Mann opted for the latter ending. Rosalie's dying words — "But how could there be spring without death? After all, death is a great instrument of life, and if for me it took on the shape of resurrection and desire, then that was not deceit but rather kindness and mercy" (*GW* 8, 950) — echo a sentiment Mann confided to his diary when he parted from Franz Westermeier: "I will live for a while longer, will still create something and die. Oh, incomprehensible life which affirms itself in love" (*Tb* 14 July 1950). In the end then both, the fictional character and her creator, welcome their last loves, despite all the inner turmoil and suffering that they entailed, as an affirmation of life.

Notes

[1] *Tb* 22 August 1950. Mann's diaries will hereafter be cited in the text.

[2] In this respect Mann shares Freud's ideas on the significance of the glance. In "Die Umgestaltungen der Pubertät" (The Transformations of Puberty, 1905), Freud states: "The eye is perhaps the zone most remote from the sexual object, but it is the one which [. . .] is liable to be the most frequently stimulated by the particular quality of excitation whose cause, when it occurs in a sexual object, we describe as beauty." In Sigmund Freud, *Three Essays on the Theory of Sexuality*, trans. James Strachey (New York: Basic Books, 1975), 75. First published in 1905 in *Drei Abhandlungen zur Sexualtheorie*, Sigmund Freud, *Gesammelte Werke chronologisch geordnet*, ed. Anna Freud, vol. 5 (London: Imago Publishing Co., 1942), 108–31.

[3] "Metaphysik der Geschlechtsliebe" appears as chapter 44 in vol. 2 of Schopenhauer's *Die Welt als Wille und Vorstellung* (1844); Arthur Schopenhauer, *Sämtliche Werke*, vol. 2, ed. Wolfgang Freiherr von Löhneysen (Stuttgart, Frankfurt am Main: Cotta/Insel, 1968), 678–727. Engl.: Arthur Schopenhauer, *The World as Will and Representation*, vol. 2, trans. E. F. J. Payne (New York: Dover Publications, 1966).

[4] *DüD* 3, 583.

[5] Heinrich Zimmer, "Die Geschichte von dem Indischen König mit dem Leichnam." The story was first published as the introduction to: *Vetalapantschavinsati: Die fünfundzwanzig Erzählungen eines Dämons* (Munich: G. Müller, 1924).

[6] *Tb* 12 November 1939. Heinrich Zimmer, "Die indische Weltmutter," *Eranus-Jahrbuch 1938* (Zurich: Rhein-Verlag, 1939).

[7] "Twenty-five Tales of a Vampire." See Wendy Doninger, *Splitting the Difference: Gender and Myth in Ancient Greece and India* (Chicago: U of Chicago P, 1999), 232–35.

[8] *DüD* 3, 587.

[9] See Hans Rudolf Vaget, *Thomas Mann: Kommentar zu sämtlichen Erzählungen* (Munich: Winkler, 1984), 253.

[10] *DüD* 3, 586.

[11] *GW* 8, 922. Mann's collected works (*GW* 1–13) will hereafter be cited in the text.

[12] Hans Rudolf Vaget, "Die Betrogene," *Thomas-Mann-Handbuch*, ed. Helmut Koopmann, 2nd. ed. (Stuttgart: Kröner, 1995), 611, 614.

[13] In Indian mythology the great mother of the world, the goddess of becoming. Also referred to as Schakti and Durgâ.

[14] *Tb* 28 August 1950, emphasis Mann's. This was an axiom that Mann shared with Goethe. Cf. Johannes von Müller, *Unterhaltungen mit Goethe*, ed. Ernst Grumach (Weimar: H. Bohlaus Nachfolger, 1956), 187–88 and Arthur Schopenhauer, *The World as Will and Representation*, vol. 2, 544.

[15] The eternal recurrence of birth, death, and rebirth.

[16] Schopenhauer, *The World as Will and Representation*, vol. 2, 539, 550.

[17] *GW* 8, 789–90. See also the narrator's comment after Aschenbach in Mann's "Der Tod in Venedig" (Death in Venice, 1912) abandons his plan to speak to Tadzio: "The step he had failed to take might readily have led [. . .] to a salutary sobering. But perhaps the aging man did not want any sobering; his rapture may have been too precious" (336).

[18] In Hindu mythology Vishnu is the preserver of the universe and the incarnation of benevolence and grace. Krishna is a semi-god who is thought of as an incarnation of Vishnu.

[19] "Es ist ja lächerlich, was du dir in deiner Neugier aus diesem Nanda gemacht hast, dessen ganzes Drum und Dran nicht mehr als normal ist. Mit solchen Armen und Beinen laufen mir Söhne millionenweise herum, du aber machstest dir einen Gandharven aus ihm" (*GW* 8, 763). Gandharven = Citraratha, the god of love. This vain attempt to sober up Sita recurs in *Felix Krull*. After Lord Kilmarnock (Lord Strathbogie) has confessed in somewhat veiled terms his attraction for Krull, the

object of his desire remarks: "If someone precisely like me occurs only once [. . .] there are nevertheless millions of young men of my age and general physique, and except for the tiny bit of uniqueness, one is made very much like another." (*Bekenntnisse des Hochstaplers Felix Krull, GW 7*, 222).

[20] Schopenhauer, *The World as Will and Representation*, vol. 2, 540, 535.

[21] Vaget, *Kommentar*, 292.

[22] Schopenhauer, *The World as Will and Representation*, vol. 2, 551.

[23] Schopenhauer, *The World as Will and Representation*, vol. 2, 536, 540.

[24] *Nb* 2 (7–14), 226.

[25] Reinhard Baumgart, "Der erotische Schriftsteller," *Thomas Mann und München* (Frankfurt: S. Fischer, 1989), 9.

[26] Peter Dettmering, *Dictung und Psychoanalyse. Thomas Mann–Rainer Maria Rilke–Richard Wagner* (Munich: Nymphenburger Verlagshandlung, 1969), 60.

[27] Peter Szondi, "Versuch über Thomas Mann." *Neue Rundschau* 67 (1956): 562; Murielle Gagnebin, "La bisexualité psychique dans 'Les têtes inverties' de Thomas Mann." *La Revue d'Esthétique* 33 (1980): 315.

[28] See Herbert Lehnert, "Idyllen und Realitätseinbrüche: Ideologische Selbstkritik in Thomas Manns 'Die vertauschten Köpfe,' in *Zeitgenossenschaft: Zur deutschsprachigen Literatur im 20. Jahrhundert: Festschrift für Egon Schwarz zum 65. Geburtstag*, ed. Paul Michael Lützeler (Frankfurt: Athenäum, 1987), 124; Monika Carbe, *Thomas Mann: "Die vertauschten Köpfe." Eine Interpretation der Erzählung*. Diss. Marburg, 1970, 184.

[29] Jürgen Rothenberg, "Der göttliche Mittler. Zur Deutung der Hermes-Figurationen im Werk Thomas Manns," *Euphorion* 66 (1977): 75.

Felix Krull

Egon Schwarz

The Unfolding of the Novel

THE HISTORY OF THE WORK *Bekenntnisse des Hochstaplers Felix Krull: Der Memoiren Erster Teil* (Confessions of Felix Krull, Confidence Man: The Early Years, 1955) extends from its conception in 1905 to the final publication in 1954, a year before the author's death. It has often been compared with Goethe's *Faust* (1790–1832) — which also parallels and reflects the poet's development from youthful beginnings to old-age maturity — particularly since Krull's confessions emit other Faustian signals as well. But in its pompous tones it also parodies the venerable German educational autobiography such as Goethe's *Dichtung und Wahrheit* (Poetry and Truth, 1811–14). This genre typically records the development of the central character toward an all-around maturity. It is one of Mann's ironies that despite his constantly switching identities Felix never really changes.

Thomas Mann's first inspiration came from a more mundane source, the confessions of George Manolescu, a Romanian confidence man whose memoirs made the rounds of all Europe at the time of their publication in 1905. Mann's first notations for his novel date from 1906, a period when he was interested in the complexities of the alienated artist's existence in modern society. The actual writing began in 1910. By 1911 he had finished Book 1, which ended with the death of Felix's father. In 1912 he had progressed to the chapter about Krull's Hungarian lover, the prostitute Rozsa. Again and again he had put aside the novel for the sake of other projects. But now ensued a gaping hiatus. It was not until 1951, after the tumultuous decade of National Socialism, the author's exile in Switzerland and the United States, and his return to Europe, that he took up his pen to continue writing on the same manuscript page where he had left off almost forty years before. This seamless resumption has been much admired. But Mann and his views of art had changed considerably. What had remained the same was a narcissistic curiosity about himself and the role of the artist in the world. The second half of *Krull* reflects these transformations, but it too has remained above all a novel about the artist, be he Krull or Thomas Mann.

According to the author's plentiful notes there were many more adventures in store for Felix, but the novel breaks off at the most exciting moment, when he finally falls into the arms of the more resolute of the two ladies he courts in Portugal's seductive capital. Thus we cannot follow Felix to Buenos Aires and the Argentinean "estancia" where he is expected, nor are we allowed to witness his subsequent career as a high-class confidence man for which we are, however, prepared by his earlier thieveries from childhood on. We are also spared his downfall, his imprisonment, his escape, his retirement and premature weariness at the age of forty, in Thomas Mann's writings a sure sign of decadence. Notwithstanding the fact that the subject of Felix Krull occupied Thomas Mann for almost half a century, the narrative remained incomplete.

The "finished fragment" was published in 1954, but portions had seen the light of day before: in 1911 the episode about the operetta singer Müller-Rosé; in 1922 "Das Buch der Kindheit" (The Book of Childhood); and in 1937 the rest, up to the scene of Krull's medical examination for the draft. After the monumental *Joseph* novels (1934–43) and the profound *Doktor Faustus* (1947), Mann, ever dependent on public opinion for his self esteem, was skeptical about the more lightweight *Krull*. But the tremendous success that immediately followed its publication restored his confidence in the book.

Krull as Artist

Thomas Mann was a *poète savant*. The learned apparatus he built up around every project would have met exacting scholarly requirements. As a result, his fictions are networks of relational references and encodements; his characters and narrative events can be described as sometimes "overdetermined." They are conglomerates of many models and resound with multiple echoes. But Mann was also a master of integration. Each little piece of mosaic snugly fits in with and complements the larger picture. The reader never feels overburdened. *Felix Krull* is no exception. In addition to Goethe and Manolescu, writers like Nietzsche, Schopenhauer, Hermann Bang, Freud, the mythologist Kerényi, Grimmelshausen, the creator of Simplicissimus, the best known German *pícaro*, and many others left their imprint on the novel. To savor the riches of such encodings fully, the critic must follow these traces. We shall try to explore a few.

For his image of the artist, even the con-artist Krull, Mann was deeply indebted to Friedrich Nietzsche, who, in his famous critique of Richard Wagner, equated the artist with the make-belief actor. Western culture abounds with skeptical representations of art, especially literature, from Plato to Dante and Flaubert. But Nietzsche goes farther than any in his psychological debunking. For him the artist is a liar, an actor who slips from one mask into another, always calculating his effects. The artist has no identity; his existence is hollow. In youth, when his views were formed, Thomas Mann was encouraged to accept and expand Nietzsche's negative portrayal of the artist. Industrialization and a crude commercialism had relegated art to the margins and made the artist an outsider in society. Understandably, artists became skeptics and critics of bourgeois society and developed the arrogant philosophy of *l'art pour l'art*. Thomas Mann, a poor student, always last in his class, a dreamer and outsider because of his homoerotic tendencies, found the symptoms of the decadent artist in himself.

Krull is a parody of the artist. He has the nervous sensibility of one, a talent for masquerades. As a boy, he slips from one disguise into another. He hones his play-acting to such perfection that, in one of the most dazzling scenes of the book, he feigns an epileptic fit, convincing an entire draft board of his unfitness for military service. He is given to self-aggrandizing fantasies. He has the narcissism of his creator, but he does not create anything. He is a talented dilettante who, at the most, fashions his own life into a work of art. Growing up in the jovial Rhineland toward the end of the nineteenth century, Krull experiences the empty "other-directed" nature of artistic performances. Since he had amusingly imitated a violinist at home, his father — himself an unscrupulous manufacturer of a champagne whose bottles are fancier than their content — engages him in a practical joke to delight as well as deceive the public. In the spa where the family is enjoying the baths, little Felix, prettily dressed, joins the resort orchestra "in the performance of a Hungarian dance, doing with my fiddle and Vaselined bow what I had done before with my two sticks."[1] But even more amazing than his perfect imitation is the reaction of the audience:

> The public [. . .] streamed up from all sides and crowded in front of the pavilion. There was a child prodigy. My abandon, my pale face, [. . .] in short my whole moving and amazing little figure captivated all hearts. When I finished with the full sweep of the bow across all strings, the garden resounded with applause mixed with high and deep shouts of "bravo." (*GW* 7, 281)

All of a sudden, the isolation in which Felix and his family are held is broken through. A Russian princess "took my head between her beringed hands and kissed my moist forehead" (*GW* 7, 281–82); and the children of a noble family, "whom I had admired from a distance while they gave me only cold looks, asked me politely to play a game of croquet with them" (*GW* 7, 282). In other words, the fraud is committed with the public's connivance. It wants to be deceived or, as Mann noted in Latin, *mundus vult decipi*.

Felix learns an even more incisive lesson when his father takes him to see an operetta; the allusions point to Franz Lehar's *Die lustige Witwe* (The Merry Widow, 1905). The star singer, a personal acquaintance of Krull senior, is Müller-Rosé, whose very name indicates the double nature of the performer: as Müller, he is the humdrum individual who works for a provincial theater, whereas Rosé suggests the glamorous transformation he undergoes on stage. His appearance is "perfect [. . .] as not of this world, so to speak" (*GW 7*, 288); and he dispenses "joy of life" (Lebensfreude). The public, composed of "male and female burghers, shop-clerks, one-year service volunteers from the upper class and young girls wearing blouses" (*GW 7*, 289), reacts with the same rapture as those who admired Felix at the music pavilion. The description of their frenzy culminates in this sentence: "Yes, this whole shadowy assembly was like an enormous swarm of nocturnal insects, silently, blindly, and blissfully rushing into a blazing fire." (*GW 7*, 290).

But this is not all. Krull takes his son behind the stage after the performance to meet the great man. And what do they see? A vulgar half-naked man wiping rouge and grease paint from his face and neck:

> Since he had taken off the beautiful chestnut-colored wig [. . .] I recognized that he had red hair. One of his eyes still had deep black shadows beneath it and metallic dust clung to the lashes, while the other squinted at the visitors nakedly, watery, pertly and inflamed from rubbing. All this could have passed if Müller-Rosé's chest shoulders back and upper arms had not been thickly covered by pimples. (*GW 7*, 292)

Mann's irony exposes with cold impartiality the regrettable weaknesses of both sides: the false pretenses of the performer as well as the social and mental inferiority of the credulous, complicitous masses, a revolting picture of society strangely at odds with Felix Krull's assertion at the beginning of his memoirs that the world was "a great and infinitely enticing phenomenon, which offered the sweetest bliss and seemed to me worthy of every effort and solicitude to a high degree" (*GW 7*, 275), a statement perhaps meant honestly by him but ironically by his creator. Krull's own life exemplifies the same lack of identity and continuity, that excess of semblance over substance which Thomas Mann attributed to the artist at that time.

> But Mann's ideas about the function of art changed in the course of his long career, and so did his view of artists. Without divesting them of each of their earlier attributes, he slowly moved his artist figures from their position of flawed outsiders to a different part of his mental map. As their creator became famous, wealthy, and a member of the international elite, the artist figures became representatives of society rather than its outcasts, indeed the moral and aesthetic conscience of the world in addition to being its critics and the exposers of its foibles.

The artistic figures and their roles in the second half of the novel reflect these shifts in conception to a certain extent. The Stoudebecker circus Felix frequents in Paris gives the author ample opportunity to invest the various types of "fabulous creatures" that dazzle a public eager for entertainment and titillation with all the traits he wishes. Mann is "historically correct" in resuscitating the circus and its denizens at this moment in Krull's experience because of the circus's ubiquitous presence in fin-de-siècle painting (e.g.

Toulouse-Lautrec and Picasso) and literature (Wedekind and Rilke) as symbols of the Bohème, indeed mankind as a whole in its loss of the rootedness and stability of yesteryear, the *saltimbanques* being only a little more obviously "Fahrende" or homeless traveling folk. Of course, the circus had been used much earlier as a metaphor for art, for example in Goethe's educational novel *Wilhelm Meisters Lehrjahre* (Wilhelm Meister's Years of Apprenticeship, 1795–96), which was one of the models Mann parodied in *Krull*. The Stoudebecker performers are called "funmaker-beings"; they are "ageless, half-grown sons of nonsense"; "monks of disharmony"; not fully human, but "part-human and part farcical art" (*GW* 7, 457–58). Krull is here describing the clowns, but the words Mann puts into his mouth are so cleverly chosen that they evoke other artists as well, any artist. No wonder they instill a "most self-reflective lure" (nachdenklichste [. . .] Hingezogenheit) (*GW* 7, 457) in Felix.

Krull then goes through a number of other circus types, the daring Hungarian horsewomen, the nimble athletes, the circus director himself who mimics bourgeois respectability with his evening clothes and the ribbon of the Legion of Honor in his lapel, each of them exhibiting this or that trait characteristic of artists in general, traits however that are not necessarily at odds with the *poète* more or less *maudit* of Thomas Mann's early conception of the artist.

It is different with the main attraction, Andromache, the "angel of daring" (Kühnheitsengel) (*GW* 7, 463). She shares with the earlier artist figures the exclusion from "life," from the participation in the ordinary pleasures and concerns of the average person. If she were to descend from her extreme "heights" to a terrestrial love affair, she would lose the ability to execute her amazing "evolutions in arial space" (*GW* 7, 458) to defy gravity as it were; "she would have lost her grip and fallen disgracefully down to earth and to her death" (*GW* 7, 463).

There are, however, several important features that point to a new conception of the artist. In contrast to the likes of Müller-Rosé, Andromache does not court the audience; "she disdained all flirtatiousness toward the crowd" (*GW* 7, 459). Self-sufficiently and self-denyingly she hovers *au-dessus de la mêlée*, an artist for the sake of art. While a good deal of animality still clings to the common man, Andromache is closer to the angels. Secondly, there is something binary, hermaphroditic about her: "Her breasts were meagre, her hips narrow," her muscles and hands suggest that she might "be a boy in disguise"; but no, the form of her thighs is definitely female. "She was not a woman, but she was not a man either" (*GW* 7, 458–60).

This binary nature is precisely what Felix Krull is obsessed with throughout his narrative. But there is even more to Andromache that appeals to him, a touch of divinity subtly alluded to by references to her Grecian nose and to "a pair of wings of white feathers" (*GW* 7, 458) attached at the shoulders to the silver armor she wears. In other words, she represents a transition to the god Hermes that Felix himself is beginning to incorporate.

No wonder he confesses, "I worshipped her" (*GW 7*, 459). This positive image is a far cry from the negativity of Mann's early artists.

While Andromache operates in ethereal realms, the next and last model Krull admires is a "blood-and-soil" artist, the *matador* Ribeiro, the star of a *corrida*. In the company of the Portuguese mother and daughter whom he woos simultaneously, Felix experiences this event as an Iberian autochthonous fertility and death rite. The bull, an "assembly of procreating and murderous force" (*GW 7*, 651), is just as mythologically enhanced as the Iberian mother goddess next to Felix, who watches the spectacle visibly enthralled. The bull is not only likened to a "god-animal" but also endowed with telltale Hermetic emblems like Andromache's "tiny wings" in the form of the "colored darts" (*GW 7*, 651) the *bandarilheiros* have planted in his back. Ribeiro, the featured artist at this primeval death festival, is young, elegant and "bildhübsch" (a poster boy) (*GW 7*, 653). The similarity between him and the narrator is made explicit by likening his embroidered costume to the disguises Felix had sported in his childhood. With the same earnest demeanor with which Andromache had performed hers, Ribeiro attends to his artistic duties. He executes the deadly game in a "extremely graceful and gently superior manner," creating "graceful dance-poses while being in danger" (*GW 7*, 654); all this to intimate the self-denial of the artist in the service of beauty. Finally, he ends this "worship of blood with folksy ingredients" by plunging his sword into the animal's neck. He too, like Andromache, seems unaware of the public. He walks away from the sacrifice unconcernedly, never acknowledging the applause (*GW 7*, 655).

Thus concludes the festival of fertility and death, paralleling in significance the mythological pair of women next to Felix, Demeter the mother goddess of fertility, and her daughter Persephone, the maiden who was abducted into the sphere of departed souls. Felix's initiation into the twin realms of art is now complete, that of above (Andromache) and that of below (Ribeiro). All this is *mutatis mutandis* reminiscent of Hans Castorp's dream in *Der Zauberberg* (The Magic Mountain, 1924) with the idyll in the foreground and the blood ritual behind it. Both are symbolic of the double nature of civilization (the word for it in *Doktor Faustus* is "unterteuft" [undermined]) of which the artist must forever remain cognizant. Krull's enjoyment of the bloody spectacle may be a reflection of the guilt that Mann assigned to the German aesthetes, including himself, for the fascist atrocities. In his discourse on the progress of life on earth, Professor Kuckuck, Krull's scientific mentor, points out the reversibility of evolution, the coexistence of the oldest and newest forms: "Yes, often the finest becomes tired of itself, is fascinated by the primitive and sinks drunkenly into barbarism" (*GW 7*, 547). Such sentences prove that they were written by an exile, by an author who had bitterly lived through the epoch of National Socialism. That Felix in the end lets himself be seduced by the Dionysian "earth mother" rather than remain with her skeptical and critical daughter is part of the same message, never mind that this reverses the original myth in which Persephone is queen of the underworld.

A Picaresque Novel?

Much has been made of Felix Krull as a *pícaro*, and there are indeed traits that place him in that tradition. Like his predecessors in that genre, Felix's life progresses in a series of episodes and changing sceneries. It could also be said that Krull, like Lazarillo de Tormes, the prototypical *pícaro*, serves a succession of masters more to his advantage than theirs; and there is no doubt that in his encounters with members of various trades, professions, and social strata, he exposes the fatuity, the egotism, and venality of society as a whole, while he shares in the moral corruption of the others.

But there are also serious deviations from the model. That Krull comes from a middle-class background, upper rather than lower, may seem to be only a minor difference. But it robs him of the proletarian resentment, the sense of grave injustice with which, say, Lazarillo views the world. On the contrary, Felix, as his name indicates, is a sunny boy whose charms pave his way everywhere. He briefly endures hard times, but on the whole he is lucky in his enterprises and well-liked by those he encounters, quite unlike the average *pícaro*. The phrase "Mais donnez donc quelque chose a çe garçon" (*GW* 7, 454) which he hears a lady whisper to her husband in the elevator he operates is indicative of the good fortune that often seeks him out without his active intervention. Above all, however, the *Bekenntnisse* are not mainly about society, it is not the social mores that the analysis focuses on but the androgynous central character, and if he loves anything besides himself, it is precisely the world that is condemned in the picaresque genre.

Sex, Sexuality, and Love

Above all, Felix Krull loves himself. His narcissism is obvious and has been much emphasized in the scholarship about the novel. But it is well to remember that it was Thomas Mann who endowed him with this trait, which indicates that the author was aware of it in himself. In projecting it onto the central character of a novel and suggesting ways of overcoming it, he is also speaking *pro domo*. While Felix's capacity for loving others is questionable, there cannot be a doubt about his capability for sexual enjoyment. Whereas he categorically forswears salacious descriptions, his memoirs are not lacking in explicitness. He often refers to the "liveliness of his senses" which "bordered on the miraculous." Sexual pleasures play such an egregious role in his mental and physical makeup that he dubs them the "Great Joy," which he first experiences as an adolescent with the housemaid Genoveva (*GW* 7, 312).

Carrying on an affair with a family servant still is very much within the bourgeois modes of sexual initiation. Soon, however, Felix embarks on a different course. There is nothing bourgeois anymore about his relationship with the Hungarian prostitute Rozsa, whose life and proceeds he shares for a few months as her "pupil," to avoid a certain reprehensible word (*GW* 7, 383) that he finds inappropriate despite all external appearances. Depraved in the eyes of the conventional world, she becomes Felix's lover and his instructress in a "naughty school of love" (*GW* 7, 385). Equally significant is the brief encounter Felix has in the Parisian hotel with an elegant lady of a certain age who commandeers the handsome lift boy — as which he begins his hotel career in Paris, perhaps to symbolize the social rise and fall — to her bedroom where she accompanies their nocturnal embraces with a stream of strange utterances beyond Felix's comprehension. Her lofty, often rhymed words reveal her as a highly educated woman, a poetess who rejects the conventions that regulate the middle-class conduct in love and marriage.

She is married to a rich manufacturer of toilets who provides her with all the luxuries of modern life but whom she despises because of his cultural vulgarity and sexual debility, against which she extols Felix's extraordinary prowess. In these details the informed reader soon recognizes an ironic portrait of Thomas Mann. Her adoration of adolescent boys, the reference to her "so-called perversion" (sogenannte Verkehrtheit) (*GW* 7, 446) to which she attributes the inspiration for her novels, the self-humiliation she seeks in the embraces of a socially and culturally inferior, the Wagnerian alliterations as well as the mixture of French and German in her conversation, reminiscent of another famous, sexually ambivalent love scene, the one in which Hans Castorp woos Madame Chauchat in *Der Zauberberg,* all point in this direction. This is why Felix's affair with Madame Houpflé has been declared to be a camouflaged homosexual encounter, among others by the author's daughter and collaborator Erika. But nothing in this scene forces the reader to make such an assumption. Mann unquestionably harbored homoerotic desires, but he wrote for a wide readership, not only for homosexuals, as some recent commentators seem to suggest. The casual reader has no compelling reason to suspect Madame Houpflé's femininity. Already in an earlier chapter Felix has confessed his true sexual orientation, his dream-like longing for an erotic union with "a double being, a pair of siblings of opposite sexes, my own and the other, that is the fair one."[2]

This duality becomes visible in his next amorous encounters, for which the hotel offers plentiful opportunities, and which present Felix with temptations for more permanent attachments than the ones he has so far experienced. Now it turns out that he is the object and not only the subject of such dual erotic yearnings. The daughter of an American millionaire, still a mere teenager, and a Scottish lord fall in love with "Armand," Felix's hotel name, in a dual simultaneousness that is not without its comic effects. It requires Felix's entire charm and diplomatic skill to extricate himself from entanglements that would have made him the unlikely husband of a rich whimsical brat or taken him to the gloomy solitudes of a Scottish castle in an ambiguous relationship with its master. While any of these possibilities would have provided him with greater security and stability, Krull recognizes that they were "path[s] that deviate from mine" (*GW* 7, 488), deviate from what he regarded his preordained route in life.

One of the self-imposed humiliations that Madame Houpflé "enjoyed" in her tryst with Armand-Felix was the theft of her jewelry, to which she directed him in the darkness of their night of love, insisting that he steal it, as it were, from under her nose. This gave her the masochistic satisfaction of having slept in the arms of a common thief. At the same time the loot lays the financial foundation for Felix's double life as a hotel employee and an elegant man-about-town which ultimately leads to his transformation into the Marquis de Venosta and to the pursuit of his nostalgia for erotic duality. Switching identities with this lovelorn young aristocrat, who, against the commands of his parents, wishes to stay in Paris with his beloved, enables Krull to travel to Portugal in grand style. The objects of his amatory zeal are this time two women of Portuguese society whom we have met before, mother and daughter, the exciting duality consisting in the juxtaposition of youth and maturity, chastity and ripe sexuality. The interplay of restraint and desire, the oscillations and vibrations within this triangle of love are enhanced by the ethnic type of the two ladies, which is described as a mixture of Celtic, Germanic, Roman, and Moorish elements, "dark-haired, somewhat yellowish in complexion, and of delicate build, with handsome, intelligent brown eyes" (*GW* 7, 532). Mann, forever on the lookout for living models, was inspired by the actress Anna Magnani at least for the older of the two ladies. He takes great care to paint a multi-ethnic world in Lisbon to make it representative of humanity as a whole. The unresolved banter between the three takes up much space in the last chapters, and we owe to it a delightful disquisition on love that Felix directs to Zouzou, the younger of the two women, in order to overcome her resistance to his advances and indeed to the sexual greed of the entire male world, a charming sermon in which the boundaries between Felix Krull's thinking and Thomas Mann's are more blurred than ever.

Shorn of its playful elements, this paean to love celebrates the ruses of nature that enact the miracle underlying the living world. In love the jealously guarded separateness of the individual is overcome; the fastidious disgust with another's body, which is normally kept at a distance, gives way to the opposite, to the yearning for the most intimate union. But Felix's speech is meant to be more than a eulogy to the procreative forces of nature. Subtly it hints at the possibility of redemption from narcissism. For Felix is not merely "talking about the blessings of parenthood and the joys of family life" but about a deeper and more universal impulse that includes the stroking of a beggar child's "louse infested hair with [one's] bare hand and afterward being happier than before," which is "perhaps more astounding evidence of love than the fondling of a beloved body" (*GW* 7, 642). This transition from *eros* to *caritas* is a cosmic principle, since everywhere there are "traces of love, allusions, concessions to it on the part of separateness and unwillingness of one body to know about another" (*GW* 7, 642). These are words from Mann's own "post-Christian, Neoplatonic" creed, to coin a phrase.

The fact that Krull hypocritically utters these lofty words in order to seduce a young woman does not detract from their veracity and intrinsic humanistic value, but illustrates the many-layered character of the discourse. Whether or not Felix's sermon is instrumental in dissipating Zousou's hesitation, she finally gives in and, still pounding his shoulder with her little fist in deference to the natural separateness of beings, while draping the other arm around the neck of her long-desired love object, she not only surrenders to his kisses but returns them greedily.

But this is not a lonely-hearts novel where such moments are frozen in perpetuity by ending the narrative abruptly. These are the vexatious memoirs of Felix Krull the Evasive. And so he is snatched from the tender embrace by the sudden appearance of Senhora Kuckuck, who interrupts the tête-à-tête. With stern motherly authority she sends Zouzou to her room, never to resurface, and, in fulfillment of his ardent quest of erotic duality, Felix is drawn to Maria Pia's heaving bosom. With this ironic twist the finished part of the novel now actually closes.

Mythology and Cosmology

Educated in the German tradition from the Romantics to Wagner and Nietzsche, Thomas Mann manifested an early interest in myth. His favored divinity in Greek mythology was the multi-faceted Hermes, who made his first appearance in "Der Tod in Venedig" (Death in Venice, 1912) in the guise of "Psychopompos," the companion of departed souls. Perhaps the author's oldest inspiration came from Gustav Schwab's *Die schönsten Sagen des Klassischen Altertums* (1838–40), must-reading for every German boy, or from the famous Mercury statue on one of the bridges in his hometown Lübeck. During the rise of the National Socialists with their myth-possessed ideology, Mann did not want to leave this fruitful field of cultural significance to their exclusive exploitation, but underpinned his own narratives with mythological frameworks. His aim was to wrest mythology from its abuse by the fascist obscurantists, imbuing it with psychology and humanistic enlightenment. In this endeavor he was aided by his study of Freud and of mythologist Karl Kerényi, whose correspondence with Mann abounds with explications of Hermes. Myth for Thomas Mann meant "walking in footprints" (In-Spuren-Gehen) (*GW* 9, 492), which for him entailed the reincarnation of divine or cultural role models whose task it was to take civilization forward to greater human achievements. In this fashion, Mann wished to become the Goethe of his epoch, whereas the central character of his monumental tetralogy, Joseph, is a reincarnation of Hermes and a precursor of Jesus.

Felix Krull is another Hermes figure, the god of thieves whose magic wand produces riches, but also the guide of travelers, interpreter of the world, and, more importantly, intellectual innovator and mediator between gods and men, and lastly, a very handsome youth. The first clear hint at a mythological dimension comes early, when Krull poses for his painter and godfather in the costume of a Grecian god. But Krull is identified with Hermes by Madame Houpflé, whose first name is Diane and who admires Felix's "Hermes legs" (*GW* 7, 444) and other bodily attributes. This identity is enhanced on various occasions, for example in a conversation with the marquis whom Krull is about to impersonate: "Do you know much about mythology? — Not very much, Marquis. There is, for example the god Hermes. But I have hardly been able to advance beyond him." (*GW* 7, 504). Hermes also comes up in Professor Kuckuck's "cosmic survey."

Andromache, with her androgynous body, her cap, wings, flight, and posture, is the full embodiment of Hermes. And in the Lisbon scenario, the author displays an almost mythological firework: Professor Kuckuck as Zeus — note his repeatedly mentioned "Sternenaugen" (starlike eyes), which the omniscient critic Hans Wysling has identified as belonging to a portrait of Schopenhauer; Maria Pia-Demeter, his wife; Zouzou-Persephone, his daughter, the *espada* Ribeiro, another Hermes figure, and the entire blood festival of the *corrida* already referred to. Felix himself has grown into his Hermes role, especially evident in the tennis game where, a complete neophyte, he exhibits unexpected skills thanks to his Hermetic "winged shoes" (beflügelnden Schuhen) (*GW* 7, 616).

More difficult than ferreting out these mythological references is explaining their effect. It is entirely possible to miss them and still enjoy the lighthearted episodes and brilliant formulations. But once aware of them the reader detects deeper significance in the mythological constellations that impart a *sub-specie-aeternitatis* feeling to ordinary events. The depth that Thomas Mann saw in the novel is measurable by his claim that it toyed with "the very idea of *Being*." This is reinforced by certain recurrences such as that of binary love objects or calculated repetitions like Felix's deliberate confusion of the Marquis de Venosta's beloved Zaza with the Portuguese Zouzou he himself courts. Such conflation seems to say: regardless of social rank there is a likeness among human beings. In fact, this observation is made explicit when, in one of his reflective moods, Felix muses about:

the idea of *exchangeability*. With a change of clothes and make-up, the servitors might often just as well have been the masters, and many of those who lounged in the deep wicker chairs smoking their cigarettes might have played the waiter. It was pure accident that the reverse was the fact, an accident of wealth (*GW* 7, 491–92).

The hotel is a mirror image of class society and the ridicule of its hierarchy part of the social satire.

Thomas Mann adopted, if it is possible to say so, a humanistic approach to nonhuman nature. His visits to museums of natural history have been recorded. To such curiosity we owe the descriptions of scientific explorations of the universe in several of his novels: in *Der Zauberberg* through the learned books Hans Castorp orders from the lowlands, in *Doktor Faustus* in the form of the natural curiosities collected by Adrian Leverkühn's father and Adrian's later visits, probably in feverish dreams, to the stellar space and the deep sea, guided by Professor Capercailzie, a demon figure. In *Felix Krull* Professor Kuckuck plays this part, Kuckuck supposedly being a nickname of the devil in keeping with the Faustian overtones of the story. Like Mephistopheles does Faust, Kuckuck takes Felix on a tour of the world, albeit a mental one. He paints a vast panorama of the universe, its origins and unfolding. In an immense monologue he guides Felix, no less feverish than Adrian, through the stellar expanses; he makes reference to the infinitesimal atomic realm and dwells on Mann's own favorite stages of creation, that of matter from nothingness, the origin of life from inanimateness and of man from myriad living things. A visit to Professor Kuckuck's museum in Lisbon completes Krull's instruction in natural history.

But even the reader who is capable of following Kuckuck's explications with critical acumen soon realizes that this display of scientific lore has one aim only: to place Krull's insignificant person, indeed man's entire ephemeral existence in perspective. Felix listens as in a trance. Time and space shrink uncannily as he is transported through the ages, and a feeling of love and compassion is engendered in his breast, a sense of "undetermined expanse" (unbestimmter Weitläufigkeit) (*GW* 7, 533) invades him, akin both to Freud's "oceanic feeling" (thematized in *Das Unbehagen in der Kultur* [Civilization and its Discontents, 1930]) and Krull's own "Great Joy." Later on this sensation is identified as "Allsympathie" (universal sympathy) (*GW* 7, 548) man's love of all the transitory phenomena between the great nothingness preceding and ensuing existence. Since he describes the same feeling in his essay "Lob der Vergänglichkeit" (Praise of Transitoriness) (*GW* 10, 383–85), it must be Thomas Mann's very own. The cosmic distance from which such a vision of life is possible also enables "a universal irony" that is fully illustrated during Felix's inspection of Kuckuck's museum. Among other phenomena he observes the chilling impartiality of nature toward its creatures, who are engendered and destroyed with equal indifference, both as individuals and as species. The giant armadillo serves as food for the sabre-tooth tiger. To protect it against its predator, nature gives it a bony armor but at the same time provides the tiger with ever more monstrous jaws and teeth, whereupon the armadillo's carapace is further strengthened in a protracted spiral until both become extinct because nature deprives them of nourishment. Nature "had been on both sides — and so, of course, on neither — had been playing with them, and when she had brought them to the pinnacle of their capacities she deserted them" (GW 7, 576). This is not only comical, it is also a programmatic statement of Mann's much admired and much maligned technique of irony.

Final Remarks

With *Felix Krull* Mann satirizes the immorality of the modern world, its hypocrisy and rapacity, its worship of rank and wealth. He has Krull talk about, certain "elements that call themselves radical, perhaps because they gnaw at the roots of society. [. . .] They call themselves men of the people, though their only connection with the people consists in subverting their sound instincts and depriving them of their natural belief in the necessity of a well graduated order of society. And how? By inoculating them with the wholly unnatural and foreign notion of equality" (GW 7, 610). These sentences sound like right-wing ideology, but as Krull addresses them to the king of Portugal, they turn into a delightful parody, particularly in the mouth of our chameleon-like character who has just expounded the theory of human interchangeability.

In this novel Mann also examines the role art and artists play in his time by absorbing cues from various sources dear to his heart: Goethe, Schopenhauer, Wagner, and Nietzsche, to name only a few. But into the figure of the charming immoralist he also projected erotic desires, mythological hopes and existential problems of his own. In the guise of a roguish hero, the old magician, the *Zauberer* as his children called him, playfully manages to convey some of his most cherished thoughts about god, man, and the world. Despite their scintillating parody and irony, these are not only the confessions of Felix Krull, but those of Thomas Mann himself.

Notes

[1] GW 7, 281; Mann's collected works (GW 1–13) will hereafter be cited in the text. The English translations rely on Thomas Mann, *Confessions of Felix Krull, Confidence Man*. Trans. Denver Lindley. New York: Vintage, 1992. Here page 18.

[2] "Mit einem Doppelwesen [. . .], einem flüchtig innig erblickten Geschwisterpaar ungleichen Geschlechtes — meines eigenen und des anderen, also des schönen" (GW 7, 346).

Female Identities and Autobiographical Impulses in Thomas Mann's Work

Hannelore Mundt

THE LUXURIOUS HOMES OF THE upper middle class during the *Gründer-jahre* of the 1870s are known for their ornate exteriors and excessively adorned interiors. With their expensive wardrobes and jewelry that demonstrated their idleness and refined social graces, bourgeois wives were expected to enhance their families' appearance of affluence; thus they functioned as part of the décor. Their daughters were to enter marriages advantageous to their families' reputations. Usually their emotional and sexual desires were ignored or denied, not only by their families, but also often by themselves, as they valued an upper-class, privileged lifestyle over sexual independence. In 1851 Louise Otto-Peters had suggested that bourgeois women should pursue ennobling virtues such as unselfish love, passive compassion, moral purity, the "Eternal-Feminine," making her equal, even superior to man.[1] This emphasis on moral superiority as a compensation for their social and sexual compliance carried into the bourgeois women's movement in the 1890s because it focused largely on charitable institutions and welfare organizations. This movement, primarily organized by women from the well-to-do, educated segment of bourgeois society, also voiced demands for more changes, stressing women's needs for educational and professional opportunities. The majority of upper-class women remained silent. When their internalization of the repressive bourgeois code of sexual morality and patriarchal standards did not stop bourgeois mothers and daughters from rebelling, the fear of losing their social privileges, of being ostracized and alienated from their social milieu surely made them reluctant to fight. Only the most feminist-oriented among them were willing and prepared to embrace a bohemian existence; only a few exceptionally creative women earned recognition, short-lived though it often was, and an independent livelihood.[2]

Thomas Mann grew up in this patriarchal world, which, despite growing demands for women's social, political, and cultural equality, was largely unaware of its anti-feminist, misogynist traditions. It is not difficult to find in his writings passages that echo this tradition. For instance, around 1904 Mann copied into his notebook the following sentence from a letter to his future wife Katia: "Only ladies and dilettantes bubble over [with creativity], only the quickly satisfied and ignorant, who do not live under the pressure and the discipline of talent."[3] That Mann could make this statement to a woman whose intelligence and education he admired indicates the level of subconscious, internalized misogyny of his age. Mann's environment taught men to be proud not to be women; it emphasized the superiority of men and solely focused on men's talents and achievements. When considering voting rights in *Betrachtungen eines Unpolitischen* (Confessions of a Nonpolitical Man, 1918) not only did Mann fail to side with the still disenfranchised women, he actually conceived of giving a man with sons more votes, because raising sons demonstrates participation in the future of the state.[4] But Mann was neither an advocate of patriarchy nor a misogynist, despite the fact that his oeuvre has a tendency not to explore the inner thoughts of many of his female characters, and that it contains unflattering portraits of women, often reduced to caricatures and archetypal beings without any discernible individuality, extraordinary artistic talents, or male discipline for distinction. Characters like Detlev Spinell in "Tristan" and Ken Keaton in "Die Betrogene" (Eng. The Black Swan, 1953) — just to name two of many male caricatures and shallow characters — should remind us that men often do not fare much better. Was Thomas Mann therefore a misanthropist? Hardly. Superficial impressions are misleading; they distort the complex, contradictory understanding and construction of both female and male identities by an author well known for his irony and ambiguity.

Mann's early works attest to a remarkable sensitivity to women's oppression in patriarchal society and to the misogynist portrayals of women that were rampant in art during his time. The first evidence of this sensitivity is "Gefallen" (Fallen, 1894), written when Mann was only nineteen years old. The story contains traces of two commonplace images of women in nineteenth-century European art and literature: the prostitute and *la belle dame sans merci*. After her first sexual relationship with the student Selten, the beautiful actress Irma Welten, now a "fallen" woman, decides to sell her body for additional income. Her portrayal as a moody, dominating, and deceitful woman is biased; it reflects Selten's reaction to an emancipated woman who rejects a passive, submissive female identity. But the story resists the misogynist tradition evoked by its title. Irma's control over her own sexuality represents female rebellion against and subversion of patriarchal Christian morality. This morality and, concomitantly, bourgeois views of women as inferior and evil, are shown to be highly questionable in "Gefallen."[5] The traditionalist Selten turns away from Irma when her economic circumstances force her to defy established morality, bourgeois narrow-mindedness, and hypocrisy. Only for a brief moment does he recognize that he is guilty of double moral standards, as he selfishly takes advantage of a woman's sexual liberation.

"Gefallen" unmasks the double standards in patriarchal sexual practices, which make allowances for sexual liberties to heterosexual men while denying these same liberties to women. While the narrative does not rebuke a woman's right to control her own sexuality, it puts that right into a negative context. Not only is an emancipated woman a destructive force, but she is also the cause of a man's disillusioned and cynical assessment of romantic, heterosexual love. "Gefallen" also associates emancipated female sexuality with an artist's bohemian, anti-bourgeois lifestyle, infidelity, and prostitution. Mann's own need to belong to the respectable bourgeois world, while yearning to escape from its narrow-mindedness into the realm of art, can explain his vacillation between exoneration and renunciation of patriarchal standards in "Gefallen." Whether the representation of a young man frustrated by a heterosexual adventure has autobiographical roots — thus representing Mann's first fictional exploration of his sexual needs and frustrations, his desire to contravene as well as to live according to accepted and respected sexual standards, possibly driven by sexual uncertainty and disappointments at this time — cannot be established with certainty.

At first sight, the soft and lethargic movements and the boneless white hand of the beautiful Ada in "Der Wille zum Glück" (The Will to Happiness, 1896) evoke the misogynist "cult of invalidism," fixated on female fragility and morbidity and rampant in nineteenth-century European art.[6] Instead of the nun-like, ephemeral, asexual woman that Mann teases his readers to expect, a sexually passionate woman evolves. She does not hesitate to display openly her sexual desire for the decadent artist Paolo, who is ill and dies shortly after their wedding night. Despite her loss, her face radiates "the solemn and powerful gravity of triumph" (*GW* 8, 61) when she stands in front of his coffin. Her triumph lies in the fact that her desire for sexual freedom has have been fulfilled.

The portrayal of a sexually active woman who chooses her sexual partner, who is not promiscuous and morally questionable, and who is not driven by primitive instincts and excessive sexual desires, is a departure from the traditional treatments found in late nineteenth-century literature and art.[7] Ada is a woman who insists upon and proudly experiences what in bourgeois-Christian culture is a taboo, even when it comes to a monogamous and socially sanctioned relationship: a woman's natural desire for and right to sexuality. With this active, life-affirming, and resolute woman who even challenges her father's authority, Mann provides an image of woman that even today's readers can appreciate as a welcome departure from the "vamp-or-virgin" dichotomy.

While Mann goes beyond demonizing or ignoring a woman's sexuality, he is, nonetheless, a writer embedded in patriarchal standards and expectations. Ambiguities in "Der Wille zum Glück" disclose his residual bonds to tradition. The spheres of life and death, sexuality and woman are woven into an ambivalent tapestry of meaning at the end, when Paolo embraces life and finds death. With this death Mann punishes the artist who makes the wrong choice, who privileges "life," that is woman, over art. Consequently, woman's sexuality becomes the subversive, even destructive force that Christian tradition has established.

In "Der kleine Herr Friedemann" (Little Herr Friedemann, 1897), Mann again resorts to the paradox of woman as harbinger of life and death. The carefully constructed ascetic life of the crippled outsider Johannes Friedemann collapses with the arrival of Gerda von Rinnlingen in town, as she brings him both passion and death. All his buried erotic desires burst into an uncontrollable longing for the woman through whom Mann challenges stereotypes and traditional classifications. These challenges coexist in the text with the representations of conventional female characters, such as Friedemann's spinster sisters and the gossiping, narrow-minded bourgeois wives.

Gerda von Rinnlingen is aloof as well as compassionate; she can be lifeless as a stone on the one hand,[8] animated and sexually enticing on the other; she appears very masculine, controlling in one instance, very feminine and sensitive in another. These ambivalences and her outsider qualities, such as her artistic inclinations and the absence of children and sexuality in her marriage, signal a non-conventional sexual orientation. On the realistic level, Gerda von Rinnlingen can be interpreted as an emancipated woman and thus as a threat to patriarchal structures; on the symbolic level, as a male character[9] and a narrative device to tell what cannot be told. In the latter case the passion of the outsider Friedemann connotes stigmatized homosexual desires, an interpretation supported by the publication of Mann's diaries and our growing insights into his repressed homosexuality.[10]

On numerous occasions Mann confounds his readers with a female character who defies fixed meaning. At the end of the narrative, Gerda von Rinnlingen's rebuff of Friedemann's sexual advances can be understood as the female outsider's disappointment that Friedemann turns out to be just another man with ordinary heterosexual desires. Her rejection of the cripple and his humiliation also conjure up the traditional image of woman as *la belle dame sans merci*. On a deeper level, her cruel reaction to an ugly, pitiful man represents the artist's arrogant, yet understandable rejection of life and also Mann's renunciation of his own homosexual desires. By coding this renunciation as a woman's defense of her bourgeois virtues, Mann subtly engages in self-censorship and thus takes the standpoint of official, sanctioned morality in "Der Kleine Herr Friedemann." Traditional constructions of female — as well as male — identities provide a safe haven for the unorthodox, yet self-doubting individual whose upholding of these constructions amounts to a compliance with patriarchal norms. But with an ambivalent character like Gerda von Rinnlingen, Mann also leaves this comfort zone, and he challenges readers to venture into a world of insecurities and unconventional sexuality.

The strikingly beautiful, aloof Gerda Buddenbrook in Mann's first novel, *Buddenbrooks* (1901) is another unconventional woman. For the Buddenbrooks this woman of affluent background is a status symbol and of ornamental value, an object on display rather than a human being. She remains astoundingly untouched by time, death, and the decline of the family. Thus she indeed resembles an artifact. One burgher proclaims that Gerda is "Hera and Aphrodite, Brünnhilde and Melusine in one person" (*GW* 1, 295). He thereby places her in the tradition of enticing, powerful women in Western art and literature. Yet one should not trust the artistically inclined burgher, as he limits his judgment to a rather comical mélange of well-established, static literary clichés.

Gerda Buddenbrook remains an enigmatic character throughout the novel, as her inner life, her thoughts and emotions remain unexplored. Bereft of compassion and physical desires, thus implicitly frigid, she neither matches the bourgeois ideal of the self-sacrificing mother and unselfish wife of ennobling virtues, nor is she the vamp-like, destructive, and promiscuous woman. She is inseparable from and considerably closer to her Stradivarius and the realm of art than to her husband and only child. *Buddenbrooks* suggests that she only gets married to satisfy bourgeois-heterosexual conventions and to provide the family with an heir, in order to escape the fate of ridiculed, pallid spinsters consumed by empty lives. Once socially established as a wife who has fulfilled her obligation, Gerda Buddenbrook feels free to snub bourgeois existence with its tedious, alienating duties. Thus she lives the life that Thomas Buddenbrook, tormented by bourgois scruples, longs to live himself but cannot. Mann does not idealize Gerda's freedom, as it has its price, the renunciation of love and compassion, a price that Gerda, with her orientation toward art, is willing to pay.

In contrast to Gerda Buddenbrook's insistence upon autonomy and her self-centered aestheticism, Mann presents Tony Buddenbrook's compassion, her self-sacrifice for and submission to her family's interests.[11] Like Gerda's freedom, this submission comes also at a high cost: the deficit of love and sexual fulfillment. When Mann wrote *Buddenbrooks* and jotted down some notes on Tony, he was familiar with Gabriele Reuter's novel *Aus guter Familie* (From a Good Family, 1895).[12] The fate of Agathe Heidling, the protagonist of Reuter's novel, which was published in the same year as Fontane's *Effi Briest* (1894/95), can shed light upon Tony Buddenbrook and her function in Mann's novel.

Aus guter Familie begins with the fifteen-year-old Agathe Heidling, who "promised obedience and humble submissiveness for her entire life." Although she resents being treated "like a dear, stupid child" by her parents and the world around her, she leads the life of a dutiful daughter in the hope of being rewarded with marriage and motherhood.[13] However, Agathe is prevented from becoming the submissive bourgeois wife because her father has spent her dowry. Within respectable bourgeois society, women have two options: either they learn self-renunciation and devote their lives to motherhood and their spousal and social obligations, or they become frustrated spinsters. To live an emancipated life is a privilege, albeit a problematic one, of men in the novel. Agathe's left-wing cousin Martin lives a life free of sexual and social restraints outside Germany. Her uncle Gustav violates bourgeois principles when he marries a woman of questionable morality and therefore becomes the black sheep of the family.[14] In both cases Gabriele Reuter associates sexual emancipation, individualism, and self-determination with a marginalized or unstable existence. Consequently, *Aus guter Familie* does not glorify an anti-bourgeois existence, even though the novel is a lucid indictment of bourgeois, patriarchal society as a cause of women's sufferings and self-effacing sacrifices.

In the introductory remarks of his essay "Gabriele Reuter" (1904), Mann praises Reuter for her detached position as an author, and recognizes that she resists using fiction as a platform for ideological solutions. Yet *Aus guter Familie* contains a feminist, accusatory slant that Mann does not acknowledge in his essay but that reverberates in *Buddenbrooks*. There are similarities between his character Tony Buddenbrook and Agathe Heidling. A religious event, confirmation, provided the occasion to teach Agathe a lesson in compliance and submission. In Tony's case, this lesson comes from the pulpit during Sunday service. Tony is asked to turn the family into a deity to whom sacrifices must be made; if she does not, condemnation will follow. Her father, eager to marry her off to the businessman Grünlich, and aware of Tony's affection for the medical student Morten Schwarzkopf, warns her not to walk a "private, disorderly path" (*GW* 1, 149); she would face expulsion from the family. In following her father's marriage plans for her, Tony suppresses her own desires and identifies with the Buddenbrooks: "Her pronounced sense of family identity nearly alienated her from the concepts of free will and self-determination" (*GW* 1, 204–5). The word "nearly" reveals that the author wants her to retain some sense of independence despite her capitulation, and moreover, that he wants his readers to perceive Tony as a woman vacillating between submission and resistance.

While Reuter's Agathe Heidling passively resents paternal authority, Mann's Tony Buddenbrook actively resists it. Unlike Reuter's figure, who concedes to despondency, Mann's character exhibits audacity, insolence, and jocularity. As an adolescent, Tony shows disrespect for an authoritarian, oppressive world when she pokes fun at the people in the streets and commits all kinds of mischief (*GW* 1, 66). Later, her mocking appraisal of Grünlich and her intuitive understanding of his true intentions set her apart from the paternal, calculating mercantile world. In a world where a woman's voice and wishes are brushed aside, her reservations and individual desires are met with a patronizing, denigrating attitude. Her father sees in the young woman an immature child in dire need of paternal guidance (*GW* 1, 105). Later, her brother Thomas calls her a child (*GW* 1, 370) and a "Kindskopf" (person with a child-like mentality) (*GW* 1, 384), when her independent decision to divorce her second husband makes him fear for his family's honor and bourgeois respectability. While the world around her dismiss her thoughts and actions,[15] Thomas Mann gives narrative signals to validate them. The narrator mentions that Tony has "an intelligent brain [. . .] which swiftly learned in school what was demanded" (*GW* 1, 65). Tony's perceptions of her surroundings surpass those of her parents, as she recognizes Grünlich's cajolery (*GW* 1, 97). Later in the novel, her brother Thomas has to admit: "A darn [verteufelt] smart person, this little Tony" (*GW* 1, 461). But sure enough, he has to disparage her in the same breath.

In Tony Buddenbrook Mann presents a woman who devotes her life to her family, but not one who uncritically embraces her bourgeois world and is a one-dimensional character.[16] When she marries Grünlich in order to meet her father's and bourgeois society's expectations, she is not simply a passive, ignorant victim and dutiful daughter who is coerced into leading an emotionally and sexually crippled life. Rather, when she breaks her engagement to Morten Schwarzkopf in order to marry Grünlich, she renounces her sexual and emotional desires to retain her privileged social and economic status; she hopes to head an ornate, affluent household. In the same chapter of *Buddenbrooks* her brother Thomas bids farewell to the flower-girl Anna. Not once, but twice Mann conveys the message that love and sexual desire are controlled by cruel, self-alienating bourgeois conventions that affect both men and women.

Like *Aus guter Familie*, *Buddenbrooks* unmasks deficits in the money- and status-oriented patrician milieu. But like Reuter's novel, it also resists providing any solutions. Even though Mann has Tony repeat verbatim sentences that reflect Morten's liberal proclivity, years after their ill-fated relationship, *Buddenbrooks* is not a call for concrete social change. Tony's quotations do not manifest her engagement in progressive, anti-bourgeois politics, nor the author's political views; they conjure up missed opportunities, a world of love and freedom from the fetters of bourgeois-patriarchal demands, and suggest all the self-sacrifices Tony and others have to undergo to keep their bourgeois world intact, albeit in vain. In voicing the thoughts of another figure — the only man whom Tony truly loved and desired — Tony rebels against her own repressive world. Yet her rebellion is not limited to words alone. She initiates the divorce from her second husband, a scandalous event for her family. This transgression does not radically change her allegiance to the bourgeois world. Openly acknowledged suffering for being a privileged bourgeois woman and deep-felt pride in being one form a paradoxical combination in Tony's character.

With Tony's fate Thomas Mann launches an accusation against bourgeois-patriarchal society and unmasks one of its blind spots. It disqualifies a woman's voice in pursuit of economic interest and barters woman's sexuality. While this society does not do justice to these women, the author of *Buddenbrooks* administers some poetic justice. Rather than the anticipated economic gains, Tony's marriages as well as that of her sister bring economic losses and assist in the family's decline.

Buddenbrooks, like *Aus guter Familie*, begs the question why critical, intelligent women like Tony do not leave their repressive surroundings. The novel suggests that Tony in particular and bourgeois women in general who are afraid to lose their social position and identity are extremely limited in forging their own destinies. Barred from higher education and any active participation in the bourgeois mercantile world of the mid nineteenth century, wives and daughters were induced to center their lives around domestic and family issues. *Buddenbrooks* expresses sympathy for women like Tony. The narrator repeatedly refers to her as "poor Tony" (arme Tony]) (e.g. *GW* 1, 365, 370), which may be an echo of the phrase "poor child" in *Aus guter Familie* (176) as well as in Fontane's *Effi Briest*. Mann shows quite realistically that women learn to live with their disappointments, even to relish what destroys them. Despite the many deaths in the family and the liquidation of the family firm, Tony has an unrivaled will to honor and perpetuate the reputation and prestige of the Buddenbrooks. Her self-identity and womanhood are inextricably bound to the name of the family. At the end of the novel, full of disenchantment, melancholy and nostalgia, Tony clings to the family papers like a religious relic to which the remaining members of the family — all females — are to undertake a pilgrimage once a week. This scene reiterates a major theme of the novel: Without their affluent families, their reputations and social position, bourgeois wives and daughters like Tony Buddenbrook feel insecure and displaced.[17]

Buddenbrooks portrays bourgeois women whose orientation and beliefs, hopes and disillusionments are engendered by their restrictive nineteenth-century space: the family. Mann was not the first male writer of the nineteenth and early twentieth centuries to unmask women's suffering under patriarchy at a time when challenges to the patriarchal structures were still in their nascent stages. However, reversing the outcome of many nineteenth-century narratives, including Fontane's *Effi Briest,* and quite probably inspired by Reuter's *Aus guter Familie,* Mann does not focus on women whom society marginalizes and alienates for violating the prevailing sexual mores. Instead Mann shows women who chose an existence *within* bourgeois society and have to pay with a sexually unfulfilled life. Despite his gloomy assessment of women's predicament, Mann does not dwell on their victimization and suffering. Even in her most desolate moments Tony does not share her brother's nihilism, his lack of enterprising spirit and courage to face life.[18] Her altruistic love for others in a loveless world, her perseverance and resolute spirit provide a counterpoint to the indifference, the loss of vitality, and the dissipating will to live that are characteristic of her brother and his son Hanno.

Inner strength and determination are positive qualities that also stand out in women in Mann's early fiction. Because Mann is not known for inventive portrayals of females with strong identities, I should emphasize that he resists a common narrative trajectory employed by both male and female writers in the nineteenth century, in which women submit to fatalism and suffer more or less passively and patiently until their death. Agathe Heidling ends up in a sanatorium; her spirit is broken. Effi Briest dies. In contrast, Tony Buddenbrook prevails, with dignity. Readers can sympathize with her suffering and admire her strength and endurance. Tony is, as Mann has her brother Thomas note so poignantly, unique (*GW* 1, 94). Her ironic yet earnest stance toward her world, her love and hate, and her hovering between affirmation and negation of reality make her Mann's most original and compelling female character to that point in his career.

Most of Mann's narratives, and many of the letters he wrote in the late nineteenth and early twentieth centuries, attest to his contradictory relationship to bourgeois society. It can therefore be assumed that in portraying Tony Buddenbrook's hovering between resistance and surrender to bourgeois society the author is expressing his own incompatible needs for emancipation and for social privileges and respectability. *Buddenbrooks* suggests that it is not worth making sacrifices for this bourgeois, mercantile world; Tony's renunciation of love and freedom in the service of the bourgeois-Christian work ethic, social respectability, and recognition cannot prevent the family's decline. It is thus pointless. Tony's wasted life provides Mann with a justification for distancing himself from the mercantile world of his father and family, and for his escape into literature.

Their love-and-hate relationship to a patriarchal world is not the only affinity between the author and Tony Buddenbrook. She is not the author's alter-ego, in particular since this female character, situated in the mid nineteenth century, remains entrapped in bourgeois society. Nonetheless, I suggest, she functions as yet another mask for the author's own repressed sexuality, his sexual frustrations and disappointment. This does not mean that Mann merely utilizes sexually disadvantaged women in bourgeois society to write about himself and the dilemma of a homosexually oriented male. It is his awareness of women's predicaments that opens up the possibility of drawing parallels between his and their repressed sexuality, and which leads to his indictment of the sexual politics of bourgeois society in general, whether its victims are heterosexuals or homosexuals.[19]

None other than Thomas Mann's brother Heinrich was the first to take notice of the complexity of Tony Buddenbrook and to admire her character — with one caveat.[20] In a notebook entry, written late 1903 or early 1904, he criticized her lack of "sexual energy" and considered her representation to be reflective of an "ostrich-like chastity" of bourgeois women and of Thomas Mann's traditional perception of them. This observation, a part of Heinrich's response to his brother's candid letter of reproach from December 5, 1904, might have been influenced by his knowledge of his brother's homosexual inclinations. In Heinrich Mann's mind, "those from the other side" (die von drüben) cannot appreciate his steamy depiction of female passion and sexuality.[21] In the same context he claims that his brother's women are castrated beings rather than true representatives of their sex. Even with today's insights into Thomas Mann's homosexual desires such a view is reductionist and one-sided. While Protestant morality and scruples, and a chaste, clandestine homosexual proclivity play an important part in Thomas Mann's constructions of women, they do not exclusively control them. His own predicaments may have directed his attention to that of contemporary women, but Mann's attention to bourgeois women's economic and social dependence goes beyond autobiographical impulses. The creative process is not a monocausal, tangible entity; in fiction, sexual and social reality, literary imagination and autobiographical impulses are intertwined.

In a letter to Ida Boy-Ed in 1904 Mann wrote that his work is full of "intimacies and confessions."[22] While the author's self-assessments cannot always be trusted, this one largely applies to texts conceived or written after *Buddenbrooks*, texts in which sexually frustrated women serve as masks for his own frustrations. The plan for a society novel tentatively entitled "Die Geliebten" occupied Mann on and off between 1901 and 1905. Its central figure is Adelaide, a married woman, who in vain loves a violinist.[23] Loathing of the beloved and self-detestation for enduring humiliation taint Adelaide's love, which reflects Mann's own tormented, secret feelings for Paul Ehrenberg.[24] With Adelaide, Mann intended to represent what he regarded at this point as the highest feminine virtues: loyalty, patience, and passive suffering. Drawing analogies between personal experiences and frustrations as a homosexual in a heterosexual world with those of women under patriarchal authority can become a problematic undertaking. This was the case when Mann eradicated the differences between the two marginalized groups in order to focus on one common denominator: suffering. Mann had planned "Die Geliebten" as an "apotheosis of the eternal feminine."[25] Traditionally, the notion of "the eternal feminine" suggests a woman's passive and compassionate nature, an innate, natural disposition for suffering.[26] Intentionally or not, in employing this notion in an attempt to come to terms with his own suffering, Mann follows in the footsteps of bourgeois-Christian beliefs that women are meant to suffer. This is certainly not the position underlying *Buddenbrooks*, in which his own social and sexual dilemma reverberates in Tony without controlling his construction of her, and in which women's suffering is a result of rigid misogynist morality and cold-hearted economic interests.

Thomas Mann's attraction to suffering is reflected in two essays on women writers. In the first essay, "Das Ewig-Weibliche" (The Eternal Feminine, 1903), Mann extolled Tony Schwabe's novel *Die Hochzeit der Esther Franzenius* (The Wedding of Esther Franzenius, 1902). Neither the novel nor its author have survived in literary history. Mann admired the work's "infinite melody of yearning" and its author's focus on "impossible passion" (*GW* 8, 385). Mann's essay does not mention that in Schwabe's novel, passion and suffering often result from lesbian and other non-conventional sexual relationships, possibly in order to veil his own stigmatized sexual proclivity.[27] Instead, he summarizes its message in one very general phrase: "Whoever knows love, also knows suffering" (*GW* 8, 387). Mann goes as far as eulogizing the novel as the epitome of a "feminine ideal of culture and art" (*GW* 8, 387) and, furthermore, suggests that one day a woman writer will achieve "leadership and mastery" (Führer- und Meisterschaft) (*GW* 8, 388). This is certainly a radical thought coming from a male writer who grew up in a patriarchal world and culture that tended to ignore the artistic achievements of women. But skepticism toward Mann's praise of female leadership is warranted. With the exception of the Russian artist Lisaveta Iwanowna in "Tonio Kröger" (1903) whose art and life remain unexplored in the narrative, the achievements of the women characters in his fiction, so highly praised in his essay, pale in contrast to those of his male characters.

Mann's resistance to established aesthetic standards, his probing into a feminine sexual identity, and feminine aesthetics all blend together in his essay "Gabriele Reuter." He finds the ideal feminine art exemplified in Reuter's presentation of a never-ending, unfulfilled yearning for love, and of traditional feminine qualities such as sensitivity, tenderness, humanity, and quiet suffering. Immediately after the essay's publication, Thomas Mann wrote to his brother Heinrich that although it ostensibly dealt with the female writer, it was meant to be general and personal.[28] Here what exists in a nascent stage in his essay on Schwabe, becomes transparent. His deliberations on women writers function as an exploration and delineation of his own literary voice in contrast to that of his brother.[29] In his letter to Heinrich of December 5, 1903, written before his essay on Reuter, Mann had candidly declared his disagreement with his brother's literary development. In this letter he accuses Heinrich of a blunt, aggressive style, a carelessness and laxity in writing and rejects his preoccupation with characters driven by excessive sexuality as designed to create effect and literary success rather than to serve legitimate aesthetic purposes. With a tone of self-assertion and confidence in his superiority as a writer, the younger brother suggests a prose closer to life, which, to put it in one word, is characterized by "yearning" (Sehnsucht). He finds this yearning missing in what he deems to be Heinrich's superfluous, exaggerated passages, which are rife with sexual overtones.[30]

In reaction to his brother's style of prose, Thomas Mann advocates one that allows readers to feel "the uncanny, the abyss, the eternal dubiousness of sexuality, one feels a suffering from sexuality, in a word, feels passion."[31] Here Mann addresses his own problematic sexuality, which is denied fulfillment and must remain in the realm of clandestine suffering and endless yearning, a realm he finds in Toni Schwabe's and Gabriele Reuter's novels.

Before discussing the intended subject of Reuter, the woman writer and her fiction, Mann emphasizes that he does not believe in anything (*GW* 13, 392). The aim of the ideal artist is to perceive and re-create reality aesthetically. Creating art is an act of resistance, but the artist should not pursue an ideological agenda. Because Reuter is sensitive to the silently suffering woman in her work and condemns bourgeois patriarchy, yet does not fight for women's emancipation, Mann praises her. One must however wonder whether he praises Reuter's writing skills primarily to advocate and praise his own. Reuter, herself an alienated bourgeois who uses her literary talents to look upon her bourgeois background with humor and irony, with sympathy and contempt, meets Mann's own need to play with sexual, aesthetic, and ideological orientations and identities.

"Ein Glück" (A Gleam, 1904), a story for which Mann used notes made for his uncompleted novel project "Die Geliebten,"[32] represents such a play. The female protagonist, Baroness Anna, is a variation of Thomas Mann/ Adelaide, the suffering woman as a mirror for the suffering male. Anna has to witness the infidelity of her husband, Baron Harry. Corresponding to Mann's covert and frustrating love for Paul Ehrenberg, Anna's love is cowardly and miserable, characterized by jealousy, yearning, hate, and self-contempt. The author gives his narrative a bold turn when he has Anna feel attracted to the little "swallow" Emmy, a showgirl and object of her husband's sexual desires. Anna experiences for Emmy a longing that is "hotter" and "deeper" than the one for Harry (*GW* 8, 359). In the scene where Emmy returns Harry's wedding ring to Anna and plays the role of male suitor who presents a ring to his beloved with a kiss of her hand, Mann presents a same-sex connection that surpasses female solidarity. This sequence, which conjures up images of lesbian love, masks and simultaneously unmasks the author's unappeasable homosexual desires. Even in the escapist world of make-believe, a fleeting moment, barely a touch, is all Mann allows himself — ever aware of and partially driven by bourgeois heterosexual mores, his striving for fame and recognition, and his internalized self-censorship.

Noteworthy are the striking parallels between the silently suffering, latently masochistic Anna and the artist figure Tonio Kröger. Both have experienced loneliness; they are both daydreamers and voyeurs, watching others dance while yearning to be part of life. But neither of them can ever belong to the world of vitality and joyful, carefree existence. In any situation, Tonio and Anna feel alienated and displaced. The sentiment that the outsider has no home, expressed at the end of "Tonio Kröger" (*GW* 8, 337), is reiterated in "Ein Glück": "it is difficult not to feel at home in either one world or in the other, — we know it. But there exists no reconciliation" (*GW* 8, 358). This feeling of being condemned to an outsider existence connects the bourgeois artist, women, and, in light of homosexual overtones at the end of "Ein Glück," the individual of non-traditional sexual orientation. All three suffer from a similar dilemma; estrangement and self-estrangement are an inevitable predicament in a world where creativity and conformity, individual desires and orthodox demands are irreconcilable.

From the essays and narratives that Mann wrote around 1903 it can be inferred that his focus on women writers and female characters coincides with his intense feelings for Paul Ehrenberg. These texts are not autobiographical testimonies; rather they provide opportunities for the author to play with and explore his insecurities about his self, his sexuality, and his identity as an artist. Such a creative play led to both Mann's second novel, *Königliche Hoheit* (Royal Highness, 1909), written after his marriage to Katia Pringsheim, the daughter of an affluent Jewish family from Munich, and his commitment to a reputable bourgeois existence that excluded homosexual and bohemian lifestyles. The fairy-tale structure of *Königliche Hoheit*, with its inevitable marriage of prince and princess at the end, can be understood as the author's fictional musing on his marriage, his vow to heterosexuality, and, concomitantly, the artist-outsider's allegiance to the bourgeois world of patriarchal norms and social expectations despite his detached artistry.[33] On another level, *Königliche Hoheit* marks Mann's continual exploration of women's morality and feminine qualities, which he had praised unequivocally in his essays on Schwabe and Reuter.

Judging by the impact of the mother, Dorothea, and the petit-bourgeois Fräulein Unschlitt upon the prince Klaus Heinrich, *Königliche Hoheit* presents a more complex, ambiguous picture of women than do the essays. Neither woman displays the feminine qualities that Mann had recently valued so highly. Dorothea is a woman obsessed with beauty and representation. She coerces her young son into a world of performance, a world dominated by traditional masculine values such as incessant discipline, self-alienating composure, and public dignity. She teaches him to deny what she, as a representative of royalty, denies herself: kindness, compassion, and spontaneity. In contrast to Dorothea, Fräulein Unschlitt is instrumental in humiliating, ridiculing, and beguiling Klaus Heinrich into dismissing his privileged social status and the central tenets of his existence: noblesse oblige. With her attempt to strip Klaus Heinrich of his dignity and discipline, and to make him stray from his public, honorable path and its masculine principles, she wants to draw him into the world of banality and ordinariness. Mann grants neither woman a positive impact on the protagonist: Dorothea wants to lead the prince away from life and emotions; under

Unschlitt's influence the prince becomes a ridiculous figure whose debasement the narrative deplores.[34]

Different from both women is the millionaire's daughter Imma Spoelmann, whose model is to some extent a real and unusual woman of her time, Mann's wife Katia Pringsheim.[35] Imma is audacious, intelligent, and explicitly associated with a masculine, active lifestyle. She is a skilled rider and lives in rooms decorated for a male rather than a female (GW 2, 283). Oblivious to protocol and ladylike manners, she does not hesitate to push through the soldiers performing the changing of the guard, although being explicitly forbidden to do so. Imma's ironic remarks reveal a young woman who questions authority and set beliefs. She is compassionate and tolerant, yet not afraid to confront Klaus Heinrich with his shallow existence and his lack of opinions and firm beliefs. Her presence undermines Klaus Heinrich's self-effacing life as a performing member of the royal family, whose every movement and gesture is calculated. Smitten by her, he appears at the Spoelmanns' residence "without will, so to speak, and as if gripped by fate" (GW 2, 267). He acts "blindly, without regard for society, obeying his inner drives" (GW 2, 293), thus suspending his commitment to the only world in which he feels secure — the shallow world of representation.

Initially, Mann presents this young woman as a subversive force. Under her influence, Klaus Heinrich questions the value of a representational life that requires discipline and aloofness. Imma makes him see that his life is loveless and empty. When he falls in love with her he hopes that his love for her will bring him "blissful happiness" (das . . . glückselige Glück; GW 2, 274). He even claims that no one but Imma can save him (GW 2, 308). Here a woman takes on the function of an educator, healer, and liberator who rescues a man, socially her superior, from his cold and empty, noncommittal existence.[36] Thus Königliche Hoheit reiterates with the character of Imma Spoelmann what his Schwabe and Reuter essays had proposed: the idea that a feminine perspective can become a guiding principle.

Imma Spoelmann's kind, altruistic relationship to the Countess Löwenjoul serves as an example for the prince to follow. When Klaus Heinrich frowns upon the countess's lack of propriety and bewildering bouts of insanity, Imma asks him to exercise "compassion and leniency and kindness" (GW 2, 255), in other words, to be guided by feminine qualities. Confronted with Löwenjoul's tragic life and — let us not forget — eager to gain Imma's affection, the prince sheds his public self, and steps out of his world of indifference, of trite, mechanical phrases and calculated effects, and into a world of kindness and caring for others. From the very beginning of the novel Mann has prepared his readers for this "feminization" of the protagonist. The prince behaves like a gracious woman in public, who, while being admired, looks past people, "a bit with a lady's glance who is aware of being observed" (GW 2, 11). Furthermore, he is generally "tender-hearted and prone to tears" (*GW 2*, 54). With Klaus Heinrich's unmanly behavior Mann gives him the necessary predisposition to learn a lesson in humanity, tolerance, and compassion.

In his Schwabe essay Thomas Mann had expressed his hope for a world in which a feminine perspective might be a guiding principle. This world exists in *Königliche Hoheit*, as Klaus Heinrich adopts feminine values, but with limitations. Less tolerant and open than Imma, he demands decency and self-discipline, while the countess displays an excessive obsession with sexuality and the corruption of morality. Initially Imma's royal student, toward the end of the narrative Klaus Heinrich becomes the royal teacher and the advocate of discipline when his presence stops the countess from losing her dignity and from escaping into a degrading trance. Since *Königliche Hoheit* presents the prince's reprimand as a beneficial pedagogical tool,[37] the novel promotes what it simultaneously scrutinizes — values associated with the masculine, patriarchal order.

That the novel moves in this direction becomes evident when Klaus Heinrich, who first admires Imma's intellectual pursuits, later asks her to put her books aside while he himself becomes an ardent reader.[38] In an interesting role reversal that befits a patriarchal world, the prince is eager to gain intellectual ground over her and enters an active, productive life. He now feels not only qualified to participate in the politics of his principality, but also to set the conditions for his relationship with Imma. Their happiness cannot be selfish: "For the public welfare and our happiness, you see, are interdependent" (*GW 2*, 337). Inversely proportional to the prince's growth in character and social conscience, Imma's initial superiority and influence decrease. In a way reminiscent of Shakespeare's *The Taming of the Shrew*, she has to give up much of her spontaneous self as she enters a world that demands representation and protocol: in other words conformity. Subtly the novel suggests that feminine qualities cannot be the only valid guiding principles. In other words, Mann undertakes a re-evaluation of his essays on Schwabe and Reuter, and, at the same time, indicates an inclination toward the masculine, patriarchal world of his father and brother, a world he had entered with his conventional marriage to Katia Pringsheim.

From a feminist perspective, *Königliche Hoheit* takes a disappointing turn. The novel not only features a patronizing tone when Imma is called a child, a little sister, and a kitten, but Mann even has his enlightened prince suggest that Imma does not know life (*GW 2*, 237). Although the narrative presents Imma as a rich man's spoiled daughter, her past experiences as an outsider in the United States and the knowledge about life that she has gained as Löwenjoul's confidante undermine the prince's assessment of her. He wants her to leave the cold and pure sphere of mathematics and her mocking attitude in order to enter the "unknown sphere, that warmer, damper, and more fertile one" (*GW 2*, 301). The reader will notice that the prince is certainly not the expert to introduce Imma to life and a world of love, compassion, and sexual passion. On the contrary, she has brought love and empathy into his solitary, representative existence. It is ironic that Mann has Klaus Heinrich claim that he can rescue Imma Spoelmann from a cold and lonely world, while he must follow his commitment to the detached world of representation. Unusual for Mann's fiction, *Königliche Hoheit* ends on a bright, harmonious note when the prince promises his new bride an existence of "Dignity and Love, — an austere happiness" (Hoheit und Liebe, — ein strenges Glück) (*GW* 2, 363), in other words, the reconciliation of social and sexual desires.

According to the prince's guidelines for their future lives, the end of the novel blends social responsibility, austerity, and aloof representation with love and compassion, thus intertwining masculine and feminine qualities, with "highness" leading the way. Subsequently, Mann shifts his focus from the sole praise of women's qualities and from their suffering, which had occupied his writings between 1901 and 1905, to a guarded acknowledgment of patriarchal power and leadership. But that is not to say that *Königliche Hoheit* indicates a radical departure from his earlier works, as another look at Imma Spoelmann reveals.

Her story is about a woman who falls in love and pays a price. In Imma's change Mann shows more than a woman's transformation from carefree adolescence to womanhood under patriarchy. Subtly woven into the narrative is the sacrifice that love demands from a spontaneous, free-spirited, young, and intelligent woman, a sacrifice, I should emphasize, that she undertakes without skepticism. However, Mann includes some reservation about this sacrifice. At the end of *Königliche Hoheit,* Imma Spoelmann appears in a silken white bridal dress. Her veil does not hide her "alien tiny child's face" (*GW* 2, 359–60). The word "fremd" appears again to underscore that conformity does not suit her: "in white glitter, the alien bride" (*GW* 2, 361). While Imma Spoelmann's fate is not identical with that of Tony Buddenbrook, as she marries the man she loves, her entrance into a world dominated by stifling conventions, imposed self-denial, and restrictions bears some similarity.

In *Der Zauberberg* (The Magic Mountain, 1924), the protagonist Hans Castorp's sympathy for death, stemming from his rejection of a lackluster bourgeois life, steers him into the arms of one of Thomas Mann's most memorable, most emancipated women: the Russian Clawdia Chauchat. The door-slamming, Kirghiz-eyed woman, whose indifference to both bourgeois etiquette and her husband's existence places her outside bourgeois norms and morality, stirs the patients' — and the readers' — imagination. References to various mythological women and fictional characters, among them Adam's first wife Lilith, Circe, Beatrice, and Carmen, suggest that Clawdia Chauchat, who leads a sexually free, promiscuous existence and dares to display her sensuality uninhibitedly, functions as the novel's femme fatale who lures her lovers, Castorp and Peeperkorn, into the realm of death.[39] In the eyes of her most severe critic, the humanist Settembrini, Chauchat is the incarnation of the uncivilized world, associated with the plains of Eastern Eurasia. She personifies all that the humanist rails against: largesse, vice, formlessness, chaos, disease, degeneration, and death.

Because Hans Castorp's infatuation with Chauchat binds him to a world of disease and death, irresponsibility and inertia, Settembrini's perception of this enticing woman seems at first glance to be justified. Eros and Thanatos are intertwined when Castorp proclaims the unity of love, body, and death, and his yearning, brought on by Chauchat, for a *Liebestod* (*GW* 3, 476–77). But this female version of Hermes is far more than death's seductress. When Castorp declares his love for her in the chapter "Walpurgisnacht," she gently caresses his hair.[40] Their subsequent sexual encounter shows not only a free woman in control of her own sexuality, but also a woman who sympathizes with the love-sick Castorp and his yearning for sexual fulfillment. In interlacing a woman's altruistic empathy, a bourgeois-Christian feminine virtue, with a sexual freedom that is customarily condemned in women, Mann erases the traditional dichotomy between sinful and virtuous woman, vamp and virgin.

Mann indicates that Chauchat's "sympathy for life" (Lebensfreundlichkeit) and "caritas" (*GW* 3, 832) result from her freedom and geniality (*GW* 3, 846). What appears from Settembrini's bourgeois-humanist perspective to be an undisciplined, promiscuous, "Asian" life can also be understood as anarchic individualism in defiance of restrictive and oppressive bourgeois mores. Because Chauchat is indifferent to these, she can practice an intuitive humanity rather than the rationalized, dispassionate one advocated by Settembrini. She demonstrates a love for life that is not tied to ideological frameworks and interests. But this love becomes questionable when Chauchat, before leaving the mountain for the last time, points out to Castorp that "passion is forgetting one's self," not egotistical "self-enrichment" (*GW* 3, 824). The narrative underscores her view. She becomes Castorp's "servant" (*GW* 3, 469) for one night; self-imposed compliance and submission, bordering on bondage (*GW* 3, 804), characterizes her relationship to Peeperkorn. Since Chauchat's caritas contains a self-effacing quality and threatens individual dignity and freedom,[41] *Der Zauberberg* evokes skepticism about participation in life, and undermines the moral point of Hans Castorp's vision in the chapter "Snow" that kindness and compassion should be guiding principles (*GW* 3, 685).

Clawdia Chauchat serves as a narrative tool to explore the proximity of life, love, and death when Mann includes a brief reference to her journey to Spain. On the symbolic level of *Der Zauberberg*, Asia, where chaos and lack of discipline reign, converges with Spain, the nation identified with the anti-humanist position of the Jesuit Naphta, inquisition, discipline, death, "torturer mentality and misanthropy" (Folterknechtsinn und Menschenfeindlichkeit) (*GW* 3, 906). Mann presents a Clawdia Chauchat who submits to neither of these worlds. Instead, in a crowd of cheerful, celebrating people in a Catalonian marketplace, Chauchat displays a social, jovial attitude, holding hands and dancing with them (*GW* 3, 774). Dance is also a motif of social interaction and harmony in the world of the sun people in Castorp's dream. This allusion accentuates the image of Chauchat as life-embracing. But it does not erase the evocation of the darker, Spanish world of anti-humanism and death. Mann positions Eastern lack of discipline, that is, anarchic autonomy, side by side with compassion for life, and Spanish terror. The gliding from one ideological framework into another, the mingling of the celebration of life and death, suggest that boundaries become unstable, that polarities are temporarily suspended, and that one principle does not overpower the other. This brief episode from Chauchat's life reflects the ambiguous, open note upon which the novel ends. Neither love nor death can proclaim victory.

Not only does Mann use a woman who is free and defies all bourgeois-patriarchal conventions, yet who is submissive, as a crystallization point in which the novel's central principles and orientations converge and become unstable, but with Chauchat he also raises the issue of Hans Castorp's as well as her own sexual identity. Various sexual personae evolve in Castorp's relationship to her. First, the virile, childless Clawdia, who appears as a reincarnation of the Slavic boy Pribislav Hippe (*GW* 3, 206, 827) on whom Castorp had a crush, is associated with Castorp's homosexual desires. When Chauchat walks through the room in an enticing gown at the Mardi Gras ball in the chapter "Walpurgisnacht" (*GW* 3, 456), he is awestruck, finding her sexually attractive as a woman. Just a few pages further, Mann has his protagonist become pale and lose his composure because Chauchat offers him a pencil, as Pribislav Hippe had done years before. Mann thereby refuses to give Castorp a fixed sexual identity and orientation, and suggests that his homo- and heterosexual desires are simultaneously fulfilled in their sexual encounter. Chauchat's sexuality is also not clearly defined. On the one hand, she likes to display her female sexuality with her wardrobe and to be the object of the male gaze (*GW* 3, 466). On the other hand, she emphasizes that, while in Spain, she put on a blue cap, traditionally worn only by men and boys (*GW* 3, 774); thus she destabilizes traditional male identity. Chauchat, whom Mann modeled to some degree after his own wife Katia,[42] addresses the author's admiration for the strong, emancipated woman and the threat that she presents to a bourgeois, patriarchal world. Mann turns this threat into an ambivalent force in which individualism and the desire for freedom alternate with the need for community and security. Clawdia Chauchat's need for independence is counterbalanced by a fear of being alone and leading a nomadic, uncommitted, and thus purposeless life — fear that compels her to become Peeperkorn's lover and to return to the Berghof and Castorp (*GW* 3, 831).

With Chauchat's swaying between asocial individualism and social integration, between autonomy and acquiescence, between traditional masculine and feminine identities, and with her transgression of bourgeois sexual morality, Mann creates a correlation to his own existence as a bourgeois artist and as a troubled male with a stigmatized sexual identity. As in the case of earlier female characters, his own longings, fears, and sexual anxieties do not determine Chauchat's portrait, but they do creep into it. With her unfettered, anti-bourgeois existence and an uninhibited sexuality that defies bourgeois morality, Mann imagines a life that was never his own, a life that is enticing, yet empty. Neither it nor its conventional bourgeois opposite is idealized in *Der Zauberberg*.

The portrayal of the biblical temptress in *Joseph und seine Brüder* (Joseph and his Brothers, 1933–1943) is informed by the author's skepticism about an existence outside bourgeois order and morality. Mann assigns a name, Mut-em-enet, which he often abbreviates to Mut in the novel, and a voice to her. No longer is she reduced to "Potiphar's wife," a man's possession. Mann gives her an identity and an entitlement to her own life. The narrator, eager to justify his exceptional interest in her and to stir the readers' curiosity, claims that he will correct the negative image of this woman (*GW* 5, 1012) who is generally known as "the shameless seductress and lure of evil" (*GW* 5, 1091).

In Mann's re-vision of Potiphar's wife the critical point of departure is a misogynist world that barters women and controls their sexuality. When the narrator informs us that Mut has been forced to marry the eunuch Potiphar, and that she consequently has been robbed of her "female humanness" (weibliches Menschentum) (*GW* 5, 1087), the oppressive sexual politics of *Buddenbrooks* comes to mind. Mann portrays Mut as a victim of a cruel patriarchal world that either ignores or looks down upon a woman's sexuality. It is understandable that her repressed sexual desires are kindled by the presence of the handsome Joseph. Mann describes Mut's love as an "affliction" that she cannot overcome (*GW* 5, 1085). Despite her gradual loss of dignity, which culminates in her asking Joseph in vain for sexual gratification, the narrator expresses his empathy for "poor Eni" (*GW* 5, 1210), a phrase reminiscent of "poor Tony" in *Buddenbrooks*.

However, the narrator's and the readers' empathy for Mut dwindles when she, hysterical and on the verge of insanity, seeks revenge for her unrequited love. Falsely she accuses Joseph of attempted rape. Not her lie, but her demagoguery leading to Joseph's arrest, is condemned by the narrator. With Mut's rhetorical skills to make socially inferior individuals and servants feel important, in calling them "brothers" (*GW* 5, 1262), Mann links his female character, initially a victim of sexual politics, to the deadly world of Nazi Germany. Her development from a rational to an irrational individual and her Dionysian rapture reflect the "Bacchanalian excess" (*GW* 11, 877) of National Socialism.[43]

From a feminist perspective, meshing a misogynist biblical narrative about a woman's revenge for sexual oppression and a nationalistic, racist rhetoric is problematic. When Mann reinscribes the image of the sex-driven, irrational, cunning, and destructive biblical woman, he not only complies with the misogynist tenets of the original source. By dwelling on her irrationality and her devious power to instigate, he even exaggerates the negative aspects of Mut's character.[44] Neither the biblical source nor the plot of *Joseph und seine Brüder* warrant such negative depiction.

Autobiographical impulses are most likely contributing factors in this shift toward a dominantly negative portrayal of Mut. With his portrayal of Mut's yearning and silent suffering Mann revives both his compassion for suffering and sexually frustrated women of the early 1900s and his own story about tormenting desires. Notebook entries reveal that Mann's past confessions of love for Paul Ehrenberg are echoed by Mut in *Joseph und seine Brüder*.[45] As Mut's yearning for a beautiful young man is associated with excessive, uninhibited sexuality and loss of dignity and honor, her presence in the text develops into Mann's private reassurance of his choice to become a disciplined, reputable artist rather than giving in to sexual needs. This reassurance of a life based on bourgeois respectability and morality is, however, undermined by the fact that Mut's story is more tragic than any of Mann's stories about an "affliction." It illustrates the self-destructive agony of an individual whose sexuality is inhibited. While Thomas Mann had to remain silent, he allowed his fictional character to cry out. He thus gave Mut a voice in literature that had previously been denied to her. Besides the voice of a lustful and vindictive woman that of an oppressed one is heard, one who deserves the readers' critical distance as well as compassion.

Unfulfilled sexual desires and love not sanctioned by society also held Mann's imagination in his last story, "Die Betrogene." Again he uses the word "affliction" (*GW* 8, 930) to describe the passionate love of an older woman, the Rhenish widow Rosalie von Tümmler, for a younger man, the American Ken Keaton. On the realistic level of the narrative, Mann presents an older woman's yearning for life and love, and her illusion that nature has rejuvenated her. On its symbolic level, this narrative can be read as another one in which Mann employs a female character to address his unfulfilled homosexual inclinations. When the author denies Rosalie sexual gratification, he echoes his own reticence to pursue his illicit desires.[46] Judging by their impact upon this middle-aged woman, such desires are a curse as well as a blessing. Rosalie, whose rapidly spreading cancer is, as the story suggests, a direct result of her desire for Keaton, feels nonetheless fortunate, and claims that, in loving the young man, she has experienced nature's "kindness and mercy" (*GW* 8, 950).

Rosalie's understanding of her love as nature's precious gift can be traced to autobiographical roots. In reaction to his infatuations with Klaus Heuser in 1927 and with Franz Westermeier in 1950, Mann disclosed in his diaries, in a gratified, nearly exultant tone, that he was able to experience love.[47] He returns to this experience with ironic distance, using as an unlikely alter-ego a naive, rather ordinary housewife (*GW* 8, 937) full of "warmth of the heart" (Herzenswärme) (*GW* 8, 878) and "simplicity of the heart" (Herzenseinfalt) (*GW* 8, 883). With her naive outlook on life, her sentimental revelry in nature, and her tendency to distort reality with her "excessive imagination" (*GW* 8, 880), Rosalie initially appears as a comical figure. However, her decision not to repress her love for the young man, not to stay within the conventional boundaries of a woman of her age, and to accept death with dignity, turn her into a free, admirable person. In unpublished manuscript fragments, Rosalie repeatedly assures her daughter that she is determined to adhere to moral conventions.[48] In the final version Mann presents a contemplative Rosalie considering renunciation of her desires (*GW* 8, 931–32), thus making her passionate declaration of love in the castle scene more plausible. Only death prevents her from transgressing bourgeois morality. With Rosalie's defiance, Mann not only underscores the fact that fiction and autobiography are not identical, but he is also able to conclude the narrative with ambiguity. "Die Betrogene" ends neither with the victory of bourgeois morality nor with its defeat.

Earlier in the narrative, when Rosalie makes the point that women are born to suffer and to endure pain (*GW* 8, 890), Mann reminds us of the silently suffering, passive women whom he had idealized five decades before. Rosalie differs from these women in that she spurns the passive female role that bourgeois-patriarchal morality had taught her.[49] The other female figure of "Die Betrogene," Rosalie's daughter Anna, whom Mann once called his "best character,"[50] is able to sublimate her suffering. Crippled, excluded from love and sexuality, Anna has learned to shun life, to become the cold, detached, and skeptical artist. Although she is artistically contented, Anna is always sensitive to the fact that she cannot participate in life. "Living with one's suffering" (*GW* 8, 931) is her inexorable predicament.

It was also Mann's predicament. In Anna, who forsakes love and finds freedom from nature in her paintings, and in Rosalie, who is willing to break with bourgeois sexual taboos, Mann has encoded his oscillation between "self-discipline and self-liberation."[51] While he had to renounce the stigmatized desires in his life, narratives like "Die Betrogene" provide a vehicle to voice them, along with his sufferings. However, this self-liberation through writing has its limits. Self-censorship, an element of Mann's writing since "Der kleine Herr Friedemann," still calls for masks such as the female character Rosalie.

Women who are not afraid to violate bourgeois morality and social boundaries, and to initiate sexual relationships and satisfy their sexual desires abound in Mann's last work, *Bekenntnisse des Hochstaplers Felix Krull* (Confessions of Felix Krull, Confidence Man, 1954). Its protagonist, the beautiful young Felix, attracts young girls as well as older, sexually experienced women of uninhibited sensuality, among them the artist figure Diane Houpflé, whom Mann characterizes as a writer who covets life. Neither her art nor her bourgeois marriage to a husband whom Mann ridicules by making him a manufacturer of water closets can appease this yearning. Diane's sexual encounter with Felix reveals her intense desire for life, leading to her demand to be humiliated and physically abused by him. Mann denies her the loss of human dignity, allowing her instead to play a game with Felix. Diane asks Felix to loot her hotel room in her presence and pretends not to notice it. This game is a construction, like her art, and gives her the delusion of participating in life. Thus she is instrumental in underscoring one of the major themes of the novel, a theme that echoes Arthur Schopenhauer's philosophy: the tangible world is appearance (Vorstellung), always close to illusion and betrayal.

Felix Krull is usually understood as a "a work of confession" (*GW* 7, 562) of a confidence man. In the figure of Diane Houpflé the novel makes another confession, that of the author's secret sexual desires and identity. The description of the gratifying sexual union between an older woman and a younger man contains a homosexual subtext. When Houpflé states that her love for young men is a tragic love, "irrational, not reputable, not practical, nothing for life, nothing for marriage" (*GW* 7, 446), Mann is reiterating the ambivalent assessment of homosexuality that is found in his essay "Die Ehe im Übergang" (Marriage in Transition, 1925).[52] Using the voice of Diane Houpflé, Mann makes another admission. He has her proclaim that she will always treasure her love for beautiful men, and that they will always be there, even when she is dead (*GW* 7, 450). They will live on in her poetry and in her novels — just as they live on in Thomas Mann's work, embodied in such characters as Tadzio, Joseph, Rudi Schwerdtfeger, and Felix Krull.

Diane Houpflé is only a minor character in *Felix Krull,* yet she is a central one in terms of Mann's confrontation with his own problematic existence as a male bourgeois artist with stigmatized desires. The fact that women rarely are the protagonists of his narratives and novels, that they are neither genial artists like Adrian Leverkühn nor architects of history like Joseph, distracts from the pivotal role that diverse and multifaceted characters such as the ones discussed in this essay play in Mann's oeuvre. Neither his homosexuality nor his bourgeois morality control the fictional identity of his female characters. It is the reciprocity of both perspectives that shaped his most memorable female characters, and which, intentionally or not, has resulted in Mann's acknowledgment of women's right to their own sexuality.

Notes

[1] Quoted in Barbara Greven-Aschoff, *Die bürgerliche Frauenbewegung in Deutschland 1894–1933* (Göttingen: Vandenhoeck & Ruprecht, 1981), 40.

[2] Among these women were Franziska von Reventlow and Gabriele Reuter. These women, quickly forgotten, have recently returned to prominence because of the interest in early feminism. See Ludmila Kaloyanova-Slavova, *Übergangsgeschöpfe: Gabriele Reuter, Hedwig Dohm, Helene Böhlau und Franziska von Reventlow* (New York: Peter Lang, 1998).

[3] *Nb* 2 (7–14), 109.

[4] *GW* 6, 268. Thomas Mann's collected works (*GW* 1–13) will hereafter be cited in the text.

[5] See also Herbert Lehnert's interpretation of Irma Welten in "Thomas Mann's Beginnings and *Buddenbrooks*" in this volume.

[6] Bram Dijkstra, Idols of Perversity: Fantasies of Feminine Evil in Fin-de-Siécle Culture (New York: Oxford UP, 1986), 25–27.

[7] Literary naturalism allows women sexuality, yet this sexuality has animal-like qualities and reduces women to instinct-driven creatures.

[8] Like Ada in "Der Wille zum Glück," Gerda von Rinnlingen is presented as a still life, a character caught in suspense (*GW* 8, 94).

[9] Smoking, riding, and driving a carriage with a pair of thoroughbreds while the groom sits behind her are all traditionally male activities that she indulges in.

[10] To his friend Otto Grautoff Mann confessed that he had found "discreet forms and masks" (*TM/OG*, 90) since "Der kleine Herr Friedemann" to write about his sexual experiences. See also Karl Werner Böhm, *Zwischen Selbstzucht und Verlangen: Thomas Mann und das Stigma der Homosexualität* (Würzburg: Königshausen & Neumann, 1991), 179.

[11] The other counter figure to Gerda Buddenbrooks is the ceaselessly pregnant child of nature Anna, a lower-class flower girl and Thomas Buddenbrook's former lover. A gender-oriented reading of Anna reveals Mann's play with and departure from traditional constructions of women. The *fille-fleur*, a popular motif in European art of the fin de siècle, became widely known through the pre-Raphaelite Millais and his painting "Ophelia" (1851), as well as through the poem inspired by it, Rimbaud's "Ophélie" (1870). Evidently, Mann's *fille-fleur* does not share her predecessors' fragility and short life. He rescues his flower girl, neither virginal nor morbid, from the stock treatment of the day. But while she is spared dire health problems that would put her on the threshold of death, she is not spared another self-effacing predicament: she becomes the epitome of self-sacrificing motherhood.

[12] *Nb* 1 (1–6), 102–3; Gabriele Reuter, *From a Good Family,* trans. Lynne Tatlock (Columbia, SC: Camden House, 1999). All future references are from this text.

[13] *From a Good Family,* 163. In her autobiography *Vom Kinde zum Menschen.* Geschichte meiner Jugend (Berlin: S. Fischer, 1921)), Reuter wrote about her protagonist's and woman's situation in bourgeois society: "Die Tragik in dem Los des Weibes: geboren zu sein, erzogen zu werden für eine Berufung, die sie gelehrt ist, als ihr einziges Glück zu betrachten" (The tragedy in a woman's fate: to be born

for, raised for a calling which she has been taught to consider as her only happiness). Gabriele Reuter, *Vom Kinde zum Menschen*, 432.

[14] Reuter, *From a Good Family*, 14.

[15] Cf. Reuter's Agathe Heidling, who pretends to be ignorant in order to meet her father's and society's expectations. Analogous to Reuter, Mann has his female character play the role of the imperceptive woman that society expects her to be, to illustrate that a woman's intelligence is dismissed in a male-dominated world.

[16] Rarely has Tony received more than sympathy from critics and readers. Negative interpretations abound, for instance: "What would a closer inspection of her inner life add? Only a confirmation that there is virtually no further substance beneath her familiar mannerisms, her repeated and usually derivative phrases." T. J. Reed, *Thomas Mann: The Uses of Tradition* (Oxford: Clarendon Press, 1974), 55–56. Nearly twenty years later this negative image still dominates. For example, Claus Tillmann states that Tony lacks ambiguity and complexity. *Das Frauenbild bei Thomas Mann: Der Wille zum strengen Glück* (Wuppertal: Holger Deimling, 1992), 42.

[17] Tony's emotional response to the sale of her parents' house reflects her need for security and orientation *within* a bourgeois world. (*GW* 1, 584–85).

[18] *GW* 1, 672. Tony is a realist rather than a fatalist. She does not like what life has is store for her, but she accepts it (*GW* 1, 639).

[19] Christian Buddenbrook's marriage, unacceptable to his family, is a marriage of love, not status. His portrayal also illustrates that bourgeois existence and sexual fulfillment are at odds with each other.

[20] Peter-Paul Schneider, "'. . . wo ich Deine Zuständigkeit leugnen muß. . . .' Die bislang unbekannte Antwort Heinrich Manns auf Thomas Manns Abrechnungsbrief vom 5. Dezember 1903," *In Spuren gehen: Festschrift für Helmut Koopmann,* ed. Andrea Bartl et al. (Tübingen: Niemeyer, 1998), 241.

[21] Schneider, "'. . . Wo ich deine Zuständigkeit leugnen muß,'" 242.

[22] *TM/OG*, 146.

[23] Over forty years later, in *Doktor Faustus,* Mann would use his notes on Adelaide to create Ines Rodde, who loves the violinist Schwerdtfeger, who resembles his close friend Paul Ehrenberg.

[24] *Nb* 2 (7–14), 46–47.

[25] *Nb* 2 (7–14), 47.

[26] The most famous representative of the "eternal feminine," Goethe's Gretchen, is overall a passive, suffering woman despite her active role in the salvation of Faust. Louise Otto-Peters's understanding of the "eternal feminine" also emphasizes the compassionate-passive nature of women.

[27] See Heinrich Detering," *Das Ewig-Weibliche:* Thomas Mann über Toni Schwabe, Gabriele Reuter, Ricarda Huch," *TMJb* 12 (1999): 150–57.

[28] *TM/HM,* 97.

[29] For a closer look at the connections between Mann, his brother Heinrich, and Gabriele Reuter, see Karin Tebben, "'Man hat das Prinzip zur Geltung zu bringen, das man darstellt.' Standortbestimmung Thomas Manns im Jahre 1904: Gabriele Reuter," *TMJb* 12 (1999): 77–97.

[30] *TM/HM,* 86–87, 82.

[31] *TM/HM,* 86.

[32] For the numerous striking parallels between "Ein Glück" and these notes see Böhm, *Zwischen Selbstzucht und Verlangen,* 184–85.

[33] *Br.* 1, 43.

[34] "Unfortunately" the prince's mentor, Raoul Überbein appears too late to rescue him from humiliation (*GW* 2, 104).

[35] With his portrayal of the quick-witted, intelligent Imma Spoelmann Mann pays tribute to his wife Katia, whose glibness was well-known. The similarities do not stop here. Both women share an interest in mathematics and a boyish appearance.

[36] For autobiographical parallels see Mann's letter to Katia at the beginning of June 1904 (*Br.* 1, 45–46).

[37] Hans Wysling, "Königliche Hoheit," *Thomas-Mann-Handbuch,* ed. Helmut Koopmann (Stuttgart: Kröner, 1990), 392.

[38] In real life, Mann, envious of his wife Katia's studies, was happy to see her neglect them. In his correspondence, he admitted his old-fashioned attitude. See *Br.* 1, 43.

[39] For interpretations of Chauchat as femme fatale see Hans Wysling (*Thomas-Mann-Handbuch,* 406) and Frederick Lubich, "Thomas Mann's Sexual Politics — Lost in translation," *Comparative Literature Studies* 31 (1994): 114.

[40] In *Doktor Faustus,* written over two decades later, Heterae Esmeralda would touch Adrian Leverkühn, resulting in his artistic elevation and illness.

[41] With this self-effacement and self-denigration Mann establishes another link between Chauchat and Leo Tolstoy, whose rejection of his own work and self-tormenting submission to religion Mann had criticized. (*GW* 9, 74–75).

[42] Wysling, *Thomas-Mann-Handbuch,* 407.

[43] Manfred Dierks, *Studien zu Mythos und Psychology bei Thomas Mann,* TMS 2 (1972), 194.

[44] Eckhard Heftrich argues that the theme of "Heimsuchung" allowed Thomas Mann "Potiphars Weib vom Schatten ihrer üblen Legende zu erlösen" (to redeem Potiphar's wife from her evil legend); *Geträumte Taten* (Frankfurt am Main: Klostermann, 1993), 245. However, Mut-em-enet fulfills the myth in the end.

[45] *Nb* 2 (7–14), 44–45, 46–47.

[46] *Tb* 10 July 1950. See also Jens Rieckmann's essay in this volume for the homosexual subtext of "Die Betrogene."

[47] *Tb* 20 February 1942; *Tb* 9 July 1950.

[48] *Tb* 23 January 1953, *Tagebücher 1953–1955,* doc. 4, 809–10.

[49] Cf. Herbert Lehnert's essay "Betrayed or Not Betrayed: A Testament," in this volume.

[50] *DüD* 3, 520.

[51] "Selbstzucht und Selbstbefreiung" ("Bilse und ich," *Essays* 1, 45).

[52] *Essays* 2, 267–82. Also under the title "Über die Ehe" (*GW* 10, 191–207). I thank Herbert Lehnert for his valuable comments and discussions.

Betrayed or Not Betrayed: A Testament?

Herbert Lehnert

THOMAS MANN'S LAST STORY IS KNOWN in English by the title of its translation: "The Black Swan." Its author called the German original "Die Betrogene," meaning "the betrayed woman." The original title seems to promise a tale of a woman betrayed by a lover. The protagonist, Rosalie von Tümmler, does have a lover, but it is not he who betrays her; rather, she is "betrayed" by herself, by her idealistic worship of nature, which makes her believe that she can rejuvenate herself through her own inner power. Dying, however, she sees that her self-induced renewal was an illusion. But even the betrayal had value, as she tells her daughter on her deathbed: "Anna, do not speak of the betrayal nor of the derisive cruelty of nature. [. . .] Not willingly do I leave you and life with its springtime. But how could there be spring without death? For death is a great means of life. While death assumed the shape of resurrection and sexual desire [Liebeslust] for me, that was not a falsehood, but goodness and mercy [Gnade]." Rosalie accepts her death in religious terms, a religion that draws from her love of nature. Her last words are: "Nature I have always loved, and it granted love to her child."[1]

The contradiction of Rosalie being betrayed and not betrayed is only one incident of Mann's multifaceted way of writing. He makes his reader see the world from different points of view or perspectives. Mann was a disciple of Nietzsche not in spite of, but because of the philosopher's contradictions. The much-discussed irony in Mann's writings expresses multivalence: not the traditional irony of two meanings of which one is valid, the other not, but a language that acknowledges that the world has many aspects which may be of different value without being arranged in a predetermined hierarchical order. Our world, the modern world, can be put into words only if more than one perspective is invoked.

The words "resurrection" (Auferstehung) and "sexual desire" (Liebeslust) appear next to each other in Rosalie's last words in the story. The resurrection of Christ is the center of the Christian faith, or myth (in the sense of a religious narration) that Jesus' self-sacrifice means his loving atonement for the sins of mankind. Rosalie's resurrection signifies her own reawakened physical love, which turns into love of nature. Nature takes the place of God. In death this love redeems her, making her life whole. Rosalie embraces a monistic belief in death as redemption into the whole of being. Monistic beliefs had been proclaimed, written about, and celebrated in Germany at the turn of the century, when, according to the time frame of the story, Rosalie would have grown up. Having celebrated her fiftieth birthday not too long before the beginning of the narration (*GW* 8, 878), she is of the same age as the author of the story in which she appears.

Monists reject the dualistic tradition that is ingrained in our culture by way of the biblical belief in an immortal human soul and a creator God existing in transcendence. The dualistic tradition is older than Christianity. The Platonic and idealistic placement of mind above matter is dualistic as well. Despite her monistic deathbed confession, Rosalie thinks in idealistic terms when she believes that her love will rejuvenate her body by reversing her menopause, because she values her mind more highly than her body, which is mere matter, and subject to her will. Rosalie does not simply switch from one philosophical view to the other. She may not even be aware of any switch. Her idealistic (dualistic) belief in the power of her mind becomes part of her (monistic) religious comfort. In addition to this philosophical confusion, there is the biblical allusion in the wording of the text. Though Rosalie uses the word for resurrection, "Auferstehung," in a completely secular sense, its presence in the text is nevertheless a signal that Christian patterns still linger. Modern consciousness is complex and cannot be grasped in consistent philosophical terms.

This mixture of worldviews may be considered realistic rather than surprising, since rejection of transcendence and appreciation of the idealistic distinction between mind and matter often go together in the modern world regardless of philosophical distinctions and the need for consistency, and biblical motifs are deeply ingrained in our culture. However, the mixture of idealistic shaping of the self, monistic coping with death, and lingering Christian faith may have significance in a text that Thomas Mann wrote under the prospect of his own death.

Mann interrupted the writing of his novel *Bekenntnisse des Hochstaplers Felix Krull* (Confessions of Felix Krull, Confidence Man, 1954) in order to write "Die Betrogene" because he realized that he might never be able to finish the Krull novel, and he needed to say something in a shorter form that could be completed. In April 1952 he had heard his wife Katia tell the story of an older woman in Munich who had passionately loved the tutor of her son and had been deceived by the apparent return of menstruation before dying of cancer.[2] This tale of an older person's sexual desire for a much younger one, and its dramatic end, implying a fight against aging and transitoriness, must have struck Mann as an opportunity to transform a similar experience of his own artistically. Less than two years earlier he had experienced a feeling of rejuvenation through his passion for the waiter Franz Westermeier,[3] a passion which he had suppressed as usual because of his "compulsion to keep the secret" (Zwang, das Geheimnis zu bewahren).[4] Throughout his life Mann had transformed his erotic desires into writing. This piece, to be finished before his death, could be enriched by probing the possibilities of coping with death.

Mann's own worldviews were most influenced by Nietzsche and Schopenhauer. Schopenhauer's system is atheistic, and Nietzsche had expressed his astonishment at the fact that so few people worried about the disappearance of religion from daily life, the "death of God."[5] Neither the teachings of Schopenhauer nor those of Nietzsche are consistently monistic, though both reject the transcendent God. Schopenhauer's system of Will and Representation is dualistic; the will is found in the human self and is considered the superior force. But since Schopenhauer's Will is identical with Kant's "thing in itself," as a pervasive force present in everything that exists, it can be regarded as a monistic conception as well. Nietzsche rejected the "true" world, the divine transcendental world, and in a radical departure from dualistic thought, even rejected the notion that contradictions (Gegensätze) were real.[6] Because Nietzsche felt challenged by the Darwinian view that man is an animal, not created in the image of God, he questioned all dualistic philosophy, including that of Plato, and denied free will. But this denial is not consistent with Nietzsche's belief in the power of human beings to surpass themselves on the way toward greatness or toward becoming "Übermenschen." He proclaimed the Will to Power to be the principle of all things and all living beings. This is an idealistic view implying human will as a superior power. Precisely this belief in superhuman will power is parodied in Rosalie's willed but then frustrated rejuvenation.

Nietzsche's monistic tendencies were derived from his reception of Darwinism and its contradiction of the Christian beliefs with which he grew up. In Thomas Mann's time, an even stronger pull towards the validity of monism as the correct view of the world as a whole was being exerted by quantum physics, because it placed into doubt the possibility of separating an observing subject from that which is observed. Heisenberg's uncertainty principle maintains that there cannot be complete objectivity because the act of observing always affects the observed object. While the disturbance of the object by the observer is negligible in classical physics, it is a fundamental principle in particle physics. Thomas Mann, while not a scientist, had knowledge of these developments. He had personal contact with physicists in Chicago, among them James Franck, and he was deeply worried about the use of the atomic and hydrogen bombs as instruments of power. Modern science excludes ideas of a spiritual afterlife of the kind Goethe still maintained a belief in despite his monistic tendencies. That Mann, in his seventies, wrote of Rosalie's acceptance of her fate can be read as his probing whether a monistic religious attitude may help in coping with death. While monism may have such an effect, dissolution into the whole of being does not offer an orientation that is usable in day-to-day life. We cannot give up observing things, like classical physics, as being something other than ourselves. In spite of scientific support for monism, the subject-object dualism retains validity. Nor can individuals give up exerting their will and considering their conscious decisions as forces superior to mere matter, including their own bodies. Strict monism, in which all being is regarded as a whole, eliminates not merely transcendence but all contradictions, contrasts, and, finally, differentiations.

This is why Thomas Mann's ironic writing reflects modernity while refusing to permit any description in philosophical terms. The modernity of his writing style perseveres even where his subjects, his material is dated. Mann's irony is to be understood in the sense of Nietzsche's perspectivism, as acceptance of a multifaceted, even contradictory world. He maintained his appreciation for Nietzsche throughout his life, even after the Nazis misused the philosopher's writings, but also did not shrink from criticizing him. It is indicative of the contradictory terms in which Mann saw Nietzsche that he insisted that Nietzsche, in spite of his violent anti-Christianity, retained at heart a love of the religion of his upbringing (*GW* 9, 684).

Thomas Mann's clinging to idealistic notions, in spite of Nietzsche's anti-idealism, is apparent in his description of his use of irony in the long essay *Betrachtungen eines Unpolitischen* (Reflections of a Nonpolitical Mann, 1918): "irony toward both sides, toward life and toward the spirit" (*GW* 12, 573). By "spirit" (Geist) he meant an attitude of critical judgment of "life," social rules as well as chaotic reality. The spirit-nature dualism is mirrored in many of Mann's works as the duality of outsider and commoner, creativeness against social adaptability, with Tonio Kröger and Hans Hansen establishing the pattern. In "Die Betrogene," Rosalie and Anna represent the duality. Their living in harmony can be read as a symbol for the "ironic" style harboring contrasts and contradictions.

Mother and daughter carry equal weight in the text. They are played out against each other, and they love each other. Anna takes the role of the outsider. She is marked by her clubfoot, much as little Herr Friedemann (of Mann's early story "Der kleine Herr Friedemann" [Little Herr Friedemann, 1897]) is by his hunchback. Fulfillment of sexual desire is denied her, as it is to Friedemann. She has to cope with her shortcoming and does it with creativity and will-power, the same will-power that is parodied in her mother's false belief in having willed her own sexual rejuvenation.

The conversations of mother and daughter in "Die Betrogene" exemplify the perspectivism of the text. During a walk in an open landscape, the two women encounter an ill-smelling pile consisting of rotten plants, human excrement, and a decaying small animal. This encounter however does not lead to Rosalie's praise of the greatness of nature regardless of its ugly aspects, as one might expect from a nature-worshiper like her. The passage is introduced as something strange that "recalled mockery" (an Spott ge-mahnte, *GW* 8, 887). To whom is it mockery? The narrator for a moment steps out of his role as narrator in the classical novella style and mocks Rosalie's selective love of nature. The two women quickly walk away from the natural, yet nevertheless disgusting phenomenon. Rosalie confirms her selective appreciation of reality by explaining her dislike for perfumes produced from animal glands because the smell produced is unlike that from flowers (*GW* 8, 887–88). Nature is good when it is growing: she loves a very old oak tree growing in a park near her house. While some branches have died, others still produce leaves in the spring (*GW* 8, 888–89).

Women, Rosalie says to her daughter, have life-giving power, of which birthing pain is an accompaniment that men do not have. Menstruation, for her, is the sign of this power. She misses it after menopause. At this point the text introduces a biblical theme. Rosalie refers to Genesis 18 (in Luther's translation): "Alas, it ceased to go with me after the manner of women, as the Bible says, wasn't it of Sarah? (*GW* 8, 891) and she uses Luther's words for sex: "der Wollust pflegen" (*GW* 8, 901, 918). The text returns to Genesis 18 when Rosalie confesses to Anna her lust for Ken Keaton, the young American with whom she has fallen in love (*GW* 8, 918). While she cites the Bible, which holds that miracles can only come from God, her modern idealism expects the miracle from herself. Her feelings, she wants to believe, can transform her body.

But not only the Bible quotations raise doubts about her self-made miracle; the language she uses also seems to refute her idealism, as she exclaims, "The miracle of my soul and my sensuality" (Wunder meiner Seele und Sinne) is "blissful pain" (selige Qual), "painful and shamefaced" (schmerz-und schamhaft) (*GW* 8, 903). She has stated earlier in the story that she had never experienced menstrual pains before (*GW* 8, 889). The words of the text call the miraculous self-made rejuvenation into question. This interpretation is confirmed by the name that Rosalie gives to her renewed love: "Heimsuchung" (visitation). This word, with connotations more ominous than ambiguous, connects "Die Betrogene" to other Mann texts, an instance of intertextuality that will be discussed later. But it is to be noted here that the word also carries biblical references, in a positive sense in the Lord's visitation of Sarah (Gen. 21:1), and as it is used in the iconography of Mary's visitation of Elisabeth (Luke 1:39–56), as well as for God's punishments, as in Leviticus 26:16 (the Luther translation uses the word).

Another religious reference appears near the end of the story. During a Sunday outing to the chateau Holterhof, where Rosalie, no longer the passive woman, will declare her love, the party encounters black swans floating on the moat surrounding the chateau. Ken Keaton has brought bread to feed the swans. Rosalie takes it from him, eating some of it because it has been warmed by his body. The wording of the text that follows, "and she took the bread and ate thereof," suggests the scene of Jesus' last supper.[7] The biblical scene is permeated by Jesus' foreknowledge of death. The text echoes this through the image of the jealous black swan, which angrily hisses at Rosalie. On her deathbed she understands the meaning of this symbol.[8] She accepts the envious and greedy animal as nature's messenger of death.

While Rosalie's last words present a possibility for coping with death in a godless world, this possibility is doubted at the same time by the presence of words of biblical origin. The biblical allusion implied when Rosalie seeks communion with her lover by her breaking of the bread, warm from his body, confronts her modernist religion with the Christian myth of death and resurrection, which reconciles imperfect "sinful" humans with a perfect God. However, instead of becoming united with her lover, the text has Rosalie die. While in her mind she transfers her love to nature and feels that her love is returned, the biblical allusions in the text object. Nature or the whole of being is not a character in a mythical narration who can return love. The totality of the world is undifferentiated and speechless. The biblical allusions cast doubts on the value of a private religion, because it does not possess a myth capable of binding a community together, a narration that is understood by all. Just as Rosalie's self-made rejuvenation is an illusion, her self-made religion may be also. The story plays with the possibility of coping with death when "God is dead." But it contains its own contradiction. It remains ironic play, and does not present a new doctrine.

In its own way, the story also touches Nietzsche's questioning of morality. The setting of the story is in the 1920s (*GW* 8, 877). Since there is no mention of the rampant inflation in Germany, which lasted into 1923, we may assume that the action takes place afterwards. Thomas Mann's fiftieth birthday occurred in 1925, which may well also be the year of Rosalie's fiftieth birthday mentioned at the beginning of the text (*GW* 8, 878). At that time, Mann, like Rosalie (*GW* 8, 927) might have considered loosening his strict moral discipline in the new atmosphere that followed after the rigid moral authority of the Wilhelminian Empire. But in reality he did not cease to suppress and keep secret his homoerotic desire. More than thirty years after the fall of the Wilhelminian Empire, in the summer of 1950, he discussed his need for that secret in his diary.[9] Similar entries can be found elsewhere in Mann's diaries. It is more than likely that "Die Betrogene" transformed Mann's memories of a temptation to break his self-imposed sexual discipline during the 1920s. A strong indication is that Mann has Rosalie live in Düsseldorf. That city was the hometown of the boy Klaus Heuser, with whom Mann had fallen in love in 1927.

"Die Betrogene" has passages that draw on Mann's most intimate and concealed desire for young men, such as when Rosalie is shaken by gazing at the naked arms of the young Ken Keaton (*GW* 8, 900).[10] In one moment Rosalie reflects on the possibility of renouncing her love and the "freedom" which would be the result of this renunciation (*GW* 8, 930, 931). Rosalie's thought of resignation is fleeting; it disappears completely. But it adds to the text's autobiographical dimension. Mann transposes his innermost experience, the renunciation of his true sexual desire, onto Rosalie. But she is a fictional character, thus free to shake off the need for renunciation and let her desire out, even talk about it, as Mann must have often wished to do.

As near as her self-liberating move may have been to Mann's wishes, Rosalie is not Mann. The autobiographical element of the text is incomplete without the contrasting figure of Anna, the artist who compensates her frustrated sexual desire by pouring it into her art. Anna's clubfoot and its consequence, her sexual frustration, has the same meaning as little Herr Friedemann's hunchback: it is a camouflaged symbol of an outsider existence forced by sexual otherness. Anna, like Rosalie, is not identical with Mann; indeed, she is not even similar. Rather, the autobiographical origin of the text can be found in two opposing fantasies: one is to give in to long-suppressed desire; the other is to continue to resist and discipline that temptation. The representation of Rosalie's sexual awakening, her self-liberation, becomes a cry for sexual liberation, as can be heard in much of Mann's work, beginning with his earliest story, "Gefallen" (Fallen, 1894).

The word "Heimsuchung" (visitation) in one passage of Mann's *Joseph in Ägypten* (Joseph in Egypt, 1936) links representations of fateful liberations of sexual repression in Mann's work. It occurs in "Die Betrogene" in a significant passage: it is the last word of the monologue in which Rosalie confesses her infatuation to herself. In Luther's Bible, the word can mean a friendly or a vengeful visitation, as we have seen. The dominant meaning in present-day German is of a catastrophic misfortune, and it is in this sense that it is used in the passage from *Joseph in Ägypten*. The word introduces the narration of the frustrated erotic sufferings of Mut-em-enet. The narrator takes the place of the author and reminisces about destructive visitations in two of his earlier works. The recurring theme, he claims, maintains a "unity" (Einheit) in his work, namely: "the invasion of intoxicated, destructive, annihilating powers into a well-framed life that had placed all its hope of dignity and a limited happiness on its self-control."[11] The two earlier works are not mentioned by name but are clearly suggested: "Der kleine Herr Friedemann" and "Der Tod in Venedig" (Death in Venice, 1912). The story of Mut-em-enet in *Joseph* will be the third work in which such a visitation takes place, and "Die Betrogene" too belongs into this sequence. In this text the word "Heimsuchung" is first spoken by Rosalie herself (*GW* 8, 903) and then by Anna, fearing for her mother: "Why do I always have the sense as if this whole visitation, whose blissful victim [beglücktes Opfer] you are, is akin to destruction?"[12] As in the cases of Friedemann, Aschenbach, and Mut-em-enet, Rosalie's blissful love is both liberation from a deprived existence and destruction.

"Die Betrogene," Mann's last completed fictional work, can be read as his testament left to the world. In his multifaceted language of several truths existing side by side, he represented one character's wish for liberation from sexual oppression and juxtaposed her with another who compensated for the renunciation of that wish by her artistic creativity, recognizing both the way he continued to live and the constant desire to break the pattern. As the liberation wish is fraught with its futility, so is the experiment with sexual love as a force connecting the self to the universe. The possibility of coping with death by way of a monistic religion remains not more than a possibility. However, the futility of creative attempts to make sense of life and death does not invalidate those attempts. In a language that rejects universal truths, they retain their worth.

Such a testament could only be written as fiction because of its many voices, its internal contrariness. Mann expressed his view of the world and his place in it much more convincingly in playful, multifaceted, ambiguous, ironic fiction than in the more direct forms of confessions or essays, because the equal or near equal value of the many voices in his texts produces their message. The irony of many voices is the essence of Mann's modernity. His writing style opposed the ideologies that were at each other's throat throughout his lifetime. Mann's ironic language is still needed in this century, which sees modernity being threatened by fundamentalisms that are as determined as past ideologies.

Notes

1 "Anna, sprich nicht von Betrug und höhnischer Grausamkeit der Natur. [. . .] Ungern geh' ich dahin — von euch, vom Leben mit seinem Frühling. Aber wie wäre denn Frühling ohne den Tod? Ist ja doch der Tod ein großes Mittel des Lebens, und wenn er für mich die Gestalt lieh von Auferstehung und Liebeslust, so war das nicht Lug, sondern Güte und Gnade. [. . .] Die Natur — ich habe sie immer geliebt, und Liebe — hat sie ihrem Kinde erwiesen" (*GW* 8, 950). Mann's collected works (*GW* 1–13) will hereafter be cited in the text.

2 *Tb* 6 April 1952.

3 For details about the entire biographical background see James N. Bade, *Die Betrogene aus neuer Sicht: Der autobiographische Hintergrund zu Thomas Manns letzter Erzählung* (Frankfurt am Main: R. G. Fischer, 1994).

4 *Tb* 11 July 1950.

5 *Die fröhliche Wissenschaft* (The Gay Science), Aphorism 125.

6 Friedrich Nietzsche, *Götzendämmerung* (Twilight of the Idols), "Wie die 'wahre Welt' endlich zur Fabel wurde" (How the "Real World" at last Became a Myth), *Jenseits von Gut und Böse* (Beyond Good and Evil), Aphorism 2.

7 "Und sie nahm von dem Brot und aß davon" (*GW* 8, 941). Cf. Matt. 26, Mark 14:22, Luke 22:19, 1 Cor. 11, 23–25.

[8] Cf. *GW* 8, 941–42, 950: "er hat mich angezischt" (he hissed at me).

[9] *Tb* 16 August 1950.

[10] See the contribution by Jens Rieckmann in this volume.

[11] "Es ist die Idee der Heimsuchung, des Einbruchs trunken zerstörender und vernichtender Mächte in ein Gefäßtes und mit allen seinen Hoffnungen auf Würde und ein bedingtes Glück der Fassung verschworenes Leben" (*GW* 5, 1085–86).

[12] "Warum muss mir immer zumute sein, als ob diese ganze Heimsuchung, deren beglücktes Opfer du bist, etwas mit Zerstörung zu tun hätte" (*GW* 8, 930).

Thomas Mann's Comedies

Herbert Lehnert

A COMEDY TRADITIONALLY IS CONSIDERED a humorous play in which a man and a woman look forward to a happy future together after having triumphed over adversities. Thomas Mann once called his second novel, *Königliche Hoheit* (Royal Highness, 1909) a "Lustspiel" (comedy), reacting to critics who had judged it to be a descent into banality. In a letter to the wife of his publisher he promised that never again would he write a comedy in which the lovers "get each other at the end."[1]

Critics were accustomed to the tragic mode in Mann's work. In *Buddenbrooks* (1901) a family lives for a business at the expense of love, but that sacrifice cannot arrest the decline of the firm. The end of the novel shows an assembly of frustrated women. In *Königliche Hoheit* love triumphs and the novel ends with a marriage. Mann was justified in calling the work a comedy, though it is, of course, not a play. Neither does it descend into banality. But more works in the tragic mode were coming, and they were considered the more relevant ones: in "Der Tod in Venedig" (Death in Venice, 1912) a great writer succumbs to passion and death; *Der Zauberberg* (The Magic Mountain, 1924) makes its reader doubt whether its protagonist Hans Castorp will survive the First World War, and *Doktor Faustus* (1947) ends with the insanity and death of a great German genius, while the narrator mourns a devastated Germany.

There is much humor in Mann's texts, including the two texts to be considered here as quasi-comedies: *Königliche Hoheit* and *Der Erwählte* (The Chosen One, published in English as The Holy Sinner, 1951). In both texts a protagonist who is alienated from the world, an outsider, and thus in a situation tending more toward the tragic than the comic, meets a happy or conciliatory end. The way the outsider is reconciled to his destiny in a comedic mode is to be understood in the light of Nietzsche's aphorism 270 from *Jenseits von Gut und Böse* (Beyond Good and Evil, 1886). In it Nietzsche claims a distinctive ("vornehm") status for humans who have suffered deeply. The ranking order among humans, Nietzsche maintains (and Mann liked to quote this statement) is almost determined by the ability to suffer.[2] A person with such an outsider status, Nietzsche continues, needs masks. There are outwardly serene individuals ("heitere Menschen") who attempt to conceal with their outward appearance that they are struggling with deep sadness.[3] In this way Mann's "comedies" stand in a reciprocal relationship to his tragedies: *Königliche Hoheit* with "Der Tod in Venedig," *Der Erwählte* with *Doktor Faustus.*

Because of this reciprocity the tragic mode in Mann's works is to be understood in Nietzsche's terms as ultimately life affirming. Tragedy, Nietzsche wrote in *Die Geburt der Tragödie aus dem Geiste der Musik* (The Birth of Tragedy, 1872), transforms tragic suffering into Apollonian serenity (Heiterkeit) and thus leads to acceptance of life as a whole.[4] In *Buddenbrooks,* the future writer Kai Graf Mölln will transform his experience of the decaying family of his friend into the realm of the symbolic. Kai's love for his friend, the last male Buddenbrook, impresses the desolate group of women in the final scene. Kai stands here for the author; the novel we read is transformed love. *Königliche Hoheit,* and also in a different fashion *Der Erwählte,* have a life-affirming element; in both texts a couple looks forward to a future without adversity.

In "Tonio Kröger" (1903), Mann's fictionalized program of writing, the alienated, lonely, singular artist is able to transform "the comical and the miserable" (Komik und Elend),[5] and this ability compensates for his feeling of exclusion. The text alludes to the homoerotic roots of Tonio's outsider position. From his distant perspective he develops a "fruitful" love for the insiders: "In it is longing and melancholic envy, and a bit of contempt and a full measure of chaste bliss" (*GW* 8, 281).[6] This sentence concludes the representation of Tonio Kröger's homoerotic love for Hans Hansen. When the same sentence appears at the end, it stands for Tonio's achievement: he has transformed his outsider situation into art (*GW* 8, 338). His alienation however remains.

The earliest record we have of Mann's conception of the story of the prince that became *Königliche Hoheit* occurs in a letter of 1903. He planned a counterpart to "Tonio Kröger," which had been published that year. A prince appears in passing in "Tonio Kröger": the artist's feeling of alienation is compared to that of a prince walking unrecognized in a crowd (*GW* 8, 297). When Mann began writing the text of the novel in 1906 (after abandoning earlier drafts), he had married, and his young family was growing. Was it possible that the lonely prince might be saved from the fate of alienation after all? Perhaps the prince could discover love and be converted into a person serving mankind? If he could still retain his elevated position while serving, his story would become a novel with a comedic end.

Königliche Hoheit

The novel begins with a short "Vorspiel" (prelude) that demonstrates Prince Klaus Heinrich's isolation. Although he wears the uniform of a mere lieutenant, a general greets him submissively in the street. Walking, the prince catches the attention of everyone, and as a consequence he is not able to walk freely; sometimes he even seems to limp. He is well known and yet "moves like a stranger" among his people, walking in the crowd "as if surrounded by emptiness" (*GW 2*, 11). The first chapter that follows is called "Die Hemmung" (the inhibition). We see the prince as a newborn infant, and see that he has been born with a deformed, withered hand. (This motif was familiar to Mann's readers at the time because Kaiser Wilhelm II was born with a withered left hand.) Even as a child Klaus Heinrich is constantly made aware of his anomaly: when he wants to embrace his beautiful mother with both arms he meets a cold glance, and she admonishes him to pay heed to his hand (*GW 2*, 59). As the prince grows older, the need to hide his left hand inhibits his freedom of movement when performing his representational duties.

To represent "highness" (Hoheit) becomes the prince's calling; but producing faultless appearances of "highness" requires almost superhuman self-discipline. The members of the prince's dynasty are called the "Grimmburger" ("Grimm" means wrath in German). The value of the strict discipline necessary for showing off "highness" is constantly reduced in the text, because a royal family is shown to be useless in a modern, early-twentieth-century state. Critics of the administration are called "die Krittler" (*GW 2*, 37 and passim), a German colloquialism referring to people who habitually offer negative and destructive criticism. The word is always to be understood ironically in this text: biting criticism cutting through the monarchical trappings describes the true decrepit state of affairs. Characters are named accordingly: one nobleman is "Trümmerhauff" (*GW 2*, 19), translatable as "pile of ruins"; he administers the finances of the court. A general is called "Graf Schmettern" (*GW 2*, 14), suggesting the empty blare of a trumpet, and the gait of the court marshal in charge of ceremonies is represented repeatedly as "schwänzelnd," a kind of cringing swagger (*GW 2*, 107, 361). The grand duke's wealth lies in his possession of farmland, but agriculture does not yield sufficient income in a modern economy; the court is deeply in debt. Decaying palaces are a recurring theme in the novel. While soap manufacturer Unschlitt can easily afford central heating in his house, the grand duke must shiver in his palace. The country is in severe debt as well.

All of this seems to change in the end, as it would in a fairy tale. But while the marriage of the prince releases him from his loneliness, and the narrator makes it appear as if the economy of the grand duchy is also improving, closer scrutiny reveals that the help of the billionaire father-in-law consists merely of buying treasury notes at normal interest rates. The influx of capital retires some but not all of the duchy's high-interest debts (*GW 2*, 353). The grand duchy's economy improves for a time, but the satiric representation of the monarchical veneer of Wilhelminian Germany remains intact. This anti-conservative message is a background concern of the novel, but more than that, it is structurally important.

The plot leads the outsider out of his lonely predicament. This movement reflects (and is motivated by) the desire of the outsider-writer, because he too wants his alienation eased. The Prince's empty ceremonial duties of representing his brother the Grand Duke, his royal family, and the country by opening fairs and holding audiences in which he is unable to really help the petitioners are similar to the formal existence of the writer whose "product" is make-believe, in contrast to the tangible goods produced by his fellow citizens. The writer's efforts can be made more useful, however, by writing in the realistic mode. Reference to the real world offers comparisons to the life of the reader; it activates his worldview, and may even hint at improvements in the social sphere. In this sense the humorous treatment of the Grand Duchy in *Königliche Hoheit,* the representation of its decay, attains both a realistic and a symbolic significance. It functions as a symbol for the alienation of the writer, and alleviates his uselessness at the same time by criticizing the anachronistic ceremonies and customs of German courtly life. The tale is neither a fantasy nor an odd private affair of no social interest. However, Thomas Mann insisted in *Betrachtungen eines Unpolitischen* (Reflections of a Non-Political Man, 1918), that whatever social or political improvements his texts may suggest, they do not subordinate themselves to a political agenda: they remain free agents (*GW* 12, 574–76). Suggesting reality, they remain free from it.

The comedic conclusion of *Königliche Hoheit,* the marriage of the prince, means the redemption of the outsider; the withered hand does not need to be hidden any longer. But at the same time the "highness" of the prince is to be preserved because his "high" appearance symbolizes, humorously, the special status of the art of writing. Literature is meant to be as free from conventional ties to reality as is the representational function of the prince. The writer needs his outsider status for his unique point of view beyond conventions and trivial obligations. The intense discipline with which Prince Klaus Heinrich exercises the art of representation in the novel stands for the disciplined language of the writer. Disciplined artistic writing must separate itself from common language, always risking the loss of its communicative function. Elevating literary language above common, ordinary speech may bring it to the point of mere self-referentiality.

At around the same time Mann wrote *Königliche Hoheit,* the literary circle around Stefan George demonstrated that very danger. George's poem "Die tote Stadt" (The Dead City) in his collection *Der Siebente Ring* (1907) juxtaposes an old aristocratic city that preserves its sacred images — its tower pointing to eternity — with a modern port city situated below the old town. The new harbor is busy with trade, industry, and pleasure, symbolizing modernity while the old town is poor. Yet the old town is healthy despite its poverty, and refuses to share its restorative climate with sick supplicants from the harbor town below, who offer valuables merely to be able to breathe the air and drink from the old town's spring.[7] The value system at work in the poem is obvious: it attributes eternal value to art and condemns all values of modernity, especially monetary value. *Königliche Hoheit,* in contrast, recognizes, even promotes change.

The comedic structure of Mann's novel aims at a move away from the self-isolation of "high" literature, its self-referentiality. This aim is recognizable when Klaus Heinrich, even as a child, develops an awareness of his growing exclusion from the reality of human experience. He goes exploring ("stöbern") in the castle, only to discover that the outside world is indeed different; yet without knowing how it differs (*GW 2*, 64). The action of the novel constantly plays with the theme of exclusion. Prince Klaus Heinrich becomes a student without really studying, and, as an adult, his "high calling" consists of representational duties that allow him to sidestep any form of reality. The parallel to literature is invoked when Prince Klaus Heinrich finds value in ceremonial representation because it heightens life by connecting the people and their community with the "highness" that royalty embodies. But this elevation is only possible in connection with strict self-discipline. Klaus Heinrich's desire to appear irreproachable at all times is symbolic of the care that the writer uses in shaping his language. The prince produces the "high-pitched moments" (hochgespannte Augenblicke) when his very presence transforms ordinary days into special occasions, and turns gray life into poetry (*GW 2*, 159), as the writer transforms chaotic reality into a sensible whole.

Constructing an imaginary world and ruling it worked as a compensation for Mann's repression of his sexuality. His sacrifice was dear, so his compensation had to be extremely valuable as well. He had followed his older brother into a life of literature, although he must have remembered how his brother had ridiculed his early homoerotic poems; now he needed the assurance that he had surpassed his model. This competitive ambition is mirrored in *Königliche Hoheit* by Klaus Heinrich's relationship to his older brother, the reigning grand duke. The fictional brothers engage in a dialogue in which the sick, neurotic, decadent Albrecht transfers most of his ceremonial and representational duties to his younger brother. When Albrecht asks his younger brother to take over all his "representative duties" (repräsentive Pflichten), Klaus Heinrich, startled, interprets his words such that he asks: "Are you thinking of abdication, Albrecht?" (Du denkst an Abdikation, Albrecht?; *GW 2*, 156). Since Mann's real-life brother Heinrich could recognize himself in some features of the fictional grand duke, this question contained a cruel message to Heinrich, who could not match the success of *Buddenbrooks.* In a letter to Heinrich, Thomas confessed to be uncomfortable thinking of Heinrich reading *Königliche Hoheit* and in it about the "play" on their sibling relations.[8] Here we are provided with a glance into the real underpinnings of the invention of the story of the lonely prince. Thomas's competition with his brother is inseparable from the difference in their sexuality. Klaus Heinrich has to hide his withered left hand; Thomas Mann needed his greater success as a writer in order to convince himself that his sexuality did not marginalize him.

Klaus Heinrich's life as prince reflects the deficiencies of the outsider-writer and their compensation by discipline. Telling are the allusive references to "Tonio Kröger." The scene in the "Vorspiel" of *Königliche Hoheit* in which the prince is shown walking awkwardly in a crowd has its parallel in Tonio Kröger's exemplification of the artist's feeling of separateness. The same feeling can be seen on the face of a prince who walks unrecognized in a crowd (*GW* 8, 297). Both texts have scenes in which a quadrille dance proves both Tonio Kröger and Klaus Heinrich to be deficient dancers and produce situations that force them to recognize their outsider status (*GW* 8, 285–88; *GW* 2, 97–105). Klaus Heinrich's teacher Überbein emphasizes the necessity of self-discipline for the prince. When his own ambition fails, and his social environment turns against him, depriving him of his honor, he commits suicide. His extreme individualism is belied by his end, which shows him dependent on his reputation, on his honor: on society after all.

Überbein's name is that of his petite bourgeois adoptive parents (*GW* 2, 81). This explanation barely camouflages a satiric reference to Friedrich Nietzsche's "Übermensch," the formula for Nietzsche's morality of a self-created higher humanity. Überbein's teachings give Klaus Heinrich a sense of self-worth and make him understand that his empty formal existence still points to a higher humanity. But the self-negating discipline Überbein demands increases rather than helps the prince's human deficiency. It takes a woman's love to heal the prince from his alienation. This stands in stark contrast to Nietzsche's tragic, even cruel, view of the world and the human condition unmitigated by love. Although he appreciated Nietzsche highly, we often find in Mann's works implied criticism of aspects of his philosophy. *Königliche Hoheit* is no exception. The change of direction is indicated in the text: Klaus Heinrich hears the news of Überbein's suicide on the day of his engagement to Imma, the billionaire's daughter, who will be able to change his life. This change does not mean a descent into conventionality, because she herself is a special person, an outsider. Her sharp-edged language and her interest in mathematics make her different from the average young woman at the time.

The prince's entrance into reality, though not into conventionality, resembles Mann's own settling down in bourgeois society. In spite of this parallel, the novel is not to be read as a veiled biography of Mann. It is much more an experiment with variants in the relationship of the writer with his public, sharpened by Thomas Mann's special status. The experiment asks whether an ambitious, original writer must remain an outsider or whether he may have a function in human society, with his outsider status merely used as a point of view. Other tragic — or tragicomic — possible ways to treat the outsider problem occupied Mann's mind at the time. Notebook entries of 1904 toy with plans for writings based on the notion that the artist will lose the creative urge when he gives up his outsider status;[9] another note of the same time problematizes the effect of success on the writer. This may be taken as the seed of the conception of "Der Tod in Venedig."[10] These ideas are found in a notebook together with notes for details of *Königliche Hoheit*, jotted down during the writing.

Königliche Hoheit contains an experimental program with no binding power. Mann playfully transforms Nietzsche's idea of a higher humanity into the image of a prince, symbolizing the writer's distance from reality. The essence of Nietzsche's higher humanity is complete creative freedom, human freedom of self-creation in the absence of a divine world order. Nietzsche's seriousness, his tragic vision of the world, is playfully and humorously transformed in *Königliche Hoheit*. Not only are the shortcomings of Überbein's ambitious seriousness exposed, but there is also a scene that makes fun of a narrow application of Nietzsche's teachings to literature: Klaus Heinrich's conversation with the poet Martini, who won a prize for composing a hymn about the joy of life. The poet, it turns out, merely acts out the joy he extols in his poem; he is unable to live it. The satire about Martini is aimed at Heinrich Mann's reception of Nietzsche and his application of Nietzsche's vitalism to his neo-Renaissance novels. With this scene Mann turns Nietzsche's description of Richard Wagner as the "actor" ("Schauspieler")[11] against Nietzsche's own glorification of Life. Such playful use of creative freedom against its prophet criticizes Nietzsche's seriousness, but it is intended to apply his basic message, not devalue it.

Freedom from set rules is what Klaus Heinrich's future bride Imma teaches the disciplined prince. She has learned to tolerate the half-mad fantasies of a noble woman hired to keep her company. Forcing Klaus Heinrich to tolerate her companion as well is the beginning of an education that leads him out of the confining aspect of his discipline. As Klaus Heinrich recognizes that the sense of form that Überbein has taught him constitutes a limitation, he begins serious studies of his country's finances in order to fill his formal existence with content.

Since the prince is a symbol for the representational function of the writer, Klaus Heinrich's new sense of reality could be misunderstood as a call for political activism in writing or for fiction produced for the acquisition of knowledge. Instead, Mann actually mocks his pretense of knowledge in his writings. The prince takes the time, before he is scheduled to perform a ceremonial function — for example, opening an exhibition or dedicating a monument — to inform himself about the historical background. He picks up learned terms and historic dates. Thus prepared, his speeches give the impression of solid knowledge (*GW* 2, 162). Mann sometimes conducted extensive studies for fictional works, for example for *Joseph und seine Brüder* (Joseph and his Brothers, 1933–43), but the aim was appearance, not scholarly solidity or historical exactness. Klaus Heinrich's studies neither advocate a return to direct monarchical government in the style of Wilhelm II before 1908, nor do they advocate that the writer become politically active. The prince studies finances so that he can support his formal existence by understanding the workings of the state that he represents and imbues with an elevated humanity, but he will still leave the affairs themselves to the care of experts. Mann's fictional prince symbolizes a writer who does not try to direct reality but who consciously and conscientiously observes the direction of human affairs. He contributes to them by representing and discussing them together with their underlying ideologies and moralities, by experimenting with them freely without the restraining considerations of social and political actuality.

Because of the nationalist ardor in some passages of *Betrachtungen eines Unpolitischen,* Thomas Mann, in contrast to Heinrich, has long been considered a conservative. *Königliche Hoheit,* with its conventional marriage at the end, could support that notion, the more so when the autobiographical parallel of Mann's own marriage is considered. The family father no longer appeared to be an outsider. By now we have enough insight into Mann's life to know that the family served him as his life's protection. He did not want to be considered a writer with a homosexual agenda, nor did he want to appear as bohemian; bohemianism being anarchic. Yet the student of Nietzsche remained anarchic at heart, and Mann put this lingering feeling into his writings. The novel about Frederick II of Prussia that he considered writing for a while would have demonstrated to himself and the public that he had arrived in the establishment so that all anarchic tendencies would be well hidden. However, not even that novel was planned as another royalty novel for well-to-do burghers of the Wilhelminian Empire; it was to analyze and critique greatness, not celebrate it. And soon Mann cast aside the plan for the Frederick novel in favor of the first few chapters of *Die Bekenntnisse des Hochstaplers Felix Krull* (written 1910–11 and 1912–13), a novel that made fun of the established order. "Der Tod in Venedig" (1912) demonstrates the powerful pull of anarchy that can slumber even in the most disciplined artist. This formal masterwork narrates the destruction of Gustav von Aschenbach, a writer of works so accepted into the canon that they were even used as teaching tools. Aschenbach is defeated by the vital power in himself, his homoerotic sexuality, a power that destroys his social as well as his artistic discipline. Nietzsche's Dionysus defeats him, and this defeat also threatens the austere happiness, "das strenge Glück," of *Königliche Hoheit.*

Der Erwählte

The novel *Der Erwählte* (1951) is not a comedy in the full sense. It ends with a couple having an intimate but non-sexual relationship, while their incestuous marriage remains a humorous hint toward tolerance. The action of *Der Erwählte* largely follows the medieval legend of Gregorius retold by Hartmann von Aue. The novel parodies sexual morality as espoused in the Bible. While Hartmann's protagonist Gregorius is eventually saved by God's will, and while the legend praises the greatness of God's grace, Mann's modernized epic parody uses the medieval narrator to transform his Christian belief into modern tolerance. While the sin that is to be forgiven is incest, not homosexuality, Mann continued to camouflage his wish for a morality that would recognize his homoerotic desire as legitimate love.

Der Erwählte again plays with the motif of the alienated outsider, and ends happily; *Der Erwählte* belongs to the comedic mode. And in more ways than one, this late novel is the continuation of *Königliche Hoheit:* Gregorius is another prince who overcomes his alienated extraordinariness, his sense of being special, which I will call singularity. At the end he becomes socially useful. The sound of the name of Grimald, Gregorius's father, appearing at the beginning of the story, reminds us of the Grimmburger family in the earlier novel. Imma in *Königliche Hoheit* has a "pearl-pale face" (*GW* 2, 203), it appears "pale like ivory" (241), and she has black eyes (209). The twins Wiliges and Sibylla in *Der Erwählte* have faces of "ivory-colored paleness," and their eyes are "night-blue" (*GW* 7, 21). The twins are special, singular as a pair, different even from their parents. Wiliges, the male twin, at fifteen, excels in knightly pursuits, but, like Prince Klaus Heinrich's achievements, his victories are only pretense. When the reader meets Pope Gregorius, his dark eyes are mentioned together with protruding cheekbones (*GW* 7, 251). This similarity to Prince Klaus Heinrich may be surprising, since the prince shared those facial features with his subjects, making him representative rather than singular. Pope Gregorius's earnestness recalls that of Prince Klaus Heinrich. At that late stage, Gregorius has overcome his pride of singularity. The Knight Gregorius's "tight clasping hand" (festhaltende Hand) (*GW* 7, 149, 151, 200, 217, 238, 254) is a contrasting motif to Klaus Heinrich's withered hand.

The playful medieval narration of *Der Erwählte* was written between 1948 and 1950.[12] After finishing *Doktor Faustus,* one of the fictional works by Leverkühn, "Gesta Romanorum," a parodic play with medieval legends, lingered in Mann's mind, specifically the legend about Pope Gregorius. Zeitblom, the narrator of *Doktor Faustus,* explains why these legends had enticed his friend, the composer. Leverkühn used them to produce a work that reacted to the "inflated pathos of an artistic era about to pass into history." Here Zeitblom is alluding to Wagner, who had taken his material from Romanticized medieval subjects (*GW* 6, 425). Leverkühn's musical puppet play is designed as a travesty of such Romantic pathos by replacing moralistic priestliness with erotic farce (*GW* 6, 426). Zeitblom narrates the comic effects of Adrian's work rather coolly and seriously, and the author makes it clear why: Zeitblom is jealous because Rudolf Schwerdtfeger expresses his appreciation for Leverkühn's composition by means of an intimate gesture (*GW* 6, 426–27). Schwerdtfeger, otherwise not very intellectual, seems to have understood that Leverkühn's facetious parody of medieval themes is aimed at the dissolution of conventional sexual morality. The musical style, with its simple instrumentation, makes fun of Wagner's pompousness and thus hints at Nietzsche's *Der Fall Wagner* (The Case of Wagner, 1888) and further to Nietzsche's criticism of morality.

The puppet play in the novel provides occasion for a passage in which Leverkühn develops his idea of a new common culture, freed from the dilemma of having the intellectual elite as its sole audience ("Bildungselite," *GW* 6, 428); the new art of the future would serve the community and, instead of *having* culture, would itself *be* culture (*GW* 6, 429). A culture serving the community does not sound like Nietzsche, but Leverkühn's vision of a new and entirely different culture does. Mann repeatedly rejected suggestions that *Der Erwählte* was meant as an example of such new art,[13] and he has Zeitblom immediately reprove Leverkühn's ideas: the lonely outsider is not to speak of community. Art, Zeitblom is convinced, is intellect (Geist), and intellect does not have to feel obligated to the community; it ought to preserve its freedom, its nobility. Ideas like the one just expressed, Zeitblom objects, do not fit Leverkühn's pride. This is Zeitblom's rather determined and narrow point of view, which is different from the experimental attitude of the author Mann. Zeitblom is a representative of the German intellectual class which insisted on "high art." Leverkühn's different vision of a new art that no longer is proud of being "high" is still in the vein of Tonio Kröger's love of the common people. While the conflict between the pride of being different and the desire to be like others is a common affliction, "Tonio Kröger" had demonstrated how central it was to Mann's aesthetics because these aesthetics were rooted in his sexuality. Mann's works are variants of problems resulting from the conflict between the pride of the outsider and the need to love and be loved.

Hartmann's *Gregorius* offered the story of a noble character condemned to singularity, and, at the same time, offered an opportunity to parody the morality that caused the condemnation. Thomas Mann came near to saying that his own homoerotic desire played a role in selecting the material. In a letter of 11 January 1951, he told the critic Walter Rilla: "The printing of the little novel of incest is finished and I read the galleys. Below the surface it suggests that the 'unnatural' actually is something natural. One is not to be surprised when equal and equal love each other."[14]

At the center of *Der Erwählte* is the resolution of the dialectic contrast between the pride of the outsider and the loving service of humanity the great pope exercises at the end. By bridging the gap between the outsider's distance from his community and his desire to be accepted by it, both "comedies" symbolize the artist's need both to be uncommon and to have his work recognized. "Der Tod in Venedig" and *Doktor Faustus* refuse to bridge the gap, treating the artist's conflicting needs in the tragic mode. In *Doktor Faustus* the alienation of the genius is connected with Christian hostility to sex. This hostility informs a significant part of traditional morality; it becomes the origin of the stigma of the homosexual. Leverkühn's pact with the devil is concluded by sexual intercourse, a deliberate infection of himself with syphilis. The devil is sin, and sin is in sex. This is the Christian valuation used in *Doktor Faustus* to signify the sinfulness of Leverkühn's deliberate acceptance of his otherness. By seeking the infection, he excludes himself from the conventional order. But when he longs for grace nevertheless, he pleads for the removal of the condemnation of the outsider-genius as sinner, and pleads in despair for a new order of things, a new morality that rewards the hard working artist with integration into the human order. *Der Erwählte* in contrast plays humorously with Christian morality. Its end is grace without despair. The plot of the legend requires penance for the sin of unknowingly committing incest, but not only the sin but also the penance appears grotesque to the modern reader. In a mock effort to make the penance more realistic, reducing Gregorius to a marmot-like creature and nourishing him with "earth milk," Mann humorously emphasizes its grotesqueness. *Der Erwählte* does not continue the theme of grace of *Doktor Faustus;* it reverses it. The tragedy is confronted with a comedy.

Moral rigidity is brought to the story not by an insisting cleric. Rather, the knight to whom the incestuous couple turns for advice forces a cruel form of atonement on the sinners. Mann calls this knight "Eisengrein." "Eisen" characterizes him as inflexible as iron, and "grein" suggests "greinen," meaning comfortless weeping. Knight Eisengrein's moral standard is not satisfied. It not only insists on the separation and penance of the sinners, it also considers it necessary to put the child, the fruit of the incest, out to sea. Eisengrein's wife characterizes his attitude as "harsh benevolence" (harte Gutmütigkeit) (*GW* 7, 54). Sibylla, the mother of the child, while first submitting to what she considers the order of the world, later calls Eisengrein an "Unhold" (fiend) (*GW* 7, 55). Not even the narrator, the faithful monk, defends Eisengrein's righteousness. Even though the characters seem to consider their incest to be a disturbance of the divine order, the seriousness of that disturbance is playfully undermined by the repetition of the many and varied kinship relations: their father is also their father-in-law, and the brother, the father of the child, is also his uncle, and so on. Eisengrein is the first to mention the odd relationships of the child (*GW* 7, 44). Mann's version of the legend provides quite a different sense of "sin," one that is similar to that of Adrian Leverkühn in *Doktor Faustus,* though it is valued differently. The "sin" of the brother-sister-parents, the twins Wiliges and Sibylla, is their pride in their distinctive singularity. Their incest means that they mutually love their extraordinariness.

Hartmann narrates the incest itself in detail; he has the brother force himself on his sister. Mann narrates the sex scene in even more detail but makes it much more mutual. As in the case of Siegmund and Sieglinde in "Wälsungenblut" (The Blood of the Walsungs, 1905), the pride of being different and the power of sexual attraction are woven together. In Hartmann's epic, the brother is not named; the name Mann gives him, Wiliges, refers to Schopenhauer's Will, which is not the free will of the individual but an irrational life-power, the focus of which is sex. Leverkühn's deliberate infection with syphilis means deliberate self-exclusion from humanity, from the chain of the generations. Wiliges and Sybilla's incest also means lack of concern for humanity. But their sex act does not remove them from the human order. Their child becomes especially beautiful and attractive; for nature there is no "sin" in their union, as the text emphasizes explicitly (*GW* 7, 53). The structure of the novel is pitched toward a happy ending, to comedy instead of tragedy. This structure ultimately justifies the twins' sense of their singularity, their faith in being different. While the tragic mode of *Doktor Faustus* associates his uniqueness with despair, the comic mode of *Der Erwählte* preserves hope for atonement.

The problems of singularity are played out in *Der Erwählte* along the plot of the legend. The child from the incest becomes the primordial outsider. Even before he is born he is marked as an "impermissible and placeless" child (unstatthafte und stättenlose Kind) (*GW* 7, 40). The word "impermissible" refers to human sexual prohibitions; he is what is placeless in God's order. The idea that there is "no place on earth" for the child (*GW* 7, 55, 114) is a basic motif that drives the text forward. It is played out when the boy is exposed to the sea in a barrel, when he leaves the monastery he considered home, when he leaves wife and children to do penance, when he stays for seventeen years on a lonely rock.

The sin for which Gregorius does his extraordinary penance is not an act of free will. According to even medieval theology Gregorius does not commit a sin when he unknowingly marries his mother. Gregorius's sinfulness, accordingly, has created much difficulty for the interpreters of Hartmann's *Gregorius.*[15] The sin is more of mythical origin: myth knows inherited guilt, and the father's actions are visited on the children. In this mythical, nontheological sense the violation of God's order is incorporated in the child of the sinful union. In Hartmann's *Gregorius* this mythical sin is heightened, since the father, the incestuous brother, does not even leave for his promised pilgrimage to the Holy Land. He suffers so much from losing his love that he dies of grief. The incest is not atoned for and thus the guilt weighs more heavily on the son, again in mythical, not in theological terms. The idea of mythical guilt is grotesque for the modern reader. Mann increases its grotesqueness by having Gregorius invoke his male prerogative of final decision when he leaves for his great penance against the more reasonable solution of the mother-wife (*GW* 7, 180).

Since the "sin" in Mann's version lies much more in the singularity of the chosen people, his Gregorius and his Sybilla know on a deep level of understanding how closely related they are. The mother remarries her beloved brother in the son, and the son marries his resemblance in his mother. In other words, both repeat the incest that produced Gregorius, loving their shared singularity. The blemish of both incests is reduced if not outright canceled by a true mutual love that produces beautiful children. In this way the text says: sexual prohibitions are not rooted in nature, but are cultural constructs. Mann had read Freud's *Totem und Tabu* (1912) with admiration. The value of prohibitive sexual rules is again questioned toward the end of Mann's text when the adultery of the woman Gudula produces a highly gifted child. Gregorius's guilt is in the narcissistic exclusiveness of love for his own self. This guilt is atoned for by extreme loneliness: Gregory on the rock lives his sin. God's grace absolves him from self-love by a call to a higher office.

Gregorius's "guilt," a condition rather than a transgression, was a very personal issue for his author. *Der Erwählte* plays with the dialectic if not the paradox in Mann's relationship to his work: high artistic quality is achieved by the artist being distant from his community, by looking into himself, by self-love; but the artist needs this high artistic quality in order for his work to be accepted by the very community from whose "normal" life, its conventions, he separates himself. Thomas Mann must have felt even more alienated from the majority of his fellow burghers because of his homosexual inclination. Relief from this alienation beckoned when the "normal" burghers read his writings. The marmot-like shape that Gregorius takes while doing penance on the rock can be read as a symbol for separation from humanity. His re-transformation into human shape is accomplished by eating bread and drinking wine. The process, emphasized by the title of the chapter, is called "Wandlung," a word that German uses for transubstantiation. The allusion to the Eucharist means communion, joining humanity. The "sin" of narcissistic separation, of singularity, is cancelled for Gregorius by being called to the service of mankind.

The motif of transubstantiation also points to a mythical element in Christianity that is associated with a motif from classical antiquity. While Hartmann nourished Gregorius only with a meager source of water, Mann has him nourished by "earth-milk," an idea and the classical origin of it he learned from an essay by his friend Karl Kerényi.[16] The implication is playful tolerance: the Greco-Roman base of our culture is more natural than Christian doctrine, but the Christian faith has remained in touch with myth, and thus its doctrines are subject to tolerant interpretations.

Mann uses a narrator as a device to soften the rigidity of Christian morality and open it to mythical-symbolic ironic play. The traveling Irish monk Clemens as "spirit of narration" claims similarity with providence — that he rejects this notion almost simultaneously is not enough to bring him back into the medieval humility (GW 7, 116). In St. Gallen, as well as in his Irish monastery, Clemens writes, moderate asceticism is combined with humanistic instruction (Bildung): "the religion of Jesus and the dedication to classical studies must go hand in hand in combating coarseness" (GW 7, 11). The voice of Clemens is used playfully to question the doctrine of papal primacy when his language undermines his own dutiful assurances of faith in the doctrine (GW 7, 12). Love scenes are not appropriate for the monk and his habit, he claims (GW 7, 159), but he obviously enjoys describing them in detail, thereby impeaching the asceticism that he represents. Contrastive humor characterizes this text and serves to reduce the dogmatism of sinfulness.

Mann made one of the two Romans who are to bring Gregorius to Rome a layman, the other a high prelate. When they meet Gregorius, who is still shaped like a marmot, it is the cleric who feels that the propriety of the church will be offended by Gregorius's appearance, while the layman, the scion of an old Roman family, has the stronger faith in God's power to engender miracles (GW 7, 227–28). Mann uses the miracle of the bells of Rome, ringing spontaneously, as an introduction to the power of the "spirit of narration" (Geist der Erzählung) at the beginning of his text. The spirit of narration identifies himself at first by "ich bin es," the formula for a divine apparition. Only then the humble monk Clemens introduces himself (GW 7, 9–10). Since the noise of the bells soon become a nuisance, weaker souls pray to heaven that it may stop. But the narrator is thoroughly informed about the goings on in heaven. He assures us how well he understands that heaven at this occasion is in too festive a mood to be inclined to lend its ear to such petty pleas. The child of disgrace (das Schandkind) was to be led to the see of St. Peter (GW 7, 234–35). The happy ending of the comedy, the scene of recognition between mother and son, wife and husband, is of a playful nature because Sibylla only pretends not to recognize her son and husband. "We thought to offer entertainment to God with our doings" (GW 7, 257), she says, revealing that the comedic character of the text is in its many details.

The medieval framework reappears when Gregorius as Pope strictly punishes heresy (GW 7, 238). This motif does not occur in Hartmann's epic but is reported of the historical Gregory the First. Gregorius's conformity with church doctrine and politics is immediately canceled by examples of his governing. He is more inclined to absolve than to bind (GW 7, 239), and his missionary plans are characterized as enlightened methods to be handled with "freedom" and latitude (Freiheit der Aufklärungsmethoden) (*GW* 7, 239). Gregorius shows as much tolerance for heathen habits as he can.

At the very end, the narrator Clemens, in his role as monk, warns against drawing false moral conclusions from the story and insists on hard penance as means of justification. But he adds: "But it is prudent to divine the chosen one in the sinner, and this is prudent for the sinner himself. Because the foreknowledge of his being chosen may dignify him and make his sinfulness fruitful, so that it may carry him high" (*GW* 7, 260).[17] This no longer refers to Gregorius, and medieval thought does not participate, even playfully, in these words. They refer instead to the writer who suffers from his singularity and who needs "high flights," high accomplishments, to be accepted by his community. After these sentences Clemens returns to his medieval voice and asks for prayers "so that we all, together with the characters of whom I have spoken, see each other again in paradise" (*GW* 7, 260). This ironic playfulness reminds the reader of the ending of *Buddenbrooks*. As Sesemi Weichbrodt's assurance is the wrong answer to the question "Was ist das" with which *Buddenbrooks* begins, so the story of sinfulness and redemptive grace ends in playful irony. It is this playful irony that carries author and reader high, though not to a definite place.

Notes

[1] *DüD* 1, 258.

[2] ". . . es bestimmt beinahe die Rangordnung, *wie* tief Menschen leiden können." *KSA* 5, 25.

[3] *KSA* 5, 225–26.

[4] Friedrich Nietzsche, *Die Geburt der Tragödie aus dem Geiste der Musik,* especially section 9, *KSA* 1, 64–71.

[5] *GW* 8, 290. Thomas Mann's collected works (*GW* 1–13) will hereafter be cited in the text.

[6] "Sehnsucht ist darin und schwermütiger Neid und ein klein wenig Verachtung und eine ganze keusche Seligkeit."

[7] Stefan George, *Werke: Ausgabe in zwei Bänden,* vol. 1 (Düsseldorf: Helmut Küpper, 1968, 1974), 243–44.

[8] *TM/HM,* 140 or *DüD* 1, 246.

[9] *Nb* 2 (7–12), 104, 107, 108, 111, 121–22, 122. Some of these notes form the idea for *Doktor Faustus.*

[10] *Nb* 2 (7–12), 120.

[11] "Die Heraufkunft des Schauspielers in der Musik" (*Der Fall Wagner, KSA* 6, 37).

[12] Ruprecht Wimmer, "Der sehr große Papst: Mythos und Religion im *Erwählten,*" *TMJb* 11 (1998): 91–107.

[13] *DüD* 3, 401, 418.

[14] DüD 3, 378: "Der kleine Inzest-Roman, der unter der Hand zu verstehen gibt, daß das 'Unnatürliche' doch eigentlich etwas recht Natürliches ist, da man sich nicht wundern darf, wenn Gleich und Gleich sich liebt, ist schon ausgedruckt und ich habe die Korrektur gelesen."

[15] Christoph Corneau, *Hartmann von Aues "Armer Heinrich" und "Gregorius": Studien zur Interpretation mit dem Blick auf die Theologie zur Zeit Hartmanns* (Munich: C. H. Beck, 1961).

[16] To Karl Kerényi, 4 January 1950, *DüD* 3, 365.

[17] "Aber klug ist es freilich, im Sünder den Erwählten zu ahnen und klug ist das auch für den Sünder selbst. Denn würdigen mag ihn die Ahnung seiner Erwähltheit und ihm die Sündhaftigkeit fruchtbar machen, so dass sie ihn zu hohen Flügen trägt."

Contributors

EHRHARD BAHR teaches German literature at the University of California, Los Angeles. He has published a history of German literature, books and articles on Goethe, and on Thomas Mann in exile.

MANFRED DIERKS is Professor of German literature at the University of Oldenburg, Germany, and a writer. He has published books and articles on the psychology of literature, on contemporary German literature with an emphasis on Thomas Mann, and two novels.

WERNER FRIZEN teaches in Cologne, Germany. He has published articles and books on Thomas Mann and other topics in modern German literature. He is the editor of Thomas Mann's novel *Lotte in Weimar* in the new Frankfurt critical edition of Thomas Mann's Works.

CLAYTON KOELB is the Guy B. Johnson Professor of German and Comparative Literature at the University of North Carolina, Chapel Hill. He has published books and articles on literary theory, Thomas Mann, and Kafka.

HELMUT KOOPMANN is Professor emeritus of modern German literature at the University of Augsburg, Germany. He has published books and articles on Heinrich Heine, Ludwig Börne, Heinrich and Thomas Mann, and on other topics in German literature of the nineteenth and twentieth centuries.

WOLFGANG LEDERER is a Clinical Professor of Psychiatry at the University of California Medical School in San Francisco. He has published books concerned with the border area of psychology and literature as well as numerous professional and popular articles.

HERBERT LEHNERT grew up in Lübeck where he attended the same school that had tormented Thomas Mann fifty years earlier — even teaching there for a while. Since 1958 in the United States, he teaches now at the University of California, Irvine, and has written on German literature from Goethe to Christa Wolf, with emphasis on Thomas Mann.

HANNELORE MUNDT teaches German and Women's Studies at the University of Wyoming. She has published on Thomas Mann, Alfred Andersch, Christa Wolf, and on other contemporary German writers. She is currently completing a book on Thomas Mann.

PETER PÜTZ was Professor emeritus for German Literature at the University of Bonn when he died in 2002. He has published books and articles on the Enlightenment, on Lessing, Nietzsche, Thomas Mann, Peter Handke, and other topics in modern German literature.

JENS RIECKMANN has written books and articles on turn-of-the-century and twentieth-century German and Austrian literature. He teaches German and Comparative Literature at the University of California, Irvine.

HANS-JOACHIM SANDBERG is Professor emeritus of German Literature at the University of Bergen. He has published on nineteenth- and twentieth-century German and Scandinavian literature, with special emphasis on Thomas Mann.

EGON SCHWARZ was exiled from Vienna in 1938 and survived barely in South America until Bernhard Blume enabled him to study German literature in the United States. He is Professor emeritus at Washington University in St. Louis and has been a visiting professor in various parts of the world. He has published books and articles on German literature, with a special emphasis on Viennese literature, culture and social conditions at the turn of the twentieth century as well as autobiographical books about his extraordinary life.

HANS RUDOLF VAGET is the Helen and Laura Shedd Professor of German Studies and Comparative Literature at Smith College, where he also teaches music history and film, and has been a visiting professor in the United States and in Germany. He has published books and articles on Goethe, Thomas Mann, Richard Wagner, and on other topics in modern German literature.

EVA M. WESSELL teaches at the University of California, Irvine. She has published on Thomas Mann's essayistic works and his *Magic Mountain*.

Select Bibliography

Adorno, Theodor. "Zu einem Portrait Thomas Manns." *Neue Rundschau* 73 (1962): 320–27.

Bade, James N. *Die Betrogene aus neuer Sicht: Der autobiographische Hintergrund zu Thomas Manns letzter Erzählung.* Frankfurt am Main: R. G. Fischer, 1994.

Baumgart, Reinhard. "Der erotische Schriftsteller." *Thomas Mann und München.* Frankfurt am Main: S. Fischer, 1989.

Biedermann, Woldemar Freiherr von, ed. *Goethes Gespräche.* Leipzig: Biedermann, 1889–91.

———, ed. *Goethes Gespräche.* 5 vols. Leipzig: Biedermann, 1909–11.

Bielschowsky, Albert. *Goethe: Sein Leben und seine Werke.* 2 vols. Munich: Beck, 1905.

Bloom, Harold, ed. *Thomas Mann's Magic Mountain.* New York: Chelsea House, 1986.

Blüher, Hans. *Die Rolle der Erotik in der männlichen Gesellschaft: Eine Theorie der menschlichen Staatsbildung nach Wesen und Wert.* 2 vols. Jena: Diederichs, 1917, 1919.

Blume, Bernhard. *Thomas Mann und Goethe.* Bern: Francke, 1949.

Bode, Wilhelm. *Goethes Sohn.* Berlin: Mittler and Son, 1918.

Böhm, Karl Werner. *Zwischen Selbstzucht und Verlangen: Thomas Mann und das Stigma der Homosexualität.* Würzburg: Königshausen & Neumann, 1991.

Bürgin, Hans, and Hans-Otto Mayer. *Thomas Mann: A Chronicle of His Life.* Trans. Eugene Dobson. University, AL: U of Alabama P, 1969.

Carnegy, Patrick. *Faust as Musician: A Study of Thomas Mann's Novel "Doctor Faustus."* New York: New Directions, 1973.

Cohn, Dorrit. "The Second Author of Death in Venice." *Probleme der Moderne: Studien zur deutschen Literatur von Nietzsche bis Brecht.* Tübingen: Niemeyer, 1983.

Collet, Helga. "Das Konvolut zu Thomas Manns Roman 'Lotte in Weimar': Eine Untersuchung." M.A. Thesis, Kingston, 1971.

Cölln, Jan. "Gerichtstag der Literatur." *Jahrbuch der deutschen Schillergesellschaft* 45 (2001): 320–43.

Corneau, Christoph. *Hartmann von Aues "Armer Heinrich" und "Gregorius": Studien zur Interpretation mit dem Blick auf die Theologie zur Zeit Hartmanns.* Munich: C. H. Beck, 1961.

Dahlhaus, Carl. "Fiktive Zwölftonmusik: Thomas Mann und Theodor Adorno." *Jahrbuch 1982: Deutsche Akademie für Sprache und Dichtung.* Heidelberg: Lothar Stiehm Verlag, 1982. 33–49.

Detering, Heinrich. "*Das Ewig-Weibliche:* Thomas Mann über Toni Schwabe, Gabriele Reuter, Ricarda Huch." *TMJb* 12 (1999): 150–57.

———. *Das offene Geheimnis: Zur literarischen Produktivität eines Tabus von Winckelmann bis zu Thomas Mann.* Göttingen: Wallstein, 1994.

Dettmering, Peter. *Thomas Mann–Rainer Maria Rilke–Richard Wagner.* Munich: Nymphenburger Verlagshandlung, 1969.

Dierks, Manfred. "Die Aktualität der positivistischen Methode — am Beispiel Thomas Mann." *Orbis Litterarum* 33 (1978): 158–82.

———. "Doctor Faustus and Recent Theories of Narcissism: New Perspectives." *Thomas Mann's "Doctor Faustus": A Novel at the Margin of Modernism.* Ed. Herbert Lehnert and Peter Pfeiffer. Columbia SC: Camden House, 1991. 33–54.

———. *Studien zu Mythos and Psychologie bei Thomas Mann.* TMS 2 (1972).

Dowden, Stephen D. *Sympathy with the Abyss: A Study in the Novel of German Modernism: Kafka, Broch, Musil, Thomas Mann.* Tübingen: Niemeyer, 1986.

———, ed. *A Companion to Thomas Mann's "The Magic Mountain."* Columbia, SC: Camden House, 1999.

Elsaghe, Yahya. *Die imaginäre Nation: Thomas Mann und das "Deutsche."* Munich: Fink, 2000.

Emig, Christine. "Wagner in verjüngten Proportionen: Thomas Manns Novelle *Wälsungenblut* als epische Wagner-Transkription." *TMJb* 7 (1994): 172–79.

Exner, Richard. "Roman und Essay by Thomas Mann: Probleme und Beispiele." *Schweizer Monatshefte* 24 (1964–65): 243–45.

Fetzer, John F. *Changing Perceptions of Thomas Mann's "Doctor Faustus."* Columbia, SC: Camden House, 1996.

Fischer, Ernst. "'Doktor Faustus' und die deutsche Katastrophe. Eine Auseinandersetzung mit Thomas Mann." *Kunst und Menschheit: Essays.* Vienna: Globus Verlag, 1949. 37–97.

Fischer, Samuel, and Hedwig Fischer. *Briefwechsel mit Autoren.* Frankfurt am Main: S. Fischer, 1989.

Frühwald, Wolfgang. "Der christliche Jüngling im Kunstladen: Milieu- und Stilparodie in Thomas Manns Erzählung 'Gladius Dei.'" *Bild und Gedanke: Festschrift für Gerhart Baumann zum 60. Geburtstag.* Ed. Günter Schnitzler et al. Munich: Fink, 1980.

Gagnebin, Murielle. "La bisexualité psychique dans 'Les têtes inverties' de Thomas Mann." *La Revue d'Esthétique* 33 (1980).

Gloystein, Christian. *"Mit mir aber ist es was anderes": Die Ausnahmestellung Hans Castorps in Thomas Manns Roman "Der Zauberberg."* Würzburg: Königshausen & Neumann, 2001.

Goethe, Johann Wolfgang von. *Goethes Werk.* Ed. at the request of Großherzogin Sophie von Sachsen. 133 vols. Weimar: Böhlaus Nachfolger, 1887–1918. [*WA*]

Gökberk, Ülker. "War as Mentor: Thomas Mann and Germanness." In *A Companion to Thomas Mann's "The Magic Mountain."* Ed. Stephen D. Dowden. Columbia, SC: Camden House, 1999. 53–79.

Goldman, Harvey. *Max Weber and Thomas Mann: Calling and the Shaping of the Self.* Berkeley: U of California P, 1991.

Gronicka, André von. "'Myth Plus Psychology': A Style Analysis of *Death in Venice*." *Germanic Review* 31 (1956): 191–205.

Hamburger, Käte. "Anachronistische Symbolik. Fragen an Thomas Manns Faustus-Roman." *Thomas Mann: Wege der Forschung.* Ed. Helmut Koopmann. Darmstadt: Wissenschaftliche Buchgesellschaft, 1975. 384–413

———. *Der Humor bei Thomas Mann: Zum Joseph-Roman.* Munich: Nymphenburger Verlagshandlung, 1965.

Hatfield, Henry. "Charon und der Kleiderschrank." *Modern Language Notes* 65 (1950): 100–102.

Haug, Hellmut. *Erkenntnisekel: Zum frühen Werk Thomas Manns.* Tübingen: Niemeyer, 1969.

Heftrich, Eckhard. *Geträumte Taten: Joseph und seine Brüder.* Frankfurt am Main: Klostermann, 1993.

———. *Vom Verfall zur Apokalypse: Über Thomas Mann.* Frankfurt am Main: Klostermann, 1982.

Heilbut, Anthony. *Thomas Mann: Eros and Literature.* Berkeley: U of California P, 1995.

Heller, Erich. *Thomas Mann: The Ironic German.* Cleveland/New York: Meridian, 1961.

Hesse, Hermann. *Hermann Hesse–Thomas Mann. Briefwechsel.* Frankfurt am Main: S. Fischer, 1968.

Höbusch, Harald. *Thomas Mann: Kunst, Kritik, Politik, 1893–1913.* Tübingen: Francke, 2000.

Hübinger, Paul Egon. *Thomas Mann, die Universität und die Zeitgeschichte: Drei Kapitel deutscher Vergangenheit aus dem Leben des Dichters 1905–1955.* Munich: Oldenbourg, 1974.

Joseph, Erkme. "Nietzsche im 'Doktor Faustus.'" *"und was werden die Deutschen sagen?": Thomas Manns Roman "Doktor Faustus."* Ed. Hans Wisskirchen and Thomas Sprecher. Lübeck: Verlag Dräger-Druck, 1997. 61–112.

Kahler, Erich. *Der deutsche Charakter in der Geschichte Europas.* Zurich: Europa Verlag, 1937.

Kaiser, Gerhard. "Thomas Manns 'Wälsungenblut' und Richard Wagners *Ring:* Erzählen als kritische Interpretation." *TMJb* 12 (1999): 239–58.

Kaloyanova-Slavova, Ludmila. *Übergangsgeschöpfe: Gabriele Reuter, Hedwig Dohm, Helene Böhlau und Franziska von Reventlow.* New York: Peter Lang, 1998.

Kluge, Gerhard. "Friedrich, der König von Preußen, in Essays von Thomas und Heinrich Mann und der Bruderkonflikt." *TMJb* 12 (1999): 259–90.

Klüger, Ruth. "Thomas Manns jüdische Gestalten." *Katastrophen: Über deutsche Literatur.* Göttingen: Wallstein, 1994. 39–58.

Klugkist, Thomas. *Glühende Konstruktion: Thomas Manns Tristan und das "Dreigestirn": Schopenhauer, Nietzsche und Wagner.* Epistemata 157. Würzburg: Königshausen & Neumann, 1995.

Koelb, Clayton, ed. and trans. *Thomas Mann: Death in Venice: A New Translation, Backgrounds and Contexts, Criticism.* New York: Norton, 1994.

Kohut, Heinz. *The Analysis of the Self.* New York: International UP, 1971.

Koopmann, Helmut, ed. *Thomas-Mann-Handbuch.* Stuttgart: Kröner, 1990, 2001.

Kropfinger, Klaus. "'Montage' und 'Composition' im 'Faustus' — Literarische Zwölftontechnik oder Leitmotivik?" *Thomas Mann: Doktor Faustus 1947–1997.* Ed. Werner Röcke. Bern: Peter Lang, 2001. 345–66.

Kurzke, Hermann. "Die Quellen der 'Betrachtungen eines Unpolitischen.' Ein Zwischenbericht." *TMS* 7 (1987). 291–310.

Kurzke, Hermann. *Thomas Mann: Das Leben als Kunstwerk.* Munich: Beck, 1999.

Lämmert, Eberhard. "Thomas Mann: Buddenbrooks." *Der deutsche Roman: Vom Barock bis zur Gegenwart.* Ed. Benno von Wiese. Düsseldorf: Bagel, 1963. 190–96.

Lange, Gerhard. *Struktur- und Quellenuntersuchungen zu "Lotte in Weimar."* Bayreuth: Tasso, 1954, 1970.

Lederer, Wolfgang. *The Kiss of the Snow Queen.* Berkeley: U of California P, 1986.

Lehnert, Herbert. "Anmerkungen zur Entstehungsgeschichte von Thomas Manns 'Bekenntnisse des Hochstaplers Felix Krull,' 'Der Zauberberg' and 'Betrachtungen eines Unpolitischen.'" *Deutsche Vierteljahresschrift für Literaturwissenschaft und Geistesgeschichte* 38 (1964): 267–72.

———. "Dauer und Wechsel der Autorität. 'Lotte in Weimar' als Werk des Exils." *Internationales Thomas-Mann-Kolloquium 1986 in Lübeck. TMS 7* (1987). 39–41.

———. "Historischer Horizont und Fiktionalität in Thomas Manns 'Der Tod in Venedig.'" *Wagner, Nietzsche, Thomas Mann: Festschrift for Eckhart Heftrich.* Frankfurt am Main: Klostermann, 1993. 254–78.

———. "Idyllen und Realitätseinbrüche: Ideologische Selbstkritik in Thomas Manns 'Die vertauschten Köpfe.'" *Zeitgenossenschaft: Zur deutschsprachigen Literatur im 20. Jahrhundert: Festschrift für Egon Schwarz zum 65. Geburtstag.* Ed. Paul Michael Lützeler. Frankfurt: Athenäum, 1987. 123–39.

———. *Thomas Mann: Fiktion, Mythos, Religion.* Stuttgart: Kohlhammer, 1965, 1968.

———. "Thomas Mann's Interpretations of *Der Tod in Venedig* and Their Reliability." *Rice University Studies* 50:4 (1964): 41–60.

———. "Thomas Manns Josephstudien 1927–1939." *Schillerjahrbuch* 10 (1966): 378–404.

———. "Thomas Manns Vorstudien zur *Joseph*-Tetralogy." *Schillerjahrbuch* 7 (1963): 458–520.

Lehnert, Herbert, and Eva Wessell. *Nihilismus der Menschenfreundlichkeit: Thomas Manns "Wandlung" und sein Essay Goethe und Tolstoi. TMS 9* (1991).

Lesér, Esther H. *Thomas Mann's Fiction: An Intellectual Biography.* London/Toronto: Associated U Presses, 1989.

Lubich, Frederick. "Thomas Mann's Sexual Politics — Lost in Translation." *Comparative Literature Studies* 31 (1994):107–27.

Mann, Heinrich. *Briefe an Ludwig Ewers 1889–1913.* Ed. Ulrich Dietzel and Rosemarie Eggert. Berlin: Aufbau-Verlag, 1980.

———. *Essays.* Berlin: Aufbau-Verlag; Hamburg: Claassen, 1960.

———. *Macht und Mensch.* Munich: Kurt Wolff, 1919.

Mann, Katia. *Meine Ungeschriebenen Memoiren.* Frankfurt am Main: S. Fischer, 1974.

Mann, Klaus. *Kind dieser Zeit.* Munich: Nymphenburger Verlagshandlung, 1965.

———. *Tagebücher 1938–1939*. Ed. Joachim Heimannsberg. Munich: Spangenberg, 1990.

Mann, Thomas. *Addresses Delivered at the Library of Congress, 1942–1949*. Washington, DC: Library of Congress, 1963.

———. *Die Briefe Thomas Manns. Regesten und Register*. Ed. Hans Bürgin and Hans-Otto Mayer. 5 vols. Frankfurt am Main: S. Fischer, 1976–87.

———. "Der Briefwechsel zwischen Thomas Mann und Gerhart Hauptmann. 'Mit Hauptmann verband mich eine Art von Freundschaft.' Teil I: Einführung. Briefe 1912–1924." Ed. Hans Wysling and Cornelia Bernini. *TMJb* 6 (1993): 245–82.

———. "Musik in München" (1917). *Im Schatten Wagners: Thomas Mann über Richard Wagner. Texte und Zeugnisse*. Ed. Hans Vaget. Frankfurt am Main: Fischer Taschenbuch, 1999.

———. *Reflections of a Nonpolitical Mann*. Trans. and with an introd. by Walter D. Morris. New York: Unger, 1983.

———. *Thomas Mann an Ernst Bertram: Briefe aus den Jahren 1910–1955*. Ed. Inge Jens. Pfullingen: Neske, 1960.

———. *Thomas Mann: Letters to Paul Amann 1915–1952*. Ed. Herbert Wegener. Trans. Richard and Clara Winston. Middletown: Wesleyan UP, 1960.

———. *The Yale Zauberberg-Manuscript: Rejected Sheets once Part of Thomas Mann's Novel*. Ed. James F. White. TMS 4 (1980).

Mann, Thomas, and Heinrich Mann. *Letters of Heinrich and Thomas Mann, 1900–1949*. Ed. Hans Wysling. Trans. Don Reneau with add. trans. Richard and Clara Winston. Berkeley: U of California P, 1998.

Mann, Thomas, and Karl Kerényi. *Thomas Mann-Karl Kerényi: Gespräch in Briefen*. Ed. Karl Kerényi. Zurich: Rhein-Verlag, 1960.

———. *Mythology and Humanism. The Correspondence of Thomas Mann and Karl Kerényi*. Trans. Alexander Gelley. Ithaka: Cornell UP, 1975.

Mann, Thomas Johann Heinrich. "Testament des Senators Thomas Johann Heinrich Mann." Thomas Mann. *Große kommentierte Frankfurter Ausgabe. Werke — Briefe — Tagebücher*. Vol 1.2. Ed. Eckhard Heftrich and Stephan Stachorski. Frankfurt am Main: S. Fischer, 2002. 629–35.

Marx, Friedhelm. "Künstler, Propheten, Heilige: Thomas Mann und die Kunstreligion der Jahrhundertwende." *TMJb* 11 (1998): 51–60.

Mendelssohn, Peter de. *Der Zauberer: Das Leben des deutschen Schriftstellers Thomas Mann*. 3 vols. Ed. Cristina Klostermann. Frankfurt am Main: S. Fischer, 1996.

Münkler, Herfried. "Wo der Teufel seine Hand im Spiel hat. Thomas Manns Deutung der deutschen Geschichte des 20. Jahrhunderts." In *Thomas Mann: Doktor Faustus 1947–1997.* Ed. Werner Röcke. Bern: Peter Lang, 2001. 89–107.

Nemerov, Howard. "Themes and Methods in the Early Stories of Thomas Mann." *Poetry and Fiction: Essays.* New Brunswick: Rutgers UP, 1963.

Neumann, Thomas. "Fast ein Frühstück bei Goethe. Thomas Mann über die Goethe-Woche in Weimar." *TMJb* 10 (1997): 237–47.

Nietzsche, Friedrich. *Kritische Studienausgabe.* Ed. Giorgio Colli and Mazzini Montinari. 15 vols. Munich: Deutscher Taschenbuch Verlag, 1988. [*KSA*]

Northcote-Bade, James. *Die Wagner-Mythen im Frühwerk Thomas Manns.* Bonn: Bouvier, 1975.

Oswald, Victor A. "The Enigma of Madame Tolna." *Germanic Review* 23 (1948): 249–53.

Pringsheim, Klaus. "Ein Nachtrag zu 'Wälsungenblut.'" *Neue Zürcher Zeitung,* 17 December, 1961. Reprinted in *Betrachtungen und Überblicke.* Ed. Georg Wenzel. Berlin: Aufbau-Verlag, 1966.

Pütz, Peter. "'Der Geist der Erzählung': Zur Poetik Fontanes und Thomas Manns." *Theodor Fontane und Thomas Mann: Die Vorträge des internationalen Kolloquiums in Lübeck 1997. TMS* 18 (1998). 99–111.

———. "Die Verwirklichung durch 'lebendige Ungenauigkeit': 'Joseph' von den Quellen zum Roman." In *Thomas Mann und seine Quellen.* Ed. Eckhard Heftrich and Helmut Koopmann. Frankfurt am Main: Klostermann, 1991. 173–88.

Radkau, Joachim. "Neugier der Nerven. Thomas Mann als Interpret des 'nervösen Zeitalters.'" *TMJb* 9 (1996): 29–53.

Reed, T[erence]. J[ames]. *Death in Venice: Making and Unmaking a Master.* New York: Twayne, 1994.

———. *The Uses of Tradition.* Oxford: Clarendon Press, 1974, 1996.

———. "*Der Zauberberg.* Zeitenwandel and Bedeutungswandel 1012–1924." *Besichtigung des Zauberbergs.* Ed. Heinz Sauereßig. Biberach: Wege und Gestalten, 1974. 84–89.

Reents, Edo. "Von der Welt als Vorstellung zur Welt als Wille: Schopenhauer und Thomas Manns *Enttäuschung.*" *TMJb* 8 (1995): 209–40.

Renner, Rolf-Günter. "Die Modernität Thomas Manns." *Die literarische Moderne in Europa.* Ed. Hans Joachim Piechotta et al. Opladen: Westdeutscher Verlag, 1994. 398–415.

Reuter, Gabriele. *From a Good Family.* Trans. Lynne Tatlock. Columbia, SC: Camden House, 1999.

Rickes, Joachim. *Der sonderbare Rosenstock*. Frankfurt am Main: Lang 1998.

Riemer, Friedrich Wilhelm. *Mitteilungen über Goethe: Auf Grund der Ausgabe von 1841 und des handschriftlichen Nachlasses*. Ed. Arthur Pollmer. Leipzig: Insel, 1921.

Roßbach, Bruno. *Spiegelungen eines Bewusstseins: Der Erzähler in Thomas Manns "Tristan."* Marburger Studien zur Germanistik 10. Marburg: Hitzeroth, 1989.

Rothenberg, Jürgen. "Der göttliche Mittler. Zur Deutung der Hermes-Figurationen im Werk Thomas Manns." *Euphorion* 66 (1977): 55–80.

Ruchat, Anna. *Thomas Manns Roman-Projekt über Friedrich den Grossen im Spiegel der Notizen. Editions and Interpretations*. Bonn: Bouvier, 1989. 159–67.

Sandberg, Hans-Joachim. "Gesegnete Mahlzeit(en): Tischgespräche im Norden." *TMJb* 15 (2002): 83–87.

Sauereßig, Heinz. "Die Entstehung des Romans "Der Zauberberg." *Besichtigung des Zauberbergs*. Ed. Heinz Sauereßig. Biberach: Wege und Gestalten, 1974. 5–53.

Scher, Steven P. *Verbal Music in German Literature*. New Haven: Yale UP, 1968.

Schmid, Bernhold. "Neues zum 'Doktor Faustus'-Streit zwischen Arnold Schönberg und Thomas Mann." *Augsburger Jahrbuch für Musikwissenschaft* 6 (1989): 149–79; 7 (1990), 177–92.

Schneider, Peter Paul. "'Wo ich Deine Zuständigkeit leugnen muß. . . .' Die bislang unbekannte Antwort Heinrich Manns auf Thomas Manns Abrechnungsbrief vom 5. Dezember 1903." *"In Spuren gehen . . .": Festschrift für Helmut Koopmann*. Ed. Andrea Bartl et al., 231–53. Tübingen: Niemeyer, 1998.

Schopenhauer, Arthur. *Sämtliche Werke*. 5 vols. Ed. Wolfgang Freiherr von Löhneysen. Stuttgart: Cotta, 1968.

———. *The World as Will and Representation*. Trans. E. F. J. Payne. 2 vols. New York: Dover Publications, 1966.

Schwarz, Egon. "Adrian Leverkühn und Alban Berg," *Modern Language Notes* 102 (1987): 663–67.

Sheppard, Richard. "Realism plus Mythology: A Reconsideration of the Problem of 'Verfall' in Thomas Mann's *Buddenbrooks*." *Modern Language Review* 87 (1994): 936–38.

Tebben, Karin. "'Man hat das Prinzip zur Geltung zu bringen, das man darstellt.' Standortbestimmung Thomas Manns im Jahre 1904: Gabriele Reuter." *TMJb* 12 (1999): 77–97.

Theilhaber, Felix Aaron. *Goethe: Sexus und Eros*. Berlin: Horen, 1929.

Tiedemann, Rolf. "'Mitdichtende Einfühlung.' Adornos Beiträge zum 'Doktor Faustus' — noch einmal." *Frankfurter Adorno Blätter* 1 (1992): 9–33.

Tillmann, Claus. *Das Frauenbild bei Thomas Mann: Der Wille zum strengen Glück.* Wuppertal: Holger Deimling, 1992.

Tobin, Robert. "Why is Tadzio a Boy?" *Thomas Mann: Death in Venice: A New Translation, Backgrounds and Contexts, Criticism.* Ed. Clayton Koelb. New York: Norton, 1994. 207–32.

Ueding, Paul. "Thomas Mann und sein Heldenbild Friedrichs des Grossen." In *Neue Jahrbücher für das klassische Altertum, Geschichte und deutsche Literatur* 19 (1916): 416–23.

Ulrich Dittmann. *Thomas Mann: "Tristan," Erläuterungen und Dokumente.* Stuttgart: Reclam, 1979. 58–62.

Vaget, Hans Rudolf. "Erich Kahler, Thomas Mann und Deutschland. Eine Miszelle zum 'Doktor Faustus.'" *Ethik und Ästhetik: Festschrift für Wolfgang Wittkowski.* Ed. Richard Fischer. Frankfurt am Main: Peter Lang, 1995. 509–18.

———. "Fünfzig Jahre Leiden an Deutschland: Thomas Manns 'Doktor Faustus' im Lichte unserer Erfahrung." *Thomas Mann: Doktor Faustus 1947–1997.* Ed. Werner Röcke. Bern: Peter Lang. 11–34.

———. "'Intertextualität im Frühwerk Thomas Manns' und Heinrich Manns 'Das Wunderbare.'" *Zeitschrift für deutsche Philologie* 101 (1982): 193–216.

———. "Mann, Joyce, Wagner: The Question of Modernism in 'Doctor Faustus.'" *Thomas Mann's "Doctor Faustus": A Novel at the Margin of Modernism.* Ed. Herbert Lehnert and Peter C. Pfeiffer. Columbia, SC: Camden House, 1991. 167–91.

———. "National and Universal: Thomas Mann and the Paradox of 'German' Music." Ed. Celia Applegate and Pamela M. Potter. *Music and German National Identity.* Chicago: U of Chicago P, 2002. 155–77.

———. *Thomas Mann: Kommentar zu sämtlichen Erzählungen.* Munich: Winkler, 1984.

———. "Thomas Mann und die Neuklassik. 'Der Tod in Venedig' und Samuel Lublinskis Literaturauffassung." In *Stationen der Thomas Mann Forschung.* Ed. Hermann Kurzke. Würzburg: Königshausen & Neumann, 1985. 41–60.

———. "Thomas Mann und Theodor Fontane: Eine Rezeptionsästhetische Studie zu 'Der kleine Herr Friedemann.'" *Modern Language Notes* 90 (1975): 448–71.

———. "The Wagner Celebration of 1933 and the 'National Excommunication' of Thomas Mann." *Wagner* 16 (1995): 51–60.

Vaget, Hans Rudolf, ed. *Im Schatten Wagners: Thomas Mann über Richard Wagner: Texte und Zeugnisse 1895–1955.* Frankfurt am Main: Fischer Taschenbuch Verlag, 1999.

Viereck, Peter. "Hitler and Wagner." *Common Sense* 8 (November 1939): 3–6.

———. *Metapolitics: From Romantics to Hitler.* New York: Knopf, 1941.

Von Rad, Gerhard. "Biblische Joseph-Erzählung und 'Joseph-Roman.'" *Neue Rundschau* 76 (1965): 546–59.

Wich, Joachim. "Groteske Verkehrung des 'Vergnügens am tragischen Gegenstand.' Thomas Manns Novelle *Luischen* als Beispiel." *Deutsche Vierteljahrsschrift für Literaturwissenschaft und Geistesgeschichte* 50 (1976): 234–36.

Wiedemann, Hans-Rudolf. *Thomas Manns Schwiegermutter Erzählt.* Lübeck: Werkstättenverlag, 1985.

Wiegmann, Hermann. *Die Erzählungen Thomas Manns: Interpretationen und Realien.* Bielefeld: Aisthesis, 1992.

Wieler, Michael. "Der französische Einfluß: Zu den frühesten Werken Thomas Manns am Beispiel des Dilettantismus." *TMJb* 9 (1996): 173–87.

Wimmer, Ruprecht. "Der sehr große Papst: Mythos und Religion im *Erwählten.*" *TMJb* 11 (1998): 91–107.

Wißkirchen, Hans. "'Ich glaube an den Fortschritt, gewiß.' Quellenkritische Untersuchungen zu Thomas Mann's Settembrini-Figur." *Das Zauberberg-Symposium 1994 in Davos.* Ed. Thomas Sprecher. TMS 11 (1994). 81–115.

———. *Zeitgeschichte im Roman: Zu Thomas Manns Zauberberg und Doktor Faustus.* TMS 6 (1986).

Wysling, Hans. "'Geist und Kunst.' Zu Thomas Manns Notizen zu einem Literaturessay." *Quellenkritische Untersuchungen zum Werk Thomas Manns.* Ed. Paul Scherrer and Hans Wysling. TMS 1 (1967). 123–233.

———. *Narzissmus und illusionäre Existenzform: Zu den Bekenntnissen des Hochstaplers Felix Krull.* TMS 5 (1982).

Wysling, Hans, and Marianne Fischer. *Dichter über ihre Dichtungen: Thomas Mann.* 3 vols. Munich: Heimeran; Frankfurt am Main: S. Fischer, 1975–81.

Young, Frank W. *Montage and Motif in Thomas Mann's "Tristan."* Bonn: Bouvier, 1975.

Index